Contents

Acknowledgments

OVER THE COURSE of the half decade that it took me to complete this book project, I benefited from the assistance of many filmmakers, scholars, research assistants, film distributors, and academic institutions. I thank them all. Without their help this multiyear, multinational, multilingual effort would not have been finished.

Many accented filmmakers generously put at my disposal their films and printed materials and agreed to be interviewed, in person, by phone, or by e-mail, sometimes several times. They are Reza Allamehzadeh, Majid Amini, Alia Arasoughly, Nezamettin Ariç, Tevfik Baser, Tina Bastajian, Nigol Bezgian, Jean Chamoun, Atom Egoyan, Hanna Elias, Shirin Etessam, Jalal Fatemi, Hamid Rahmanian, Joris Ivens, Erica Jordan, Ann Kaneko, Kuch Nai Collective, Kamshad Kushan, Marceline Loridan, Ara Madzounian, Joan Mandel, Mai Masri, Jonas Mekas, Nina Menkes, Smihi Moumen, Marva Nabili, Amir Naderi, Meena Nanji, Shirin Neshat, Rafigh Pooya, Prajna Parasher, Walid Raad, Mehrnaz Saeed Vafa, Jayce Salloum, Sohrab Shahid Saless, Elia Suleiman, Mitra Tabrizian, Nancy Tong, Caveh Zahedi, and Ilan Ziv. Unfortunately, not all made it into the final manuscript, which because of its length, had to be reduced considerably.

Several film programmers helped with information and videos: Edith Kramer of the Pacific Film Archive; Marian Luntz of Houston Museum of Fine Arts: Linda Blackaby of Philadelphia World Film Festival; Christine Gardner and Liz Empelton of Rice Cinema; Isa Cucinnotta of the Lincoln Center Film Society; and Hossein Mahini of Exile Film Festival in Sweden. Debra Zimmerman, executive director of Women Make Movies, provided several tapes and agreed to interviews about her company's operation. John Sinno of Arab Film Distribution also provided tapes. I thank them both. Dagmar Spira, acting director of Villa Aurora in Los Angeles, facilitated my interview with Nizamettin Ariç.

Various university professors, scholars, and film critics supplied their own or others' writings or helped me track down information. Their contribution was valuable: Mehdi Bozorgmehr put at my disposal his papers and information on Middle Eastern and Iranian immigrants, Livia Alexander her paper on Michel Kheifi's films, Janet Bergsrom her information about Chantal Akerman's films, Persis Karim and Peter Bloom their information on the *beur* literature and cinema, and Mousumi Roy Chowdhury her material on daughter-texts. Mary Elena de las Carreras shared her dissertation and tapes of Fernando Solans's films, Jonathan Friedlander various film tapes, Sam Ho film reviews and films, Scott MacDonald information about filmmakers, Adrian Miles her bibliography on Chris Marker, Holly Willis her writings on independent film-makers, Gerald O'Grady his material on Jonas Mekas, and Michael Renov his paper on video confessions. Stella Grigorian helped with Armenian transla-tion, Anita Brown and Gudrun Klein with German translation, and Julie Tay-lor with Spanish translation of films. José Aranda helped with Chicano terms. My brother Mehdy Naficy provided assistance for my research and interviews in Germany; additionally, he and his family, Fariba and Setareh, nurtured me during my stays, providing meals, shelter, and companionship.

Allen Matusow and Judith Brown, Deans of Humanities at Rice University, provided me with the much-needed summer research money over several sum-mers, which made possible my travels, research, and interviews. Their assis-tance was essential to this project. I also want to thank the University of Cali-fornia Humanities Research Institute and its director, Pat O' Brien, at the University of California, Irvine, for providing me with a Humanities Fellow-ship and for hosting me for the winter 1997 term as a participant in the Media and Nations Study Group, which was convened by Anton Kaes. That period proved to be very useful in shaping my ideas and allowing me time to write. I benefited greatly from the critical comments of the members of the group, which consisted of: Sara Banet-Weiser, Peter Bloom, Iain Chambers, Edward Dimemberg, Anton Kaes, Susan Larsen, Roland Marchand, Mark Poster, Erick Rentschler, and Vanessa Schwartz. Katie Stewart of the Histories of the Future Group at the institute also commented on parts of my work. Bernard Aresu commented on the *beur* cinema section, and George Marcus critiqued an early version of the manuscript. I particularly want to thank Ron Burnett and the anonymous reviewers, who read the entire manuscript (more than once) and offered extensive, substantive advice.

Over the years, several graduate students helped me as research assistants: Molly Rogers, Stephanie Smith, Celeste Roberts, James Ellis, and Betsy Mul-lins. Sandra E. Edwards of Rice University's Fondren Library assisted me in tracking down library citations. Travis Johnson and Jeff Fegley helped me with scanning videos and preparing the film stills. Media Center administrator Cindy Wunder assisted with tabulating information on Middle Eastern and North African filmmakers. I appreciate all their help.

Mary Murrell, senior editor for literary and cultural studies at Princeton University Press, who shepherded this project through its various iterations to fruition, deserves special credit. She supported the project as it expanded, evolved, and found its right length and shape. Finally, I want to say how much I appreciate the way my immediate family, Kelly, Cameron, and Shayda, not only tolerated my absences, or absent presences, but also in ways big and small supported me with their love and presence at all times.

List of Illustrations

AN ACCENTED CINEMA

Introduction

IN JUNE 1995, while conducting research in Paris for this book, I attended a private screening of Mohsen Makhmalbaf's *A Time to Love* (*Nowbat-e Asheqi*, 1991) at MK2 Productions, which was considering the film for distribution. Made by the best-known new director to emerge since the revolution of 1979, the film had been banned in the director's home country, Iran, for its theme of love, in essence a ménage à trois. My friend Azadeh Kian and I were the only spectators in the comfortably appointed screening room. Perhaps partly to avoid the Iranian censors, Makhmalbaf had shot the film in Turkey, with all the dialogue in Turkish, a language I did not know beyond certain words. The film was subtitled, but in French, which at times passed too fast for my understanding, especially since I was trying to take notes. On these occasions, I would nudge Azadeh to translate for me. Reading the French subtitles, she would whisper the Persian translation into my ears. Trying to keep up with her translation and with the ongoing film and its subtitles, I was forced to take notes hurriedly in English and Persian, whichever served the moment best. Thus, watching this single film involved multiple acts of translation across four cultures and languages. This chain of linguistic and cultural signification pointed to the radical shift that has occurred in the globalization of cinema since my childhood. In those days, cinema screens were monopolized by the West, particularly by American films, and the Third World people were more consumers of these films than producers of their own narratives. But now people of the Third World are making and exhibiting films not only in their own countries but also increasingly across national boundaries, finding receptive audiences in Western film festivals and commercial theaters and on television. This book is centrally concerned with the films that postcolonial, Third World filmmakers have made in their Western sojourn since the 1960s, but several key Russian, European, Canadian, and American filmmakers in exile are also featured.

In an earlier work, I focused on the particularity of a specific group's televisual productions in exile, that of the Iranians in Los Angeles (Naficy 1993a). The present volume, on the other hand, seeks to identify and analyze the common features of the cinematic productions of a number of filmmakers from diverse originating and receiving countries. My contention is that although there is nothing common about exile and diaspora, deterritorialized peoples and their films share certain features, which in today's climate of lethal ethnic difference need to be considered, even emphasized. While stressing these features, the book continually engages with the specific histories of individuals and groups that engender divergent experiences, institutions, and modes of cultural production and consumption—hence the use of close-up sections throughout.

Significantly, what occurred in the MK2 screening room involved not only watching and listening but also reading, translating, and writing—all of which are part of the spectatorial activities and competencies that are needed for appreciating the works of these filmmakers, which I have termed "accented cinema." This is by no means an established or cohesive cinema, since it has been in a state of preformation and emergence in disparate and dispersed pockets across the globe. It is, nevertheless, an increasingly significant cinematic formation in terms of its output, which reaches into the thousands, its variety of forms and diversity of cultures, which are staggering, and its social impact, which extends far beyond exilic and diasporic communities to include the general public as well. If the dominant cinema is considered universal and without accent, the films that diasporic and exilic subjects make are accented. As discussed in chapter 1, the accent emanates not so much from the accented speech of the diegetic characters as from the displacement of the filmmakers and their artisanal production modes. Although many of their films are authorial and autobiographical, I problematize both authorship and autobiography by positing that the filmmakers' relationship to their films and to the authoring agency within them is not solely one of parentage but also one of performance. However, by putting the author back into authorship, I counter a prevalent postmodernist tendency, which either celebrates the death of the author or multiplies the authoring effect to the point of de-authoring the text. Accented filmmakers are not just textual structures or fictions within their films; they also are empirical subjects, situated in the interstices of cultures and film practices, who exist outside and prior to their films.

Another aspect of the accent is the style characterizing these films, whose components, discussed in various chapters and at various points throughout, are open-form and closed-form visual style; fragmented, multilingual, epistolary, self-reflexive, and critically juxtaposed narrative structure; amphibolic, doubled, crossed, and lost characters; subject matter and themes that involve journeying, historicity, identity, and displacement; dysphoric, euphoric, nostalgic, synaesthetic, liminal, and politicized structures of feeling; interstitial and collective modes of production; and inscription of the biographical, social, and cinematic (dis)location of the filmmakers.

Accented films are interstitial because they are created astride and in the interstices of social formations and cinematic practices. Consequently, they are simultaneously local and global, and they resonate against the prevailing cinematic production practices, at the same time that they benefit from them. As such, the best of the accented films signify and signify upon the conditions both of exile and diaspora and of cinema. They signify and signify upon exile and diaspora by expressing, allegorizing, commenting upon, and critiquing the home and host societies and cultures and the deterritorialized conditions of the filmmakers. They signify and signify upon cinematic traditions by means of their artisanal and collective production modes, their aesthetics and politics of smallness and imperfection, and their narrative strategies that cross generic boundaries and undermine cinematic realism. Chapters 2 and 3 are devoted to an extensive examination of the accented production modes and their politics and aesthetics.

One of the most intriguing features of the films' narratives is their epistolarity, involving the use of the formal properties of letters and telephony to create and exchange meaning. Exile and epistolarity necessitate one another, for distance and absence drive them both. However, by addressing someone in an epistle, an illusion of presence is created that hovers in the text's interstices. As a result, address is not just a problem but the problematic of these films. Epistolarity is also counterhegemonic because it challenges the authority of the classic realist films and their omniscient narrator and narrative system by its multivocal, multiauthorial, calligraphic, and free indirect discourses. Chapter 4 examines these and other issues in the context of three main types of epistolary films: film-letters, telephonic epistles, and letter-films.

Despite the recent overcelebration of the extranational and extraterritorial cyber communities created by computer connectivity, interactivity, and bandwidth, and the popularization of the notions of travel, traveling aesthetics, and traveling identity, many accented films emphasize territoriality, rootedness, and geography. Because they are deterritorialized, these films are deeply concerned with territory and territoriality. Their preoccupation with place is expressed in their open and closed space-time (chronotopical) representations. That of the homeland tends to emphasize boundlessness and timelessness, and it is cathected by means of fetishization and nostalgic longing to the homeland's natural landscape, mountains, monuments, and souvenirs. The representation of life in exile and diaspora, on the other hand, tends to stress claustrophobia and temporality, and it is cathected to sites of confinement and control and to narratives of panic and pursuit. While the idyllic open structures of home emphasize continuity, these paranoid structures of exile underscore rupture. Significantly, the paranoid structures also serve the comforting and critical functions of embodying the exiles' protest against the fluid and hostile social conditions in which they find themselves. However, some accented films are freed from such territorial imperatives. These issues and films are explored extensively in chapters 5 and 6.

Then there are the important transitional and transnational places and spaces, such as borders, tunnels, seaports, airports, and hotels and vehicles of mobility, such as trains, buses, and suitcases, that are frequently inscribed in the accented films. I have chosen these places, spaces, and vehicles as privileged sites for my examination of journeys of and struggles over identity. Accented filmmakers are subject to momentous historical dynamism and to intense national longings for form. They cross many borders and engage in many deterritorializing and reterritorializing journeys, which take several forms, including home-seeking journeys, journeys of homelessness, and homecoming journeys. However, these journeys are not just physical and territorial but are also deeply psychological and philosophical. Among the most important are journeys of identity, in the course of which old identities are sometimes shed and new ones refashioned. In the best of the accented films, identity is not a fixed essence but a process of becoming, even a performance of identity. Indeed, each accented film may be thought of as a performance of its author's identity. Because they are highly fluid, exilic and diasporic identities raise important questions about political agency and about the ethics of identity politics. These issues of journeying, border crossing, and identity crossing are investigated in chapter 7.

Although driven by the aesthetics of juxtaposition and by the binary structures that nostalgically repress, fetishize, and favorably compare there with here, then with now, home with exile, accented films in general derive their power not from purity and *refusal* but from impurity and *refusion*. The acts of signification, signifying upon, and refusion that are hinted at in this introduction constitute the "work" of the accented style. Importantly, the style not only signifies the endemic *dislocation* of our times in general and of these filmmaker in particular but also serves to *locate* the filmmakers as authors of their films and to some extent of their own destiny.

Accented films are in dialogue with the home and host societies and their respective national cinemas, as well as with audiences, many of whom are similarly transnational, whose desires, aspirations, and fears they express. However, displacement creates its own peculiar spectatorial environment that produces different demands and expectations, which are torqued not only by market forces but also by nationalist politics and by politics of ethnic representation. While the general public may prefer accented films that are entertaining and enlightening, sometimes at the expense of the integrity of the filmmakers' native culture, displaced communities often demand "authentic" and corrective representations. Such conflicting demands may "distort" the accented films, exposing them to criticism from all sides. Consequently, the accented style continually grapples with the politicized immediacy of the films and with their collective enunciation and reception—that is, with the manner in which politics infuses all aspects of their existence. The study of a transnational cultural phenomenon such as the accented cinema is always haunted by the particularity of its autochthonous cultures. Within every transnational culture beats the hearts of multiple displaced but situated cultures interacting with one another. By continually incorporating the novel aspects of these local cultures into the universal, the dominant society and cinema renew themselves and remain dominant. To resist total absorption, one may follow Deleuze and Guattari's advice and intensify capitalism's schizophrenic tendencies to such an extent that its integrity is threatened (Larsen 1991, xviii). Alternatively, one may create paranoid structures and citadel cultures of withdrawal or may engage in

rhizomatic group affiliations—vertical, horizontal, and transverse—across deterritorialized social formations. The dynamics of such incorporative and resistive strategies in accented cinema are discussed throughout.

Although accented cinema is unprecedented in its cultural and linguistic diversity and its global dispersion, it has had predecessors, and immigrants everywhere have been key players in the development of the literature and cinema
of their adopted countries. Indeed, "foreigners and émigrés" have dominated
the pinnacles of modern English literature (Eagleton 1970, 9) and of American
cinema, which from the beginning was immigrant, transnational, and American all at the same time. Although the contribution of immigrants has continued throughout the century of cinema's existence, its greatest impact in the
United States was cyclical, rising with displacement of populations abroad or
within the country. Two major immigration waves occurred in this century,
the first peaking around 1915 and the second in the mid-1980s. These waves
were markedly different from each other, and smaller-waves and countercur-
rents that involved national, religious, racial, and inter- and intraethnic differences and conflicts further complicated this picture.

The immigrants contributed to the American cinema as spectators and as
producers. At the dawn of cinema, immigrants-as-spectators were important
to the medium's evolution from an artisanal enterprise to an industrial system;
likewise, cinema played a crucial role in their transformation from immigrant
to American (Ewen and Ewen 1982; Hansen 1991). This social transformation
was intimately tied to a textual transformation of the audience. For the films
gradually moved away from the primitive cinema's conception of a collective
"audience" to the classical cinema's individually addressed "spectator," who was
thought to be "a singular, unified but potentially universal category" that tran-
scended rooted categories of the immigrants. This facilitated the interpellation
of spectators as a classless mass audience (Hansen 1991, 84–85).

The immigrants' impact extended to their indispensable contribution to the
production, distribution, and exhibition of the movies. The trajectory of their
varied contributions in the United States is sketched briefly here. From cinema's inception, émigré and ethnic filmmakers attempted to make films for
their own specific audiences, with little sustained success or with mixed results.
The most extended and successful efforts were Yiddish films that Jews made
for the Jewish diaspora (Hoberman 1991a) and "race movies" that African-
Americans made for African-Americans (Cripps 1988; Green 1993; Gaines
1993). However, the first generation of Jews and Jewish immigrants, primarily
from Eastern Europe and Russia—dubbed the Hollywood "pioneers"—were
instrumental in building the motion picture industry and the studio system
(Gabler 1988). Between the two world wars, a second group of European
immigrants and exiles, particularly from Germany and Austria, who had left

their homelands to advance professionally or to escape the Nazis, entered the American cinema. Working for the studios in various capacities, they proved to be pivotal in consolidating the studio system and in internationalizing the American cinema. Unlike the "pioneers," these "émigrés" and "exiles" were not given to a totalizing image of assimilation, and they engaged in various performative strategies of camouflage in their films and self-fashioning in their lives (Elsaesser 1999). The poststudio "ethnics," the children of Irish, Italian, and Jewish immigrants, contributed to the emergence of the New Hollywood postindustrial cinema. They produced quintessentially American films that were nonetheless suffused with manifest or submerged ethnicity. Since the 1960s, "identity" and "postcolonial" filmmakers have dealt with particularistic and minoritarian affiliations and with the dynamics of assimilation and resistance. Group affiliation and identity politics often take precedence over adherence to cinematic and generic categories. Thus, only in the best of their films (such as those of Spike Lee, Charles Burnett, Julie Dash, and Haile Gerima, among African-Americans) is there much experimentation and innovation in style and content.

Since the 1960s, we have been living in a rapidly globalizing world and media environment. Indeed, globalization is the norm against which people are now determining their individual and national identities (Hall 1996). Access to multiple channels and types of local and transnational media and the displacement of an unprecedented number of people have challenged our received notions of national culture and identity, national cinema and genre, authorial vision and style, and film reception and ethnography. In such a mediated world, imagination itself must be regarded as a social practice. As Arjun Appadurai notes, "The imagination is now central to all forms of agency, is itself a social fact, and is the key component of the new global order" (1996, 31). In this book, I direct attention to a new and critical imagination in the global media: an accented cinema of exile and diaspora and its embedded theory of criticism. This is both a cinema *of* exile and a cinema *in* exile. It concerns deterritorialization and is itself produced in the interstices of cultures and cinematic production practices. However, since it has not been made by cohesive, programmatic, or generic production practices backed by the studios, it is currently a category more of criticism than of production.

The close-up sections placed throughout the book offer case studies that are devoted to an extended analysis of a single film (such as Fernando Solanas's *Tangos: Exile of Gardel,* 1985) or to the career of individual filmmakers (such as Atom Egoyan, Jonas Mekas, Mira Nair, and Miguel Littín), which contextualize their lives and times for a better understanding of their films. Sometimes the sections focus on a collective filming formation, examining less the specific films than the emergence, evolution, and impact of lines of forces on those formations. Examples are the sections on Asian Pacific American cinema, *beur* cinema in France, black and Asian collectives in Britain, and Iranian filmmaking in Europe and the United States. Attention to the specificity and situatedness of each displaced filmmaker, community, or formation is an important safeguard against the temptation to engage in postmodernist discursive tourism or the positing of an all-encompassing grand Exile or great Diaspora—or a homogeneous Accented Cinema.

1

Situating Accented Cinema

Accented Filmmakers

The exilic and diasporic filmmakers discussed here are "situated but universal" figures who work in the interstices of social formations and cinematic practices. A majority are from Third World and postcolonial countries (or from the global South) who since the 1960s have relocated to northern cosmopolitan centers where they exist in a state of tension and dissension with both their original and their current homes. By and large, they operate independently, outside the studio system or the mainstream film industries, using interstitial and collective modes of production that critique those entities. As a result, they are presumed to be more prone to the tensions of marginality and difference. While they share these characteristics, the very existence of the tensions and differences helps prevent accented filmmakers from becoming a homogeneous group or a film movement. And while their films encode these tensions and differences, they are not neatly resolved by familiar narrative and generic schemas—hence, their grouping under accented style. The variations among the films are driven by many factors, while their similarities stem principally from what the filmmakers have in common: liminal subjectivity and interstitial location in society and the film industry. What constitutes the accented style is the combination and intersection of these variations and similarities.

Accented filmmakers came to live and make films in the West in two general groupings. The first group was displaced or lured to the West from the late 1950s to the mid-1970s by Third World decolonization, wars of national liberation, the Soviet Union's invasions of Poland and Czechoslovakia, Westernization, and a kind of "internal decolonization" in the West itself, involving various civil rights, counterculture, and antiwar movements. Indeed, as Fredric Jameson notes, the beginning of the period called "the sixties" must be located in the Third World decolonization that so profoundly influenced the First World sociopolitical movements (1984, 180). The second group emerged in the 1980s and 1990s as a result of the failure of nationalism, socialism, and communism; the ruptures caused by the emergence of postindustrial global economies, the rise of militant forms of Islam, the return of religious and ethnic wars, and the fragmentation of nation-states; the changes in the European, Australian, and American immigration policies encouraging non-Western immigration; and the unprecedented technological developments and consolidation in computers and media. Accented filmmakers are the products of this dual postcolonial displacement and postmodern or late modern scattering. Because of their displacement from the margins to the centers, they have become subjects in world history. They have earned the right to speak and have dared to capture the means of representation. However marginalized they are within the center, their ability to access the means of *reproduction* may prove to be as empowering to the marginalia of the postindustrial era as the capturing of the means of *production* would have been to the subalterns of the industrial era.

It is helpful, when mapping the accented cinema, to differentiate three types of film that constitute it: exilic, diasporic, and ethnic. These distinctions are not hard-and-fast. A few films fall naturally within one of these classifications, while the majority share the characteristics of all three in different measures. Within each type, too, there are subdivisions. In addition, in the course of their careers, many filmmakers move not only from country to country but also from making one type of film to making another type, in tandem with the trajectory of their own travels of identity and those of their primary community.

Exilic Filmmakers

Traditionally, exile is taken to mean banishment for a particular offense, with a prohibition of return. Exile can be internal or external, depending on the location to which one is banished. The tremendous toll that internal exile, restrictions, deprivations, and censorship in totalitarian countries have taken on filmmakers has been widely publicized. What has been analyzed less is the way such constraints, by challenging the filmmakers, force them to develop an authorial style. Many filmmakers who could escape internal exile refuse to do so in order to fight the good fight at home—a fight that often defines not only their film style but also their identity as oppositional figures of some stature. By working under an internal regime of exile, they choose their "site of struggle" and their potential social transformation (Harlow 1991, 150). When they speak from this site at home, they have an impact, even if, and often because, they are punished for it. In fact, interrogation, censorship, and jailing are all proof that they have been heard. But if they move out into external exile in the West, where they have the political freedom to speak, no one may hear them among the cacophony of voices competing for attention in the market. In that case, Gayatri Spivak's famous question "Can the subaltern speak?" will have to be reworded to ask, "Can the subaltern be heard?" Because of globalization, the internal and external exiles of one country are not sealed off from each other. In fact, there is much traffic and exchange between them.

   In this study, the term "exile" refers principally to external exiles: individuals or groups who voluntarily or involuntarily have left their country of origin and who maintain an ambivalent relationship with their previous and current places and cultures. Although they do not return to their homelands, they maintain an intense desire to do so—a desire that is projected in potent return narratives in their films. In the meantime, they memorialize the homeland by fetishizing it in the form of cathected sounds, images, and chronotopes that are circulated intertextually in exilic popular culture, including in films and music videos. The exiles' primary relationship, in short, is with their countries and cultures of origin and with the sight, sound, taste, and feel of an originary experience, of an elsewhere at other times. Exiles, especially those filmmakers who have been forcibly driven away, tend to want to define, at least during the liminal period of displacement, all things in their lives not only in relationship to the homeland but also in strictly political terms. As a result, in their early films they tend to represent their homelands and people more than themselves.

   The authority of the exiles as filmmaking authors is derived from their position as subjects inhabiting interstitial spaces and sites of struggle. Indeed, all great authorship is predicated on distance—banishment and exile of sorts—from the larger society. The resulting tensions and ambivalences produce the complexity and the intensity that are so characteristic of great works of art and literature. In the same way that sexual taboo permits procreation, exilic banishment encourages creativity.[1] Of course, not all exilic subjects produce great or lasting art, but many of the greatest and most enduring works of literature and cinema have been created by displaced writers and filmmakers. But exile can result in an agonistic form of liminality characterized by oscillation between the extremes. It is a slipzone of anxiety and imperfection, where life hovers between the heights of ecstasy and confidence and the depths of despondency and doubt.[2]

   For external exiles the descent relations with the homeland and the consent relations with the host society are continually tested. Freed from old and new, they are "deterritorialized," yet they continue to be in the grip of both the old and the new, the before and the after. Located in such a slipzone, they can be suffused with hybrid excess, or they may feel deeply deprived and divided, even fragmented. Lithuanian filmmaker and poet Jonas Mekas, who spent some four years in European displaced persons camps before landing in the United States, explained his feelings of fragmentation in the following manner:

> Everything that I believed in shook to the foundations—all my idealism, and my faith in the goodness of man and progress of man—all was shattered. Somehow, I managed to keep myself together. But really, I wasn't one piece any longer; I was one thousand painful pieces. . . . And I wasn't surprised when, upon my arrival in New York, I found others who felt as I felt. There were poets, and film-makers, and paint-ers—people who were also walking like one thousand painful pieces. (quoted in O'Grady 1973, 229)

Neither the hybrid fusion nor the fragmentation is total, permanent, or pain-less. On the one hand, like Derridian "undecidables," the new exiles can be "both and neither": the pharmacon, meaning both poison and remedy; the hymen, meaning both membrane and its violation; and the supplement, mean-ing both addition and replacement (quoted in Bauman 1991, 145–46). On the other hand, they could aptly be called, in Salman Rushdie's words, "at once plural and partial" (1991, 15). As partial, fragmented, and multiple subjects, these filmmakers are capable of producing ambiguity and doubt about the taken-for-granted values of their home and host societies. They can also tran-scend and transform themselves to produce hybridized, syncretic, performed, or virtual identities. None of these constructed and impure identities are risk-free, however, as the Ayatollah Khomeini's death threat against Salman Rush-die glaringly pointed out.[3]

Not all transnational exiles, of course, savor fundamental doubt, strive to-ward hybridized and performative self-fashioning, or reach for utopian or vir-tual imaginings. However, for those who remain in the enduring and endearing crises and tensions of exilic migrancy, liminality and interstitiality may become passionate sources of creativity and dynamism that produce in literature and cinema the likes of James Joyce and Marguerite Duras, Joseph Conrad and Fernando Solanas, Ezra Pound and Trinh T. Minh-ha, Samuel Beckett and Sohrab Shahid Saless, Salman Rushdie and Andrei Tarkovsky, Garcia Mar-quez and Atom Egoyan, Vladimir Nabokov and Raúl Ruiz, Gertrude Stein and Michel Khleifi, Assia Djebar and Jonas Mekas.

Many exilic filmmakers and groups of filmmakers are discussed in this book—Latin American, Lithuanian, Iranian, Turkish, Palestinian, and Rus-sian. They are not all equally or similarly exiled, and there are vast differences even among filmmakers from a single originating country.

Diasporic Filmmakers

Originally, "diaspora" referred to the dispersion of the Greeks after the de-struction of the city of Aegina, to the Jews after their Babylonian exile, and to the Armenians after Persian and Turkish invasions and expulsion in the mid–sixteenth century. The classic paradigm of diaspora has involved the Jews, but as Peters (1999), Cohen (1997), Tölölyan (1996), Clifford (1997, 244–77), Naficy (1993a), and Safran (1991) have argued, the definition should no longer be limited to the dispersion of the Jews, for myriad peoples have histori-cally undergone sustained dispersions—a process that continues on a massive scale today. The term has been taken up by other displaced peoples, among them African-Americans in the United States and Afro-Caribbeans in En-gland, to describe their abduction from their African homes and their forced dispersion to the new world (Gilroy 1993, 1991, 1988; Mercer 1994a, 1994b,

1988; Hall 1988). In these and other recodings, the concept of diaspora has become much closer to exile. Consequently, as Khachig Tölölyan notes, "diaspora" has lost some of its former specificity and precision to become a "promiscuously capacious category that is taken to include all the adjacent phenomena to which it is linked but from which it actually differs in ways that are constitutive" (1996, 8).

Here I will briefly point out the similarities and differences between exile and diaspora that inform this work. Diaspora, like exile, often begins with trauma, rupture, and coercion, and it involves the scattering of populations to places outside their homeland. Sometimes, however, the scattering is caused by a desire for increased trade, for work, or for colonial and imperial pursuits. Consequently, diasporic movements can be classified according to their motivating factors. Robin Cohen (1997) suggested the following classifications and examples: victim/refugee diasporas (exemplified by the Jews, Africans, and Armenians); labor/service diasporas (Indians); trade/business diasporas (Chinese and Lebanese); imperial/colonial diasporas (British, Russian); and cultural/hybrid diasporas (Caribbeans). Like the exiles, people in diaspora have an identity in their homeland *before* their departure, and their diasporic identity is constructed in resonance with this prior identity. However, unlike exile, which may be individualistic or collective, diaspora is necessarily collective, in both its origination and its destination. As a result, the nurturing of a collective memory, often of an idealized homeland, is constitutive of the diasporic identity. This idealization may be state-based, involving love for an existing homeland, or it may be stateless, based on a desire for a homeland yet to come. The Armenian diaspora before and after the Soviet era has been state-based, whereas the Palestinian diaspora since the 1948 creation of Israel has been stateless, driven by the Palestinians' desire to create a sovereign state.

People in diaspora, moreover, maintain a long-term sense of ethnic consciousness and distinctiveness, which is consolidated by the periodic hostility of either the original home or the host societies toward them. However, unlike the exiles whose identity entails a vertical and primary relationship with their homeland, diasporic consciousness is horizontal and multisited, involving not only the homeland but also the compatriot communities elsewhere. As a result, plurality, multiplicity, and hybridity are structured in dominance among the diasporans, while among the political exiles, binarism and duality rule.

These differences tend to shape exilic and diasporic films differently. Diasporized filmmakers tend to be centered less than the exiled filmmakers on a cathected relationship with a single homeland and on a claim that they represent it and its people. As a result, their works are expressed less in the narratives of retrospection, loss, and absence or in strictly partisanal political terms. Their films are accented more fully than those of the exiles by the plurality and performativity of identity. In short, while binarism and subtraction in particular accent exilic films, diasporic films are accented more by multiplicity and addition. Many diasporic filmmakers are discussed here individually, among them Armenians. Black and Asian British filmmakers are discussed collectively.

Postcolonial Ethnic and Identity Filmmakers

Although exilic, diasporic, and ethnic communities all patrol their real and symbolic boundaries to maintain a measure of collective identity that distinguishes them from the ruling strata and ideologies, they differ from one another principally by the relative strength of their attachment to compatriot communities. The postcolonial ethnic and identity filmmakers are both ethnic and diasporic; but they differ from the poststudio American ethnics, such as Woody Allen, Francis Ford Coppola, and Martin Scorsese, in that many of them are either immigrants themselves or have been born in the West since the 1960s to nonwhite, non-Western, postcolonial émigrés. They also differ from the diasporic filmmakers in their emphasis on their ethnic and racial identity within the host country.

The different emphasis on the relationship to place creates differently accented films. Thus, exilic cinema is dominated by its focus on there and then in the homeland, diasporic cinema by its vertical relationship to the homeland and by its lateral relationship to the diaspora communities and experiences, and postcolonial ethnic and identity cinema by the exigencies of life here and now in the country in which the filmmakers reside. As a result of their focus on the here and now, ethnic identity films tend to deal with what Werner Sollors has characterized as "the central drama in American culture," which emerges from the conflict between descent relations, emphasizing bloodline and ethnicity, and consent relations, stressing self-made, contractual affiliations (1986, 6). In other words, while the former is concerned with being, the latter is concerned with becoming; while the former is conciliatory, the latter is contestatory. Although such a drama is also present to some extent in exilic and diasporic films, the hostland location of the drama makes the ethnic and identity films different from the other two categories, whose narratives are often centered elsewhere.

Some of the key problematics of the postcolonial ethnic and identity cinema are encoded in the "politics of the hyphen." Recognized as a crucial marker of ethnicity and authenticity in a multicultural America, group terms such as black, Chicano/a, Oriental, and people of color have gradually been replaced by hyphenated terms such as African-American, Latino-American, and Asian-American. Identity cinema's adoption of the hyphen is seen as a marker of resistance to the homogenizing and hegemonizing power of the American melting pot ideology. However, retaining the hyphen has a number of negative connotations, too. The hyphen may imply a lack, or the idea that hyphenated people are somehow subordinate to unhyphenated people, or that they are "equal but not quite," or that they will never be totally accepted or trusted as full citizens. In addition, it may suggest a divided allegiance, which is a painful reminder to certain groups of American citizens.[4] The hyphen may also suggest a divided mind, an irrevocably split identity, or a type of paralysis between two cultures or nations. Finally, the hyphen can feed into nativist discourses that assume authentic essences that lie outside ideology and predate, or stand apart from, the nation.

In its nativist adoption, the hyphen provides vertical links that emphasize descent relations, roots, depth, inheritance, continuity, homogeneity, and stability. These are allegorized in family sagas and mother-daughter and generational conflict narratives of Chinese-American films such as Wayne Wang's *Eat a Bowl of Tea* (1989) and *The Joy Luck Club* (1993). The filmmakers' task in this modality, in Stuart Hall's words, is "to discover, excavate, bring to light and express through cinematic representation" that inherited collective cultural identity, that "one true self" (1994, 393). In its contestatory adoption, the hyphen can operate horizontally, highlighting consent relations, disruption, heterogeneity, slippage, and mediation, as in Trinh T. Minh-ha's *Surname Viet Given Name Nam* (1985) and Srinivas Krishna's *Masala* (1990). In this modality, filmmakers do not recover an existing past or impose an imaginary and often fetishized coherence on their fragmented experiences and histories. Rather, by emphasizing discontinuity and specificity, they demonstrate that they are in the process of becoming, that they are "subject to the continuous 'play' of history, culture and power" (Hall 1994, 394). Christine Choy and Rene Tajima's award-winning film *Who Killed Vincent Chin?* (1988) is really a treatise on the problematic of the hyphen in the Asian-American context, as it centers on the murder of a Chinese-American by out-of-work white Detroit autoworkers who, resentful of Japanese car imports, mistook him for being Japanese.

Read as a sign of hybridized, multiple, or constructed identity, the hyphen can become liberating because it can be performed and signified upon. Each hyphen is in reality a nested hyphen, consisting of a number of other intersecting and overlapping hyphens that provide inter- and intraethnic and national links. This fragmentation and multiplication can work against essentialism, nationalism, and dyadism. Faced with too many options and meanings, however, some have suggested removing the hyphen, while others have proposed replacing it with a plus sign.[5] Martin Scorsese's *ITALIANAMERICAN* (1974) cleverly removes the hyphen and the space and instead joins the "Italian" with the "American" to suggest a fused third term. The film title by this most ethnic of New Hollywood cinema directors posits that there is no Italianness that precedes or stands apart from Americanness. In this book, I have retained the hyphen, since this is the most popular form of writing these compound ethnic designations.

The compound terms that bracket the hyphen also present problems, for at the same time that each term produces symbolic alliance among disparate members of a group, it tends to elide their diversity and specificity. "Asian-American," for example, encompasses people from such culturally and nationally diverse roots as the Philippines, Vietnam, Cambodia, Korea, Japan, Thailand, China, Laos, Taiwan, Indonesia, Malaysia, India, Bangladesh, and Pakistan. To calibrate the term, such unwieldy terms as "Southeast Asian diasporas" have also been created. Similar processes and politics of naming have been tried for the "black" British filmmakers.

Independent film distributors, such as Third World Newsreel, Icarus-First Run Films, and Women Make Movies, exploit the hyphen and the politics of the identity cinema by classifying these films thematically or by their hyphenated designation. Such classifications create targets of opportunity for those interested in such films, but they also narrow the marketing and critical discourses about these films by encouraging audiences to read them in terms of their ethnic content and identity politics more than their authorial vision and stylistic innovations. Several postcolonial ethnic and identity filmmakers are discussed individually and collectively.

Diaspora, exile, and ethnicity are not steady states; rather, they are fluid processes that under certain circumstances may transform into one another and beyond. There is also no direct and predetermined progression from exile to ethnicity, although dominant ideological and economic apparatuses tend to favor an assimilationist trajectory—from exile to diaspora to ethnic to citizen to consumer.

Mapping Accented Cinema's Corpus

It may be difficult to appreciate the geographic dispersion and the massive size of the accented cinema and the wide range of films that it has produced since the 1960s. To get a grip on this amorphous entity, I conducted a case study of Middle Eastern and North African accented filmmakers, a summary of which is presented in the following close-up section.

Close-Up: Middle Eastern and North African Filmmakers

These filmmakers are a prime example of the new postcolonial, Third World, and non-Western populations in the West whose work forms the accented cinema. Although their emigration to Europe and the Americas is not new, there has been a massive surge in their transplantation since the 1960s. Accurate figures for their various population types (refugees, émigrés, exiles, etc.) are difficult to obtain and vary based on the definition of each type and the data sources that are consulted. In the United States, the 1990 Census Bureau data showed that the total number of those who trace their ancestry to the

Middle East is nearly 2 million (exact figure: 1,731,000) out of a total U.S. population of approximately 250 million. Among these, there are 921,000 Arabs, 308,000 Armenians, 260,000 Iranians, and 117,000 Israelis. The largest concentration of Middle Easterners in the United States, and in the Western world, some 300,000 people, is found in Los Angeles (Bozorgmehr, Der-Martirosian, and Sabagh 1996).

The Middle Eastern and North African filmmakers form a surprisingly large and diverse group, numbering 321 filmmakers from sixteen sending countries who made at least 920 films in twenty-seven receiving countries, mostly in Europe and North America.[6] In terms of output, Iranian filmmakers topped the list (with 307 films), followed by Armenians (235), Algerians (107), Lebanese (46), Palestinians (35), Turks (25), Moroccans (25), Tunisians (23), and Israeli/Jewish filmmakers (24). The majority of the filmmakers were men, reflecting the dominance of patriarchy within the sending nations and the general pattern of migrations worldwide, which have favored the emigration of men ahead of their families to establish a beachhead for chain migration. This gender imbalance also reflects the belief, common to many Middle Eastern and North African societies, that cinema is not a socially acceptable, religiously sanctioned, and economically feasible enterprise for women. The patriarchal ideologies of the receiving countries, too, contributed to women's underrepresentation.

The historical factors that caused the migration and the density, variety, and cultural and economic capital of the displaced populations in the receiving countries are factors that favored accented filmmaking. Algerian filmmakers made their films almost exclusively in France, the country that until 1961 colonized Algeria and to which Algerians emigrated in massive numbers after their independence. Likewise, the majority of Turkish filmmakers worked in Germany, where historical relationship favored Turkish guest workers. On the other hand, Armenians made films in a number of European and North American countries, commensurate with their worldwide diaspora. Likewise, a social revolution dispersed many affluent Iranians to North America, where they made most of their films. European countries with receptive immigration policies toward Iranians, such as France, Germany, Holland, and Sweden, also proved favorable to the filmmakers.

The accented filmmakers' films, too, form a highly diverse corpus, as many of them are transnationally funded and are multilingual and intercultural. They range widely in types, from amateur films to feature fiction films, and from animated films to documentaries to avant-garde video (television films and series were not considered).

The magnitude, diversity, and geographic reach of the Middle Eastern and North African immigration give us an idea of the larger scattering of the peoples across the globe and of the movement of cultural and intellectual capital from the Third World to the First World.[7] Clearly, we are facing a mammoth,

emergent, transnational film movement and film style. However, unlike most
film movements and styles of the past, the accented cinema is not monolithic,
cohesive, centralized, or hierarchized. Rather, it is simultaneously global and
local, and it exists in chaotic semiautonomous pockets in symbiosis with the
dominant and other alternative cinemas.

The Stylistic Approach

How films are conceived and received has a lot to do with how they are framed
discursively. Sometimes the films of great transplanted directors, such as Alfred
Hitchcock, Luis Buñuel, and Jean-Luc Godard, are framed within the "international" cinema category.[8] Most often, they are classified within either the
national cinemas of their host countries or the established film genres and
styles. Thus, the films of F. W. Murnau, Douglas Sirk, George Cukor, Vincent
Minnelli, and Fritz Lang are usually considered as exemplars of the American
cinema, the classical Hollywood style, or the melodrama and noir genres. Of
course, the works of these and other established directors are also discussed
under the rubric of "auteurism." Alternatively, many independent exiled filmmakers who make films about exile and their homelands' cultures and politics
(such as Abid Med Hondo, Michel Khleifi, Mira Nair, and Ghasem Ebrahimian) or those minority filmmakers who make films about their ethnic communities (Rea Tajiri, Charles Burnett, Christine Choy, Gregory Nava, Haile
Gerima, and Julie Dash) are often marginalized as merely national, Third
World, Third Cinema, identity cinema, or ethnic filmmakers, who are unable
to fully speak to mainstream audiences. Through funding, festival programming, and marketing strategy, these filmmakers are often encouraged to engage
in "salvage filmmaking," that is, making films that serve to preserve and recover
cultural and ethnic heritage. Other exilic filmmakers, such as Jonas Mekas,
Mona Hatoum, Chantal Akerman, Trinh T. Minh-ha, Isaac Julien, and Shirin
Neshat, are placed within the avant-garde category, while some, such as Agnès
Varda and Chris Marker, are considered unclassifiable.

Although these classificatory approaches are important for framing films to
better understand them or better market them, they also serve to overdetermine
and limit the films' potential meanings. Their undesirable consequences are
particularly grave for the accented films because classification approaches are
not neutral structures. They are "ideological constructs" masquerading as neutral categories (Altman 1989, 5). By forcing accented films into one of the
established categories, the very cultural and political foundations that constitute them are bracketed, misread, or effaced altogether. Such traditional schemas also tend to lock the filmmakers into discursive ghettos that fail to reflect
or account for their personal evolution and stylistic transformations over time.
Once labeled "ethnic," "ethnographic," or "hyphenated," accented filmmakers

remain discursively so even long after they have moved on. On the other hand, there are those, such as Gregory Nava, Spike Lee, Euzhan Palcy, and Mira Nair, who have made the move with varying degrees of success out of ethnic or Third World filmmaking and into mainstream cinema by telling their ethnic and national stories in more recognizable narrative forms.

One of the key purposes of this study is to identify and develop the most appropriate theory to account for the complexities, regularities, and inconsistencies of the films made in exile and diaspora, as well as for the impact that the liminal and interstitial location of the filmmakers has on their work. Occasionally, such a theory is explicitly embedded in the films themselves, such as in Jonas Mekas's *Lost, Lost, Lost* (1949–76), Fernando Solanas's *Tangos: Exile of Gardel* (1985), and Prajna Parasher's *Exile and Displacement* (1992). More often, however, the theory must be discovered and defined as the film moves toward reception, by marketers, reviewers, critics, and viewers. Such a deductive process presents a formidable challenge. It requires discovering common features among disparate products of differently situated displaced filmmakers from varied national origins who are living and making films in the interstices of divergent host societies, under unfamiliar, often hostile, political and cinematic systems. I have opted to work with a stylistic approach, designating it the "accented style."[9] Stylistic history is one of the "strongest justifications for film studies as a distinct academic discipline" (Bordwell 1997, 8). But stylistic study is not much in vogue today. Fear of formalism, lack of knowledge of the intricacies of film aesthetics and film production techniques, the importation of theories into film studies with little regard for the film's specific textual and spectatorial environments—all these can share the blame.

In the narrowest sense, style is the "patterned and significant use of technique" (Bordwell and Thompson 1993, 337). Depending on the site of the repetition, style may refer to a film's style (patterns of significant techniques in a single film), a filmmaker's style (patterns repeated in unique ways in a filmmaker's oeuvre), or a group style (consistent use of technique across the works of several directors). Although attention will be paid here to the authorial styles of individual filmmakers, the group style is the central concern of this book. In general, the choice of style is governed by social and artistic movements, regulations governing censorship, technological developments, the reigning mode of production (cinematic and otherwise), availability of financial resources, and the choices that individual filmmakers make as social and cinematic agents. Sometimes group style is formed by filmmakers who follow certain philosophical tendencies and aesthetic concerns, such as German expressionism and Soviet montage. The accented group style, however, has existed only in a limited, latent, and emergent form, awaiting recognition. Even those who deal with the accented films usually speak of exile and diaspora as themes inscribed in the films, not as components of style. In addition, the overwhelming majority of the many valuable studies of filmmaking in exile and diaspora have been narrowly focused on the works of either an individual filmmaker or a regional group of filmmakers. There are, for example, studies (both lengthy and brief) devoted to the filmmakers Raúl Ruiz, Fernando Solanas, Valeria Sarmiento, Amos Gitai, Michel Khleifi, Abid Med Hondo, Chantal Akerman, Jonas Mekas, Atom Egoyan, and Trinh T. Minh-ha, and there are studies centered on Chilean exile films, Arab exile cinema, *beur* cinema, Chicano/a cinema, Iranian exile cinema, and black African, British, and American diasporic cinemas. While these works shed light on the modus operandi, stylistic features, politics, and thematic concerns of specific filmmakers or of regional or collective diasporic films, none of them adequately addresses the theoretical problematic of an exilic and diasporic cinema as a category that cuts across and is shared by all or by many of them.[10] My task here is to theorize this cinema's existence as an accented style that encompasses characteristics common to the works of differently situated filmmakers involved in varied decentered social formations and cinematic practices across the globe—all of whom are presumed to share the fact of displacement and deterritorialization. Such a shared accent must be discovered (at least initially) at the films' reception and articulated more by the critics than by the filmmakers.

The components of the accented style, listed in Table A.1 (Appendix A), include the film's visual style; narrative structure; character and character development; subject matter, theme, and plot; structures of feeling of exile; filmmaker's biographical and sociocultural location; and the film's mode of production, distribution, exhibition, and reception. I have devoted entire chapters to some of these components or their subsidiary elements, while I have dealt with others in special sections or throughout the book.

Earlier, I divided accented cinema into exilic, diasporic, and postcolonial ethnic films—a division based chiefly on the varied relationship of the films and their makers to existing or imagined homeplaces. Now I draw a further stylistic distinction, between feature and experimental films. The accented feature films are generally narrative, fictional, feature-length, polished, and designed for commercial distribution and theatrical exhibition. The accented experimental films, on the other hand, are usually shot on lower-gauge film stock (16mm and super-8) or on video, making a virtue of their low-tech, low-velocity, almost homemade quality. In addition, they are often nonfictional, vary in length from a few minutes to several hours, and are designed for nontheatrical distribution and exhibition. The feature films are generally more exilic than diasporic, and they are often made by older émigré filmmakers. On the other hand, the experimental films and videos are sometimes more diasporic than exilic, and are made by a younger generation of filmmakers who have been born or bred in diaspora. The experimental films also tend to inscribe autobiography or biography more, or more openly, than the feature films.[11] In them, the filmmakers' own voice-over narration mediates between film types (documentary, fictional) and various levels of identity (personal, ethnic, gender, racial, national). Although narrative hybridity is a characteristic of the accented cinema, the experimental films are more hybridized than the feature films in their intentional crossing and problematization of various borders, such as those between video and film, fiction and nonfiction, narrative and nonnarrative, social and psychic, autobiographical and national.[12]

Accented Style

If the classical cinema has generally required that components of style, such as mise-en-scène, filming, and editing, produce a realistic rendition of the world, the exilic accent must be sought in the manner in which realism is, if not subverted, at least inflected differently. Henry Louis Gates Jr. has characterized black texts as "mulatto" or "mulatta," containing a double voice and a two-toned heritage: "These texts speak in standard Romance and Germanic languages and literary structures, but almost always speak with a distinct and resonant accent, an accent that Signifies (upon) the various black vernacular literary traditions, which are still being written down" (1988, xxiii). Accented films are also mulatta texts. They are created with awareness of the vast histories of the prevailing cinematic modes. They are also created in a new mode that is constituted both by the structures of feeling of the filmmakers themselves as displaced subjects and by the traditions of exilic and diasporic cultural productions that preceded them. From the cinematic traditions they acquire one set of voices, and from the exilic and diasporic traditions they acquire a second. This double consciousness constitutes the accented style that not only signifies upon exile and other cinemas but also signifies the condition of exile itself. It signifies upon cinematic traditions by its artisanal and collective modes of production, which undermine the dominant production mode, and by narrative strategies, which subvert that mode's realistic treatment of time, space, and causality. It also signifies and signifies upon exile by expressing, allegorizing, commenting upon, and critiquing the conditions of its own production, and deterritorialization. Both of these acts of signifying and signification are constitutive of the accented style, whose key characteristics are elaborated upon in the following. What turns these into attributes of style is their repeated inscription in a single film, in the entire oeuvre of individual filmmakers, or in the works of various displaced filmmakers regardless of their place of origin or residence. Ultimately, the style demonstrates their dislocation at the same time that it serves to locate them as authors.

Language, Voice, Address

In linguistics, accent refers only to pronunciation, while dialect refers to grammar and vocabulary as well. More specifically, accent has two chief definitions: "The cumulative auditory effect of those features of pronunciation which identify where a person is from, regionally and socially" and "The emphasis which makes a particular word or syllable stand out in a stream of speech" (Crystal 1991, 2). While accents may be standardized (for example, as British, Scottish, Indian, Canadian, Australian, or American accents of English), it is impossible to speak without an accent. There are various reasons for differences in accent. In English, the majority of accents are regional. Speakers of English as a second language, too, have accents that stem from their regional and first-language characteristics. Differences in accent often correlate with other factors as well: social and class origin, religious affiliation, educational level, and political grouping (Asher 1994, 9). Even though from a linguistic point of view all accents are equally important, all accents are not of equal value socially and politically. People make use of accents to judge not only the social standing of the speakers but also their personality. Depending on their accents, some speakers may be considered regional, local yokel, vulgar, ugly, or comic, whereas others may be thought of as educated, upper-class, sophisticated, beautiful, and proper. As a result, accent is one of the most intimate and powerful markers of group identity and solidarity, as well as of individual difference and personality. The flagship newscasts of mainstream national television and radio networks have traditionally been delivered in the preferred "official" accent, that is, the accent that is considered to be standard, neutral, and value-free.

Applied to cinema, the standard, neutral, value-free accent maps onto the dominant cinema produced by the society's reigning mode of production. This typifies the classical and the new Hollywood cinemas, whose films are realistic and intended for entertainment only, and thus free from overt ideology or accent. By that definition, all alternative cinemas are accented, but each is accented in certain specific ways that distinguish it. The cinema discussed here derives its accent from its artisanal and collective production modes and from the filmmakers' and audiences' deterritorialized locations. Consequently, not all accented films are exilic and diasporic, but all exilic and diasporic films are accented. If in linguistics accent pertains only to pronunciation, leaving grammar and vocabulary intact, exilic and diasporic accent permeates the film's deep structure: its narrative, visual style, characters, subject matter, theme, and plot. In that sense, the accented style in film functions as both accent and dialect in linguistics. Discussions of accents and dialects are usually confined to oral literature and to spoken presentations. Little has been written—besides typographical accentuation of words—about what Taghi Modarressi has called "writing with an accent":

> The new language of any immigrant writer is obviously accented and, at least initially, inarticulate. I consider this "artifact" language expressive in its own right. Writing with an accented voice is organic to the mind of the immigrant writer. It is not something one can invent. It is frequently buried beneath personal inhibitions and doubts. The accented voice is loaded with hidden messages from our cultural heritage, messages that often reach beyond the capacity of the ordinary words of any language. . . . Perhaps it is their [immigrant and exile writers'] personal language that

can build a bridge between what is familiar and what is strange. They may then find it possible to generate new and revealing paradoxes. Here we have our juxtapositions and our transformations—the graceful and the awkward, the beautiful and the ugly, sitting side by side in a perpetual metamorphosis of one into the other. It is like the Hunchback of Notre Dame trying to be Prince Charming for strangers. (1992, 9)

At its most rudimentary level, making films with an accent involves using on-camera and voice-over characters and actors who speak with a literal accent in their pronunciation. In the classical Hollywood cinema, the characters' accents were not a reliable indicator of the actors' ethnicity.[13] In accented cinema, however, the characters' accents are often ethnically coded, for in this cinema, more often than not, the actor's ethnicity, the character's ethnicity, and the ethnicity of the star's persona coincide. However, in some of these films the coincidence is problematized, as in the epistolary films of Chantal Akerman (*News from Home*, 1976) and Mona Hatoum (*Measures of Distance*, 1988). In each of these works, a filmmaking daughter reads in an accented English voice-over the letters she has received from her mother. The audience may assume that these are the voices of the mothers (complete coincidence among the three accents), but since neither of the films declares whose voice we are hearing, the coincidence is subverted and the spectators must speculate about the true relationship of the accent to the identity, ethnicity, and authenticity of the speaker or else rely on extratextual information.

One of the greatest deprivations of exile is the gradual deterioration in and potential loss of one's original language, for language serves to shape not only individual identity but also regional and national identities prior to displacement. Threatened by this catastrophic loss, many accented filmmakers doggedly insist on writing the dialogues in their original language—to the detriment of the films' wider distribution. However, most accented films are bilingual, even multilingual, multivocal, and multiaccented, like Egoyan's *Calendar* (1993), which contains a series of telephonic monologues in a dozen untranslated languages, or Raúl Ruiz's *On Top of the Whale* (1981), whose dialogue is spoken in more than a half dozen languages, one of them invented by Ruiz himself. If the dominant cinema is driven by the hegemony of synchronous sound and a strict alignment of speaker and voice, accented films are counterhegemonic insofar as many of them de-emphasize synchronous sound, insist on first-person and other voice-over narrations delivered in the accented pronunciation of the host country's language, create a slippage between voice and speaker, and inscribe everyday nondramatic pauses and long silences.

At the same time that accented films emphasize visual fetishes of homeland and the past (landscape, monuments, photographs, souvenirs, letters), as well as visual markers of difference and belonging (posture, look, style of dress and behavior), they equally stress the oral, the vocal, and the musical—that is, accents, intonations, voices, music, and songs, which also demarcate individual and collective identities. These voices may belong to real, empirical persons, like Mekas's voice narrating his diary films; or they may be fictitious voices, as in Marker's *Letter from Siberia* (1958) and *Sunless* (1982); or they may be accented voices whose identity is not firmly established, as in the aforementioned films by Akerman and Hatoum. Sergeï Paradjanov's four feature films are not only intensely visual in their tableau-like mise-en-scène and presentational filming but also deeply oral in the way they are structured like oral narratives that are told to the camera.

Stressing musical and oral accents redirects our attention from the hegemony of the visual and of modernity toward the acousticity of exile and the commingling of premodernity and postmodernity in the films. Polyphony and heteroglossia both localize and locate the films as texts of cultural and temporal difference.

Increasingly, accented films are using the film's frame as a writing tablet on which appear multiple texts in original languages and in translation in the form of titles, subtitles, intertitles, or blocks of text. The calligraphic display of these texts de-emphasizes visuality while highlighting the textuality and translational issues of intercultural art. Because they are multilingual, accented films require extensive titling just to translate the dialogues. Many of them go beyond that, however, by experimenting with on-screen typography as a supplementary mode of narration and expression. Mekas's *Lost, Lost, Lost*, Trinh's *Surname Viet Given Name Nam*, and Tajiri's *History and Memory* (1991) experiment with multiple typographical presentations of English texts on the screen linked in complicated ways to the dialogue and to the voice-overs, which are also accented in their pronunciation. In cases where the on-screen text is written in "foreign" languages, such as in Suleiman's *Homage by Assassination* (1991) and Hatoum's *Measures of Distance*, both of which display Arabic words, the vocal accent is complemented by a calligraphic accent. The inscription of these visual and vocal accents transforms the act of spectatorship, from just watching to watching *and* literally reading the screen.

By incorporating voice-over narration, direct address, multilinguality, and multivocality, accented films, particularly the epistolary variety, destabilize the omniscient narrator and narrative system of the mainstream cinema and journalism. Film letters often contain the characters' direct address (usually in first-person singular), the indirect discourse of the filmmaker (as the teller of the tale), and the free indirect discourse of the film in which the direct voice contaminates the indirect. Egoyan's *Calendar* combines all three of these discourses to create confusion as to what is happening, who is speaking, who is addressing whom, where the diegetic photographer and his on-screen wife (played by Egoyan and his real-life wife) leave off and where the historical persons Atom Egoyan and Arsinée Khanjian begin. The accented style is itself an example of free indirect discourse in the sense of forcing the dominant cinema to speak in a minoritarian dialect.

Embedded Criticism

As Dick Hebdige has noted, style—any style—is "a gesture of defiance or contempt, in a smile or a sneer. It signals a Refusal" (1979, 3). The accented film style is such a gesture, smile, or sneer of refusal and defiance. Although it does not conform to the classic Hollywood style, the national cinema style of any particular country, the style of any specific film movement or any film author, the accented style is influenced by them all, and it signifies upon them and criticizes them. By its artisanal and collective mode of production, its subversion of the conventions of storytelling and spectator positioning, its critical juxtaposition of different worlds, languages, and cultures, and its aesthetics of imperfection and smallness, it critiques the dominant cinema. It is also highly political because politics infuses it from inception to reception. For these reasons, accented cinema is not only a minority cinema but also a minor cinema, in the way that Deleuze and Guattari have defined the concept (1986).

However, this should not be construed to mean that the accented cinema is oppositional cinema, in the sense of defining itself primarily against an unaccented dominant cinema. Produced in a capitalist (if alternative) mode of production, the accented films are not necessarily radical, for they act as agents not only of expression and defiance but also of assimilation, even legitimization, of their makers and their audiences. As such, accented cinema is one of the dialects of our language of cinema.

Accented Structures of Feeling

Since the accented style is not a programmatic, already formed style, one may speak of it as an emergent "structure of feeling," which, according to Raymond Williams, is not a fixed institution, formation, position, or even a formal concept such as worldview or ideology. Rather, it is a set of undeniable personal and social experiences—with internal relations and tensions—that is

> still in process, often indeed not yet recognized as social but taken to be private, idiosyncratic, and even isolating, but which in analysis (though rarely otherwise) has its emergent, connecting, and dominant characteristics, indeed its specific hierarchies. These are often more recognizable at a later stage, when they have been (as often happens) formalized, classified, and in many cases built into institutions and formations. (1977, 132)

The accented style is one such emergent category—not yet fully recognized or formalized. Its structure of feeling is rooted in the filmmakers' profound experiences of deterritorialization, which oscillate between dysphoria and euphoria, celibacy and celebration. These dislocatory feeling structures are powerfully expressed in the accented films' chronotopical configurations of the homeland as utopian and open and of exile as dystopian and claustrophobic (to which I devote two chapters of this book).

In some measure, what is being described here is similar to the feeling structures of postmodernism. In speaking about the formation of a new mass audience for postmodernist art, Fred Pfeil notes that experiencing such art is characterized by "a very unstable play between a primal delight and primal fear, between two simultaneous versions of the primary aggressive impulse, that which seeks to incorporate the world into itself and that which struggles to prevent its own engulfment. This dialectic is the postmodern 'structure of feeling' (1988, 386). To the extent that the accented and postmodernist cinemas both immerse us in these dystopic and euphoric moments of unresolved polarity, they are similar. However, not all postmodernist films are diasporically or exilically accented, while all accented films are to some extent postmodernist. Accented films differ from other postmodernist films because they usually posit the homeland as a grand and deeply rooted referent, which stops the postmodernist play of signification. Since exile (more than diaspora) is driven by the modernist concerns and tropes of nationalism and state formation, which posits the existence and realness of the earth, mountains, monuments, and seas as well as of the peoples, histories, politics, and cultures of the homeland, many exilically accented films are intensely place-bound, and their narratives are driven by a desire either to recapture the homeland or to return to it. As a result, during the liminal period of displacement, the postmodernist playfulness, indeterminacy, and intertextuality have little place in exilic politics and cinema. The referent homeland is too powerfully real, even sacred, to be played with and signified upon. It is this powerful hold of the homeland that imbues the accented structures of feeling with such sadness and sense of terminal loss as described by Edward Said:

> Exile is strangely compelling to think about but terrible to experience. It is the unhealable rift forced between a human being and a native place, between the self and its true home: its essential sadness can never be surmounted. And while it is true that literature and history contain heroic, romantic, glorious, even triumphant episodes in an exile's life, these are no more than efforts meant to overcome the crippling sorrow of estrangement. The achievements of exile are permanently undermined by the loss of something left behind for ever. (1990b, 357)

Sadness, loneliness, and alienation are frequent themes, and sad, lonely, and alienated people are favorite characters in the accented films.

Only when the grand return to the homeland is found to be impossible, illusory, or undesirable does the postmodernist semiosis set in. Then the nostalgia for the referent and the pain of separation from it may be transformed into a nostalgia for its synecdoches, fetishes, and signifieds—the frozen sounds and images of the homeland—which are then circulated in exilic media and pop culture (including wall calendars, as in Egoyan's *Calendar*).[14]

Multiple sites, cultures, and time zones inform the feeling structures of exile and diaspora, and they pose the representation of simultaneity and multisitedness as challenges for the accented films. Citing Sergei Eisenstein, George Marcus offered montage as a methodology that not only encodes multiple times and sites but also self-consciously problematizes the realist representation of the world. In the accented cinema, as in the multisited ethnography that Marcus describes, this is achieved by critical juxtapositions of multiple spaces, times, voices, narratives, and foci (1994).

Tactile Optics

The human body is experienced from both sides of the phenomenological divide: externally, by means of mirrors, photography, film, electronic sensors, and other peoples' reactions; and internally, by means of our own vision, organs of balance, and proprioception (Sobchack 1999). In traumatic forms of expulsion and exile, especially when they are coupled with racism and hostility in the new country, the certainty and wholeness of the body (and of the mind) are often put into doubt. The body's integrity, requiring a coincidence of inside and outside, is threatened, as a result of which it may be felt to be separated, collapsed, fractured, eviscerated, or pithed. The exilic dislocation can be experienced simultaneously both at quotidian and profound and at corporeal and spiritual levels. The impact of dislocation on language has already been discussed. The dominance of vision—an accepted fact of modernity (Jay 1993)—is attenuated for the exiles by the prominence of the other senses, which continually and poignantly remind them of their seemingly irrevocable difference, loss, or lack of fit. A particular fragrance on a hillside, a stolen glance in a restaurant, a body brush in a crowded street, a particular posture by a passenger in an elevator, a flash of memory during daily conversations, the sound of familiar words in one's native tongue heard from an adjoining car at a red traffic light—each of these sensory reports activates private memories and intensifies the feeling of *displacement*, a feeling that one may have suppressed in order to get on with life. However, just as frequently and powerfully, these very reports may serve the opposite function of restoration and *emplacement*—by reestablishing connections.

Since some of the most poignant reminders of exile are non-visual and deeply rooted in everyday experiences, they tend to emphasize tactile sensibilities. As formulated by Michael Taussig, the sense of everydayness includes "much that is not sense so much as sensuousness, an embodied and somewhat automatic 'knowledge' that functions like peripheral vision, not studied contemplation, a knowledge that is imageric and sensate rather than ideational" (1992, 8). This peripheral, distracted, tactile vision of the new location is replicated in the accented films' "tactile optics," that is, their nonlinear structure, which is driven by the juxtaposition of multiple spaces, times, voices, narratives, and foci—the montage effect. This effect, in turn, is propelled by the memory, nostalgic longing, and multiple losses and wishes that are experienced by the diegetic characters, exilic filmmakers, and their audiences. Significantly, such a distracted mode of being in the world is also characteristic of postmodern living. Given that distracted vision and glance are also characteristic of televisual viewing, as opposed to film spectatorship, which is largely gaze-driven, this may partially account for the affinity of the accented experimental filmmakers for televisuality.

In addition to the distracted aesthetics of montage, the tactile optics involves the style of filming. Some filmmakers force the audience to experience the diegesis by means of the texture of the film, video, and computer screens (as in Egoyan's *Next of Kin*, *Speaking Parts*, and *Calendar* and in Marker's *Sunless*). Some use long takes, which allow the spectators time to leisurely project themselves into the diegesis to the point of occupying it (as in Tarkovsky's *Nostalgia* and in Michael Snow's *Wavelength*, 1966–67). Single-frame filming and audio sampling capture fleeting moments of vision, memory, and voice, replicating distracted attention (as in Mekas's *Walden*, part of which is filmed in single frame, or in Trinh's *Reassemblage* (1982), in which unfinished words and sentences are repeated in different iterations). Texture is suggested by emphasizing aromatic and sensual experiences (as in Ang Lee's *Eat Drink Man Woman* [*Yinshi Nan Nu*] 1994); by showing nature's elemental forces (as in Artavazd Pelechian's *Seasons* [1982] and in Ivens and Loridan's *A Tale of the Wind* [1988]); or by inscribing extremely claustrophobic urban spaces (as in Yilmaz Güney's *The Wall* [1983], Tevfik Baser's *40 m² Germany* [1986], Sohrab Shahid Saless's *Utopia* [1982], Yuri Ilienko's *Swan Lake: The Zone* [1990], and Yilmaz Arslan's *Passages* [1982]). A thematic focus on journey, traveling, and nomadic wandering (as in Tarkovsky's *Stalker* [1979], Ulrike Ottinger's *Johanna d'Arc of Mongolia* [1989], and Rachid Bouchareb's *Cheb* [1990]) can also be a source of varying textures.[15]

Tactility is also promoted by the nonaudiovisual ways in which displaced people experience the audiovisual media. Located at the intersection of difference and alterity, they experience every film in the context of awareness of that difference. Certain images, sounds, characters, actors, accented speech, gestures, stories, locations, and quality of light within the film may remind exilic spectators of what Laura Marks calls their private "sense memories" (1994, 258), that is, each spectator's recollections of the images, sounds, smells, people, places, and times they have left behind.

The exilic structures of feeling and the tactile optics are reminiscent of Dudley Andrew's designation of "poetic realism" as an "optique" that characterizes the classic French films of the late 1930s. By his formulation, optique "suggests the ocular and ideological mechanisms of 'perspective,' both of which aptly play roles in the medium of film" (1995, 19). In its multiple contract with

industry and audiences, optique is similar to genre, and in positing a spontaneous, idiosyncratic, and authentic relationship between films and their makers,
it resembles style. The accented style is an exilic optique because it provides
both an ocular and an ideological perspective on deterritorialization. The ocular is encoded in the tactile optics and the ideological in the structures of feeling
and synaesthetic sensibilities of the style.

Third Cinema Aesthetics

The genealogy of the accented style may be traced not only ato the epochal
shifts of postcolonialism and postmodernism but also to the transformation of
cinematic structures, theories, and practices since the 1960s. Specifically, it begins with the emergence and theorization of a Latin-American cinema of liberation, dubbed "Third Cinema," and its later elaboration by Teshome H. Gabriel
and others. Drawing upon the Cuban revolution of 1959, Italian neorealist film
aesthetics, Griersonian social documentary style, and Marxist analysis, Brazilian filmmaker Glauber Rocha issued his passionate polemic, "The Aesthetics
of Hunger," and Argentinean cinéastes Fernando Solanas and Spanish-born
Octavio Getino, makers of the massive film *The Hour of the Furnaces* (*La Hora
de los Hornos*, 1968), published their famous manifesto, "Towards a Third Cinema." These were followed by an avant-gardist manifesto, "For an Imperfect
Cinema," written by the Cuban filmmaker Julio Garcia Espinosa.[16] Other "revolutionary" cinematic manifestos were issued in North Africa and the Middle
East.[17] In France, the SLON (later ISKRA) and Dziga Vertov groups, among
others, and in the United States, Newsreel and other groups picked up the
clarion call of these manifestos and issued their own summons for new radical
cinematic practices. The Latin-American polemics and manifestos in particular, including *The Hour of the Furnaces*, critiqued the mainstream, capitalist,
"first cinema" and the petit bourgeois, authorial "second cinema"; in their place
they proposed a new research category of "Third Cinema"—a cinema that is
not perfect, polished, or professional.[18] Indeed, in its formal practices, *The Hour
of the Furnaces* is a clear progenitor of the accented style.

The accented cinema is one of the offshoots of the Third Cinema, with
which it shares certain attributes and from which it is differentiated by certain
sensibilities. As Gabriel elaborated, although Third Cinema films are made
chiefly in the Third World, they may be made anywhere, by anyone, about any
subject, and in a variety of styles and forms, as long as they are oppositional and
liberationist (1982, 2–3). As a cinema of displacement, however, the accented
cinema is much more situated than the Third Cinema, for it is necessarily
made by (and often for) specific displaced subjects and diasporized communities. Less polemical than the Third Cinema, it is nonetheless a political cinema
that stands opposed to authoritarianism and oppression. If Third Cinema films
generally advocated class struggle and armed struggle, accented films favor

discursive and semiotic struggles. Although not necessarily Marxist or even socialist like the Third Cinema, the accented cinema is an engagé cinema. However, its engagement is less with "the people" and "the masses," as was the case with the Third Cinema, than with specific individuals, ethnicities, nationalities, and identities, and with the experience of deterritorialization itself. In accented cinema, therefore, every story is both a private story of an individual and a social and public story of exile and diaspora. These engagements with collectivities and with deterritorialization turn accented films into allegories of exile and diaspora—not the totalizing "national allegories" that Jameson once characterized Third World literature and cinema to be (1986).

Third Cinema and accented cinema are alike in their attempts to define and create a nostalgic, even fetishized, authentic prior culture—before contamination by the West in the case of the Third Cinema, and before displacement and emigration in the case of the accented cinema. Like *The Hour of the Furnaces*, accented films are hybridized in their use of forms that cut across the national, typological, generic, and stylistic boundaries. Similarly, many of them are driven by the aesthetics of provisionality, experimentation, and imperfection—even amateurness—and they are made in the artisanal, low-cost mode of "cinema of hunger." In sum, despite some marked differences, both accented films and Third Cinema films are historically conscious, politically engaged, critically aware, generically hybridized, and artisanally produced. The affinity of the two cinemas and the impact of the one on the other are paralleled in the lives of some of the filmmakers, such as Fernando Solanas from Argentina and Miguel Littín from Chile, who moved from the Third Cinema in the 1960s to the accented cinema of the 1980s and beyond.

Border Effects, Border Writing

Border consciousness emerges from being situated at the border, where multiple determinants of race, class, gender, and membership in divergent, even antagonistic, historical and national identities intersect. As a result, border consciousness, like exilic liminality, is theoretically against binarism and duality and for a third optique, which is multiperspectival and tolerant of ambiguity, ambivalence, and chaos.

The globalization of capital, labor, culture, and media is threatening to make borders obsolete and national sovereignty irrelevant. However, physical borders are real and extremely dangerous, particularly for those who have to cross them. In recent years no region in the world has borne deadlier sustained clashes over physical (and discursive) borders than the Middle East and the former Yugoslavia. The collisions over physical and literal lands, even over individual houses and their symbolic meanings, are also waged in the accented films. Since their widely received formulation by Anzaldúa (1987), borderland consciousness and theory have been romanticized, universalized, and co-opted by ignoring the specific dislocatory and conflictual historical and territorial grounds that produce them. However, borders are open, and infected wounds and the subjectivity they engender cannot be postnational or post-al, but interstitial. Unequal power relations and incompatible identities prevent the wound from healing.

Since border subjectivity is cross-cultural and intercultural, border filmmaking tends to be accented by the "strategy of translation rather than representation" (Hicks 1991, xxiii). Such a strategy undermines the distinction between autochthonous and alien cultures in the interest of promoting their interaction and intertextuality. As a result, the best of the border films are hybridized and experimental—characterized by multifocality, multilinguality, asynchronicity, critical distance, fragmented or multiple subjectivity, and transborder amphibolic characters—characters who might best be called "shifters." Of these characteristics, the latter bears discussion at this point.

In linguistics, shifters are words, such as "I" and "you," whose reference can be understood only in the context of the utterance. More generally, a shifter is an "operator" in the sense of being dishonest, evasive, and expedient, or even being a "mimic," in the sense that Homi Bhabha formulated, as a producer of critical excess, irony, and sly civility (1994). In the context of border filmmaking, shifters are characters who exhibit some or all of these registers of understanding and performativity. As such, they occupy a powerful position in the political economy of both actual and diegetic border crossings. For example, in Nava's *El Norte*, a classic border film, the shifters consist of the following characters: the *pollo* (border-crossing brother and sister, Enrique and Rosa); the coyote (the Mexican middleman who for a fee brings the *pollo* across), the *migra* (the U.S. immigration officers who chase and arrest Enrique); the *pocho* (Americans of Mexican descent who speak Mexican Spanish imperfectly, the man in the film who turns Enrique in to the immigration authorities); the *chola/cholo* and *pachuca/pachuco* (young inhabitants of the border underworld who have their own dialect called *caló*); and the U.S.-based Mexican or Hispanic contractors who employ border crossers as day laborers (among them, Enrique).[19] The power of these border shifters comes from their situationist existence, their familiarity with the cultural and legal codes of interacting cultures, and the way in which they manipulate identity and the asymmetrical power situations in which they find themselves.

Accented films inscribe other amphibolic character types who are split, double, crossed, and hybridized and who perform their identities. As liminal subjects and interstitial artists, many accented filmmakers are themselves shifters, with multiple perspectives and conflicted or performed identities. They may own no passport or hold multiple passports, and they may be stranded between legality and illegality. Many are scarred by the harrowing experiences of their own border crossings. Some may be energized, while others may be paralyzed by their fear of partiality. Their films often draw upon these biographical crossing experiences.

Themes

Understandably, journeys, real or imaginary, form a major thematic thread in the accented films. Journeys have motivation, direction, and duration, each of which impacts the travel and the traveler. Three types of journeys are explored in this book: outward journeys of escape, home seeking, and home founding; journeys of quest, homelessness, and lostness; and inward, homecoming journeys. Depending on their directions, journeys are valued differently. In the accented cinema, westering journeys are particularly valued, partly because they reflect the filmmakers' own trajectory and the general flow of value worldwide. The westering journey is embedded, in its varied manifestations, in Xavier Koller's *Journey of Hope* (1990), Nizamettin Ariç's *A Cry for Beko* (1992), and Ghasem Ebrahimian's *The Suitors* (1989). In Nava's *El Norte*, a south-north journey lures the Mayan Indians from Guatemala to the United States.

There are many instances of empowering return journeys: to Morocco in Faridah Ben Lyazid's *Door to the Sky* (1989), to Africa in Raquel Gerber's *Ori* (1989), and to Ghana in Haile Gerima's *Sankofa* (1993). When neither escape nor return is possible, the desire for escape and the longing for return become highly cathected to certain icons of homeland's nature and to certain narratives. These narratives take the form of varied journeys: from the dystopic and irresolute journey of lostness in Tarkovsky's *Stalker* (1979) to the nostalgically celebratory homecoming journey in Mekas's *Reminiscences of a Journey to Lithuania* (1971–72) to the conflicting return journey to Japan and China in Ann Hui's *Song of the Exile* (1990).

Not all journeys involve physical travel. There also are metaphoric and philosophical journeys of identity and transformation that involve the films' characters and sometimes the filmmakers themselves, as in Mekas's films or in Ivens and Loridan's *A Tale of the Wind*.

Authorship and Autobiographical Inscription

If prestructuralism considered authors to be outside and prior to the texts that uniquely express their personalities, and if cinestructuralism regarded authors as structures within their own texts, poststructuralism views authors as fictions within their texts who reveal themselves only in the act of spectating. Poststructuralist theory of authorship is thus embedded in theories of ideology and subject formation, and it privileges spectatorial reading over that of authoring. Roland Barthes went so far as to declare that "the birth of the reader must be at the cost of the death of the Author" (1977, 148). In this figuration, the author as a biographical person exercising parentage over the text disappears, leaving behind desiring spectators in search of an author. This author whom they construct is neither a projection nor a representation of a real author but

a fictive figure within the text (Barthes 1975, 27). According to this formulation, the fictional structure or subject "Atom Egoyan" whom the spectators
discover in the films of Atom Egoyan is not the same as, and does not necessarily map out onto, the empirical person named Atom Egoyan. Since texts create
subject positions for both authors and spectators, poststructural theory must
deal with the construction of both authors and spectators. Spectators, however,
like authors, are not only subjects of texts but also—Barthes to the contrary—
subjects in history, negotiating for positions within psychosocial formations,
producing multiple readings and multiple author and spectator effects. The
classical Hollywood cinema's invisible style creates filmic realism by promoting
the impression of cohesiveness of time, space, and causality. As a result, diegetic
reality appears to be authorless, natural, and mimetic, in an organic relationship
to the profilmic world. As John Caughie notes, "The removal or suppression
of the clear marks of 'authored discourse' transforms ideology from something
produced out of a locatable, historical, determined position into something
natural to the world" (1981, 202).

My project in this book is precisely to put the locatedness and the historicity
of the authors back into authorship. To that extent, accented cinema theory is
an extension of the authorship theory, and it runs counter to much of the
postmodern theory that attempts to either deny authorship altogether or multiply the authoring parentage to the point of "de-originating the utterance."[20]
However, film authors are not autonomous, transcendental beings who are
graced by unique, primordial, and originary sparks of genius. Accented film
authors are literally and figuratively everyday journeymen and journeywomen
who are driven off or set free from their places of origin, by force or by choice,
on agonizing quests that require diplacements and emplacements so profound,
personal, and transformative as to shape not only the authors themselves and
their films but also the question of authorship. Any discussion of authorship
in exile needs to take into consideration not only the individuality, originality,
and personality of unique individuals as expressive film authors but also, and
more important, their (dis)location as interstitial subjects within social formations and cinematic practices.

Accented films are personal and unique, like fingerprints, because they are
both authorial and autobiographical. Exile discourse needs to counter the move
by some postmodern critics to separate the author of the film from the enunciating subject in the film, for exile and authorship are fundamentally intertwined
with historical movements of empirical subjects across boundaries of nations—
not just texts.

To be sure, there are postmodern accented filmmakers, such as Egoyan and
Caveh Zahedi, in whose films the relationship of the authoring filmmaker to
both the text and the authoring structure within the text is one not of direct
parentage but of convoluted performance. However, the questioning of the
bond linking autobiography to authorship should not be used as a postmodern-

ist sleight of hand to dismiss the specificity of exilic conditions or to defuse their subversive and empowering potentiality. Such a move comes at the very moment that, for the diasporized subalterns of the world, history, historical agency, and autobiographical consciousness have become significant and signifying components of identity, artistic production, and social agency. Accented authors are empirical subjects who exist outside and prior to their films.

In the accented cinema, the author is in the text in multiple ways, traversing the spectrum of authorship theories, from prestructuralism to poststructuralism. In a longitudinal and intertextual study of the films of individual filmmakers, we may discover certain consistencies from which we can construct an authorial presence within the films. It is thus that authors become discursive figures (Foucault 1977) who inhabit and are constructed not only by history but also by their own filmic texts. How they inhabit their films, or, in Bordwell's term (1989, 151–68), how they are "personified" varies: they may inhabit them as real empirical persons, enunciating subjects, structured absences, fictive structures, or a combination of these. In the accented films, determining the mode of habitation of the author within the text is a complex task, even in films in which the filmmakers appear as empirical persons and as themselves either audiovisually (Mekas's films, including *Lost, Lost, Lost*), or only visually (Suleiman's *Chronicle of Disappearance*), or only vocally and as the film's addressee (Akerman's *News from Home*), or as fictional characters (Egoyan's *Calendar*), or as author surrogates (Naderi's *Manhattan by Numbers* and Shahid Saless's *Roses for Africa*, 1991). In all these cases, filmmakers are engaged in the performance of the self. In short, because of their interstitiality, even in situations of self-inscription exilic authors tend to create ambiguity regarding their own real, fictive, or discursive identities, thus problematizing Phillipe Lejeune's "autobiographical pact," which requires that the author, the narrator, and the protagonist be identical (1989, 5).

Exilic authorship is also a function of the filmmakers' mode of production. In fact, in their multiple incarnations or personifications, the authors are produced by their production mode. If the cinema's dominant postindustrial production modes privilege certain kinds of authorship, then the artisanal accented production modes must favor certain other authorial signatures and accents. It is worth bearing in mind that such signatures or accents signify both the various incarnations of their authors and the conditions of exile and diaspora. The interpretation of these signatures and accents depends on the spectators, who are themselves often situated astride cultures and within collective formations. Hence, the figures they cut in their spectating of the accented filmmakers as authors are nuanced by their own extratextual tensions of difference and identity.

To further demonstrate the explanatory power of the accented style, a case study of Atom Egoyan's style is presented in the next close-up section, based on an examination of his feature films, a review of the literature by and about him, and my extensive discussions with him (Naficy 1997a). Although some of the components of Egoyan's accented style constitute his personal authorial signature, there are many components that he shares with other accented filmmakers.

Close-Up: Atom Egoyan's Accented Style

In the early 1990s, Atom Egoyan was considered to be the "most original" Canadian director next to David Cronenberg (Atamian 1991, 70; Ansen 1992). He was also called "the most accomplished Canadian director of his generation" (Johnson 1991, 68) and Canada's first multicultural feature filmmaker, "grant-magnet and prize pony" (Balley 1989, 46), a characterization he derided. His films occasionally received criticism on grounds of being "dishonest and posturing, more like intellectual masturbation" (Kempley 1990, D3), or for being "pretentious" and "elegantly empty" (Maslin 1989, C16). However, they were such a favorite of international film festivals and critics that he was regarded as "a child of the festival circuit" (Handling 1993, 8). It was at these festivals that his films received high praise and almost universal critical acclaim. Calling him one of the most talented directors at the 1987 Montreal Film Festival, Wim Wenders publicly turned over his $5,000 award for *Wings of Desire* (1988) to Egoyan for directing *Family Viewing* (1987). *The Adjuster* (1991) won the Special Jury Prize at the 1991 Moscow Film Festival, and the Cannes International Film Festival gave Egoyan the International Critics Prize for *Exotica* in 1993 and the Grand Prize for *The Sweet Hereafter* in 1997. With each film, both his cult following and his general popularity grew.

Egoyan was born in Egypt in 1960 to two artists, who were descendants of Armenian refugees. His parents ran a successful furniture store until the rising tide of Nasserist nationalism and the parochialism of the local Armenian community encouraged their emigration in 1962 to Victoria, British Columbia. Egoyan was three years old at the time. The only Armenian family in the area, they set up another furniture store called Ego Interiors (Atom Egoyan's film company is called Ego Film Arts). Although Egoyan spoke Armenian as a child, he gave it up when he entered kindergarten to forestall ethnic embarrassment and harassment. He also refused to speak Armenian at home, and whenever his parents spoke Armenian to him, he covered his ears. At eighteen, he moved to Toronto and became what he thought was a fully assimilated Canadian, graduating with honors in international relations from the University of Toronto. While there, he led a socially active life, writing plays, publishing film criticism in the school paper, and working on student films. Egoyan's first short film, *Howard in Particular* (1979), was made in Toronto and was followed by several more shorts. His contact at the university with nationalist Armenian students placed him on a trajectory of increased ethnic awareness.

Egoyan's output may be divided into three general categories: short films, television films and episodic series, and feature films. Despite the increasingly wide reception, even popularity, of some of his features and television films, so far Egoyan has remained an independent filmmaker, relying on a variety of funds from local and regional arts councils, private sources, his own earnings, and Canadian and European television networks. This independent and alternative mode of production is a characteristic of the accented film practice and is constitutive of its accented style. Another contributor to this style and to his authorship is Egoyan's multiple functions in his films: he has written and directed all of his features; edited several of them (*Next of Kin* [1984], *Family Viewing*, and *Calendar*); functioned as executive producer or producer in many of them (*Next of Kin, Family Viewing, Speaking Parts, Calendar, Exotica*, and *The Sweet Hereafter*); and acted in one feature (*Calendar*) and several shorts. He has also played the classical guitar sound track for two of his features (*Next of Kin* and *The Adjuster*). In addition, his wife, Arsinée Khanjian, has starred in all of his features and coproduced *Calendar* with him. Other on-camera talent and off-camera crew members have been regular participants in his films. As I discuss in the section on the mode of production, performing multiple functions and employing a repertory of talent and crew give accented filmmakers, such as Egoyan, fuller control over both the authorship and the cost of their projects. At the same time, however, this control deepens their interstitiality by limiting their options. As such, Egoyan's films tend to inscribe more fully his own biography, personal obsessions, and auteurist vision and style.

Issues of race, ethnicity, and submerged ethnicity are not limited to "ethnic" films. In fact, much of the mainstream Hollywood cinema is "saturated" with submerged ethnic and racial resonances (Shohat 1991, 219). On closer examination, it will be seen that Egoyan's films are also suffused with such submerged resonances and that his filmic career is one of increased ethnicization, which emerges fully in *Calendar*. His films embody many attributes of the accented style, including the inscription of closed and claustrophobic spaces both in the films' mise-en-scène and in the filming; ethnically coded mise-en-scène, characters, music, and iconography; multilinguality and accented speech by ethnic characters and actors; epistolarity by means of letters, video, and the telephone; tactile uses of video and technological mediation of all reality; slippery, guarded, and obsessive characters who camouflage or perform their identities and secret desires; ethnic characters who either are silent or are present but only on video; inscription of journeys of identity and of return journey to the homeland; the instability and persistence of memory that can be recorded, recorded over, remembered nostalgically, erased, and played back repeatedly; and fragmented structures of feeling and narratives.[21]

Certain Armenian sensibilities further accent Egoyan's films: looks, gestures, expressions, postures, and certain thematic concerns with family structures, Armenian history, religiosity, ethnicity, and diasporism. Added to these ethnocultural sensibilities are Egoyan's personal proclivities and his feeling structures as a subject inhabiting the liminal slipzones of identity, cultural difference, and film production practice. Another enabling component of his accented style is his expression of those sensibilities and feelings in certain juxtapositions, narratives, and themes that are at times so paradoxical as to require a knowing audience for their full appreciation. Like all accented speech, Egoyan's style has produced results that are fabulous and grotesque, charming and offensive.

These components of the accented style are present in the corpus of Egoyan's feature films, and to a large extent in each of his films. It is important to emphasize, however, that the identification of the accented style in his work in no way diminishes the heterogeneity of his films and the multiplicity of their meanings. My intention is not to reduce Egoyan to an essential exilic or ethnic subject. There is none! Rather, it is to analyze his accented style and the hitherto more or less latent currents, crosscurrents, and structures in his public image and films.[22] By neither conforming to nor exhausting the paradigm of the accented style, Egoyan's films confirm the importance of authorship as a marker of difference. His most glaring differences with the paradigm are his suppression of orality and his intense emphasis on the visual, vision, and voyeuristic structures of looking. In addition, although memory is significant in all his films, it does not particularly promote tactility or "tactile vision" (*Speaking Parts* excepted). There is almost no significant scene in any of Egoyan's films, except *Next of Kin*, in which the synaesthesia of meal preparation or of eating of food is figured. Likewise, open spaces, landscape, nature, and the human relation with them had no place in any of his feature films until *Calendar*—his most exilic work.

This examination of Egoyan's works also demonstrates the elasticity of the concept of style as a critical approach to exilic and diasporic cinema. Like many of the filmmakers discussed, both Egoyan and his cinema are nomadic and hybridized. The films combine aspects of exilic feature films and diasporic experimental films. His early features, especially the exilically pivotal *Calendar*, integrated the high-gloss, narrative-driven attributes of the former with the small-scale, experimental, home-video dimensions of the latter, while his later films—*The Adjuster, Exotica*, and *The Sweet Hereafter*—belong almost entirely to the feature film form. His wider critical and commercial success since *Exotica* is pushing him across another divide: away from the alternative and interstitial modes of production and toward the mainstream independent mode of production. By traveling across forms and modes, Egoyan himself is transformed. How he will respond to the undeniable allure of the big budgets, high gloss, and massive audience that the postindustrial cinema promises remains to be seen.

Like all approaches to cinema, the accented style attempts to reduce and to channel the free play of meanings. But this approach is driven by its sensitivity to the production and consumption of films and videos in conditions of exilic liminality and diasporic transnationality. The style designation also allows us to reclassify films or to classify certain hitherto unclassifiable films. Thus, Mekas's *Lost, Lost, Lost*, which has been variously regarded as documentary, avant-garde, or diary film, will yield new insights if reread as an accented film. If one thinks of Buñuel as an exilic filmmaker, as does Marsha Kinder (1993), further understanding about his films, hitherto unavailable, will be produced. Likewise, a rereading of Miguel Littín's docudrama *The Jackal of Nahueltoro* (*El Chacal de Nahueltoro*, 1969), turns it into a protoexilic film containing many components of the accented style in emergent form, even though at first blush the story does not warrant such an interpretation.

The accented style helps us to discover commonalities among exilic filmmakers that cut across gender, race, nationality, and ethnicity, as well as across boundaries of national cinemas, genres, and authorship. References to filmmakers in this book range far and wide, from Godard to Mekas, from Akerman to Med Hondo, and from Solanas to Trinh. Approached stylistically, films can be read, reread, and back-read not only as individual texts but also as sites of struggle over meanings and identities. By problematizing the traditional schemas and representational practices, this approach blurs the distinction, often artificially maintained, among various film types such as documentary, fictional, and avant-garde. All of these types are considered here.

The accented style is not a fully recognized and sanctioned film genre, and the exilic and diasporic filmmakers do not always make accented films. In fact, most of them would wish to be in Egoyan's place, to move out of marginal cinema niches into the world of art cinema or even popular cinema. Style permits the critics to track the evolution of the work of not only a single filmmaker but also a group of filmmakers. As I discuss in the chapters on mode of production, Asian Pacific American filmmaking has gradually evolved away from an ethnic focus toward diasporic and exilic concerns, while Iranian exilic filmmakers have evolved toward a diasporic sensibility. These evolutions signal the transformation of both filmmakers and their audiences. They also signal the appropriation of the filmmakers, their audiences, and certain features of the accented style by the mainstream cinema and by its independent offspring. Because it goes beyond connoisseurship to situate the cinéastes within their changing social formations, cultural locations, and cinematic practices, the accented style is not hermetic, homogeneous, or autonomous. It meanders and evolves. It is an inalienable element of the social material process of exile and diaspora and of the exilic and diasporic mode of production.

2

Interstitial and Artisanal Mode of Production

Postindustrial Mode of Production

In addition to the (dis)location of the filmmaking authors, another defining characteristic of the accented style is the mode of production, distribution, and consumption of this cinema (referred to as mode of production for convenience). This takes a number of forms, chief among them the interstitial and collective forms, dealt with here in two separate chapters. Cinema's mode of production is influenced by and modeled after the reigning mode of production in society, and, like that mode, it specifies a relationship between forces of production and social relations of production. The product of cinema is film, a commodity that in capitalist regimes must return a profit to its investors at the box office, video stores, television outlets, and cash registers (for tie-in products). Thus mode of production also specifies a social relation of consumption. The industrial mode of production, exemplified by the classical Hollywood cinema and the studio system in its heyday (1920s–1960s), was characterized by centralized control of production, distribution, and exhibition; division and hierarchy of labor; mass production of standardized products and their continual variation; and creation, attraction, and manipulation of mass publics and taste cultures.[1]

The industrial mode of production underwent a massive transformation that began long before its eventual demise, a transformation that was rooted in a new global economy. In July 1944, delegates from forty-four countries gathered at Bretton Woods, New Hampshire, to devise a monetary system that would encourage international cooperation and economic stability by preventing the kind of chaos and dramatic boom-and-bust fluctuations that had characterized the 1930s. The conference created a framework for a new payment system. Instead of being based on gold convertibility, it was based on pegged, but adjustable, exchange rates. And it created two institutions that have since played an increasingly important role in institutionalizing the liberal capitalist system within the world's economy and politics. The International Monetary Fund (IMF) operates as a central bank for central banks and assists countries that experience short-term balance-of-payments difficulties. The International Bank for Reconstruction and Development (World Bank), on the other hand, makes long-term loans to needy countries. Both institutions are dominated by the United States, making it the controlling global economic and political force in the post–cold war world. Both the IMF and the World Bank have favored stringent austerity programs, free markets, open societies, and reduced government involvement in business decisions—policies that have brought increasing attacks on them as "pawns" of the United States and "agents" of the destruction of national economies (Stevenson and Gerth 1997, A1). The Bretton Woods payment system collapsed in August 1971, when the United States cut the dollar loose from gold. Soon the exchange rate of all major industrial countries began to float against the dollar, and the regime of fixed exchange rates was gradually replaced with one based on managed but relatively flexible exchange rates (Canoni and Hellerstein 1994, 66).

These and other financial and sociopolitical transformations consolidated the primacy of private enterprise globally and helped usher in a shift in the American cinema's dominant production mode. The studio system's industrial mode faded away, gradually giving way since the mid-1970s to what has become known as the "New Hollywood cinema" and its postindustrial mode, which is less involved in the production than in the global acquisition, distribution, and marketing of films and various multimedia products and related merchandise and services. The postindustrial system is possible thanks to both vertical integration and a widening horizontal integration, once outlawed by the U.S. Supreme Court in its 1948 *Paramount* decision, which have come back since the 1980s in a vastly increased and globalized form, driven partly by corporate mergers of an unprecedented scale. The merger of Walt Disney and Capital Cities/ABC, and Time Warner's acquisition of the Turner Broadcasting System in the mid-1990s provide examples of this accelerating vertical and horizontal integration of media, entertainment, and merchandising companies at the global level. This has brought together, under one roof, movie production and distribution, music production and distribution, broadcast television, cable television, foreign television, satellite television, video distribution, radio broadcasting, film library acquisition, book and periodicals publishing, theme parks, sports teams, and merchandising and retailing.[2]

To these so-called synergistic trends must be added the technological convergence that promises to standardize and digitize all forms of communications, on the one hand, and to fuse telephone, cable television, and computer technologies and services, on the other. The proposed acquisition by America Online of Time Warner in 2000 extends the synergistic tendencies between the old analog media and the new digital media.

Movies are no longer what they used to be: films shown to a group in a theater according to a schedule. Instead, they have become the "intertextual products," "franchises," or "software" that nourish this integrated postindustrial system of production and consumer services. This development has, likewise, deeply influenced the films' choice of stories and their manner of storytelling, as Tom Schatz astutely observes: "The vertical integration of classical Hollywood, which ensured a closed industrial system and coherent narrative, has given way to 'horizontal integration' of the New Hollywood's tightly diversified media conglomerates, which favors texts strategically 'open' to multiple readings and multimedia reiteration" (1993, 34).

The key words that summarize the postindustrial system—globalization, privatization, diversification, deregulation, digitization, convergence, and consolidation—are all associated with centralization of the global economic and media powers in fewer and more powerful hands. However, this market-driven centralization masks a fundamental opposing trend at social and political levels, that is, the fragmentation of nation-states and other social formations, and the scattering, often violent and involuntary, of an increasing number of people from their homelands—all of which are driven by divergence, not convergence. The accented cinema and its mode of production are the products of these centripetal and centrifugal developments since the 1960s.

The postindustrial mode of production is dominant not because it is homogeneous or because it obliterates all opposition. In fact, it contains many cracks, tensions, and contradictions that encourage alternative modes and innovations. To satisfy its unsatiable appetite for new material, it continually cultivates, incorporates, or marginalizes those very alternatives. The American postindustrial cinema tends to hegemonically absorb or dominate its alternatives not only at home but also abroad, including in Europe, where in 1990 its share of the European Community's box office amounted to a surprising 77.4 percent, and of the British market reached a staggering 89 percent (Hill 1994, 59, 75). Realizing the futility of competing with such a juggernaut on its own terms, European countries attempted to protect their film industries by regulating the importation of American films by quota and tariff restrictions, engaging in coproductions with American concerns for the purpose of exporting their products, and aggressively financing their own filmmakers and national cinemas. This resulted not only in a number of national film "movements" but also in lengthy debates about the possibility, the desirability, and the epistemology of a "postnational" European cinema and television (Sorlin 1991; Drummond et al. 1993; Petrie 1992; Lev 1993; Vincendeau 1996; Sinclair et al. 1996). However, as Stuart Hall noted some time ago, " 'Europe' remains an ambiguous and contested signifier" (1992, 45), and the concept of a European identity or a European cinema or television remains elusive—even after the formation of the European Union. In the meantime, the radicalism, pluralism, and specificity of the various cultures, social formations, and individual filmmakers within Europe were recruited in the service of an author-based cinema that was "artisanal in scale, in intention and in mode of production" (Stoneman 1996, 131). The "black British" films and "*beur* cinema" films in France are examples of such an artisanal cinema in Europe.

Accented Mode of Production

Because of the inherent dynamism and contradictions of the postindustrial mode, there are always pockets of alternative film practice that escape the mode's panoptic lights, voracious gaze, and alluring temptations. In his thought-provoking book *Allegories of Cinema* (1989), David James formulated the "alternative" mode of production that emerged during the 1960s in the United States as a counterpractice to the capitalist and industrial mode of production. In a later work, he quoted Karl Marx: "In all forms of society there is one specific kind of production which predominates over the rest, whose relations thus assign rank and influence to the others. It is a general illumination which bathes all the other colours and modifies their particularity. It is a particular ether which determines the specific gravity of every being which has materialized within it" (1996a, 12). The dominant mode of cultural production exists side by side with the alternative and emergent modes, which serve other functions and can mobilize other values. Although it may circumscribe, influence, and modify those modes, it does not obliterate either their particularity or their alterity, for it needs both in order to flourish and to remain dominant.

The accented cinema's mode of production stands in relation to the new Hollywood's postindustrial cinema in the way James's alternative practice stood in relation to the classical Hollywood's industrial mode. Although it is not strongly motivated by money, accented cinema is, nevertheless, enabled by capital—in a peculiar mixed economy consisting of market forces within media industries; personal, private, public, and philanthropic funding sources; and ethnic and exilic economies. It is thus not entirely free from capital, nor should it be reduced to it.

The accented cinema's mode of production is divided into the interstitial and the collective modes, which are explored extensively in this and the next chapters by means of a number of close-up sections. These modes are undergirded by rhizomatically interlinked independent, nonprofit, political, and ethnoreligious organizations and by a variety of mediating cultural institutions. As Douglas Gomery shows, since the mid-1960s, the specialty theaters that offered art cinema, black films, and ethnic films expanded the commercial venues of the independent and alternative films (1992, 155–96). With the influx of new non-Western immigrants, some theaters in major cities became in effect segregated by their exclusive screening of films that interested this rising population—Asian and Hispanic in particular. In the meantime, important noncommercial venues began offering the accented films, among them museums, film archives, repertory theaters, university cinemas, and university film classes. Since the 1980s, film festivals and touring programs that featured these films also multiplied.[3] Established distributors of independent and avant-garde films, such as Canyon Cinema, Film-Makers' Cooperative, and Anthology Film Archives, continued to handle some accented films. Microdistributors began acquiring and organizing their products into multicultural and diaspora packages, with special brochures and publicity material that made them attractive to grassroots organizations and educators.[4] They created crossover audiences by cross-listing and cross-packaging diaspora-made and exile-made films with their films by and about immigrants and other traditionally disenfranchised populations, such as ethnic minorities, women, and gays and lesbians.[5]

The rise of global television multiplied the channels of transmission and intensified the need for new software, thus causing an extraordinary proliferation of programming sources and contents. Broadcast and cable television, especially Channel Four (in the United Kingdom), ZDF (in Germany), Canal Plus (in France), Arté (in Germany and France), and PBS, Bravo, Independent Film Channel, and Sundance Film Channel (in the United States), became important sources of financing and broadcasting for the independent and alternative films, including the accented films. Indeed, according to a recent study, television supplies between 30 and 74 percent of the financing for feature film production in Europe, depending on the country (Hohenadel 2000, AR32). In addition, by offering public access and leased access, cable television opened the airwaves to accented transnational, ethnic, and exilic media producers who could not gain entry into the big medium of broadcast television (Naficy 1993a, 1998b). These narrowcast, even lowcast, forms of TV and low-cost video were instrumental in helping ethnic and displaced populations form and maintain cultural identities from a distance and across national and geographic borders (Burnett 1995, chaps. 5, 6). Many of the accented filmmakers and videographers air their products on, and work for, such minority television outlets.

Critical and postcolonial theories entered film studies, and seminars and symposia began to explore exilic and diasporic subjectivity, identity, and agency.[6] These and other allied concepts became topics of papers and panels and the overarching themes of major academic conferences.[7] Significantly, the small-scale, viewer-oriented technologies of production and consumption, such as hi-8 and digital video cameras, VCRs, CD-ROMs, computers, and cable TV, as well as the World Wide Web, with its global reach and massive capacity for distributing and exhibiting films, became the linchpins linking the products of the most advanced postindustrial mode to those of the most artisanal mode. These technologies made possible the kind of low-tech, personal, impulsive, and contingent filmmaking and film viewing, demanded by the accented cinema, that was difficult or impossible before.

The totality of this rhizomatic organism that produces and facilitates the consumption of exilic and diasporic films is called the "accented mode of film production." As Fredric Jameson stated, in the "decentered and 'schizophrenic' world of late capitalism," the organic relationship among Althusserian apparatuses may "melt down," thereby opening up semiautonomous levels or spheres in which local or cellular struggles could take shape (1984, 192). The accented mode is born out of moments of autonomy that are ephemeral but sufficiently real, such as the liminality of exile, and it serves not only to renew the dominant mode of production but also to enrich the plurality of what is collectively called cinema. Dependence and autonomy, therefore, are the dual, differentially torqued, engines of the accented mode. That is why this discussion is driven not only by the limitations and constraints of dependence but also by the freedom and enablement promised by interstitial cellular autonomy.

The output of the accented mode is a cinema of alterity whose films, in David James's words, are "(un)popular" in that they are "contradictory, unstable, and usually short-lived," made by displaced and minority persons in liminal circumstances under "their own volition, rather than by corporations" (1996a, 18). These films are fundamentally "critical," in Scott MacDonald's term, for they are often noncommercial and usually artisanal and collective in their production. They either refuse to use (or else use in order to critique and undermine) the conventions of funding, production, storytelling, and spectator positioning so naturalized by mainstream cinema (MacDonald 1988, 2). Criticism is, therefore, embedded both in their mode of production and in their visual style.

The accented mode of production is not only alternative and critical but also "minor," in the sense that Deleuze and Guattari formulated. They ascribed three characteristics to "minor literature": "the deterritorialization of language, the connection of the individual to a political immediacy, and the collective assemblage of enunciation" (1986, 18). This production mode encourages the development of an accented and deterritorialized style, which is driven by its own limitations, that is, by its smallness, imperfection, amateurishness, and lack of cinematic gloss (many of the films are low-tech shorts with extremely low budgets and small crews and casts). It is also driven, in the exemplars of the style, by the style's textual richness and narrative inventiveness (deterritorialized language). The expected imbrication of exile and politics in this cinema goes beyond the inscription of political content, or of the films' mimetic, autobiographical, and theoretical criticism, which MacDonald describes. Because it involves inserting politics at the point of the film's origination and reception, the accented mode of production offers, by the fact of its existence, a powerful criticism of dominant film practices (political immediacy). Inserting politics at the point of origination may take the form of interstitial or collective production. This latter means working collaboratively and collectively and considering filmmaking to be a type of "collective enunciation" in which filmmakers and audiences are conjoined by their membership in communities of address that consist of émigrés, exiles, ethnicized, and otherwise otherized subjects (collective assemblage of enunciation). If the postindustrial mode tends to situate the directors as manufacturers and the spectators as consumers, the accented mode's collective enunciation and reception potentially blur the line that separates producers from consumers, corroborating the poststructural shift from the independent autonomous author to the readers as coauthors.

Significantly, the accented filmmakers' enunciating work is not only interstitial and/or collective but also multifunctional and integrated. It is multifunctional because filmmakers are involved in all aspects of their films horizontally, often serving as producer, director, screenplay writer, editor, and sometimes as on-camera talent and cinematographer. It is integrated because they are involved in all phases of their films vertically, from preproduction financing to exhibition.

Formulated as an intercultural practice by situated filmmakers working at a specific historical juncture and organized around an unorthodox mode of production, accented cinema generates both situated minor filmmakers and filmic forms. By making their films, the filmmakers can move out of their disempowered "minority" status, conferred upon them by the majority, into becoming "minor," a self-designated, self-actualizing category. This is because making accented films is, in the words of Deleuze and Guattari, like "setting up a minor practice of major language" (1986, 18)—a practice that defines the major. The minor practice of accented filmmaking supplies the sculpting lights that help define the major cinema's glowing visage. As a result, any definition of the dominant cinema must necessarily and centrally involve consideration of its alternatives. In terms of filmic forms, as James argues, "A given stylistic vocabulary is never merely itself; rather, it is the trace of the social process that constitutes a practice" (1989, 23). The accented style inscribes the social processes of exile and diaspora. By internalizing the conditions of their own production, accented films become allegories of exile and diaspora. Indeed, every accented film is at once an allegory of both exile and cinema.

Interstitial Mode of Production

It would be inaccurate to characterize accented filmmakers as marginal, as scholars are prone to do, for they do not live and work on the peripheries of society or the film and media industries. They are situated inside and work in the interstices of both. As Homi Bhabha has noted, it is "theoretically innovative and politically necessary" to think beyond singular categories and dominant designations, to focus on "those *interstitial* moments or processes that are produced in the articulation of 'differences' " (1994, 269). It is in these interstitial spaces that "minorities translate their dominant designations of difference—gender, ethnicity, class—into a solidarity that refuses both the binary politics of polarity, or the necessity of a homogeneous, unitary oppositional 'bloc' " (270). To be interstitial, therefore, is to operate both within and astride the cracks of the system, benefiting from its contradictions, anomalies, and heterogeneity. It also means being located at the intersection of the local and the global, mediating between the two contrary categories, which in syllogism are called "subalternity" and "superalternity." As a result, accented filmmakers

Figure 1. Worn-out but determined: allegorical inscription of filmmakers' search for funding. George Murphy (John Wodja) in Amir Naderi's *Manhattan by Numbers*. Courtesy Rising Star Productions.

are not so much marginal or subaltern as they are interstitial, partial, and multiple—not only in terms of their identity and subjectivity but also in terms of the various roles they play in every aspect of their films, from inception to consumption.

One characteristic of the interstitial production mode is the financial provisions under which it operates. Filmmakers often have to either invest in their own films or work in technical or routine capacities in the entertainment industries and ethnic media to raise funds.[8] Their work involves a range of cinematic practices, from professional to amateur, and a range of television, from broadcast to narrowcast TV, and from art video to lowcast video to webcast video. Such forced employment facilitates textual crossovers in their films. However, since working in these fields usually does not generate sufficient funds, filmmakers must seek additional financing from a range of public and private sources. Perhaps the lion's share of their time is spent on financial and producerly functions. Amir Naderi's *Manhattan by Numbers* (1993) provides an allegorical, if dystopic, inscription of such fund-raising problems. The film is also an allegory of the conditions of exile itself. It focuses on the fruitless efforts of a laid-off journalist to find a moneyed friend from whom to borrow cash to forestall eviction from his apartment. Like a filmmaker who is trying to tap into every resource and connection to generate funds, the journalist searches Manhattan from one end to the other. But his friend has vanished like scarce filmmaking resources. Naderi confirms that the film could be read as a metaphor for independent filmmakers' search for funds (Anderson 1993). The low budgets of accented films, however, do not necessarily translate into unpolished products, as will be seen in the close-up section on Atom Egoyan later in this chapter.

In the careers of the accented filmmakers, there often are long periods of distressing and dispiriting down time spent waiting for financing to come through. Sohrab Shahid Saless, a filmmaker of Iranian origin who for over two decades made celebrated but difficult films in Germany, captures this state of mind and characterizes the political economy of such waiting periods as a form of censoring of unpopular films:

> You feel badly frustrated when you stay at home for months looking out through the window and wishing you could film your ideas; but everybody else is trying to block your way or stop your project from being fulfilled. Let me tell you this: unlike what many people may think, censorship is not only in the Third World countries. But it also exists in countries such as Germany, France or Britain. The difference is that here they are more experienced in this regard. They stop it [the project] before it is begun, saying there is not enough budget or this film will fail. (1993, 65)

A second characteristic of the interstitial mode is the multiplication or accumulation of labor, particularly on behalf of the director, instead of the division of labor that characterizes the postindustrial production mode. Directors often act in principal roles in their films to control the project, keep down the cost, or make up for a lack of appropriate, bilingual actors.[9] Solanas appears in a small role in his *Tangos: Exile of Gardel*; Parviz Sayyad stars in his films *The Mission* (1983) and *Checkpoint* (1987); Akerman stars in many of her films, including in *Je Tu Il Elle* (1974); Suleiman stars in *Homage by Assassination* and *Chronicle of Disappearance*; Jonas Mekas and his brother Adolfas are prominent presences in almost all of Jonas's films, including *Lost, Lost, Lost*; Littín appears in *General Statement on Chile* (*Acta General de Chile*, 1988); and Nina Menkes's sister, Tina Menkes, is the star of all her films, including *The Great Sadness of Zohara* (1983). The voices of Hatoum and Akerman are the sole voices heard in their respective films, *Measures of Distance* and *News from Home*. Both Mahnaz Saeed Vafa, the director, and her mother appear in *A Tajik Woman* (1995).

Sometimes, such self-inscriptions are not included for financial reasons or to maintain tighter control over the film. In these cases, self-inscription is often autobiographical (as in the films of Mekas, Hatoum, and Saeed Vafa). Whatever the motivation, self-inscription—an attribute of the accented style—tends to implicate the author as the actor, thus collectivizing the films' enunciation, which is another attribute of the style.

Accented filmmakers not only act in their own films but also perform multiple other functions. Jewish-American filmmaker Nina Menkes is director, cinematographer, art director, coeditor (with her sister), and fund-raiser for all her films. Unlike many diasporic, Third World, and avant-garde filmmakers, she does not consider performing multiple functions to be a form of victimization and poverty. On the contrary, she considers multifunctionality a proactive strategy:

> Doing all these functions is an active choice because my work is intensely personal. I would never have anyone else shoot my movies or be the art director. If I would get more help on my future projects I would get more help on the production manager level and have more production assistants. . . . I feel like I am the enemy of Hollywood. I am in direct opposition to everything Hollywood stands for politically, socially, emotionally. (Oswald 1991, 27)

Perhaps for similar reasons, Iranian-American filmmaker Marva Nabili directed, wrote, and photographed *Nightsongs*, and her husband, Thomas Fucci, produced the film. Caveh Zahedi wrote, codirected, and starred in *A Little Stiff* (1992), and he also wrote, directed, and starred in *I Don't Hate Las Vegas Anymore* (1994)—a film in which his father and brother also act in prominent roles. Naderi, another Iranian-American filmmaker, wrote, directed, and edited *Manhattan by Numbers*. The Ethiopian-American filmmaker Haile Gerima produced, directed, wrote, and edited his latest film, *Sankofa* (1993). Pakistani-British filmmaker Jamil Dehlavi was producer, director, writer, editor, cinematographer, and a key actor in his avant-garde film *Towers of Silence* (1975). Kurdish filmmaker Nizamettin Ariç directed, cowrote, starred in, composed and performed the music, and supervised the makeup and costuming of his German production *A Cry for Beko* (*Klamek ji bo Beko/Ein lied für Beko*, 1992). As noted in chapter 1, Atom Egoyan has also functioned in a variety of positions in his films: as writer, producer, director, editor, actor, and musician.

By performing multiple functions, the filmmaker is able to shape a film's vision and aesthetics and become truly its author. Authorship, therefore, is not only in the economic and aesthetic but also in the total control of the film. Laws and regulations define authorship differently in each country, and this may also influence the filmmaker's decision to serve multiple functions. The 1957 intellectual property law in France, for example, confers authorship on the film's director and not to the producing, funding, or institutional agency. In other countries where authorship is not so clearly ascribed to the director, performing multiple functions helps to settle the question. However, multiple involvement in all phases and aspects of films is not a universally desired ideal; it is often a stressful condition forced by exile and interstitiality.

Multilinguality is a third characteristic of the accented mode, which is driven by the many languages of the filmmakers and their crew, the stories they por-

Figure 2. Anthro-
pologist attempting
to discover the name
of ordinary objects,
such as an iron, in
Patagonian, in Raúl
Ruiz's *On Top of
the Whale.*

tray, and the situated audiences whom they address. Multilinguality makes
intelligibility more complex, contributing to the accent. Importantly, in these
films language is almost never taken for granted. In fact, it is often a theme
and the self-reflexive agent of narration and identity. Raúl Ruiz's *On Top of the
Whale* (*Het Dak Van de Walvis*, 1981) is about an anthropologist traveling to
Tierra del Fuego, at the southernmost tip of Chile, to study the language of
two remaining members of a Patagonian tribe. As the French anthropologist,
in a situation typical of ethnographic fieldwork, points to everyday objects and
asks the Patagonians to name them, he discovers to his dismay that their language consists of only one phrase, *yamas gutan.* By varying the pattern of stress
on the syllables, the Patagonians imply different meanings. Even more distressing for him, the meanings derived are not stable; they change almost daily.
This both disturbing and droll use of language in the film invokes multiple
interpretations. The invention of a shifting language can be read as the Patagonians' resistance to their colonizers. By rendering themselves unintelligible,
they become a moving target that cannot be comprehended and apprehended.
The reduction of a tribe to only two surviving members bespeaks the massacre
of indigenous peoples at the hands of their European invaders. The anthropologists' methodology and their complicity with colonial powers are also ridi-
culed and criticized. Finally, the film points to the constructedness of all languages—a fact that becomes more apparent in exile and displacement, where
language ceases to be "natural."

Most exilic and diasporic films are bilingual, but many are multilingual,
necessitating varied types of dubbing, translation, and titling. Marilu Mallet's
Unfinished Diary (*Journal Inachevé*, 1986) is spoken in French, Spanish, and
English, which are subtitled in English. *On Top of the Whale* is spoken in
English, Spanish, French, Dutch, German, and the Ruiz-invented "Patagonian" language, all of which are subtitled in English. Egoyan's *Calendar* contains telephonic confessions of love and lust in more than half a dozen lan-

guages, none of which is translated or subtitled. Likewise, Suleiman's *Homage by Assassination* contains Arabic proverbs and text on the screen that are neither translated nor subtitled. The lion's share of the dialogue in Ann Hui's *Song of the Exile* (1990) is in English, but the portions spoken in Chinese and Japanese are subtitled. Multilinguality, like politics, permeates all aspects of accented films, not only those that are on the screen, such as character speech, dialogue, and subtitles, but also those, like the multinational composition of the production crew, that remain behind the cameras.[10] It also impacts the films' reception, as different languages serve multiple communities of address, often privileging one over another.

The production process of the accented films is convoluted: funding sources, languages used on the set and on screen, nationalities of crew and cast, and the functions that filmmakers perform are all multiple. This complexity includes the artisanal conditions and the political constraints under which the films are shot—forming a fourth characteristic. The Kurdish filmmaker Ariç, who lives in Germany, filmed most of his *A Cry for Beko* in Armenia in the early 1990s near the Armenian-Turkish border. As an exile from Turkey, condemned by the government, he could not film his Kurdish nationalist saga in his country of origin. However, filming in Armenia presented difficulties of its own. Because there were no processing labs nearby in Armenia, he had to ship the exposed footage to Leningrad. For various reasons, the lab did not deliver the footage in time, forcing Ariç, who was operating under a tight temporal and financial budget, to continue filming without seeing any of the dailies until long after the cast and crew had left the location—all this during his directorial debut! The telltale signs of these production difficulties are the traces they sometimes leave on the films, which give a certain look and feel of "imperfection" that signifies or allegorizes exilic condition and production.

A fifth characteristic of the interstitial mode is the length of time it may take to distribute and exhibit the films. For example, it took Jocelyne Saab of Lebanon four years to make *The Razor's Edge* (*Ghazal al-bant*, 1985) and three years of court battle to get it released commercially (Rosen 1989, 35). Akerman's great film *Jeanne Dielman, 23 Quai de Commerce, 1080 Bruxelles* (1975) did not open commercially in New York for eight years, even though it was discussed widely and favorably by feminists and film critics (Rosenbaum 1983a, 31). An analysis of Akerman's career makes clear that the disparity between generous press coverage, especially in France, where she made many of her films, and small audiences is not limited to this demanding film but is characteristic of the bifurcated responses to her films in general (McRobbie 1993, 200). This split reception—motivated by a combination of political and commercial forms of censorship—applies to the works of many accented filmmakers.

In general interstitial filmmakers must be satisfied with a limited distribution and exhibition of their films; often they must spend extra effort to obtain even that level of exposure. Spectators for their films are not a given but must be nurtured by means of specialized film tours, festivals, and distribution companies and by relying on video to enter college libraries, university courses, and academic conferences. The emergence of webcasting is likely to considerably improve the distribution and exhibition of their films.

One major consequence of the difficulties of making and exhibiting films under artisanal conditions is the very meager output of many of the filmmakers. In tabulating the output of the Middle Eastern and North African filmmakers working in exile and diaspora in the West, I discovered that some 306 cinéastes had made 920 films (mostly shorts), with an average ratio of 3 films per filmmaker—not a high output. Although certain individuals are more prolific than others, for filmmakers years sometimes pass without their making a new film: Argentine filmmaker Solanas made his second film in exile, *Tangos: Exile of Gardel* (1985), eight years after his first, *The Sons of Fierro* (1975–78). Iranian filmmaker Sayyad made his second film in America, *Checkpoint* (1987) only four years after his first, *The Mission* (1983); however, he has yet to make a third film. Naderi emigrated to the United States in 1986 to make films, but it took him seven years to produce his first English-language film, *Manhattan by Numbers* (1993) and another four years for his second film, *Avenue A.B.C. . . . Manhattan* (1997). Palestinian filmmaker Michel Khleifi, working in Belgium, made his first film, *The Fertile Memory* (*Surat min mudhakkirat khusbah*), in 1981. It took him six years of making films and programs for Belgian TV to produce his own celebrated second feature *Wedding in Galilée* (1987). Algerian writer Assia Djebar made her first film, *La Nouba des Femmes du Mont Chenoua*, in 1978, followed four years later by her second film, *La Zerda et les Chants de l'Oubli* (1982). Since then, however, she has made no other film and appears to have abandoned filmmaking altogether. Sometimes it takes years to film a single project: Mauritanian exile filmmaker Abid Med Hondo, working in France, relates how it took him a year and a half just to film *Soleil O* (*Sun Oh*) and three and a half years to film *Les Bicots-Nègres: Vos Voisins* (*The Nigger-Arabs: Your Neighbors*) (Hondo 1987, 75). French ethnographic filmmaker Jean Rouch, whose decades of intense engagement with and filming in Niger and other African countries turned him into a hybridized French-African transcultural figure, took years to complete certain film projects. For example, because of ill health, magical interference with the hunt, and other reasons, it took him seven years to complete his powerful film *The Lion Hunters* (*La Chasse au Lion à l'Arc* [1957–64].)

This time lag between accented film projects is only one of many. There often are other lags between filming and editing, and between filming and the recording of the voice-over narration. These are particularly relevant to Mekas's works, as discussed elsewhere. Finally, this production time lag allegorizes other more general disruptions and lags brought on by exile and diasporic existence.

Low output may be a function not only of economic forces and the film-makers' interstitial location but also of antagonistic state-artist relations. Armenian filmmaker Sergeï Paradjanov provides an example in the context of internal exile. Born in Georgia, Paradjanov made his early brilliant films in Ukraine under the Soviet Union's state-sponsored mode of production (*Shadows of Our Forgotten Ancestors*, 1964; *The Color of Pomegranates*, 1969). Despite such support, however, he was accused of homosexuality, currency fraud, Ukrainian nationalism, and incitement to suicide and was forced to spend six years of the 1970s in labor camps. An international campaign on his behalf led to Paradjanov's release in 1978, but he was blacklisted, blocked from working in cinema, and rearrested for attempted bribery (the real reason may have been his interviews with foreign journalists). He began making films again only on the eve of Mikhail Gorbachev's presidency and reforms, resulting in only two more features: *The Legend of the Suram Fortress* (1984) and *Ashik Kerib* (1988). All in all, Paradjanov's meager life's output was four feature films and a number of documentaries, made in two working periods separated by fifteen years (Alekseychuk 1990–91; Hoberman 1991b).

For accented filmmakers, the dream of transcendence and transformation that their liminality and interstitiality promise must constantly be checked against the realities of state encroachment and free-market competition. Some of their output is entertaining, even though often ironically and parodically critical of the host and home societies and of the exilic communities. But as artists who often make distressing and dystopian films, accented filmmakers inhabit a realm of incredible tension and agony, as Shahid Saless sarcastically noted: "People like us who make somber and hardly entertaining films are not fortunate. They write letters, come up with treatments, put together scripts that are never filmed and once in a while a good soul appears, gestures to them and says—just like in Kafka—: it's your turn now. You too can have a chance" (1988, 56). Straddling more than one culture, diasporic filmmakers are sometimes in a position to play funding agencies from different countries against each other to receive financing. Sometimes they attempt to get ahead by cashing in on the newsworthiness and popular stereotypes of their country of origin. Such efforts pay off more when newsworthiness is based on positive attributes, but they can backfire badly if negative connotations are involved, as in the case of *Veiled Threat* (1989), by Iranian-American filmmaker Cyrus Nowrasteh. The Los Angeles International Film Festival canceled the film's premiere in April 1989 at the last minute because of a bomb threat—an action that caused controversy about the festival's responsibility for public safety and First Amendment rights protection. However, it was difficult to sort out definitively the real reasons behind the bomb threat or the cancellation of the screening. The festival director claimed that the producers had brought the threat on themselves as a publicity stunt by publicly linking their film and its anti-Islamist content to the Ayatollah Khomeini's *fatwa* against Salman Rushdie, the author of *The Satanic Verses*. The producers responded by saying that the threat was real enough for the Federal Bureau of Investigation to have taken it seriously. This low-budget, low-velocity, lowbrow thriller finally opened in Los Angeles theaters to dismal reviews and attendance. Trying to recoup their losses by downplaying its Islamic connotations, the producers dropped the "veil" from the title. Apparently the ploy did not help the film's box office.

The kafkaesque situation that Shahid Saless speaks about is certainly real. It becomes more personally painful when national representation in festivals is involved, raising anew such vexing questions as to which nation the filmmakers belong and which national cinema they represent. In the 1970s, scores of films were made by Chilean exiles who had escaped the military dictatorship of Augusto Pinochet, constituting a Chilean cinema of resistance. This classification, however, excluded certain exile-made films, such as Raúl Ruiz's works after *Dialogue of Exiles* (*Dialogue d'éxilés*, 1974), which had critiqued the exiles (Pick 1987, 41). The politics of exilic filmmakers, which is usually directed against their home governments, often forces them into painful positions. For example, the Turkish government revoked Yilmaz Güney's citizenship after he escaped to Europe to complete his film *Yol* (*The Way*, 1982), which powerfully critiqued Turkish society under military rule. Thus the most famous Turkish filmmaker, who was also a very popular actor, could not represent his own country abroad. Parviz Sayyad could not enter in the Cannes International Film Festival as an Iranian product his film *The Mission*, an anti–Islamic Republic film made in the United States, forcing him to enter it as a U.S. production. By doing so, he was made in effect to admit that he represented neither Iranian cinema nor Iranians. With Sayyad unable to represent his own country and unwilling to represent the host country, his film was in essence made "homeless." This kind of homelessness, of course, is not limited to Third World or non-Western films or to their makers in the West. An increasing number of transnationally financed films and filmmakers have found it difficult to land a home, so to speak. Angieszka Holland's *Europa, Europa* (*Hitlerjunge Solomon*, 1991), made in Germany, is an example of a European film threatened with homelessness. The German Export Film Union refused to nominate it for an Academy of Motion Picture Arts and Science foreign film Oscar, claiming it was too "international." According to the Union, the film's Polish director, French cofinancing, and Russian assistance disqualified it as a German entry. Critics, however, surmised that the real reason behind the government action was that the Germans were uncomfortable with the film's depiction of a young Jew who opportunistically survives in the Hitler Youth (Breslau 1992; McBride 1991). The case of Luis Buñuel's exilic film career, spent largely in Mexico but also in France and the United States, provides a more complex and long-term view of artistic homelessness and its nemesis, internationalization, that exile is capable of producing.

Buñuel made most of his films in exile, subverting Catholicism, Francoism, and Hollywoodism, and he faced controversy and threat in all the countries in which he worked. He lived in Mexico for thirty-six years and became a Mexican citizen in 1949. However, the unsentimental realism with which his *Los Olvidados* (1950) portrayed the hand-to-mouth existence of Mexico City's abandoned slum children brought on hostility toward him from all sides. Labor unions demanded his expulsion, and the press attacked him "with nothing short of vitriol." His friends refused to speak to him; one even charged him with committing a "crime against the state" (Buñuel 1983, 200). If with *Los Olvidados* Buñuel raised the wrath of his adopted homeland, with *Viridiana* (1961) he created a heated controversy both among the Spanish expatriates in Mexico and in his original homeland of Spain. The Vatican also denounced the film. When it was shown in Milan, the public prosecutor closed the theater, impounded the film, and condemned Buñuel to one year in jail should he enter the country. His troubles were not limited to France, Spain, Mexico, or Italy. During the McCarthy era in the United States, Buñuel was blacklisted because of his leftist opinions and political affiliations (although he never joined the Communist Party). Until 1975, when his name was removed from the list, he had to submit to what he characterized as an "inquisition" every time he entered the United States (Buñuel 1983, 194).

Yet this most exilic of filmmakers, as Marsha Kinder tells it, is considered by the English-speaking world to be the most Spanish and Mexican of all directors—in fact, he is regarded as the embodiment of the national cinemas of both Spain and Mexico (1993, 289–91). His multifaceted situation as an "exilic," "Spanish," "Mexican," and "international" director demonstrates that as partial and multiple subjects of nation-states, accented filmmakers not only are in a position to critique the home and host societies but also are themselves poised to receive intense criticism from their compatriots everywhere. It is unlikely that all of these differently situated, and often antagonistic, publics can be satisfied. And yet, as filmmakers with an eye to the market and to public recognition, they must somehow reconcile their publics. Buñuel is both the epitome of exile and its most prominent exception. Few exile filmmakers have achieved his international status or have been subjected to such vehement criticism and praise in their home, host, or other countries. Although many strive to become major, most remain only interstitial.

Loneliness is an inevitable outcome of transnationality, and it finds its way into the desolate structures of feeling and lonely diegetic characters. For accented filmmakers, loneliness has an additional structural basis, which is rooted in their interstitial mode of production. As Robert Kolker aptly notes, while the disappearance of the classic studio system liberated the directors of the

New Hollywood cinema, it also tended to isolate them, since they could no longer rely on a centralized community of craftspeople, technicians, and administrators to support them from film to film, or on a stock company of experienced actors, or on a consistent source of funding, or on an articulated studio philosophy. The freedom they won was the "freedom to be alone" (1988, 7). For the accented filmmakers working interstitially or collectively, the structural loneliness that their mode of production imposes is magnified. As authors of their texts (and to some extent of their own lonely lives), their biography is not just implicitly coded in their films. Often autobiography and self-inscription are the forces that drive the lonely diegetic characters and the tropes of loneliness that structure their films. Any cultural space, such as exilic liminality and the interstitial mode of production, is capable of generating films that inscribe at a fundamental level their makers' station in life and their location in culture, stamping them with an accent. Tragically, loneliness is also the fate of the accented films. Although today's postindustrial film conglomerates have belatedly begun to rigorously archive, preserve, and restore their own film prints, independent and alternative films do not benefit from such infrastructural support. As a result, they are basically homeless (or "orphan" in the language of film archivists), like their makers.

Two important aspects of the interstitial mode of production, multisource funding and academic distribution, are explored more fully in the next sections.

Multisource Funding and Coproduction

Located astride cultures and addressing multisited and multilingual audiences, accented filmmakers naturally seek funding from multinational sources. The most successful are able to obtain financing from funding agencies, ethnic communities, filmmaking institutions, and television networks of several countries. In the following close-up sections, the multisource financing of Atom Egoyan and Michel Khleifi are explored. These sources are equally available to the accented filmmakers who work collectively.

Close-Up: Atom Egoyan

Despite the wide reception of his later feature films, Atom Egoyan has remained an independent filmmaker, relying on various personal, private, ethnic, public, and commercial funds. The sources listed in the ending credits of his feature films indicate both the diversity and the regularity of his funding sources in terms of the institutions and countries involved. Table B.1 (Appendix B) demonstrates that Egoyan partially funded all his films through his production company, Ego Film Arts. He tapped regional film funds of Ontario, as well as national film funds (National Film Board of Canada) and television funds (Telefilm). In addition, international film and TV agencies, from Rome to London to Germany, contributed funds, sometimes by purchasing the films' broadcasting rights. Finally, assistance from his ancestral homeland (Armenian National Cinématheque) was also obtained.

The overall high production values of Egoyan's films belie his extremely low budgets. *Next of Kin* was made for $37,000, *Family Viewing* for $160,000, and *Speaking Parts* for £600,000, £75,000 of which (or 13 percent) was supplied by Channel 4 (Pym 1992).[11] *Calendar* was made for $100,000, *Exotica* for $2 million, and *The Sweet Hereafter* for $5 million. The low budgets of these films, their varied sources, and the game of resistance and co-optation that Egoyan has played with the dominant cinema are characteristic of accented filmmakers. Clearly, the steep rise in the budgets of his last few films is an indication of both his success in this game and the high quality of his films. Such low budgets, especially for his earlier films, were made possible thanks to the multiple functions that he performed in them and the fact that in *Next of Kin* most of the talent and crew were paid little or nothing, and the equipment and services were obtained mostly on the cheap.

The theatrical release of Egoyan's last three films, which testifies to his increased popularity, offers one possible, and enviable, trajectory for accented filmmakers. *The Adjuster* was released in a limited fashion in a few U.S. cities, but it did much better in Canada and Europe. *Exotica* was also at first released cautiously by Miramax only on 7 screens in six cities. However, it generated $14,379 per screen, an amount considered "huge," encouraging the distributor to release it on 433 screens nationwide (Parks 1995, 3c). In its marketing and advertising campaign for *Exotica*, Miramax emphasized the film's sexual and mystery dimensions by labeling it an "erotic thriller." Genre designation is an important marketing strategy by which alternative, minor, or accented films are reinscribed in recognizable cinematic forms to attract larger audiences. This may lead to the domestication and transformation of their makers from minor into major filmmakers. After *The Sweet Hereafter* won the Grand Prize at the 1997 Cannes International Film Festival and received rave reviews, Fine Line Features opened it widely in Canada and the United States and placed full-page ads in mainstream national publications such as the *New York Times*.[12] It was nominated for two Oscars, both of them for Egoyan, for directing and screenplay adaptation. Until the success of *The Adjuster*, Egoyan's director's fee had been deferred pending his films' box office successes. Interestingly, his least expensive films, *Next of Kin*, *Family Viewing*, and *Calendar*, all made a profit.

The Canadian film market has been so dominated by American films and distributors that independent indigenous productions have limited access to their national screens (Pendakur 1990, 183–85). Television, on the other hand, has been instrumental in projecting the Canadian accented films into the national and transnational spheres. For example, Egoyan's telefilm about hockey, *Gross Misconduct* (1992), which he made for CBC, was watched by 3 million viewers—many more than the 10,000 people he estimates watched *The Adjuster* in Canadian cinemas.

Close-Up: Michel Khleifi

Khleifi is a Christian Palestinian, born in 1950 to a middle-class family in Nazareth, Israel, where he lived until his emigration to Belgium in 1970. He was an auto mechanic who went abroad to specialize in that field. After a while, however, he chose a completely different course of study. In Brussels he received his diploma in directing theater, radio, and television in 1977 and began working for the French-language Belgian television. There he made documentaries and short pieces for newsmagazines and other shows, including the notable documentary *Ashrafieh*, which won him a top award (Elena 1993, 242; *l'Avant Scène Cinéma*, 87). Simultaneously, he established his own film company, Marisa Films, through which he made a number of feature-length documentary and fictional films.[13] Most were coproduced with financial assistance from European countries, and several won international praise. An examination of the coproduction arrangements for his *Wedding in Galilée* (1987) provides a more detailed look at a single film's transnational financing (Table B.2, Appendix B).

Thanks to its activist governmental policies, France has the largest film industry in Europe, producing and coproducing more films than any other country. After World War II, Centre nationale de la cinématographie (CNC) was charged with supporting the indigenous French cinema, which was suffering both from the war's destruction and from the postwar competition from U.S. imports. The CNC film fund is continually replenished by taxing the box office receipts of movie houses and TV networks that broadcast films.[14] All films produced in France are entitled to some CNC support, which partially shields filmmakers from the vagaries of the market and allows practitioners of alternative cinemas to obtain sufficient funds to begin their films. This support is given in the form of a production advance that is considered a loan that must be paid back should the film make a profit. As Table B.2 shows, Khleifi received a production advance of 1.6 million French francs. CNC support also takes the form of distribution assistance (for which Khleifi received 175,000 francs) and direct payment to film laboratories to strike film prints (Khleifi received three such prints). This latter assistance not only helps the filmmakers by providing free distribution prints but also helps the film industry by providing employment. These forms of CNC support, as well as those provided by Sociétés de financement du cinéma et de l'audiovisuel (SOFICA), a government-approved tax-sheltering company that procures investment for film and TV productions, go a long way in accounting for the large number of *beur*, émigré, and diasporic films that are made in France.[15] On the Belgian side, in addition to obtaining aid from commercial entities, Khleifi received financial assistance from the Ministry of the French Community, a Belgian government agency that supports French cultural forms.

Manjunath Pendakur defines coproduction as "the principal mechanism used by film and television producers to pool capital and labor from around the world and gain market access globally" (1990, 194). In its simplest form, a film is coproduced when two or more firms are involved in funding it. However, coproductions usually involve more complex situations. Pendakur identifies four general categories of coproduction: public- and private-sector coproductions in a given country, public- and private-sector coproductions of different countries, private capital from different countries, and treaty coproductions (195). European countries are mobilizing coproductions of all four types to compete with the onslaught of the American movie machine, becoming "the center of international coproductions," where in 1992 some 32 percent of all films were coproductions (Moore 1994, 289).

Khleifi mobilized these coproduction strategies to make and market his films. In the case of *Wedding in Galilee*, he seems to have employed the second and fourth strategies. That is, he used public and private capital obtained from film and TV agencies of several countries (Belgium, France, Britain, and Germany) and relied on legal agreements between France and Belgium to support film coproduction and codistribution. As the number of television channels and networks has increased following privatization of the former state monopolies in Europe, the need for programming has increased manyfold, turning television into a key supplier of funds for alternative filmmaking. These entities sometimes pay for the production of films and sometimes for the rights to broadcast them. Khleifi received the latter support from ZDF in Germany and from Canal Plus in France.

In addition to obtaining funds, accented filmmakers obtain assistance by in-kind arrangements with a variety of businesses, including airlines, national and local tourism boards, multinational companies, film distributors, film labs, and ethnic businesses. Sometimes, too, the performers, musicians, and technical crew donate all or part of their services to the film to show their solidarity. The ending credits of independent transnational films are filled with the names of such benefactors, as well as those of family members, friends, nonprofit agencies, and the like.

The contribution of the homeland's institutions to the production and distribution of the accented films is fraught with additional politics and controversy. Table B.2 lists only the financial aid of Belgian, French, and other European institutions to *Wedding in Galilee*, but Khleifi himself has said that he considers the film to be a Belgian-French-Palestinian coproduction. However, it is not clear what the Palestinian financial contribution was, other than his own investment in the film. As a person born in Israel, he could have applied for

Israeli funding. Apparently, he did not do so because he feared either contamination or co-optation. His fears were strong enough that he refused to show the film at the Jerusalem Cinématheque. The film's commercial release in Israel also encountered obstacles. One distributor who expressed interest in it wanted its title shortened to *The Wedding* and its length reduced by fifteen minutes. Although the distributor cited commercial reasons for demanding these modifications, Khleifi surmised that the true reasons were political, stemming from the distributor's objection to the film showing Shimon Peres's official portrait and the Israeli military's occupation of Arab villages. The film's reception among Arabs in North Africa was also controversial and political. In certain Egyptian and Moroccan circles, *Wedding in Galilée* was considered a shocking film for its extensive female nudity (the actresses were Tunisian and French-Armenian), the impotence of the groom, and the village headman's invitation to Israeli soldiers and officers to attend the wedding as guests (Hoberman 1988, 84). Political issues crop up time and again during both production and reception of accented films.

Distribution to Academic Institutions

The academic market is an influential specialized public that provides a viable and growing alternative to the commercial and ethnic publics. This market includes universities, colleges, and art museums that program films as part of their classroom instruction or public outreach function. Thousands of films are screened annually in these settings, only some of which are accented films. Since the number of courses that use film and video in the United States has grown to several thousand, this academic market is large, forming the lion's share of the sales of microdistributors that cater to alternative films.[16] The following case study of Women Make Movies describes one company's distribution to the academic market.

Close-Up: Women Make Movies

Women Make Movies (WMM) was established as a nonprofit company in 1972 to distribute films made for, about, and by women. With a full-time staff of six and part-time staff of seven, the company currently distributes over 400 titles that include documentary, animated, experimental, and fiction films. Debra Zimmerman, executive director of WMM, told me in an interview that 80 percent of the company's revenues came from academic distribution (Naficy 1996f). Its overall revenue grew from gross receipts of less than $15,000 in 1983 to nearly $800,000 in 1996 and to $1,053,635 in 1999.[17] There are several reasons why universities and colleges are such important markets for independent films: academic institutions are proven media users;

they are particularly interested in independent and alternative cinemas; their gatekeeping functions are more liberally defined than those of other large nontheatrical markets (high schools, for example); they form a market that is large enough, but not too large, for direct-mail marketing;[18] and their film audiences are socially significant because of their future impact as filmmakers, film critics, and policy makers.

Although some universities continue to show 35mm prints for their public screenings and 16mm prints in their classrooms, an increasing number of them use video screening only. This is due to the high cost of film rental, the small departmental budgets for such purposes, the difficulty of locating good-quality film prints, and the proliferation of film classes requiring a large number of film prints. In general, WMM bases its prices for the rental and sale of its films and videos not on the home consumption formula, which presupposes individual or small-group viewing, but on the model of a large group setting (such as classrooms).[19] This and the lack of economy of scale are two reasons why the rental fee for videos of independent films is much higher than for mainstream films. In exceptional cases, when filmmakers, such as Trinh Minh-ha, set the rental fee, the price far exceeds the average figures, making even the rental of alternative films on video prohibitive for many film classes.[20]

Ironically, this crisis of funding is occurring at the same time that the student demand for courses on alternative and minority cinemas is on the rise due to changing demography in the United States and the increasing diversity of student bodies and curricula.[21] WMM has responded by lowering the sale and rental fees for selected titles whose audience the company has determined to be primarily "activist" or "community-based." Currently, titles dealing with AIDS and with Native American issues are discounted on those grounds.

The situation is more ironic, even kafkaesque, in the case of the accented films that are dystopic and critical of the society's cultural norms and yet must be distributed like any other film within the marketplace. For even though distributors such as WMM are nonprofit, they still operate commercially. With the slashing of the federal and state budgets for the arts in the 1990s, the support that WMM was receiving from these sources decreased dramatically. As a result, in 1996, some 90 percent of its operating budget came from funds generated by the sale and rental of films and videos. The remaining 10 percent came from foundations (3–5 percent), the New York State Council on the Arts (3 percent), the National Endowment for the Arts (1 percent), individual donors (1 percent), and the New York City Department of Cultural Affairs (0.5 percent).[22]

Like Third World Newsreel, WMM regards its distribution activity as a form of advocacy and a means by which women can inject or "infiltrate" their voices and works into the interstices of the dominant culture.[23] More than half of the works it distributes are by "women of color," who are "the most marginalized by the mainstream media" (Kolson 1992, D1). WMM's nontheatrical entry points for infiltrating the system include—in addition to universities and colleges—museums, film festivals, alternative cinemas, television, media arts centers, libraries, high schools, labor unions, government agencies, corporations; women's centers, hospitals, and prisons.

Although women exiles, émigrés, refugees, and expatriates make many of the films distributed by Women Make Movies, until recently the company's penetration was limited to the North American market. The chief reasons are the complications and the high cost of negotiating rights in different countries. Other reasons include the politics of the accented films, which are often critical of their home governments, their high rental cost, the incompatibility of technical standards for television in different countries, the smaller market for such products outside North America, the dominance of the English language in the films, and the high cost of subtitling, dubbing, or TV standards conversion. Ironically, the postindustrial synergy created by the mergers of media, computer, and cable TV giants, along with digitization of television, increased bandwidth via cable for Internet access, and the widening use of the World Wide Web as a transmitter of films, is likely to solve some of these problems by providing new distribution and exhibition venues for accented films.

3

Collective Mode of Production

ONE OF the legacies of the 1960s is the ascendance of a collective basis for personal identity and political action, best expressed at the time in the emergence of various forms of collective living,[1] collective action,[2] and collective countercultural productions, including film and video collectives.[3] Although the fortunes and lifelines of the film collectives fluctuated and many of them disbanded, several survived by evolving. San Francisco Newsreel, for example, evolved into California Newsreel, and New York Newsreel became Third World Newsreel.[4] In the meantime, new collectives such as Women Make Movies emerged.

Collective filmmaking, identified earlier as one of the characteristics of being minor, is being renewed and reexamined as a viable alternative film practice. For example, the 1995 Margaret Mead Film Festival celebrated films made by "international film collectives" that are collaborative in their organizational and work structures and experimental in their approaches to narratives, mixing genres and types. Collectivism, however, involves not only the collaborative production of the films but also their collective reception. I noted earlier that the classical Hollywood cinema transformed the conception of the filmgoer from the collective "audience" to a universalized, individually addressed "spectator." I also noted that despite the classical mode's hegemony, specialized movies continued to be made that addressed small collectivities based on race and ethnoreligiosity—such as race movies for blacks and Yiddish films for Jews. These films were often exhibited in specialty movie houses or at specific times in public theaters. With the emergence of the postindustrial New Hollywood cinema, which thrives not only on globalized mass audiences but also on their segmentation for better targeting, and with the rise of the accented cinema in Europe and North America, which inscribes a collective enunciation and whose distribution, exhibition, and reception are also often collective, the notion of what is collective requires further examination. Here I examine a number of ethnic, exilic, and diasporic filmmaking collective formations in the United States, Great Britain, and France whose works fall within the accented style.

Ethnic Collectives: Asian Pacific American Film Collectives

Asian-American media arts organizations, of which there are many, provide an example of ethnically accented film collectives. The most important and enduring of these are Visual Communications in Los Angeles, Asian CineVision in New York, and the National Asian-American Telecommunication Association in San Francisco. Two common beliefs appear to bind these collectives: being Asian-American transcends the experience of being only Korean-, Chinese-, Japanese-, Vietnamese-, Filipino-, or Indian-American, and working in media can bring about social and attitudinal change, especially by countering negative stereotyping of Asian-Americans (Gong 1991, 2). Founded largely by UCLA-trained filmmakers and incorporated in 1971 as an independent, nonprofit organization, Visual Communications (VC) took advantage of its not-for-profit status to obtain support from a broad range of funding sources, especially from publicly legislated programs such as the Comprehensive Employment and Training Act (CETA), Emergency School Aid (ESSA), and the Media Arts and Expansion Arts programs of the National Endowment for the Arts.[5] VC has operated collectively, with its members involved in deciding on projects, writing grant proposals, and producing and exhibiting films. In the last two decades, its mission, which at first was limited to making films from an Asian-American point of view, has grown to include supporting Asian-American film production, distribution, exhibition, training, and advocacy—very similar to Third World Newsreel and Women Make Movies. Its members have made a range of films by Asian-Americans, about Asian-Americans, and for Asian-Americans, from documentary to animation to their first feature fiction film, *Hito Hata: Raise the Banner* (directed by Duane Kubo and Robert Nakamura, 1980).

In its first six years, VC produced nearly a dozen films, but with them it encountered one of the key paradoxes of accented filmmaking, that is, the "burden of representation" that subjects ethnic and identity filmmakers to sometimes impossible demands and to criticism from both within and outside the community. As Robert Nakamura, one of the founders of VC and the director of some of its early films, including *Manzanar* (1971) and *Wataridori: Birds of Passage* (1976), notes, "The radical left and the conservatives of the community had very different ideas about the role of media. We were criticized by both sides" (quoted in Gong 1991, 3). Criticism ranged from charges of historical inaccuracy to lack of technical proficiency to failure to adequately represent the community.

One factor that distinguishes ethnic media collectives such as VC from other, nonethnic collectives such as Third World Newsreel is the intimate vertical and horizontal ethnic, cultural, linguistic, and national ties that ethnic collective members must maintain with the community, or communities, they serve. These ties can produce harmony and support, or they can result in discord and unfulfilled expectations. Having faced historical discrimination, hostility, and stereotyping, ethnic communities are highly sensitive to how they are represented by both by outsider and insider filmmakers.[6] They often feel protective and proprietary about their "image," sometimes even defensive—all of which forces accented filmmakers either to accede to the community's self-perception and demands or to take an independent path at the expense of alienating the community and losing its support. What is more, defensiveness and the desire for counterhegemonic representations often create communal pressure for each film to contain all of the best that the "original" or the "authentic" culture is perceived to possess *and* to represent as fully as possible the diaspora community. Arthur Dong's hour-long documentary *Claiming a Voice: The Visual Communication Story* (1990) supplies one example of how community pressure and criticism determined the filmmaker's agenda. *Omai Fa'atasi* (directed by Takashi Fujii, 1979) is about an organization (named in the film's title) that was devoted to helping Samoan youths in Los Angeles. The film contained such frank language and antisocial attitudes by the young people that the community elders and parents criticized it harshly, prompting Fujii and VC to make *Vitafe: Running Water* (1981), a more positive film about the educational achievements of the youth.

The various ties that bind may bring accented filmmakers into direct conflict with their communities at the same time they are doing their best to counter negative or inaccurate stereotypes. These filmmakers also must take into consideration the expectations and dictates of nonethnic funding agencies. These multiple demands and expectations create a heavy burden that is unlikely to be met by any single film or filmmaker. Further, the ethnic communities' influence on the film collectives is not limited to their sociocultural ties and pressures. It extends to the financial realm, since ethnic civic organizations, businesses, and individuals are both funders of and paying audiences for ethnic films. Because of these pressures and linkages, ethnic films tend to be on the whole rather conservative, emphasizing descent relations, ethnic continuity, and sociocultural achievements.

An increasingly popular and significant strategy in the collective mode of film production, distribution, and reception is to organize ethnic film festivals. By showing a number of films to insider and outsider audiences over a short time, and by bringing together filmmakers, producers, financiers, and media critics, such events make a claim on public consciousness, facilitate collective identity formation, and enable the kind of discursive and financial networking that encourages further productions.

Established in 1976 in New York City, Asian CineVision (ACV) began its first Asian-American Film Festival two years later—a festival that has continued to date and has spawned other festivals on the West Coast. In addition, since 1985, Visual Communications, in conjunction with UCLA and the American Film Institute, has organized an annual Asian Pacific American International Film Festival. What is interesting about these festivals is that the process of selecting the films, conducted by committees, has tended to define not only what constitutes the Asian-American media arts but also what constitutes Asian-American identity. They became engaged in the politics of the hyphen and naming and renaming. In 1992, the ACV festival changed its title from Asian Pacific American International Film Festival to the Los Angeles Asian Pacific Film and Video Festival. The change was designed to reflect the achievement of those working in video and to acknowledge the "notion that 'community' as it pertains to people of color is a diasporic one."[7] Since its redefinition as a diasporic festival, its offerings have included films and videos by Asian and Pacific Islands filmmakers and videomakers working not only in the United States but also in the United Kingdom, Canada, Hong Kong, Latin America, and Europe. This diaspora category is far more inclusive than the Asian-American category, in which Asians from Japanese and Chinese backgrounds living in the metropolitan centers of the West Coast (San Francisco and Los Angeles) and the East Coast (New York City) predominated.

This remapping of ethnic identity is reflected in the programming of National Asian-American Telecommunication Association (NAATA) as well. Since the early 1980s, with support from the Corporation for Public Broadcasting, NAATA has been acquiring, packaging, and distributing television, radio programs, and films on Asian-American concerns. One of these is a series called "Video Titles from the Asian Diaspora" (NAATA CrossCurrent Media 1995). While inclusiveness and coalition politics are welcome strategies in the age of deadly difference and ethnic cleansing, there is a danger that these mapping and remapping dynamics may lead to the erasure of differences and of specific histories.

However, there are both demographic and marketing reasons for this diasporizing shift. While the filmmakers of the 1960s and 1970s were chiefly Asian-American in the sense of being born or bred in the United States, the crop from the 1980s and 1990s contains a number of Asian émigrés, born in Asian countries, who came to live and work in the United States relatively recently. For these recent émigrés and exiles, their primary relationship of identity may initially be more with the homeland and the Asian diaspora than with the host society and Asian-Americans. In addition, Asian filmmakers are now finding that international television, particularly in Asia, is a lucrative market for their products. These issues are considered in the next close-up section.

Close-Up: Nancy Tong and Christine Choy's In the Name of the Emperor *(1995)*

According to Tong, producer and with Choy codirector, Asian and foreign television networks and stations are less interested in Asian-American matters than in Asian diaspora subjects. The marketing of their film provides a case study of the dynamics of globalization of the media markets and diasporization of the Asian populations and filmmakers. The film centers on a particularly gruesome but suppressed history: the Japanese invasion of China, particularly what became known as the "rape" of Nanjing in 1937, during which more than 300,000 people (among them many women and children) were tortured, raped, mutilated, and murdered. It contains graphic footage of the massacre filmed with a hidden camera by an American clergyman and candid interviews with both the aging Chinese and Korean victims and Japanese perpetrators. In the tradition of prosecutorial films, it powerfully recounts this history and condemns both the Japanese acts of violence and the Japanese government's denials that such acts took place. It also takes the U.S. government to task for downplaying, in the interest of building a united front with Japan against the Soviet Union, the Tokyo war crimes tribunal, which was charged with investigating the atrocities.

According to Tong in her interview with me (Naficy 1996e), she had no difficulty selling the film to Arté (the European transnational network), TV Ontario in Canada, and television networks in Taiwan, Hong Kong, Korea, Australia, Spain, Finland, and Bulgaria. However, despite several attempts with PBS—even during the anniversary year of the end of World War II, when many films and programs on war issues were aired, she was unable to have the film broadcast in the United States. The PBS stations' primary objections were to the film's visual horror and to the preponderance of subtitles and intertitles (the calligraphic component of the accented style). By selling the film to international television networks, however, the filmmakers recouped one-third of the film's $250,000 budget.[8] Although it has been shown in New York City, Houston, and elsewhere, it is unlikely to be released theatrically (it is only fifty minutes long). Without national exposure on movie and television screens, the film will have a short life in its country of origin.

Politically charged accented films naturally arouse different responses in different settings, contributing to the liminality and homelessness of both films and filmmakers. The Asian audience response in Canada and Hong Kong to *In the Name of the Emperor* was either enthusiastic or polite but hostile. The latter reaction stemmed from the criticism that the film failed to show more graphically and condemn more emphatically the suppressed history of the massacre. The film has not been shown publicly in Japan for an opposite reason: the sensitivity of the Japanese to its graphic visuals and testimonials. Ironically, the producers have not distributed the film in the People's Republic of China because of fear of copyright violation, which has been rampant there.

The politics of location in the accented cinema is further complicated by the desire of the ethnic community and others to distinguish between insiders and outsiders. An aspect of these issues has already been addressed in the section on the politics of the hyphen. As Trinh T. Minh-ha has noted in an article appropriately titled "Outside In Inside Out" (1989), whites and First Worlders have traditionally been authorized to make films about both themselves and their others. Third Worlders and exiles, on the other hand, are deemed best qualified and authorized to make films about themselves and their own cultures. They are generally not expected to make films about either outsiders or other insider groups. The reason is that as intellectuals they are generally thought to be subjective, personal, emotional, highly political, and locally authoritative because of their purported authenticity. White outsiders, on the other hand, are generally considered to be objective, universal, abstract, individual, and globally authoritative because of their ability to reason. Although such strict binarism and racialist essentialism are on the wane, their reductive vestiges are still in play, forcing accented filmmakers to either stay exilic and diasporic or at best become ethnic. Other questions that this insider-outsider schema raises are: Who should draw the dividing line between self and other, insider and outsider? Should the line be drawn according to differences in language, ethnicity, race, religion, skin color, geography, gender, nationality, politics, or some other criteria? What about exilic liminars and hybrids who occupy interstitial and multiple spaces of identity and cultures and who do not fully belong to any single category? What about those who venture outside their circumscribed spaces? Several close-up sections provide examples of perils and promises of crossing the boundaries of identity.

Close-Up: Mira Nair's Salaam Bombay! (1988)

Although Nair is an independent director from India and not a member of an Asian or other filmmaking collectives, she is nonetheless an important contributor both to the collective Indian identity in diaspora and to the Indian cinema. Her *Salaam Bombay!* illustrates the problematic of the collective identity and the politics of location of an insider who makes films about the insider's own native culture from a position of exile. Born in Orissa, India, in 1957, Nair studied sociology in the elite Miranda House, Delhi University, worked for a few years as an amateur actor on the Delhi stage, and finally received her filmmaking degree at Harvard University in 1979. She was based in the United States for many years but made all her documentaries and two of her feature films in India: *Salaam Bombay!* and *Kama Sutra: A Tale of Love* (1997).[9] In between the latter two films, she directed two other features, *Mississippi Masala* (1992) and *The Perez Family* (1995), which are about ethnic and diasporic issues involving African-Indian immigrants and Cuban immigrants in the United States, respectively.

A number of Indian scholars and reviewers, both inside and outside India, criticized *Salaam Bombay!* by contending that its "realistic" depiction of the desperate lives of young subaltern girls and boys living in the streets, brothels, and detention centers of Bombay was an outsider's "fantasy."[10] These critics emphasized Nair's privileged upbringing in India, her higher education in a leading American university, her membership in an elite diaspora population, and her film's textual and other politics. According to these critics, the film's textual and class politics are such that they sentimentalize, romanticize, homogenize, and universalize the lives of Indian subalterns without analyzing the underlying causes and the specific power relations that perpetuate their poverty, prostitution, homelessness, drug addiction, and drug dealing (Dayal 1992; Bharucha 1989). Arora Poonam argued that although *Salaam Bombay!* is a

Figure 3. Krishna, aka "Chaipau," is defeated by Bombay at the end of Mira Nair's *Salaam Bombay!*

"feminist ethnography" that advertises itself as an indigenous insider account of India, it is produced for consumption by outsiders, its appeal resulting "precisely from its ability to produce the Indian subject in terms dictated by the representational codes of the West" (1994, 294). Because it elides power relations and targets foreign audiences, Nair's cinematic gaze upon her native home is considered touristic, voyeuristic, and superficial—the kind of gaze that is produced by "facile interculturalists" (Bharucha 1989, 1277).

Nair's characterization as a facile interculturalist is a reference to her multicultural and hybridized perspective, with which she is comfortable and in which she takes pride: "As a brown person, between black and white, I could move between these worlds very comfortably because I was neither" (quoted in Foster 1997, 111). Some insiders have criticized her work for not sufficiently presenting the "good" India or the whole of India to outsiders. For example, her father and other South Asians protested against her documentary *India Cabaret* (1985), about the lives of female exotic dancers, on grounds that it objectified women and washed India's dirty linen in the public.[11]

On the other hand, to outsiders, that is, to non-Indians such as Caryn James of the *New York Times*, *Salaam Bombay!* appeared to be an insider's account, displaying authenticity and authoritativeness (1988, 3). The factors that heightened the film's reality effect for them were its linear, comprehensible, and engaging fictional narrative told in the best tradition of the classical Hollywood cinema style, its sympathetic characters, and its use of real (nonactor) children. Another contributor to the film's realism is the peculiarity of cross-cultural viewing, which positions fictional films made in one cultural context to be read by those in another culture as if they were documentaries. American fictional films, for example, are routinely read by audiences in other countries not only as fictional stories but also as documentaries of the American way of life, culture, and values ("This is the way the United States looks; this is how Americans behave, work, and play"). These factors made the authenticity, authoritativeness, and realism of Nair's view (the insider) so compelling that American mainline reviewers (outsiders) spoke of *Salaam Bombay!*'s "documentary feel" (James 1988, 3). However, a native reviewer (insider) criticized it for its "fabricated realism" and "insidious humanism" (Bharucha 1989, 1275).

By dint of their education, class affiliation, multilingualism, cosmopolitanism, and distance from the homeland, accented filmmakers are structurally outsiders, however much they desire to be considered insiders, either within their own native culture or in the host society. Nair's documentaries, her feature films, and her book about *Salaam Bombay!* (Nair and Taraporevala 1989) show her deep interest in the lives of social outcasts and liminals. She states that she has always been "drawn to stories of people who live on the margins of society; people who are on the edge, or outside, learning the language of being in between; dealing with the questions, 'What, and where is home'" (Simpson 1992, 67). Whether considered as an authentic autochthonous view or as an exoticizing outsider's fantasy, the fact remains that the current globalization and deterritorialization have made Nair's films part of the cultural identity of Indians everywhere. As such, her films are part of not only accented cinema but also Indian cinema because all accented films contribute to constructing both what is exilic and diasporic and what is national.

Had *Salaam Bombay!* been more self-reflexive about its own status as a diasporic rumination about India, and had it highlighted Nair's own in-betweenness, the film's politics of location may have been less subject to question. However, self-reflexivity as a cinematic methodology for deconstructing ideology does not guarantee authenticity, transparency, or radical politics, for it can be performed and co-opted, as it has been by the myriad television shows, both fictional and reality based, mainstream films, and television ads that adopt a knowing, ironic, and self-reflexive stance to better sell dominant ideologies and consumer products.

Close-Up: Trinh T. Minh-ha

The reactions of African, African-American, and Chinese audiences to Trinh's films about Africa and China demonstrate that Third World films about other Third World peoples (not one's own) can provoke similar controversies even if self-reflexive strategies are employed. Therefore, although Trinh's film production practice is not collective in the sense described here, the reception of her films collectivizes them.

As she relates her story, Trinh was born to a large family in which three different Vietnamese political factions coexisted. Her own biography represents two of these. She was born in Hanoi, then the capital of North Vietnam, but was compelled to move to Saigon, then the capital of South Vietnam, where she grew up. A third faction was involved with the National Liberation Front in the South. "This is why the dualistic divide between pro- and anti-Communists has always appeared to me as a simplistic product of the rivalry between (what once were) the two superpowers. It can never come close to the complexity of the Vietnam reality" (quoted in Chen 1992, 83). This positionality is inscribed in the nonbinarist but ambiguous attitude with which she treats the South Vietnamese and North Vietnamese in *Surname Viet Given Name Nam* and Mao in *Shoot for the Contents* (1991). It also accounts for some of the criticism of her work on the basis of its ambivalent and conservative politics.

Seeking a "rupture" with the Vietnamized French model of education, Trinh sought her higher education elsewhere. Like throwing bottles in the sea, she sent many letters to American universities, seeking admission. Wilmington College, a small school in Vermont, accepted her, and she migrated to the United States in the 1970s, at the height of the American war in Vietnam. There, as an "international" student, she developed close contacts with other foreign students, especially those from Africa, and with minority students, particularly African-Americans. These contacts continued as she moved on to pursue higher degrees, and they influenced her filmmaking career and her films, made in various African countries, China, and Vietnam. She received a master of arts degree in French literature and music and another in music composition, as well as a doctorate in comparative literature from the University of Illinois.

In her two dense, essayistic films about Africa, *Reassemblage* (1982) and *Naked Spaces—Living Is Round* (1985), Trinh not only explored the relationship of African women to spatial configuration but also critiqued religious missionaries, tourists, and her own role as an observer of foreign cultures. She criticized the received notions and practices of realist ethnographic films by embodying their opposite: a nonrealist, nonlinear, fragmented, and self-reflexive narrative, containing a multivocal sound track that included her own voice-over narration. Many Euro-American anthropologists objected to her work, as did some minority filmmakers and critics. In 1986, at the Fortieth Edinburgh International Film Festival's conference on Third Cinema, she was taken to task by African-American and black British filmmakers for homogenizing and aestheticizing Africans, for elitist theorization, and for crossing the insider-outsider divide (an Asian making films about Africa). In response to these criticisms, she later acknowledged that "any attempt at blurring the dividing line between outsider and insider would justifiably provoke anxiety, if not anger" (1989, 137). However, as a hybridized filmmaker who has crossed the lines of disciplines, national identities, and national imaginaries, she is clearly not comfortable with the politics of essentialism. And in her writings since then, she has opposed them because of the limitations they impose on filmmakers: "Every time you hear similar reactions to your films, you are bound to realize how small the limits and the territory remain in which you are allowed to work. And such reactions come as much from your community or from the communities of people of color as it comes from the dominant group" (1992, 164).

In her film practice Trinh has worked in opposition to binarist limitations by making films about other Third World cultures not her own and by having Third World insiders comment in her films on other Third World insiders not their own. *Shoot for the Contents* is a case in point: a black African, Clairmonte Moore, comments on Chinese culture and politics without the film invoking the usual attributes of authenticity and authority, such as the speaker's insider status or academic expertise in the topic. While such crossing of boundaries can be productive, it can also lead to superficial engagement with other cultures and societies. Vertical, historical engagement is a necessary antidote to the horizontal, surface traveling promoted by postmodernism.

For accented filmmakers, the choice of what film to make is often determined less by economic necessity than by their personal quest, which strengthens the autobiographical and authorial dimensions of their work. As Trinh has said, "Every work I have realized was designed to transform my own consciousness" (Chen 1992, 87). By using film, in the words of Alexander Astruc, as a *caméra stylo* to think and theorize with, Trinh has created her own unique accented style. She is an insider who acts like an outsider and also is an outsider who investigates the inside. Even in *Surname Viet Given Name Nam*, which is about insiders (Vietnamese and Vietnamese-Americans), she occupies both the inside and the outside positions, that is, the intersubjective and interstitial spaces that are characteristic of the accented cinema. Appropriately, her film style has been labeled "subjective documentary" (Kuhn and Radstone 1990, 403). By mixing and juxtaposing poetry, interviews, songs, dances, musical passages, talking heads, on-screen text, translation, foreign languages, archival footage, and documentary and staged footage, she documents, dramatizes, and theorizes from both sides of the divide. Her films are thus allegories, artifacts, and effects of multiple border crossings.

In the case of Trinh's work, what is at stake is not only the politics of hybridity and ambivalence but also the form of her films. Whereas Nair's linear, realist narratives are comprehensible and pleasurable for viewers, the nonlinear, essayistic, self-reflexive, and experimental style of Trinh's films problematizes not only the African, Chinese, and Vietnamese realities that are out there but also the realities that are shaped by the filmic apparatuses and narratives. This makes for films that are not narratively pleasurable or easily assimilable, requiring proactive spectatorship. If realism in Nair's films covers up the essential ambivalence of the postcolonial diasporic existence, Trinh's films tend to fully inscribe and embrace them.

Close-Up: Marva Nabili's Nightsongs *(1984)*

The reaction that Iranian exile filmmaker Marva Nabili received from the New York Chinese community when she was filming *Nightsongs* provides another example of intraethnic controversy, which is integral to the politics of postcolonial identity cinema. Trained in painting in Iran in the 1960s (Tehran University) and in film production in the United States in the 1970s (City University of New York and Vermont's Goddard College), Nabili returned to Iran in 1975, where she wrote and directed a series of hour-long films based on traditional folktales (called *Afsanehha-ye Kohan/Ancient Fairy Tales*) for the national television network. Under the guise of filming one such film, she and her small crew shot a feature film in southwestern Iran in just six days, without official authorization, using a nonprofessional cast. As the anti-Shah revolution was gaining momentum, Nabili smuggled the negatives and a rough cut to the United States. Completed and released in 1978, *The Sealed Soil (Khak-e Sar Behmohr)* has never been shown publicly in its country of origin. This slow-paced film, which uses Brechtian distantiation technique and is filmed almost entirely in long shots, centers on the personal transition of its protagonist from girlhood to womanhood—a transition that parallels that of her nation from traditionalism to modernism (Naficy 1985).

For her first fully exilic film, *Nightsongs*, Nabili again turned her attention to the life of a young woman in transition. Shot in Cantonese, the film centers on the struggle of a Chinese immigrant family from the perspective of a female Chinese-Vietnamese relative who is staying with them in New York City's Chinatown. Apparently, the first feature to be shot entirely in Chinatown, with a budget of $400,000, the filming encountered protest from the Chinese community, particularly from Asian-American filmmakers. They reportedly objected to the film's funding by the PBS *American Playhouse* series and the director's alleged "exploitation" of Chinese-Americans (Taylor 1983, pt. 6, p. 9). Nabili, who had spent nearly two years in Chinatown cultivating community contacts and doing research, including a four-month period of working in a sweatshop, denied the charge of exploitation and pointed out that fourteen members of her thirty-two-member nonunion crew were Chinese.[12] Instead, she claimed that this was "a case of my not being accepted because I am not Chinese" (9). Clearly in this last statement, she, like Trinh, is referring to the strict demarcation that is often drawn between outsiders and insiders. As an Iranian exile, Nabili was viewed with suspicion and considered unqualified to make a film about Chinese immigrants; PBS was criticized for funding an outsider project. The protest paid off: Nabili filmed additional "approved" scenes, including a new ending. A serious and uncompromising view of émigré alienation, *Nightsongs* subsequently received critical acclaim in the United States and abroad, but it did not do well at the box office.[13] Now, over a dozen years later, Nabili has yet to make another feature film.

Iranian Accented Film Production and Reception

Many accented filmmakers operate interstitially and artisanally by working outside both the mainstream film industry and the collective film environments. Yet some of these filmmakers have a strong affiliation with some type of collective identity in their production and/or exhibition practices. Unlike the Asian Pacific American groups, Iranian filmmakers have not created any formal collective organization for producing and distributing their films, videos, and television programs—even though, as the close-up section in chapter 1 showed, they are the most active among Middle Eastern and North African filmmakers in the West, with some 307 films and videos to their credit. Instead, because of their historical experiences, their orientational framework of mistrust, their class capital, and their phobic and conflicted exile politics, they have generally preferred individual enterprise to collective effort. Despite this interstitial production mode, the filmmakers' shared experience of otherness, their films' common themes, and the manner of the films' exhibition have served to construct an Iranian collective consciousness. Here I explore both the interstitial production and the collective exhibition practices.

Interstitial Production

There are many reasons for the absence of collective enterprise in the face of exilic onslaught. These reasons shed light on how the history of a particular group shapes its experience of exile and the institutions and cultures it creates there. Unlike the North African, South Asian, East Asian, and Caribbean countries whose exiles and émigrés formed the "postcolonial" category and created the *beur* cinema in France, Asian Pacific film and video collectives in the United States, and black and Asian film and video collectives in Britain, respectively, Iran was never colonized by the West directly, and Iranian exiles cannot accurately be called postcolonial. Although colonialism was brutal and unjust for the colonized subjects, the shared experience of colonialism and the imposed colonial language ironically produced certain positive side effects for the postcolonial subjects who emigrated to Western metropolitan centers. The most important of these is, in Gayatri Spivak's words, "access to the culture of imperialism," which allowed postcolonials to "critique, yet inhabit intimately," that culture (1993, 60). This access created the necessary distance that also positioned them to critique their own native culture and to create counterhegemonic identities. At the same time, shared history encouraged consolidation of identity among the disparate, formerly colonized populations now in diaspora, while linguistic commonality facilitated communication among them, and between them and the colonizing host societies. The formerly imposed colonial language, therefore, became an unexpected asset for the postcolonial subjects in diaspora, particularly for the intellectuals. As such, they are more prone to invest in the constitution of a new society here and now than in a nostalgic reconstitution of an imaginary homeland elsewhere. The impact of postcolonial critical thinkers such as Frantz Fanon, Edward Said, Gayatri Spivak, and Homi Bhabha on theorizing and dramatizing the postcolonial and postmodern conditions would have been at best modest were it not for their mastery of the colonizers' languages, cultures, and philosophical traditions. With some exceptions, most postcolonial and *beur* literature is written in the colonizers' languages, and sometimes these works are best-sellers. As a result, their output forms not only the postcolonial and *beur* literatures but also the national literatures of the former colonizing countries—much like the way in which accented films contribute to national cinemas.

Iranians, who had not experienced direct colonialism and its imposed language and culture at home, could not benefit in exile from the collective identity, the ease of communication, and the intimate access and cultural mastery that these vestiges of colonialism offered. However, from the nineteenth century onward, Iran was an arena of intense machinations, first between the Great Powers (imperialist England and czarist Russia) and later between the superpowers (the United States and the USSR). Foreign and Iranian leaders manipulated these rivalries to benefit themselves and to overdetermine Westernization in Iran.[14] These and other experiences since the 1950s, culminating in the 1979 revolution, which drove a great many Iranians into exile, produced a deep sense of deep paranoia, conspiracy thinking, and ambivalence, which compounded the general mistrust that comes with political exile. What exacerbated not only governmental relations but also personal relations was the taking of some fifty Americans hostage in the U.S. embassy in Tehran in 1979; the Iranian government's involvement in terrorism at home and abroad, in alleged nuclear and chemical arms buildup, and in opposing the Israeli-Palestinian peace process; and the continually tightening economic boycott of Iran by the West, particularly by the United States. All this led to a complexly negative representation of Iran and of the United States in the respective national media and pop cultures (Naficy 1995d) and to ambivalent feelings among the exiles about the Iranian and American governments. This ambivalence is inscribed in the films they produced.

The 1990 United States Census shows a total of 285,000 Iranians in the country—both foreign-born and native-born—of whom 100,000 (35 percent) live in the Los Angeles metropolitan area (Bozorgmehr 1997, 445). The largest influx of Iranians into the United States occurred in two broad phases: the first between 1950 and 1977, and the second between 1979 and 1986. These two waves, one motivated by a rapid, top-down Westernization spearheaded by the Shah, and the other by a bottom-up popular social revolution eventually led by the Ayatollah Khomeini, produced two different types of populations. While the first wave was composed chiefly of permanent economic immigrants or of temporary immigrants such as a large number of students, much of the second wave—forming a majority—is made up of political refugees and exiles. According to Mehdi Bozorgmehr and Georges Sabagh, the exiles are on average older than immigrants, have less education, are forced to accept jobs that are less desirable than what they had in Iran or what they would like to have, and have a lower mastery of the host country's language and culture (1991, 126–31). These trends show that exile, at least for the first generation, involves drastic shifts in status, often in the form of downward mobility. This partially explains the propensity toward dystopia and dysphoria, particularly among the intellectuals. Significantly, these data also show that the exile and immigrant categories are not fixed, since the former can transform into the latter. This evolution is reflected not only in the contents and forms of the exile-produced televisual cultures (Naficy 1993a) but also in the thematic trajectory of the films (discussed later).

Most of the exiles opposed the postrevolutionary Islamist government, but for different reasons, and they supported divergent alternatives. This political diversity, even divisiveness, was undergirded by mistrust, a tendency especially among the older generation to suspect collective work and to reward situationist individualism. In addition, because of their generally high class capital and aspirations (high education, income, professional jobs, and self-employment) and their religious diversity and subethnic affiliations, Iranian exiles were able to leapfrog the traditional low-paying émigré jobs, ethnic employment, and residency, which favor place-bound ethnic formations. On the other hand, these very factors favored the creation of a dynamic, advertising-driven exilic pop culture and ethnic economy, which consolidated a symbolic and discursive Iranian collective identity. Ironically, these same factors, along with the host society's discrimination and prejudice, prevented exiles from fully participating in the social and political life of the host countries, slowing their assimilation. As a result, many Iranians remained in an agonistic exilic mode of cultural otherness and psychic split for over two decades. This tendency was fed by the relative recency of their emigration, which meant that they occupied the liminal space of exile more than the settled niche of ethnicity. Their wide dispersion to over a dozen countries, however, helped temper the binarist attachment to the homeland, preparing the ground for lateral diasporist affiliations. Finally, the Islamist regime's gradual move toward increasing openness in the 1990s and the prospect of future rapprochement between Iran and the United States made possible the thought of return and reconciliation.

It is in the light of these evolving historical, psychological, and social forces that exiled Iranian filmmakers and cultural producers generally preferred interstitiality to collective effort. As a result, unlike other ethnic groups, they did not form credible media associations to represent their professional interests; and only in the late 1990s did they form watchdog organizations to monitor media representation of Iranians. However, a younger generation, raised in

Europe and North America and schooled in the media, has come to the fore; and it is more aware of the importance of professional and ethnic associations for collective bargaining and corrective representation, and it is less exilic than the older generation.

Diversity among the exiles is not only generational but also geographic and historical, for they evolve differently across national boundaries and over time. The exilism of Iranians in the United States has toned down over the years to the point of assuming for many an émigré, ethnic, or hyphenated character, while the exilism of those in Europe—particularly of the political exiles— seems to have remained more or less intact, or even hardened. This is evident in the far less political contexts in which Iranian films are screened and received in the United States than in Europe. For example, there are no regularly scheduled festivals of Iranian "exile films" in the United States, while several have surfaced in Europe. It is also evident in the evolution of the Iranian accented feature films, from an overcathected preoccupation with homeland and the culture of politics toward a concern with life in exile and the politics of culture.

This evolution, which may be charted in a six-part thematic trajectory, demonstrates the exile's processual nature. These categories are not entirely distinct, however, since some films partake of the politics and aesthetics of more than one category. It is for clarity that films are predominantly assigned to only one category.

In its first thematic category, Iranian exile cinema was a *cinema of denial*; physically located in exile, mentally it was situated at home, and it largely disavowed the fact of exile. For example, although the story of Sayyad's film *The Mission* (1983) occurs in the United States, involving an Islamic Republic terrorist on a mission to assassinate an ex-Savak agent (Shah's security police), it emphasizes the politics of the homeland. Likewise, Cyrus Nowrasterh's *Veiled Threat* (1988) concentrates on the problems an Iranian exile faces when he attempts to track down the Islamic government's agent who had tried to assassinate his family. In Arby Ovanessian's *How My Mother's Embroidered Apron Unfolds in My Life* (*Le tablier brodé de ma mère s'étale dans ma vie*, 1983– 85), the director's ancestral homeland of Armenia is explicitly encoded, not his homeland (Iran), nor his host country (France). Exilic denial is not accidental. It is motivated by both the desire to disavow the ruptures of exile and the wish that it will be short-lived, culminating in a glorious return.[15]

In the second category, *cinema of panic and pursuit*, there is a sense of both spatial claustrophobia in the films' mise-en-scène and shot composition and of temporal claustrophobia and panic among diegetic characters whose actions are driven by chase, stalking, assassination, and terrorism. Sayyad's *The Mission* and Hassan Ildari's *Face of the Enemy* (1989) provide examples.

In the third category, *cinema of transition*, the films focus on Iranians who are in transit in third spaces, where they attempt to obtain passports, visas, and plane tickets. Sayyad's *Checkpoint* (1987), for example, charts the heated political debate among a group of Iranian and American students who are caught in a geographic and legal limbo at a Canadian-American border checkpoint because of the cancellation of their visas due to hostage taking in Tehran. *The Guests of Hotel Astoria* (1989) is about a group of Iranian refugees in a hotel in Istanbul, Turkey, and the tragic efforts of a young couple to gain entry to the United States and of an older couple to return to Iran.

The diegesis of the fourth category, *liminal cinema*, is both physically and mentally located in the host country, and its narrative is centered on the life and clash of cultures in exile. *The Nuclear Baby* (1990) is an experimental feature video that evokes a nightmarish post–nuclear war vision in which past, present, and future, as well as Iranian and American landscapes, are critically juxtaposed. Erica Jordan and Shirin Etessam's *Walls of Sand* (1996) charts the deepening relationship of an Iranian illegal immigrant with a young Anglo mother who suffers from agoraphobia. The mere exposure to Shirin Neshat's two-monitor avant-garde video installations, *Turbulent* (*Biqarar*, 1998), *Soliloquy* (*Zemzemeh*, 1999) and *Rapture* (*Owj*, 1999), reproduces the duality, fragmentation, and simultaneity of exilic liminality (Naficy 2000).

A fifth category, *transnational cinema*, made in part by hyphenated Iranians, does not necessarily deal with Iranian issues but instead with universal issues of love and displacement. Many of them are dystopic. Sohrab Shahid Saless's uncompromising *Utopia* (1982) focuses on the painful lives of a group of prostitutes in Germany, and his *Roses for Africa* (*Rosen für Afrika*, 1991) centers on the dystopic, fruitless efforts of a German to reach his continent of dream, Africa. Amir Naderi's visually stunning films *Manhattan by Numbers* (1993) and *Avenue A.B.C. . . . Manhattan* (1997) chart various states of displacement and disconnection in New York City. Marva Nabili's first fully exilic film, *Nightsongs* (1984), is about the difficult life of a young Vietnamese woman in New York City's Chinatown. Mitra Tabrizian's *Journey of No Return* (1993) explores the angst-ridden exile of a young woman in Britain and her unresolved epistolary relationship with her father. Caveh Zahedi's minimalist comedy *A Little Stiff* (1991), codirected with Greg Watkins, deals with the unceasing efforts of a young man to win the attention of a girlfriend. Iran, Iranians, and Iranian politics are not an issue in these films.

A sixth category, *cinema of return*, emerged early, led by documentarists who returned to document the 1979 revolution and its aftermath. Among these films are Rafigh Pooya's *Bloody Friday* (1979) and *In Defense of People* (*Dar Defa' az Mardom*, 1981) and Bigan Saliani's *Iran: Inside the Islamic Republic* (1980). Pooya's subsequent feature fiction thriller *Broken Bridges* (1996), shot in the United States, Russia, and Azerbaijan, is also driven by the return narrative that examines Azeri nationalism. Persheng Sadegh Vaziri's *Journal from Iran* (1986) and *A Place Called Home* (1988) are return films of a different kind, in that they document the filmmaker's own return visits to Iran in search of a home, visits that seem to have paved the way for her eventual return home to

Figure 4. Politics of return and nationalism. Jeff (right, Peter Reckell), returning to Azerbaijan, enlists Michael's help (Behrouz Vossooghi), in Rafigh Pooya's *Broken Bridges*. Courtesy International Home Cinema, Inc.

live and make films. Her return is emblematic of the developing exchange relations between the Iranian cinemas in exile and at home. In the ascendance of the reformist movement since the election of Mohammad Khatami, former minister of culture and Islamic guidance, to the presidency, it is inevitable that some exile filmmakers and their films will be welcomed inside Iran. This was borne out by the 2000 Fajr International Film Festival in Tehran, in which films of exiled and formerly exiled directors were screened for the first time.[16] This sort of return and exchange enriches filmmakers on both sides of the exilic divide.

These evolving thematic categories were products of the specific Iranian history and politics and the Iranian exiles' ethnoreligious affiliations and gender relations. Interethnicity and religiosity were suppressed in the interest of promoting nationalistic politics. As a result, although ethnoreligious minorities (such as Jews, Armenians, and Bahais) were involved in cinema, few films foregrounded interethnic issues or singled out religious minorities as protagonists. Exilic deterritorialization destabilizes the traditional Iranian patriarchy, bringing prominence to women's social and political status. Many exile-made films featured strong women, including Ghasem Ebrahimian's *The Suitors* (*Khastegaran*, 1989).

Such a thematic classification is not unique to Iranians. A similar schema may be charted for the accented filmmakers of other nations. Indeed, evolution is constitutive of the accented cinema for the accented style is not stabilized by the apparatuses of cinematic genres and production, and its audiences are not normalized by their legal status.

Stylistically, with the exception of the liminal and transnational films, Iranian accented features were highly invested in mimetic realism and in the classical cinema's invisible style. Their accent lay not so much in their alternative visual style as in the prevalence of the following features: the accented speech or the Persian-language dialogue of their diegetic characters; themes of displacement, journey, search, politics of blame, family unity, history, and obsession with the homeland; structures of feeling and narratives of panic and phobia, as well as of memory and nostalgia, that are inscribed in closed and open chronotopes; and the allegorization of the filmmakers' interstitial and authorial positions. The highly politicized films (such as *The Mission, Checkpoint, Veiled Threat*, and *The Guests of Hotel Astoria*) were ideologically complicit with the dominant view in the United States that regarded the Islamic Republic as a "terrorist" and "rogue" state, Iran under that regime to be a ruin, and Iranians at home to be nothing but victims. Such comforting polar views suppressed, or misrepresented, the evolution of and the differences between the exiles and those at home.

The interstitial filmmakers' dilemma is to determine for whom they speak, whom they address, and to whom they must turn for financing and distribution of their films. The films of denial, panic, and transition addressed only Iranian audiences, in Persian, which required their casts and stories to be strictly Iranian and their distribution limited to the exile outlets (bookstores, grocery stores, and music stores). Indeed, most of the 307 films made abroad are not available even in those outlets, making access to them extremely difficult. However, the liminal, transnational, and return films moved away from such narrow conceptions and became truly accented. They dealt with both Iranian and non-Iranian subjects, involve bilingual worlds and speech, and are experimental and authorial in style. They also addressed a crossover nonethnic audience, and several of them were critically acclaimed and commercially distributed in theaters and on video. As such, these film are part of both the accented cinema and the national cinemas of the countries in which the filmmakers reside. Such moves inevitably have entailed a physical and mental relocation, from "there" to "here," which in turn has necessitated a toning down of the films' political rhetoric, even a depoliticization of sorts, and an integration of the particular (Iranian) with the general (universal).

As expected, the filmmakers' politics of location and the films' narrative shifts have alienated compatriot and crossover audiences, as was the case with Nair's *Salaam Bombay!*, Trinh's *Naked Spaces*, and Nabili's *Nightsongs*, since in the process they signified upon both the homeland's culture and the exiles' lifestyle. A case in point is Ebrahimian's *The Suitors*, discussed in the following close-up section. These reactions demonstrate again that because of their textual politics and exhibition practices, accented films, collectively made or not, are often received collectively. Textually, Iranian films' overwhelming concern with national politics and exilic politics, as well as their Persian-language dialogue, encouraged ethnic consolidation. Certain exhibition practices also favored high ethnic attendance: most films were on the screen for only a short period, from one to several nights, and in only one theater at a time, and most were not commercially distributed by mainstream video stores. The screening venues were generally repertory theaters, rented commercial theaters, or university cinemas. Each screening was heavily promoted in the Iranian media and often was attended by families, increasing ethnic affiliation and collective celebration.

Close-Up: *Ghasem Ebrahimian's* The Suitors (Khastegaran, *1989)*

Filmed in Persian, *The Suitors* shows a group of Islamist expatriates in New York City slaughtering a sheep in the bathtub of their apartment in a traditional ritual that celebrates the arrival of guests, in this case, a married couple from Iran. The blood from the slaughter seeps into the apartment below, causing a neighbor who is watching a Christian TV show to call in the SWAT team, which attacks the premises on the assumption that there are terrorists inside. In the confusion, the newly arrived husband is killed. The rest of the film is the story of Maryam, his young, attractive, veiled wife, attempting to rid herself of her veil and of her various persistent suitors—all of whom were close friends of her dead husband and were involved in sacrificing the sheep.

The film caused strong and divergent reactions. It was critically well received by mainline American and European presses, was selected for the Directors' Fortnight at the 1988 Cannes International Film Festival, and was released commercially in a number of U.S. cities.[17] The exile media, on the other hand, reacted defensively, and many condemned it. Acculturated Iranians regarded the film—despite its narrative flaws, uneven pacing, and some crude characterization—as a feminist corrective to the dominant view of Iranian women as backward, dependent victims. The film's feminism and critical edge, which were clearly pointed at men and at patriarchy, were partially responsible for the negative reaction of the exile media, which is heavily male-dominated.

Specifically, what seems to have offended most of the critics were the "savage" scenes of the sheep's slaughter in a bathtub, the callous pursuit of Maryam by the suitors, and her cold-blooded murder of one of them. The critics appear to have understood that in portraying the traditional customs of slaughtering

animals and seeking a spouse, Ebrahimian was signifying upon those customs
and in the process criticizing them. Maryam's murder of her persistent suitor
was also condemned for portraying Iranian women as uncharacteristically ruthless and violent.[18] These readings, however, contradicted the director's purpose
of depicting Iranians as "humans," not "terrorists" (Dowlatabadi 1989, 31).
These reactions (similar to the criticism leveled at Nair's *Salaam Bombay!*) show
that the exiles felt betrayed by a director who exposed and signified upon aspects of the native culture from an insider perspective but did so for the benefit
of outsider audiences. This is because Ebrahimian violated two norms of Iranian collective identity: maintaining a clear separation between self and other,
and loyalty to the insider group. That traditional customs are interpreted so
negatively by some has more to do with the exilic context of the film's reception
than with its production. When indigenous practices are both produced and
viewed outside their naturalized contexts, they become defamiliarized and may
be devalued, particularly if viewers are defensive about those practices. If viewers are not defensive, then defamiliarization may produce the promised critical
awareness and pedagogical effect that Bertold Brecht theorized. Such defamiliarization may lead to viewer self-awareness and empathy with Maryam. As
Ann Kibbey notes in her extensive study of the film, "It is through self-refer-
ence to her own consciousness, her own experience of the film, that the viewer
articulates what *The Suitors* is about" (1993, 7).

The controversy surrounding this film shows again the accented films' extraordinary burden of representation. Thus, to the accented filmmakers' dilem-
mas, the following two must be added: how to balance ethnic and national
loyalty with personal and artistic integrity, and how to reconcile universality
with specificity. Each director must determine for herself what constitutes the
universal or the specific. However, as Abid Med Hondo, a Mauritanian exile
filmmaker in France, declared, "Let us be suspicious of the concept of universalism, which is a dangerous thing" (1978, 71), especially the hegemonic form of
universalism that is undergirded by an oppressive will to power. The localist
universalism that is intended here is obtainable only through specificity, which
can be had if, instead of focusing on the homeland alone and on copying cinematic formulas, accented filmmakers turn, like Gypsy filmmaker Gatlif, Argentine director Solanas, Iranian filmmaker Shahid Saless, and Mauritanian director Med Hondo, to their indigenous "local cultures" or to their own individual
experiences in exile to create a thirdspace of alterity, creativity, and insight.

Achieving universal truths by way of cultural specificity is a route taken not
only by important Third World filmmakers in exile but also by eminent First
World directors who made films outside their own countries, such as Jean
Renoir, who worked in the United States. Renoir, described by Georges Sadoul
as "the most French of prewar film makers," poignantly articulated this dynamics between the local and the universal:

Naïvely and laboriously, I did my best to imitate my American teachers; I had not understood that a Frenchman living in France, drinking red wine and eating Brie cheese in front of a grisaille of Paris, could only create works of quality by following the traditions of people like himself. . . . Now I am beginning to be aware of how I must work. I know that I am French and that I must work in an absolutely national sense. I know also that, by doing this, and only by doing this, I can reach the people of other countries and create works of international standing. (quoted in Sadoul 1972, 213–14)

This knowledge became truly available to him only after he experienced exile. That exile can move a filmmaker to become simultaneously more local and more universal is gleaned from André Bazin's insightful assessment of Renoir after the latter's return from the United States:

Let those who have known and loved Renoir be reassured. America has not devoured him. At the very most, and this is hardly a misfortune, it has distilled his French virtues, eliminating the impurities and leaving only the essentials. A kind of Franciscan serenity and tenderness tempers his Rabelaisian paganism now. A sense of the universal, of the relativity of history and geography, situates and confirms his Frenchness. (1973, 101)

Collective Exhibition and Exile Festivals

The collective mode involves not only film's collective production or reception but also their collective distribution and exhibition. The collective exhibition is highly complicated, particularly in the case of festivals that screen both the homeland's films and the exile-made films. The animus and anxiety that film festivals provoke are due not only to the antagonistic politics, cinemas, filmmakers, and audiences, which are brought together across the exilic divide, but also to the cultural translations and mistranslations that occur on these occasions.

One of the first exhibition venues for Iranian exiles in the early 1980s was the screening of over 130 fiction films made before the revolution in rented commercial theaters of Los Angeles (and a few other major American cities). Most of them were B-grade movies, with comedies, melodramas, and *jaheli* (tough-guy action) genres predominant.[19] A sprinkling of A-grade features and documentaries were also exhibited.[20] Although these were not exilic films, their screening in exile played an important homeostatic function for the newly displaced people who, initially at least, desired cultural continuity. Like much of Iranian exile television, these films offered frozen, fetishized images of the country and the nation before the exilic fall. The result was a rekindling of the viewers' nostalgic memories of the "good old days" back home and of their first experience of these films there—thus deepening their colonization by the home. This exhibition venue did not last long, however. The exhibitors were soon forced out of business because of their inability to compete with the low-cost videos of the films or with the emerging exilic television. In addition, there was a finite supply of such films, whose production had stopped with the revolution. Finally, as exile wore on, these films became less relevant to an increasingly acculturated audience.[21]

For almost a decade, the mutual hostility between the American and Iranian governments discouraged the exhibition of postrevolutionary films in the United States. Consequently, Iranian cinema remained largely unknown here, even though Iranian films had begun to appear at international film festivals in increasing numbers, receiving generally high honors.[22] The situation changed in the late 1980s thanks to a variety of factors.

A major festival at UCLA in 1990 that showed a large number of postrevolutionary films (eighteen fictional features and a number of shorts) proved to be a seminal event for Iranian films in the United States.[23] The festival was criticized harshly by some exiles, particularly by media producers and film-makers,[24] who condemned it for helping to whitewash the Islamist government by putting a humane face on its inhumane deeds.[25] The attacks began before the festival screenings, and some continued for years after the event.[26] However, despite the call to boycott the festival, spectators embraced it enthusiastically. They flocked to the theater in large numbers from all over the country, at times standing in line for more than eight hours to obtain tickets. The few television producers who supported the festival were also attacked by the opposing factions and embraced by the filmgoers.[27] The vehemence of the attack suggested that the debate was as much about exilic politics as it was about the Iranian government's politics. The protesting media producers and entertainers wanted to maintain the comforting psychological barriers that they themselves had created by their fetishized and frozen representations of Iran. The intense audience involvement with the movies, however, showed that the films had succeeded in breaking through those barriers, unleashing the threat that had been kept in check—that of the homeland unfettered by repressions and distortions of exilic politics. Peter Bloom's account of the "emotionally charged" festival that caused the spectators to contemplate the unthinkable—the possibility of reconciliation, even return—attested to such a breakthrough (1990, 95). Both the vehemence of the opposition and the cathartic enthusiasm of those embracing the festival revealed that the exilic media's fetishization of Iran under the Islamic Republic as a backward and ruined land served the political and economic interests of only a segment of the exiles. Even those who benefited were perhaps torn by the conflicting needs both to repress and reconnect.

The festival created an emotionally strong sense of collective identity among the exiles, and the festivals and touring programs of Iranian films that since then have become annual events in many cities have sustained this identity. Filmmakers such as Abbas Kiarostami, Mohsen Makhmalbaf, Dariush Mehrjui, Bahram Baizai, Jafar Panahi, Majid Majidi, Rakhshan Banietemad, Samira Makhmalbaf, and Tahmineh Milani gradually entered the established venues of "international cinema," and their films are now routinely reviewed, exhibited, and distributed commercially.[28] Film festivals are appropriate forums not only for screening films but also for their critical discussion, which will inevitably touch upon the political climate at home and abroad. This criticism, person-to-person contact, and professional exchange that festivals promote are necessary to keep filmmakers from both sides of the exilic divide from becoming ossified in inflexible positions based on politically motivated repressions and manipulations.

At the same time that festivals of films made in Iran prospered, an exhibition venue for exile-made films emerged, particularly in Europe, with collectivizing consequences. In 1993 the first major festival of Iranian films in exile was held in Göteborg, Sweden, by dissident filmmaker Hossein Mahini. It showed sixty-four films made by Iranian filmmakers in the United States and in seven European countries. The second festival, held in 1995, featured fifty-eight exile films, forty-four of which were made by Iranians, and the rest by other exiled filmmakers.[29] With the second festival, the geographic distribution of Iranian participants increased to twelve countries, mapping out the global distribution and concentration of the Iranian diaspora communities.[30] In so doing, the Göteborg festival added a diasporic dimension to the Iranian filmic identity, which previously had been limited to a national or an exilic identity. It is in this emerging thirdspace of diaspora in which Iranian filmmakers may finally find a collective voice.[31] This entails creating vertical, horizontal, and transverse group affiliations across social formations and nation-states. It also requires suppressing insider group differences in order to move out of cellularity into coalitional agency. Finally, it means becoming, in the words of Neil Larsen, a postnational border subject (1991, xviii). For Iranians, such diasporic rhizomaticity, coalitional agency, and postnational subjectivity are present in only an inchoate state.

By including exile films from non-Iranians and by programming the films of both political and nonpolitical exiles, the Göteborg festival has moved toward a pan-exilic identity that transcends the filmmakers' place of birth and place of residence. Like the Asian-American expansion of the Asian diaspora, this move points to an important direction in globalized alliance politics among the displaced filmmakers worldwide that argues for comparative exilism and diasporism.

Festivals that cater to exilic films define the accented cinema in contradistinction to the home cinemas. At the same time, home governments, fearing contamination, ban exile-made films from their own national festivals and tend to pressure international festivals to not show exile-made films. According to refugee filmmakers Parviz Sayyad and Reza Allamehzadeh, the Islamic Republic shut them out of international festivals in which Iran-made films were entered.[32] However, in at least one instance Sayyad himself withdrew his film *The*

Figure 5. Politics of the exile film festivals. Postal card of the Festival of Iranian Exile Cinema, which is subtitled "The World Is My Home," Gothenburg, Sweden, 1996. © 1996 FRI FILM.

Mission from the 1992 Los Angeles Festival because the festival was screening films from Iran. While festival organizers are subject to governmental pressures, they do not acquiesce to them routinely. It is also disingenuous to say that foreign audiences will ignore the human rights violations of a government, particularly one as notorious as the Islamic Republic, because of the exhibition of the country's films—many of which contain social criticism. Such blanket statements and calls for boycotts do the exiles a disservice because they simplify complex situations and fail to give audiences and critics the credit they deserve in judging the films and the home country's politics for themselves.

The exilically accented filmmakers and festivals are caught in the vise of other political relationships. As Marsha Kinder, in her perceptive discussion of the films of the Spanish exile directors Luis Buñuel and José Luis Borau, states, "The fate of all films at international festivals and in the world market is largely determined by the position of their home nation in global politics" (1993, 383). A weak country's films may be excluded from the international festivals and other exhibition venues because the country does not matter politically. On the other hand, the political notoriety of "rogue" regimes from small countries with dismal human rights records, such as that of Francisco Franco in Spain, Fidel Castro in Cuba, or the ayatollahs in Iran, may make them sufficiently attractive for the international festivals to invite their quality films. Such invitations often cause controversy.[33] Foreign film festivals can construct a national cinema identity and an auteur identity, but they can also distort both. And if a notorious government is removed, those identities are likely to be readjusted. As Borau notes:

> Franco's death did not improve matters much. To a certain extent it even made things worse. Spain is no longer the victim of a Fascist dictatorship. Our books and our films don't arrive abroad bedecked with the palm of martyrdom. No one has to listen to us because it is humane or politically expedient to do so. The waters have finally returned to the river bed: the situation has returned to "normal." (1983, 86)

After the demise, or liberalization, of the Islamist government, a similar readjustment or "normalization" may befall the Iranian cinema and those exiled filmmakers whose popularity is dependent on the unpopularity of the government.

British Postcolonial Workshops and Collectives

The British workshop and collective phenomenon of the 1980s dates as far back as John Grierson's General Post Office and Empire Marketing Board film units in the 1930s and the "free cinema" group in the 1950s. This latest postcolonial manifestation emerged in the aftermath of the black and youth "riots" in Notting Hill and Brixton districts of London in 1976 and 1981, which were protests against police harassment, racism, and unemployment and

Figure 6. "Street riots"
in *Handsworth Songs.*

for "black representation." Both the radical labor administration of the Greater
London Council and Channel 4 Television set aside funds to create workshops
and collectives in which minority artists could be trained to produce their own
self-representational films and videos. In this manner, the children of the first
generation of the immigrants from the former British colonies gained a collective, creative voice. For example, those primarily from the West Indies created
Black Audio Film Collective, Ceddo Film and Video Workshop, and Sankofa
Film and Video Collective, and those from India and Pakistan formed Retake
Film and Video Workshop.

Driven by the politics and poetics of decolonization, postcolonial diasporism, and critical theory, the workshops became an integral part of the new
politics of representation, which questioned not only the mainstream media's
stereotyping and misrepresentation of the black and subaltern subjects but also
representation itself. Despite their differences, the works of Sankofa, Ceddo,
and Black Audio shared certain features. They were of varying lengths, thus
breaking the length requirement of both commercial cinema and television.
They critically juxtaposed news footage, interviews, polemical narration, political analysis, and dramatization. They questioned the official "history" of the
blacks in Britain and attempted to discover behind it multiple "histories" of
slavery, racism, sexism, colonialism, and diaspora, or, in the words of *Handsworth Songs'* narration, "the ghosts of other stories." Indeed, these films,
through their accented themes and visual style, allegorized the contentious and
hybridized black diaspora conditions and the very double consciousness that
gave rise to their making. The fragmented and self-reflexive strategies of films
such as *The Passion of Remembrance* (directed by Maureen Blackwood and Isaac
Julien, 1986), *Territories* (Isaac Julien, 1985), and *Handsworth Songs* (John
Akomfrah, 1986) subverted the master codes of realist aesthetics and race relation narratives, which had traditionally posited blacks and minorities as invisi-

ble problem figures or victims.[34] These strategies opened up for discussion not just the (mis)representations of such aesthetics and narratives but also their "politics of representation" (Hall 1988, 27).

In their collective practice, too, workshop participants offered an alternative model to the traditional conception of the director as "auteur director" or independent "filmmaker" and to that of the audience as "passive consumers of a predetermined product" (Akomfrah, quoted in Diawara 1993b, 152). Like the Asian Pacific American diaspora collectives and the Iranian exile filmmakers, these black British collectives did not hold the production of the films and videos to be the end of their task. If they wanted to effect a cultural shift, from individualized to collective mode of production, they would have to consider as integral to the process the reception of their films at the community level. As Ceddo noted in an early handout at the Third Cinema conference in Edinburgh, "Our common interest is the involvement of black people in all aspects of film/video production, thereby contributing to the development of an independent film/video culture. Linking our work with the community is an important part of the Workshop's function, as it is from this source that we will gain our strength and support" (1986). Although through their integrated practice the workshops tried to link up with their communities, their dense accented style created problems of comprehension for audiences and critics alike. Salman Rushdie, for one, mockingly criticized *Handsworth Songs* for, among other things, its limited representation of "blacks" and its penchant for using "the dead language of race industry professionals" (1988, 16).[35] As has been noted, ethnic and disaporic filmmakers must continually wrestle with the problem of multiple reception communities, each of which may demand a different contractual relationship with a film.

Since the late 1980s, a number of black collective filmmakers have worked on projects of their own, moving from the "collective" to the "independent" mode of production, and moving from the "experimental" to the "feature" category of the accented films—Isaac Julien, among them. This shift in production mode happened concurrently with a thematic shift. Julien's independent films began to examine more openly black homosexuality and gender inscriptions. As though heeding Judith Williamson's recommendation (1988, 112), his independent films also adopted more popular forms, such as *Young Soul Rebel* (1991), which employed a thriller narrative. These textual shifts created crossover audiences that in turn energized Julien's own geographic crossover from the United Kingdom to the United States.[36] These crossovers were undergirded by Julien's identity crossovers as "a product of a diasporan culture," traveling among a number of subjectivities: Caribbean, gay, British, black British, and black American (Julien, quoted in Grundmann 1995, 30).

Of course, what is called the "black independent cinema" or the "black British cinema" is not limited to the works of the grant-supported black collectives operating in the public sector. There are many other independent black film-makers (and production companies) in Britain, among them the prolific Trinidadian filmmakers Horace Ové and Melenick Shabazz, who work on commission for the television industry.[37] In addition, there are many independent black filmmakers working in other European countries.[38]

The workshop phenomenon was not limited to the black collectives, although from journalistic and academic writings, particularly in the United States, one would not know otherwise.[39] The highly celebratory discourse about the black collectives overshadowed the works of other minority and immigrant workshops, such as the Asians (chiefly from India, Pakistan, and Bangladesh), which also dealt with similar postcolonial and late-modern diaspora issues but from distinctly different perspectives and with a different stylistic accent. The almost systematic exclusion of Asian perspectives by both white and black critics was due partly to the normalization throughout much of the 1980s of the definition of "black" as a political, not a racial, category. Although the term was intended to include all nonwhites in Britain, in practice, as Dhillon-Kashyap explains, it ended up being used very narrowly: "The narrow use of the term 'black' in Britain to refer mainly to those of Afro-Caribbean origin, and the fact that much of the black independent film sector in Britain has engaged in debate with black writers and critics in the US, where black experience is very different, has meant that the Asian perspective in British film culture has tended to be excluded" (1988, 121). The restricted interpretation of the "black" and "diaspora" concepts is not limited to the popular discourses. The works of astute observers on diaspora matters, such as Paul Gilroy (in *The Black Atlantic*, for example), are hobbled by their inability to fully figure in the non-African diasporas. In addition, attempts by critics such as Gilroy to posit diaspora as antecedent to or exceeding the nation ignore the constitutive contribution that national consciousness makes to diaspora formations, even when nation-states are in the process of disintegration or (re)formation. Nation and diaspora thus must be thought of in relationship to each other, which means that one must recognize that there are multiple diasporas-in-relation. There is no single, hegemonic, autonomous, homogeneous, or all-encompassing grand diaspora; nor are there a series of isolated, hermetic, and cellular diasporas. While recognizing commonalities, it is important to keep in mind the specificity of the cultures and the locatedness of the identities that produce the different diasporas and their relations with each other. Positing a grand diaspora (such as the black diaspora or the Jewish diaspora) calls also for positing a grand homogeneous Other. The result is a simplification and polarization of the world, which distorts the optic through which identities are formed.

Afro-Caribbean and Asian diasporas in England are different from and are in relations with one another, and so are the many internal minidiasporas that in turn constitute them—each of which is driven by specific histories, politics, memories, and power relations. By beginning with short excerpts from interviews with four South Asian British youths—interspersed with Bhangra music performed in the streets of London—Gurinder Chadha's *I'm British But . . .* (1989) succinctly establishes the variety of minidiasporic identities and their inherent ambivalence and hybridity, which constitute the British Asian diaspora subjectivity.

MALE: I see myself as British . . . maybe Welsh . . . I am Welsh, one of *them*, I suppose.

FEMALE: I am Asian, this is what you do. You see, I am Asian. . . . I feel no affiliation to any one city or to any one country.

MALE: I am Irish. Hybrid, is the way I describe myself, and very happy with that!

FEMALE: I would prefer to be described as a Scottish Pakistani, rather than British. . . . It doesn't bother me the fact that I've been born here and [that] I am British as well as Asian.

The film argues that what constitutes Asian British subjectivity is a syncretic combination of the specificity of the individuals' emplacement as ethnic subjects and the commonality of their collective displacement as postcolonial, diasporic subjects in Britain. What is more, the multiple diasporas that constitute this new Britishness are neither static nor isolated, and they interact with one another. South Asian youths, for example, do not just draw upon or follow music, fashion, and dance trends set by Afro-Caribbeans in order to transform, reconstruct, and enrich their diasporic identities. Their borrowings and transformations do not leave the Afro-Caribbean diaspora cultures untouched. Indeed, the multiplicity and reciprocality, even the competitiveness and antagonism, of the diaspora flows ensure that trendsetters and borrowers change places from time to time and that both are enriched by cultural exchange and hybridization.[40]

These exchanges extend far beyond the shores of the British Isles, and they are facilitated by the epistolary and electronic media of the telephone and the Internet, transnational satellite television, and the global marketing of videocassettes. In 1992, some 750 specialist video shops provided feature films from the home countries to the Indian, Pakistani, and Bangladeshi communities in the United Kingdom (Dean 1992). Like most ethnic video distribution, this Asian system is replete with piracy and uneven quality. However, the increasing availability of movies and television programs through direct satellite transmission and the Internet is likely to rival the tape-based industry. As a result of these intra- and international exchanges, diaspora cultures and cinemas have truly become polyphonic, multicultural, multisited, and relational, and the accented style, too, has become multiaccentual, breaking down both the universalism of modernism and the essentialism of postmodernism.

Retake Film and Video Workshop was set up in 1982 as an Asian collective to challenge the stereotyped images of South Asians in British mass media. As with the other arts organizations, much of its early effort was spent in coalition building and fund-raising, leading to its full franchisement in 1984 under the Workshop Declaration. The Greater London Council was the first organization to commit funds for Retake's initial production, *Majdhar* (1984), directed by Ahmed Jamal.

Similar to the black British collectives and Asian-American Visual Communications, corrective representation was a key starting mission for Retake. Negative and demeaning stereotyping is painful for minorities, and it is encountered daily in both private and public situations, thus demanding forceful and all-out neutralization. However, this reaction may lead to oversensitivity and overcorrection and to a defensive binarism that demands that negative "unrealistic" representations be replaced with positive "realistic" ones. As Mahmood Jamal of Retake notes: "Being constantly misrepresented in the media can make one unbearably sensitive to issues of stereotyping and lead us into protecting and defending every stain that shows up when we wear our badly washed cloths" (1988, 21).

Historicizing, documenting, and dramatizing the problems besetting the Asian communities in Britain constituted Retake's other missions. Historicizing was important, for unlike the other colonized people, the Asian presence in Britain was not a recent phenomenon. It dated back to the eighteenth century, and this long history colored and accented the relationship of the Asians to Britain in specific ways at the same time that it produced commonalities with other colonized people. Among the characteristics that Asian and black workshops (as well as the American Asian collectives) shared was their interest in archaeology of knowledge, ethnic genealogy, and historiography. These were crystallized in the Retake Workshop's name and also in that of the Sankofa Collective. Retake implies filming/refilming, making/remaking, viewing/reviewing, and revising. Borrowed from the Akan culture of Ghana, *sankofa* refers to a mythical bird and to its ability to visualize both the past and the future. The idea was to return to the past in order to understand it and go forward.[41] As such, these collectives countered the postmodern emphasis on surfaces and on ahistorical synchronicity. Their cultural politics, in Gilroy's words, were "not about depthlessness but about its preservation and reproduction, not about the suppression of temporal patterns but about history itself" (1988, 46).[42]

Retake's style was aesthetically less innovative and politically more conservative than that of the black collectives. Unlike the latter's nonlinear and experimental films, Retake's films, whether documentary (*Poets in Exile*, 1982; *Living in Danger*, 1984; *It's Our Right*, 1985) or fictional (*Majdhar*; *An Environment of Dignity*, directed by Mahmood Jamal, 1985; *Hotel London*, 1987), were made in a more or less linear, realist, and narrative mode that did not self-consciously question cinematic apparatuses and their representational regimes. This made Retake's films more comprehensible; however, their narrative and stylistic familiarity failed to attract the kind of high-level critical discourse and theorization that the works of the black collectives garnered. Nevertheless, the films raised important questions about Indian and Pakistani politics, as well as about British colonial and immigration politics. Retake's films thus generated controversy. Ahmad Jamal's assimilationist *Majdhar*, about the conflicting choices that independence brings a young Pakistani woman, provoked heated criticism not only within Asian communities in Britain but also in the front pages of national papers in Pakistan (Mercer 1988, 4; Malik 1996, 208). Jamal found out, as did Nair, Trinh, and Nabili, that occupying multiple diasporic positions exposes accented filmmakers to both the rewards and the liabilities of the multiple receptions of their works.

The two highly successful films written by Pakistani-British writer Hanif Kureishi (both directed by Irish-British Stephen Frears), *My Beautiful Laundrette* (1985) and *Sammy and Rosie Get Laid* (1987), became popular and controversial. According to Kureishi, both films were characterized by a critic of the *Sunday Times* as "sick," "disgusting," and "worthless and insulting" (1988, 24). Apparently, the emphasis in *Laundrette* on what the reviewer called the "depressing aspects" of life in Britain, such as "homosexuals," "grim concrete," and "race riots," was an attempt by the filmmakers to "run down" Prime Minister Margaret Thatcher. Kureishi, for his part, complained that under Thatcher's administration everyone was expected to "bat for Britain or shut up"— something he was not prepared to do. Instead, he issued the following angry and damning assessment of England in the late 1980s, which, like much of the black and Asian collectives' output, painted in words the distressing picture that his own writings and films offered: "England seems to have become a squalid, ugly and uncomfortable place. For some reason I am starting to feel that it is an intolerant, racist, homophobic, narrow-minded authoritarian rathole run by vicious, suburban-minded, materialistic philistines who think democracy is constituted by the selling of a few council houses and shares" (1988, 24). Although of Pakistani émigré parentage, Kureishi is a thoroughly British author. However, he is part of the new multicultural Britain whose literature, arts, and cinema speak with a decidedly postcolonial accent. As he stated: "We are part of English literature. . . . Whatever I've written about, it's all been about England in some way, even if the characters are Asian or they're from Pakistan or whatever" (quoted in Kaleta 1998, 3). Other accented Asian filmmakers in England also have chosen to make feature films independently instead of making experimental works using a collective production mode. Gurinder Chadha's hybridized and exuberant *Bhaji on the Beach* (1993), like Kureishi's films, is fundamentally about being British but also about being dual, even multiple. However, in *Bhaji on the Beach*, which focuses on the heterogeneous lives of a group of Asian women, there is more pleasure and playfulness in hybridization than there is in Kureishi's critical and edgy *My Beautiful Laundrette*, *Sammy and Rosie Get Laid*, and *London Kills Me* (1991), which he directed himself.

Unlike other forms of alternative cinema, the accented cinema inevitably arouses patriotic sentiments, for every accented film is also in some measure a state-of-the-nation film that takes stock of the nation and passes judgment on its values and performance. No other cinema is so irrevocably implicated at one and the same time in the individual, communal, and national definition and redefinition. Likewise, no other cinema is so intimately political, even though it may not be about politics.

In working collectively and in focusing on issues that minority and subaltern communities face, Asian and black collectives in Britain made films that, in Teshome Gabriel's words, were the "auto-biographies" of their communities (1987, 2). Many of them operated within and served a very specific community or locality. For example, Retake operated chiefly in Camden, and Black Audio operated in the borough of Hackney, both in London. This geographic locatedness tied the collectives to their respective communities, both empowering them and simultaneously confining them as captives of the community's expectations, support, and pressures. One method for moving out of communal dependence was for the workshops to simultaneously be both local and exilic, and global and diasporic. This is what Sankofa and, to a lesser extent, the Black Audio and Ceddo collectives were able to accomplish, chiefly by integrating film production and cultural criticism and by engaging in alliance politics with African-American and supportive academic critics in the United States. Retake did not significantly engage in either the politics of theory or alliance politics with Asian diasporas in the United States. It remained localized, and, instead of looking beyond to Asian diasporas elsewhere, it looked primarily back, to the Asian homelands, and to the present, to the Asian immigrants in Britain. Asian-Americans, on the other hand, with the infusion of a crop of recent exiles and émigrés from China, Vietnam, the Philippines, Korea, Hong Kong, and Taiwan, made both diasporic connections with Asian mediamakers elsewhere and exilic linkages with those in the homelands. By thus opening or closing their vistas, these filmmakers expanded or contracted both the potential markets for their products and their dependence on those markets.

Although the black British and Asian-British workshops and collectives operated more or less independently of one another, there was cooperation among them, and they belonged to an umbrella organization that represented them collectively (Association of Black Workshops). Starting as a handful of community videomakers and filmmakers, these collectives grew to form a national network of film and video workshops that spanned the British Isles. By the mid-1980s, the British Film Institute's yearbook was listing some seventy active film and video workshops nationwide (MacPherson 1986, 32), a figure that grew to nearly ninety by the mid-1990s (Dija 1995, 351–60). However, the structural underpinning of the workshops was shattered in 1986 when Margaret Thatcher's government abolished the Greater London Council and other metropolitan councils and reduced public funding for the arts. Unlike the U.S.-based collectives, which traditionally relied on a mixture of public and private funding, the British workshops did not receive significant private support. Ironically, the ethnic media's dependent political economy seemed to replicate, on a smaller scale, and in the belly of the former colonial power, the larger scale national dependency of the former colonies during the colonial era. This was a subject to which many of the black and Asian filmmakers—themselves children of the formerly colonized people who had been subjected to dependent development—were very sensitive.

Channel 4 Television, however, continued its support of the workshops. Its policy of commissioning, purchasing, and airing nontraditional and experimental material from independent and minority filmmakers turned it into a major cultural and cinematic force in Britain. Between 1981 and 1990 it funded the production of some 170 films by independent companies (Giles 1993, 74). In the same period, Channel 4's drama department commissioned 136 feature or near-feature films (Pym 1992). However, its impact on the independent cinema reaches far beyond the British shores.[43] The list of films that it funded, commissioned, or aired makes a veritable who's who of the best alternative and independent cinema of the 1980s and 1990s from Israel to the United States, including many accented films.[44] The amount of support that each film received varied, from a small percentage of its budget to its entire budget.[45] These films were aired primarily by Channel 4's key film series, *Film on Four*, *The Eleventh Hour*, and *People to People*, and were released theatrically as well.

Although Channel 4 continued to support, commission, and broadcast independent films and videos, it ended its support of the workshops in 1991 for commercial reasons and to accommodate changes in governmental policies. It did this primarily by abandoning the separate budget that it had set aside for the workshops, thus forcing them to compete for resources on the open market like other producers (Hill 1996a, 170). Some of the workshops, such as Sankofa and Black Audio, continued to operate by competing for funds. Others, like Retake, went into hibernation as a collective, although individual members continued to make films independently.

The crossover impact of the black and Asian workshop films demonstrates one of the arguments of this book: that accented cinema not only constitutes a transnational cinema and identity but also is a constitutive part of the national cinemas and national identity. As Sarita Malik observes, "The emergence of a wide range of Black British films in the 1980s and 1990s has broadened the somewhat narrow repertoire of British national cinema by interrogating otherwise taken-for-granted notions of British culture and British film" (1996, 214).

Beur Cinema in France

North African filmmakers in France form sufficient cohesiveness by their concentration in a single "host" country over a long period for their films to assume a kind of collective identity. This identity is also partly a result of the unifying structures of colonization (including the imposition of the French language) and the subsequent circumstances of decolonization, particularly in the case of an assimilationist Algeria. The term *beur* refers to Algerians and North Africans of Arab origin who were born or bred in France. For the most part, this second generation of French citizens was raised in housing projects (called *banlieue*) in the suburbs of major French cities.[46] Although the word *beur* is a self-descriptive back slang (called *verlan*) for *arabe*, it is not an exact inversion but a deliberate mixing up of the letters in the word. As a result, *beur* is "a sign of creolization and cultural ambiguity" (Chambers 1994, 94). Initially a self-designated term, it has gradually lost its use among educated North Africans in France because of its growing pejorative connotations and its lack of geographic specificity (Gross, McMurray, and Swedenburg 1994, 13).

Beur entered what Battegay and Boubeker call the French "media space" (1993, 60) in the aftermath of housing project riots in Lyon in which cars were torched (known as *festival des voitures brûlées*, or festival of burning cars), intermittent clashes with the police (known as *rodéos*), and a massive antiracist march in 1983, which brought some 100,000 demonstrators on foot from Marseilles to Paris. These widespread incidents of social unrest, or "fractures," like the riots in London, Birmingham, and Manchester that fed the British film and video collectives, were created by large numbers of young, nonwhite immigrants and children of immigrants in the context of the larger tendencies toward political conservatism, social exclusionarism, anti-immigrant intolerance, heavy-handed policing, and racial fears fanned by racist parties such as the National Front. The collective identity of the youthful population of *beurs* was formed during these public contestations for the soul of France.

During the tumultuous 1980s, a genre of *beur* literature was identified in which some twenty writers commercially published (Hargreaves 1990, 4). These were the first novels of their authors, who were by and large male, young, and beset by a "dual cultural heritage" that pitted their internal and external cultures against each other (Hargreaves 1989, 661). While their internal culture in France is predominantly Islamic and Algerian, their external culture is secular and mediated by Western mass media and pop culture. However, the increasing antiforeign and anti-Muslim mood in the 1990s and the contestatorial public positions of Muslims, such as girls insisting on wearing the *hijab* in schools, gradually dislodged the neat divide implied by the "dual cultural heritage." Indeed, these uncertainties, tensions, and militancies, associated with divided, contested, and hybridized identities, form the central drama of many *beur* novels and films.

In the mid-1980s, *beur* novelist and filmmaker Farida Belghoul divided *beur* cinema into three categories: films made by *beur* filmmakers such as Mehdi Charef and Rachid Bouchareb, who were born and bred in France; those made by émigré filmmakers such as Ali Ghalem and Mahmoud Zemmouri, who were born and raised in Algeria but are conflicted about national identity; and those made by French filmmakers such as Gérard Blain and Serge LePéron, which portray the *beur* communities (*Cinématographe*, no. 112 [July 1985]: 19). Each type of filmmaker produced a different perspective, ranging from insider to outsider, on what it is to be a *beur*. Christian Bosséno has offered a narrower definition: "A *beur* film is one which was made by a young person of North African origin who was born or who spent his or her youth in France, and which features *beur* characters" (1992, 49). While Belghoul's definition is too general, Bosséno's is too restrictive, for it ignores the pervasive effects of French colonialism, which has created a kind of exile in situ, or internal exile, within the former colonies. This is particularly true for Algerian filmmakers who because of their organic contact with the French cultural institutions, media, and language did not have to leave their country to face exile. In addition, due to the impoverished national film production budget, a number of Algerian filmmakers, among them Merzak Allouache and Mahmoud Zemmouri, turned to outside sources in France to make their films. The experience of being displaced internally or being forced to make films outside the country opened Algerian filmmakers to exilic tensions and to hybridized identities—central themes in *beur* cinema. From this perspective, therefore, it is valid to include in the taxonomy of *beur* cinema the films that Algerians have made in Algeria about *beur* issues. Finally, not all the films of *beur* directors are *beur*, since some of them deal with non-*beur* characters and issues.

However defined, *beur* cinema does not qualify as a collective mode of production, distribution, or exhibition in the sense discussed in this chapter, although small *beur* collectives were formed. One of these was the Mohammed Collective, from Vitry-sur-Seine, whose members in the late 1970s and the early 1980s produced a number of super-8 short-subject films. These films, among them *The Garage* (*Le Garage*, 1979), *They've Killed Kadar* (*Ils Ont Tué Kadar*, 1980), and *Immigrant Zone* (*Zone Immigrée*, 1981), were either aired in segments on French national television or later incorporated into, or led to, longer films.[47] Unlike the U.S.-based Asian Pacific American film collectives or the British black and Asian workshops, *beur* filmmakers do not generally work within an institutional structure or collective setting. However, they have benefited from and are dependent on public funds—from the French Ministry of Culture, other public institutions, and French and European television. State funding ensures both the films' distribution and a steady supply of products for television transmission that satisfies the quota of domestic productions.[48]

Beur cinema has evolved in several stages. In the 1970s, *beur* filmmakers produced realist shorts and documentaries about the conflicts and experiences of racism, unemployment, and immigration in France, which depended almost exclusively on alternative exhibition circuits. By the mid-1980s, commercially made feature-length fictional films with similar themes achieved popularity beyond the ethnic communities (Dhoukar 1990). The country of origin, about which émigrés dream and to which they desire to return, is also a perennial theme. However, return journeys, in such films as Rachid Bouchareb's *Cheb* (1990), are almost always experienced as a trauma and they end in failure (Bosséno 1992, 53). Perhaps this results from the *beurs'* bitter realization that they are French but not quite, that they are North African but not quite, and that they have no home to which they can return. This split and ambivalent subjectivity finds its way into the films that internalize and replicate the dominant stereotypes of the *beurs* in France as victims and delinquents—similar to some of the Iranian émigré filmmakers, who, having internalized negative views of Iranians in the West as terrorists, reproduced them in their films. In terms of gender representation, *beur* cinema is primarily a male cinema, made chiefly by men and containing stories about men (Tarr 1993). A few women, such as Farida Belghoul and Aïssa Djabri, made short and feature-length films, respectively.

Unlike some of the films of the black British and Asian-British workshops and independent filmmakers, which are antirealist and nonnarrative and target small audiences, *beur* cinema is generally a realist, narrative, commercial, and popular cinema in France.[49] It embodies the accented style more in its themes, characters, and structures of feeling than in its style of visualization or narration.

Beur cinema has continued to evolve toward auteurism and professionalism. While auteurs still deal with multicultural and multiracial issues, professional cinéastes are less concerned with the political contingencies of a second generation's coming of age (Bloom 1995, 4). Many of them no longer want to be considered émigré or ethnic filmmakers. Two well-known cinéastes of Algerian descent spoke to this point. Mehdi Charef declared: "I don't have any desire to be labeled immigrant filmmaker. I'm a filmmaker, that's all." Merzak Allouache echoed: "I'm a filmmaker in transit, not an émigré. A filmmaker who wants to make films where they can be made. My own dream is to say that I'm someone who just makes films" (quoted in Rosen 1989, 37). Yet, the burden of representation and the politics of interstitiality dog accented filmmakers like Allouache, who was accused of abandoning his homeland and culture and of selling out—a charge he disputed after a screening of his film *Bab El-Oued City* (1993) at the 1994 Cannes International Film Festival: "I have made 5 pictures so far, I consider myself an independent filmmaker, and I believe so far I have not been bought by the West or by any other country. The idea that we have been bought because we work in the West or that we are imprisoned by the western people is purely the critics' conception. My cinema is a dialogue I have with my people" (Mehrabi 1994, 35). However, deeper immersion in one's culture and locality, often can produce more universal truths. In this regard, the case of the Gypsy filmmaker Tony Gatlif is instructive. Born in Algeria, as a teenager in the early 1960s he fled to France, where he entered the world of cinema. At first, he wished to make his name as a director—not just a Gypsy director—but apparently not much came of that. However, like many auteur and exilic filmmakers who find their most inspiring material in their own lives, only after he again "assumed his identity as a Gypsy" did he discover his own "hybrid voice" (Riding 1997, H16). This newfound voice is inscribed in a number of critically acclaimed and award-winning films that focus on Gypsy lives and stories in Europe and that also are deeply universal. An essential component of this voice is music, which plays a pivotal role in Gatlif's films as well as in those of other Romany filmmakers because, according to him, "music is the only authentic document that the Roma have; any written documents are police records" (Siberok 1997, C2). The Romas' highly developed musical tradition helps them to both preserve and express their odyssey of displacement and cohesiveness. Music is perhaps their true home.[50]

Because of various pressures and counterpressures, the concept of "*beur*" and the category of "*beur* cinema" are neither stable nor universally accepted (Rosello 1996). What keeps the terms and their referents in continual flux are the evolution and contestation of the *beurs* themselves and the manner in which the dominant culture works hegemonically to isolate or absorb them in order to revitalize itself. As *beur* culture and cinema and the hybridized North African–French music known as *raï* have become popular, certain aspects of these cultural forms have been appropriated by the culture industries, thereby defusing their original critical or oppositional edge.[51] At the same time, however, this appropriation has expanded the *beur* cinema aesthetics and enriched the repertoire of the French cultural idioms.

One instance of such enrichment is the emergence of what is called *le film de banlieue* (suburb film, or films of the 'hood), a term inspired by suburban housing projects in which poor, working-class, and émigré populations have coexisted for a long time. The films of this genre share some features of the *beur* style, but these are not necessarily made by the *beurs*. An example of such an expanded *beur-banlieue* film identity is *Hate* (*La Haine*, 1995), winner of the Best Director Award at the 1995 Cannes International Film Festival. Directed by Mathieu Kassovitz (a Jew of Hungarian origin), it deals with the desperate and futureless lives of three boys: a white Jew, a *beur*, and an African black. What brings the three protagonists together in this film, as in *beur* and *banlieue* films in general, are the shared experiences of unemployment and cohabitation by disadvantaged populations of *beur* and poor whites and the concomitant shared anomie, alienation, and anger.[52]

Although *beur* and *banlieue* films and *raï* music have become chic, not all aspects of the North African culture are popular. In the meantime, however, certain strata of the *beur* population have been moving up the social ladder, entering the middle class, and funding the building of mosques and other Islamic civic institutions. Consequently, the new *beur* lifestyle can no longer be characterized solely by poverty, unemployment, and living in the suburban projects. The new *beur* is part of the French "*beur*-geoisie," no longer a threat to the dominant culture. Likewise, for many filmmakers, *beur* cinema is a transitional phase in their evolution from "émigré" to "French" filmmaker. But like all terms that refer to social imaginaries, *beur* is likely to remain an organic concept, which is held in reserve, to be reinvoked and redefined when needed.

By their mode of production, accented filmmakers define and transform both themselves and the accented cinema. To paraphrase Walter Benjamin, to be oppositional it is not enough that accented filmmakers have oppositional politics. They must also act oppositionally by engaging in alternative practices that have an "organizing function"—a function whose usefulness extends beyond politics or propaganda (1978, 233). Hallmarks of this organizing function, as amply demonstrated here in the two chapters on mode of production, are the interstitial and collective production modes and the integrated film practices that entail the accented filmmakers' horizontal and vertical involvement in all aspects and phases of their works. Their oppositionality is further enhanced by their films' textual politics, characterized by the accented style. By means of these organizational and textual counterpractices, the filmmakers are transformed from displaced subjects into active agents of their own emplacement. However, their agency is limited, for they operate within a globalized capitalist system—even though in its interstices—and, with some exception, they remain primarily the "suppliers" of the postindustrial productive processes and not the "engineers" of revolutionary change—the function that Benjamin had envisioned for artists as producers.

4

Epistolarity and Epistolary Narratives

EXILE and epistolarity are constitutively linked because both are driven by distance, separation, absence, and loss and by the desire to bridge the multiple gaps. Whatever form the epistle takes, whether a letter, a note scribbled on a napkin, a telephone conversation, a video, or an e-mail message, it becomes, in the words of Linda Kauffman, a "metonymic and a metaphoric displacement of desire" (1986, 38)—the desire to be with an other and to reimagine an elsewhere and other times. Epistolarity, defined as "the use of the letter's formal properties to create meaning (Altman 1982, 4), is an ancient and rich genre of imaginative and critical literature. As Derrida (1980), Altman (1982), and Kauffman (1986, 1992) have demonstrated, epistolarity involves the acts and events of sending and receiving, losing and finding, and writing and reading letters. It also involves the acts, events, and institutions that facilitate, hinder, inhibit, or prohibit such acts and events. In the classical fictional cinema, letters figured large, and a number of films can be classified as epistolary.[1]

Epistolarity is a chief contributor to the accented cinema's style. Accented epistolary films are divided into three main types: film-letters, telephonic epistles, and letter-films. Film-letters inscribe letters and acts of reading and writing of letters by diegetic characters. Likewise, telephonic epistles inscribe telephones and answering machines and the use of these devices by diegetic characters. Letter-films, on the other hand, are themselves in the form of epistles addressed to someone either inside or outside the diegesis, and they do not necessarily inscribe the epistolary media. Like the other classification schemes in this book, the epistolary division is used for greater clarity and convenience, since differences are not clear-cut in all cases, and many epistolary films contain more than one epistolic medium and narrative system.

Film-Letters

Mode of Address

Modern realist novels and classical Hollywood films are generally driven by an omniscient narrator and narrative system. Modern journalism, too, has encouraged "objective" reporting and omniscient narration. The authority of these types of narrators and narrative systems, however, has been challenged in various ways—by the stream-of-consciousness technique, free indirect style, and epistolary form. In the traditional epistolary literature, the story is told by direct narration, that is, by means of letters written by one or more of the characters without the apparent intervention of the novelist. Through these letters, readers gain direct access to the characters' subjective viewpoints and emotional states and are affected by the intimacy, immediacy, and intensity of their interiority. Because it provides access to multiple viewpoints and voices, the epistolary form enhances the work's verisimilitude and psychological depth.

However, epistolary works are not only mimetic but also diegetic. They involve both the direct discourse of the characters (usually in the first person) and the indirect discourse of the novelist (usually in the third person). There is yet a third, free-indirect discourse, which initially appears to be in the indirect style, written by the author. However, upon scrutiny it will become clear that this discourse is contaminated by the enunciative properties of the characters' speech (Ducrot and Todorov 1983, 303). If the early novels were written largely in the direct and indirect styles, many modern and postmodern novels employ all three, especially the free-indirect style. As Henry Louis Gates Jr. has demonstrated (1988), African-American novels, particularly Alice Walker's *The Color Purple* and Zora Neale Hurston's *Their Eyes Were Watching God*, make very creative, intricate use of the free-indirect style. One of the key contributions of this style is to force the dominant language (standard English, the language of indirect narration) to speak with a minoritarian voice (spoken black English, the language of direct speech). This free-indirect voice is not a dual voice of both a character and a narrator but a bivocal utterance that fuses both direct and indirect elements to express dramatically the double consciousness of a divided self (Gates 1988, 207–8). As such, free-indirect discourse expresses well the bifurcated consciousness of exile and diaspora.[2]

In film narratology, the direct style would include the characters' speech ("I am hungry") and point of view, or what Edward Branigan has called the character's "direct subjectivity" of "I am hungry." In the indirect style, a character's speech or thoughts are reported without quotation (1984, 125–26). The indirect style includes reflection of the characters and objects, by means of mirror shots and eyeline matches; and projection of the character's mental processes, such as thinking, dreaming, fearing, desiring, and remembering, by means of expressive camera movements and editing (98–99). The free indirect style may include the interjection of the personal/direct discourse into the narratorial/indirect discourse. Point-of-view shots, cutaways, perception shots, even certain shot reverse-shot configurations may be considered cinematic instances of free indirect style. Reflection, projection, and introjection subjectivize the films and their characters and may create ambiguities about what is happening on the screen and who exactly are the subjects—that is, the owners or the objects of the gaze, thought, voice, and the epistles. Such narrative ambiguity re-creates and expresses the ambivalent subjectivity and hybridized identity of exilic and diasporic conditions.

The epistolary form is intensely dialogic. Address is not just a problem in the epistolary films but also a problematic of the films, as they inscribe several sets of dialogic relations: the relations between diegetic addressers and addressees who write and read each other's letters or who converse on the phone on-camera; the relations between diegetic addressers and some off-screen interlocutor whom they address with their epistles and whose epistles they receive; and the intertextual relation of the film text with itself, either addressing itself by means of self-reflexivity and self-referentiality or addressing its audience by means of direct address, captions, and titling. Accented films are replete with this latter form of address, which turns them into both epistolic and calligraphic texts.

The very fact of addressing someone in an epistle creates an illusion of presence that transforms the addressee from an absent figure into a presence, which hovers in the text's interstices. As "speech-for-another," the letter, in Terry Eagleton's words, is "overhearing itself in the ears of the addressee" (1982, 52). The scene of the letter's reception is always already embedded in its scene of production (and vice versa). In the classical realist cinema, letters function differently from film to film, entering or exiting the plot at different points. For example, they may set off the plot or end it; they may complicate or clarify the plot's trajectory or the characters' motivations and psychology; they may mislead, be mislaid, or be misdelivered.[3]

In the case of accented films, however, epistolarity appears to be less a function of plot formation and character motivation than an expression and inscription of exilic displacement, split subjectivity, and multifocalism. Freed from traditional linear, realist narration, these films tend to juxtapose direct, indirect, and free indirect discourses in novel and varied ways to produce a bewildering array of address forms. In the process, they raise fascinating questions about the identity of author, addresser, addressee, reader, reciter, and translator of the letters, and about their narratological functions and power relations. In accented epistolaries, letters are not written or delivered only to the diegetic characters. In Chantal Akerman's *News from Home* (1977) and in Mona Hatoum's *Measures of Distance* (1988), the addressee of the letters in each case is the filmmaker, who never visually appears in the film but whose voice reads her mother's letters on the sound track. Without access to extratextual information, it would be impossible to ascertain from the films that the voices reading the letters belong to the directors, not to their mothers or to a third party. On the other hand, Akerman appears in her *Je Tu Il Elle* (1974) as a diegetic character who attempts to write letters to a lover who is not definitively identified, and it is her own voice that reads the letters on the sound track. In *Lost, Lost, Lost* (1949–76), the voice of filmmaker Jonas Mekas addresses not only the diegetic characters (including himself) but also audience members. In Agnès Varda's *One Sings, the Other Doesn't* (1976), two women maintain their close friendship through a decade of separation by writing to each other and by reading each other's letters on camera. In Solanas's *Tangos: Exile of Gardel* (1985), a fictitious Juan Uno sends letters and scraps of paper from Argentina to Juan Dos, his real-life double, in Parisian exile. In some accented epistolaries, the voice-over narration that contains the letters dominates the visual letters to the point that they may be called "image-over" films.[4]

In letter-films, such as in Chris Marker's *Letter from Siberia* (1957), letters address the spectators. Jean-Luc Godard and Jean-Pierre Gorin, in *Letter to Jane: Investigation of a Still* (1972), do not actually deliver a letter to a diegetic character named Jane Fonda; rather, the film is their letter to the real-life actress Fonda, whose news photograph taken in North Vietnam instigated the letter-film. If in *Letter to Jane* the addressee is a real person who appears in the film, in Marker's *Sunless* (*Sans Soleil*, 1987), the addressee is some fictional character who is absent from the film. The variety and complexity of the modes of address and the juxtaposition of direct, indirect, and free indirect discourses in accented epistolaries are staggering.

In addition, the epistles are not limited to written letters delivered, undelivered, or misdelivered by the postal system. Electronic epistolary media, such as the telephone, answering machine, e-mail, fax, audiocassette, and videocassette, are widely employed, resulting in fragmented, multifocal, multivocal, and emotional narratives. As part of the problematic of address, many accented films are self-reflexive about their own status as autonomous and sovereign texts. Jayce Salloum and Walid Ra'ad's film *Lebanon: Up to the South* (*Tale'ain Aljonub*, 1993) opens with an interviewee, Zahra Bedran, challenging the off-camera filmmakers:

> If I simply wanted to refuse, I would not be doing this interview. But if I don't do this interview, I cannot express this refusal. You put me in an uncomfortable position, because even this refusal you will use to your advantage. Your question is actually an accusation. You are demanding that I behave well. I reject this demand. Your question relegates me as either terrorist or hero. Why do you simplify the issues?

With these point-blank observations she acknowledges the presence of the off-screen filmmakers and questions their politics; she also challenges the tradition of objective, journalistic interviews and the realist documentary form. By opening up the film with these questions posed by their subject, the filmmakers in turn create a self-reflexive dialogue with their audience about these issues.

Epistolary filmmaking also entails a dialogue with the self by the filmmaker, as well as self-evaluation. No other exile film so relentlessly and complexly addresses the self as does Mekas's *Lost, Lost, Lost*. Since in exile the traditional definitions and boundaries of self, nation, and culture are seriously questioned and tested, epistolarity becomes an important instrument of self-exploration and self-narrativization. That is why many epistolaries, including Mekas's, are autobiographical or contain elements of autobiography and of the diary cin-

because even this refusal
you will use to your advantage.

Figure 7. Self-reflexive
mode of address.
Interviewer questions
filmmakers Jayce
Salloum and Walid
Raad in their *Lebanon:
Up to the South.*

ema. However, since in exile personal identity is more than ever enmeshed
with identities of other sorts, autobiographical films are concerned not only
with self and individual but also with shared elements on which group affiliation are based.

Communitarianism

Epistolary media are generally communitarian; they link people across time,
space, and cultural difference. In this, they work in opposition to transportation
means, also frequently inscribed in accented films, that usually function to keep
people apart. Epistolary films are driven in part by scopophilia, but the object
of the scopic drive is not solely another person; more often, it is one's homeland
or culture—a homeland that is usually gendered as female and a culture that
is often coded as maternal and nurturing. The epistolaries are also driven by
epistephilia, which often involves a burning desire to know and to tell about
the causes, experiences, and consequences of disrupted personal and national
histories. As such, they are films of social engagement that, like documentaries,
have "a less incendiary effect on our erotic fantasies and sense of sexual identity
but a stronger effect on our social imagination and senses of cultural identity"
(Nichols 1991, 178). Because of the coexistence of the scopophilic and epis-
tephilic structurations, accented epistolary cinema is both fictional and documentary, and it is simultaneously personal and social. However, because of the
fragmented, nonlinear, dialogic, self-reflexive, multivocal, multiauthorial, and
defamiliarizing structures and narratives of some of the films, the relationship
between authorship and authenticity, personal and social, fictional and nonfictional, narrative and nonnarrative, is never a given. Instead, it is continually
posed as a question and, characteristically, is often left unresolved.

Letters stand in for those who are absent and inaccessible. They are awaited with bated breath, kissed, cried over, kept close to the heart, shared with friends, protected, dreaded, mutilated, and destroyed. As in Solanas's *Tangos: Exile of Gardel*, letters not only link people who are separated but also remind them of their separation. In this, they act fetishistically, both disavowing and acknowledging the trauma of displacement.

Close-Up: Fernando Ezequiel "Pino" Solanas

Solanas was born in 1936 to an upper-middle-class family in Olivos, near Buenos Aires, Argentina, where he studied piano and musical composition, theater, and painting at the National Conservatory of Dramatic Arts. Rebelling against his family's conservative and anti-Perónist politics, he joined Buenos Aires's progressive circles. He made his first film in 1962 (a short entitled *Keep Going/Seguir Andando*), after which, according to his curriculum vitae, he made "hundreds of documentary shorts and commercials" throughout the 1960s. In 1966 he cofounded, with Octavio Getino and Cesar Vallejo, the collective Grupo Cine Liberación to make underground films. He was placed on the Third Cinema map with the four-hour-and-twenty-minute prizewinning agit-prop film *The Hour of the Furnaces* (*La Hora de los Honros*, 1968). A landmark work that embodies both the theory and the practice of Third Cinema, this film and the 1974 manifesto "Toward a Third Cinema," which Solanas and Getino coauthored, further secured their place within the emergent militant cinema.[5] Juan Perón, who returned to Argentina from his long political exile in 1973, died a year later, and a coup brought a ruthless military regime to power in 1976. The new regime's brutal "dirty war" on civilians involved torture, murder, and the disappearance of thousands of people by diabolical means that included "death flights"—flights in which prisoners, sedated but still alive, were dumped into the ocean from planes (Sims 1995, A5).

This turn of events pushed the Perónist Solanas (and his family) into exile, first to Madrid and then to Paris. He stayed there until 1984, when the Argentine military relinquished power in the aftermath of its disastrous defeat in the Malvinas/Falklands War with Britain. Just before his exile, Solanas had filmed *The Sons of Fierro* (*Los Hijos de Fierro*, 1973–78), but he was unable to complete it until he went abroad. An exilically inflected film, this is as an homage to Argentina's epic 1870s poem *The Gaucho Martin Fierro* by José Hernandez, about a displaced gaucho of the pampas.

Displaced at the age of forty, Solanas had to start his career all over again. This period of displacement and disempowerment put him in touch with the deep existential meanings of exile, which he described as "a feeling of absence, a sense of loss."[6] These feelings powerfully shape *Tangos: Exile of Gardel* (*Tangos: El Exilio de Gardel*, 1985), a sensual musical that he began while in Parisian exile but completed after returning home. A paradigmatic exilic film, it won international awards, including the Silver Lion at the 1985 Venice Film Festival. Since his return to Argentina, Solanas has pursued a dual-track career as politician and filmmaker. He founded with others Frente Grande, a coalition of left-wing parties, and he directed two major fictional coproductions on themes that are exilically nuanced: *South* (*Sur*, 1988) and *The Journey* (*El Viaje*, 1992). That the Argentine postmilitary democracy is fragile, and that his dual-track careers are interwoven, were proven when, during *The Journey*'s production, President Carlos Menem took Solanas to court on the charge that he had slandered him in an article in the journal *Noticias* by accusing him of corruption and treason. The day after giving his court testimony, Solanas was shot in the leg outside the Cinecolor Lab where he was editing his film. The government attempt to cover up the investigation of the attack was countered by an international solidarity campaign.[7] Solanas publicly declared, "I am not leaving the country, and I am not going to keep quiet" (Rich 1991, 64). He was true to his declaration, for although his injuries immobilized him for many months and delayed the film's editing, he was able to complete it a year later and get elected to the Congress a year after that in 1993.

Solanas evolved from a guerrilla filmmaker to an independent cinéaste who uses the mainstream cinema's production mode and narrative conventions experimentally and critically to create hybridized films. Since *Tangos* he has set aside his underground production mode and noncommercial distribution in the interest of coproduction (principally between France and Argentina) and commercial distribution. Despite these moves toward the mainstream, however, he remained steadfastly critical of the hegemonic Hollywood cinema, which he characterized as a "mechanical shark" that devours other cinemas (de las Carreras 1995, 324). According to Solanas, his critical appropriation of popular genres, such as the tango, "bothers the system," which is more comfortable with pigeonholing him as a militant filmmaker who has a limited appeal and is therefore irrelevant: "They wanted to exclude me from cinema, so I said I'm going to annoy them. I'm going to make a film about the everyday problems of exile. I'm going to present it as a spectacle, as a work of art" (quoted in Fusco 1987–88, 59). He was an innovator in his militant Third Cinema phase (in the 1960s and 1970s), and he remained a stylistic trailblazer in his films of the 1980s and 1990s, in which exile in its external and internal configurations, as well as history, memory, and longing for a return, are shaping presences. These thematic concerns with displacement, along with his mixing film genres, adding fantasy to everyday life, injecting comedy into tragedy, assembling nonlinear anecdotes, heightening the emotionality, sensuality, and tactility of situations, setting forth exilic structures of feeling, inscribing double or split characters, and embodying self-reflexivity and epistolarity, turn these films into exemplars of the exilically accented cinema.

Tangos: Exile of Gardel is a French-Argentine coproduction, and its binational financing is undergirded by its biculturality, which involves French and Spanish dialogue (spoken with varying accents) and French and Argentine locations. *Tangos* was filmed in two six-week periods in Paris and Buenos Aires; however, the film's spatial configuration is exilic. Because all the interior scenes, even those purported to be in Paris, were filmed in Buenos Aires, home (Argentina) uncannily occupies the interior space of exile.

Like many exilically accented filmmakers, Solanas performed multiple functions in this film, which is dedicated to the Turkish exile director Yilmaz Güney. He functioned as director, producer, screenplay writer, composer, lyricist, and actor.[8] *Tangos* is, therefore, multiply authorial; it is also biographical, for it is based on the filmmaker's own experiences, as well as those of his friends who spent nearly a decade in exile. As such, it is about the experience of a specific exile, as Solanas emphasizes: "This is a story of exile in France, which in no way pretends to analyze exile, or to be *the* film about exile. It is, rather, a few stories, a few songs, a few confessions, a few poems about exile that I have seen and lived in Paris" (quoted in Fusco 1987–88, 59). Yet the film's very specificity and situatedness give it its emotional power and its insight into the general condition of exile. "A film of great emotional impact, perhaps the best-known film of Latin-American exile" (Newman 1993, 244), *Tangos* explores the anguish and the daily dramas of a group of left-wing Perónist intellectuals and artists in their Parisian exile. The exiles are collaborating to stage an Argentine tango, which they call *tanguedia*—a hybridized genre consisting of a tango that is infused with elements of tragedy and comedy (referred to hereafter as "tango-dy"). The film's chief characters are the actress Mariana, her daughter María, the writer and composer Juan Dos, his family, and a number of artists, friends, and other real and imagined figures. Its drama centers on the performers' artistic and political struggles to stage such a specifically national performance as tango outside its national context, their trials and tribulations in obtaining French sponsorship, and their nostalgic and emotional epistolary relationship with their homeland and their memories of it. More generally, theirs is the classic drama of assimilation, which pits descent relations against consent relations: "They are torn between the desire to become integrated into French society and the need to preserve an Argentine identity" (de las Carreras 1995, 325). In the end, the film's older generation opts for the homeland, while the younger generation, the "children of exile," remains in Paris. For them, what Solanas has called the exile's "eternal desire to return" is indefinitely postponed. Despite such a tidy resolution to the assimilation drama, the film is suffused with the aesthetics of absence, loss, and longing and with the problematic of exile, the tango-dy, and, by extension, the film itself not having an ending. As a structurally open-ended process, exile encourages films that are both unfinished and unpolished.

Solanas stated in a postscreening discussion of his film at UCLA on June 26, 1988, that "exile is an experience in which one lives expecting and waiting to receive letters." This conception is overdetermined in *Tangos*, which inscribes epistles and epistolarity extensively and in ways that affirm the commu-

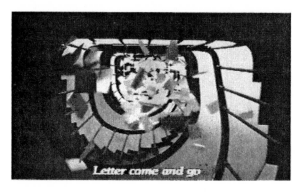

Figure 8. Icons of homelessness. Letters and papers pouring down the stairwell during a "letter song" in Fernando Solanas's *Tangos: Exile of Gardel.*

nitarian urges of the exiles to connect with those at home. A woman sobbingly reads a letter from home to a tearful group of exiles: "For three years I have thought of nothing but you." In private moments, people in a pensive mood are alone with their letters, writing or reading them. Visitors from Argentina bring with them letters for the anxiously awaiting exiles. A long sequence of the film's second act is devoted to exilic letters. It shows various acts of reading and writing of letters, accompanied by a song whose refrain is "Letters, more letters. Letters come and go." Because these epistolary acts both disavow and acknowledge the exile's separation from home, they promote the bittersweet emotions that can temporarily bridge the exilic gaps. As a result of its communitarianism, *Tangos* embodies an optimistic structure of feelings, which is emphasized by the film's closing line, delivered to the camera by María: "I've learned this from exile and suffering: We have so many years to live. No tragedy lasts very long!"

A persistent visual motif in many of the tango-dy scenes is the presence of letters and assorted papers that rain down the stairwell of a multistory building, pour out of a mail delivery truck, or scatter on the stage and are blown about by the fast movements of actors and dancers. These loose papers may refer to exilic epistolarity, or they may symbolize exilic provisionality. However, their pervasiveness underscores the importance of "papers" in the life of the exiles— identity card, passport, refugee paper, work permit, residency permit, social security card, certificate of citizenship, and driver's license—papers that mark their status as exile, refugee, alien, resident, immigrant, or citizen. No one who has undergone the by turn frightening and liberating experiences of crossing of borders, immigration, and resettlement in another country is likely to forget or take for granted the importance of identity papers. Loose papers in *Tangos* are iconographic, symbolic, and indexical reminders of such identity papers and the various states of displacement and placement that they imply.

Juan Dos and Juan Uno are linked not only by the telephone (see later discussion) but also by scraps of papers stuffed in a rickety suitcase, itself a symbol of exilic provisionality. In a sequence entitled "Poetics of Juan Uno,"

Pierre and Juan Dos, desperate to work up a story for their tango-dy, go through this suitcase, which is filled with notes that Juan Uno has written in Argentina on scraps of paper, backs of envelopes, and napkins. These epistles magically inspire his displaced counterparts to better express their exile. Their task is to "find the logic" and the stories that link these chaotic bits of writings. Constructing stories, however, as the film reminds us, is inevitably risky, for it entails making commitments in the face of doubt. For Argentines, this poetics of risk is necessary to overcome not just the ambivalence of this particular exile but also the general Argentine self-doubt—a poetics best expressed by the tango itself, which is both a dance and a form of cultural orientation and a means of personal expression and national identity formation. As Julie Taylor explains:

> For Argentines, this dance is deadly serious. In the tango, as in their personal lives and their politics, they tend to dwell on real or imagined affronts. In response, they attempt to seek out and affirm self-definition. They resort to elaborately staged behavior as a way of confronting the result of their search—a self-definition whose very essence is doubt. The tango proclaims this doubt and reveals the intensity and depth of Argentine feelings of insecurity, but it also insists that an aggressive facade should betray no hint that it could have arisen from an anguished sense of vulnerability. (1992, 377–78)

Although like many accented filmmakers, the Belgian-born French filmmaker Agnès Varda tends to make gritty and dystopic films, her epistolary *One Sings, the Other Doesn't* (*L'Un Chante, l'Autre Pas*, 1976) is communitarian and optimistic, like other epistolaries. The film, a "feminist musical," traces the development of the women's rights movement and pop culture in France in the 1960s and 1970s by means of the friendship of two young women. In a characteristic move, Varda juxtaposes documentary footage (of the women's movement) with fictional scenes (involving the two protagonists). Pauline is a high school student who helps her friend Suzanne, an unmarried mother of two, to obtain an illegal abortion. Suzanne's boyfriend, a bohemian French photographer, commits suicide, and Pauline falls in love with an Iranian whom she marries in Iran.[9] In the meantime, Suzanne opens a family planning clinic and raises her children, while Pauline returns to France to give birth to her child and to pursue her career as a singer in a women's band. In the course of these plot moves, Varda provides a veritable catalog of the women's issues, throughout which she remains rather conventional and essentialist in her construction of femininity (Kuhn and Radstone 1990, 411; Flitterman-Lewis 1996, 216).[10]

During the years of separation, the two friends keep in touch by exchanging letters and postcards. The film contains many scenes in which Suzanne and Pauline are writing, mailing, or reading each other's letters and cards in different times and places (even while walking in the busy street). Sometimes, the postcards are arranged in colorful displays within the frame as they arrive.

The contents of the epistles are recited not by the two epistolary parties but by Varda herself. In this manner, the filmmaker inscribes herself into the film as a third character, similar to the way that Mona Hatoum, Chantal Akerman, and Trinh T. Minh-ha inscribe themselves in their epistolary films by means of their voices. Occupying such an intermediary position is very powerful, for these women directors can thereby act as shifters or translators between diegetic characters and between film and audience to not only present but also represent, and even misrepresent, the epistles. However, because of Varda's straightforward and realistic treatment of the third, epistolary, voice, this subversive potentiality does not materialize in *One Sings, the Other Doesn't* as it does in *Measures of Distance*, *News from Home*, and *Surname Viet Given Name Nam*.

Unlike Solanas's epistolic communitarianism, Varda's is driven not by ethnic, national, or exilic affiliation but by gender alliance, and her optimism is based not on closing the exilic gap but on the potentiality of female friendship. In the film, two women of different ages, classes, and temperaments are united by adversity and life's challenges and by the epistolary communications that bridge the various spatial and temporal distances that separate them.

Epistolarity is constitutionally a discourse of desire, for it mediates between distanced but desiring subjects. Desire can be transgressive when it is driven by the wish—made possible by exilic estrangement—to cross the naturalized boundaries of self, society, and nation. One such desire is to rebel against the traditional notions and practices of sexuality that privilege heterosexual relations. In recent years several accented films have questioned and subverted these traditions, favoring homosexual relations.[11] In the epistolary form, Akerman's *Je Tu Il Elle* (*I You He She*, 1974) is notable.

Close-Up: Chantal Akerman

Akerman was born in 1950 in Brussels, Belgium, to Jewish parents who had emigrated from Eastern Europe in the late 1930s. Their emigration, however, did not protect them from the Nazi onslaught. Akerman's mother and maternal grandparents were sent to Auschwitz, and her father spent World War II hiding in a small apartment in Brussels. Her exposure to Jean-Luc Godard's *Pierrot le Fou* (1965) transformed Akerman literally overnight, from a casual filmgoer to a filmmaker-to-be: "I got crazy about movies immediately and I decided to make movies the same night" (Walker Art Center 1995, 67). Arriving in New York City in the early 1970s, she spent some time at Jonas Mekas's Anthology Film Archives, where she watched many avant-garde films. She was particularly taken with Michael Snow's structuralist films and with the diarist sensibility of Mekas's films, which she described as "like homemade cooking" (68). In New York she worked as a waitress, a sculpture class model, and a porn theater cashier. Like a number of accented films, her first exilic film, *Hôtel Monterey* (1972), centered on life in a hotel; however, the hotel

Figure 9. Prohibition against epistolary communication. Unable to write letters, Chantal Akerman compulsively eats spoonfuls of sugar from a bag in *Je Tu Il Elle*.

housed people on welfare instead of émigrés and exiles (internal exiles, so to speak). With this silent film, what became Akerman's signature style, static framing and long takes, surfaced.

Akerman appears as a character in many of her films—an attribute of the accented style. She stars as Julie in the black-and-white feature *Je Tu Il Elle*, about a woman's tripartite sexual journey that divides the film into three equal-length segments. This film won critical acclaim, but it was only after her next film, *Jeanne Dielman, 23 Quai de Commerce, 1080 Bruxelles* (1975), that Akerman was catapulted into international fame. The first segment of Je Tu Il Elle shows Akerman in her austere, claustrophobic apartment, struggling for twenty-eight days to write a letter to someone whose identity and gender are not disclosed. During her epistolary ordeal, she compulsively eats powdered sugar from a paper bag. Having failed to complete the letter, in the film's second segment, Akerman hitches a ride from a truck driver, eats and smokes with him in truck stop restaurants and bars, watches him shave in a bathroom, and masturbates him (off camera) while he drives. In the final segment, Akerman arrives at the house of a girlfriend, who initially rejects her but then changes her mind, fixes her a sandwich, and allows her to stay for one night of passionate lovemaking.

In the first section, which is the film's epistolary heart, Akerman's desire and attempts at writing are thwarted by her various avoidance activities: she paints her room (the first day blue, the second day green!); rearranges the furniture; undresses; writes a bit; sleeps; eats spoonfuls of sugar from the bag (her voice-over reading the letter says, "I ate powdered sugar for eight pages"), arranges the many pages of the letter she has written on the floor; carelessly spills sugar on them; and waits. Like the austere visuals, the voice is matter-of-fact and emotionless, and the words, too, are mostly descriptive. Postponing or avoiding writing are constitutive of the epistolary structure, and there is an overpowering sense here of some deep psychic inhibition or social prohibition that prevents her from completing her letter. This makes the film extremely claustrophobic not only spatially (because it is shot in tight quarters with a stationary camera and static framing) but also emotionally. The unstated inhibitory force may be related to the character's (or the film's) anxiety in the first two parts about engaging in lesbian sex. However, the last part, devoted to lesbian lovemaking, is uninhibited and emotional, and it is refreshingly bereft of the usual voyeuristic gaze of male-staged lesbian relations. Even in this scene, however, desire and passion are somewhat flattened by the complete absence of sound.

Ultimately, *Je Tu Il Elle* is similar to the epistolary films of Naderi (*Manhattan by Numbers*, 1993), Egoyan (*Calendar*, 1990), and Tabrizian (*Journey of No Return*, 1993) in its doubt about the epistles' ability to break through the inhibitions and prohibitions against writing and speaking. In the first episode, Akerman cannot write, and in the second, she does not speak. Even when, in the third episode, a personal visit is substituted for the failed epistolary communication, it is short-lived and muted. Another fascinating aspect of the epistolary desire that the film brings up is the relationship of epistolarity to orality, in its widest interpretation. It seems that Julie consumes sugar compulsively to compensate for her inability to complete the letter, but since sugar does not fully compensate and the desire to write is not fully suppressed, the cycle of writing and eating must continue. Akerman is clearly concerned with the dynamics of the different types of orality (speaking, listening, eating, oral sex), epistolarity (writing, reading), and sexuality (straight, lesbian).[12]

Epistolarity demands seriality. The serial and palimpsestic structure of epistolary films intensifies the desire of the diegetic characters and the spectators for knowledge and identification. Each letter in the communicative chain fulfills or thwarts a previous anxiety or expectation: "A letter which has been passionately awaited should be immediately supplemented by another one, to counteract the feeling of flatness that comes upon us when the agonizing delights of anticipation have been replaced by the colder flood of fulfillment" (Sackville-West 1990, 25). In Akerman's *News from Home*, her mother's letters continually complain of the infrequency and late arrival of her daughter's letters, urging her to write more often. Psychologically, the interrupted structure of seriality intensifies the desire for more letters, and the successive addition of each letter builds a palimpsestic narrative structure.

One must view Hatoum's *Measures of Distance* and Akerman's *News from Home* more than once to appreciate their serial and palimpsestic structuration. Visually, *Measures of Distance* consists of still pictures of the filmmaker's mother's nude body and the handwritten text of her letters in Arabic to her daughter. The sound track consists of Hatoum's voice reading those letters. The first letter (quoted later) centers on the nuclear family and the intimate, mother-daughter relationship developed under the patriarchal censure of the husband/father. The second letter informs viewers of the mother's longing to be united with her daughter and of her recollection of her daughter's first menstruation. The third letter speaks about an afternoon when Hatoum's father discovers with disapproval his wife and daughter naked, taking photographs and taping their conversations. The fourth letter highlights the mother's sadness at her family's fragmentation due to the Lebanese civil war, double exile, and diaspora. The fifth letter adds the last layer to this palimpsest. It recounts the car bombing of the post office that brings to a close the mother-daughter communication. Likewise, the first letter of *News from Home* (quoted later) centers on the nuclear family relations, particularly the mother-daughter intimacy and their respective birthdays. Later letters bring new pieces of information, new concerns, or an added nuance to an old item.

The viewing of the epistolary films resembles an archaeological expedition in reverse: instead of digging deeper for information, it is added layer by layer.[13] As a result, theoretically, epistolary spectatorship is more congruent with cognitive psychology than with Lacanian psychoanalysis. Each letter compels viewers to revise their earlier hypotheses about the writer(s), addressee(s), and reciter(s) of the letters, the world they inhabit, and the desires and prohibitions under which they are attempting to connect. This spectatorial activity is congruent with the epistolary's repetitive structure that results from the inability to close the gap of exile. The gap is reiterated with each letter, turning epistolarity into, if not communication, at least a ritual of communication.

Another important structural and thematic component of epistolary communitarianism is the trial motif, by which diegetic characters and filmmakers seek to redress a historical wrong by appealing to spectators' sense of morality and justice. Trial films are not epistolary in the strict sense of the term, involving letters. However, they are often made under the regimes of erasure and desire that are similar to the letter-films, and their diegetic characters address the audience directly, using the film itself as an epistle. In this manner, the trial motif transforms a film from film-letter to letter-film. Jean Chamoun and Mai Masri's *Wildflower: Women of South Lebanon* (1988) and Maysoon Pachachi's *Iraqi Women: Voices from Exile* (1994) attempt to redress the historical wrongs perpetrated on the Lebanese and Iraqi people by the Israeli and Iraqi governments.[14]

In many Third World societies from which accented filmmakers have emerged, confession is highly political and public. Authoritarian regimes routinely use the mass media to transmit coerced confessions from their opponents in order to discredit them. In turn, exiled filmmakers, such as Rafigh Pooya in *In Defense of the People* (*Dar Defa' az Mardom*, 1981), sometimes use these confessions deconstructively to prosecute the regimes that obtained them. Pooya used the footage from a nationally televised military court trial of a group of Iranian leftists during the Shah's time to critique and prosecute his regime.[15] Stylistically, prosecutorial films, which form a vast and rich genre, make heavy use of archival footage, testimonials, and interviews, as well as compilation and reconstruction techniques, and they fit into Bill Nichols's "interactive mode" of documentary (1991).

These protest-laden confessional and testimonial films, along with calligraphic films and daughter-films, provide alternative discourses to officially produced and sanctioned history and cinema. Appealing to individual and collective experience is a postcolonial, Third Worldist, and exilic oppositional strategy to create locality, local knowledge, and located knowledge in the face of the tendency of hegemonic powers toward abstraction and universalization. These are some of the ways in which the subalterns speak.

Inhibition and Prohibition

Another characteristic of epistolarity is that it is produced under erasure, for epistolary narratives invariably spring from an injunction or a prohibition against writing and connecting, which takes many forms. Linda Kauffman demonstrated that many amorous epistolaries are driven by an injunction against writing put into effect by one of the lovers (1986, 1992). In certain circumstances, familial and social norms prohibit the lovers from contacting one another. However, prohibition may also stem from personal refusal to engage in communication, as in Tarkovsky's *Nostalgia*, in which a ringing telephone is not answered. The prohibition may represent, as in the muteness of the lead character in Suleiman's *Chronicle of Disappearance*, either a strategy of political resistance by means of silence or the difficulty of coming to speech in exilic situations. In Tabrizian's *Journey of No Return*, a psychosexual resistance to patriarchal connection prevents the female character from either mailing the letter that she has written to her father or deleting it from her computer. The injunction may be instituted by authoritarian regimes bent on controlling communication, which often results in countermeasures such as clever encoding of key terms in letters and phone conversations to camouflage intention. There are times when the post office is blown up (as in Hatoum's *Measures of Distance*) and phone conversations are either tapped (as in Kieslowski's *Red*) or disrupted by bad connection (as in Egoyan's *Calendar*). The prohibitive cost of long-distance phone calls is another form of prohibition, which compels the Argentines in *Tangos: Exile of Gardel* to develop ingenious methods of rigging the public telephones. Military censorship prohibits communitarian urges, but it also incites its violations, as in Chamoun and Masri's *Wildflower: Women of South Lebanon*, which contains a harrowing sequence of car bombing that was recorded secretly in violation of Israeli military censorship (Naficy 1987).

The following two close-up studies of Palestinian filmmakers working in Europe and the United States further bring out the dynamics of exilic epistolary desire as deflected by various forms of inhibition and prohibition.

Figure 10. Epistolarity
as performative expres-
sion of nationhood.
Elia Suleiman's writ-
ings at the computer
("mourning and dig-
nity") are reflected on
his face in his *Homage
by Assassination.*

Close-Up: Elia Suleiman

Suleiman was born in 1960 in Nazareth, Israel, to a Palestinian family and
has lived in New York City periodically since the early 1980s. During this
intermittent exile, he made two experimental, but substantial, shorts and one
feature film. In collaboration with Jayce Salloum, a Lebanese-Canadian filmmaker and artist, he made *Introduction to the End of an Argument (Intifada):
Speaking for Oneself . . . /Speaking for Others* (*Muqaddimah Li-Nihayat Jidaal,*
1990). This is a biting collage-essay (forty-five minutes in length) that by
means of critical juxtaposition of bitterly funny filmed and appropriated footage, from Henry Kissinger's news clips to Looney Tunes cartoons, critiques
the dominant representation of Arabs and Palestinians in Western media as
terrorists. Subsequently, Suleiman made *Homage by Assassination* (35mm,
twenty-eight minutes in length, 1991) about one night of his exilic existence
in New York City during the 1991 Persian Gulf war with Iraq. Although this
is a quiet and reflective film, its form is as experimental as that of the boisterous,
humorous *Introduction.* In his first feature film, *Chronicle of a Disappearance*
(1996), Suleiman appears as a diegetic filmmaker who returns to his homeland.[16] Like a number of accented filmmakers, Suleiman also plays himself in
Homage and *Chronicle,* turning these films into personal and autobiographical
ruminations about exile and cinema.[17] The more nuanced techniques of critical
and ironic juxtaposition that emerge in these films also express and embody
exilic contradictions and thirdspace ambivalence.

   Homage by Assassination shows the filmmaker cloistered in his claustrophobic
apartment in New York City during the war as his birthplace, Nazareth, is
threatened by the Iraqi Scud missiles launched against Israeli cities. Like a
letter, the film reports on the routines of Suleiman's day, which he performs
mutely: he ties his bootlaces, boils milk on the stove, observes from the window
a couple's quiet quarrel in the street below, weighs himself on the scale repeatedly, goes to the bathroom, and attempts to make phone calls, write, photo-
copy, fax, and edit his film. These routine activities are what Homi Bhabha has
called the "performative" expressions of nationhood, "the everyday, unofficial

representation of the nation" (quoted in Marks 1991, 64–65). These expressions take on a higher significance when the nation is either coming into being or being lost to exile—both of which are true with Palestinians. The performative expression of dailiness by exiled and disenfranchised peoples is a countermeasure to the official pedagogical representation of them, which tends to abstract them by stereotyping, exoticizing, and otherizing. This may account for the emphasis in the films of the Third World cinema, Third Cinema, and accented cinema on "documentary-like" descriptions of mundane routines and detailed activities that slow the films' pacing. However, these routines and details carry with them highly significant cultural, national, and critical import; they are not empty gestures or bad filmmaking!

Another performative strategy of the nation is engagement in counter-representations. While *Introduction to the End of an Argument* engages in a point-by-point counterrepresentation by making fun of, subverting, and directly critiquing American media's representations of Arabs and Palestinians, counterrepresentation in *Homage by Assassination* is more subtle. The souvenirs and fetishes of a Palestinian homeland-in-the-making are displayed throughout the apartment: the map of Palestine on the wall, the Palestinian flag on a remote-control toy car and on the TV screen, the native Arabic language on the computer screen and reflected on Suleiman's face sitting at his Macintosh computer, and the exilic desire to return to the homeland signaled in the close-up shot of the "return" key on the keyboard.

The diegetic Suleiman, in his small apartment, is at the nexus of a technologized communication and epistolary network consisting of computer, copier, fax, telephone, answering machine, radio, and television, all capable of both representing and misrepresenting the Palestinians. They can also put him in touch with the world. In a humorously touching sequence, he picks a bouquet of flowers from a vase, places it on the copy machine, and faxes the copied flowers to an Iraqi Jewish friend in Israel. The friend is not identified, but it is film scholar Ella Shohat, whose response to Suleiman also arrives by fax. In it, she recounts (in her own voice) the story of her family's displacement from Iraq, years of living with a split identity in Israel/Palestine, and finally her arrival in the United States (Shohat and Stam 1994: 319).

Because of its live ontology and the concomitant immediacy, intimacy, and intensity, the telephone is most susceptible to both epistolary prohibition and transgression. The inability to contact at critical moments, and the overwhelming desire to do so, turns the telephone into a highly cathected, even magical, instrument. But Suleiman is pessimistic about the epistolary media's communitarian potentials, for despite their clamor, there is a strong sense of prohibition and deliberate silence at work. The sole diegetic character, the filmmaker, appears to be under siege and paralyzed by technological mediation. He seems to be waiting, unable to speak and impossible to reach. The voices of people attempting to reach him are heard on the answering machine: a talk radio host interested in a "Palestinian angle" on the Gulf War, his friend telling him of his success at reaching Nazareth by telephone, and another one telling the latest joke about Palestinians. When Suleiman attempts to call home, the dreaded recorded message familiar to exiles from war-torn countries is heard: "All lines to the country you've dialed are temporarily disconnected."

Ensconced in his "safe zone" of an apartment, where all the shades are drawn, Suleiman edits his epistolic film, like all epistolaries, in a state of deep loneliness, which allegorizes the loneliness of the film's interstitial production mode. Loneliness, which motivates epistolary writing, can be solipsistic. However, since exile structurally involves questions of collective belonging, exilic epistles are less prone to this affliction than amorous ones. As a result, despite the character's refusal, silence, and loneliness, and despite the film's austere, even pessimistic, tone, *Homage by Assassination* is Suleiman's impassioned letter-film to the world, giving voice to a few moments in the life of Palestinian exiles. If, in Israel, Palestinian youths by means of the *intifada* (uprising) gave voice to the stones, Suleiman in New York City gives voice to the film—with all the muteness, inarticulateness, and trauma of coming into language that are hallmarks of his works. Although the character's defiant silence and the film's elegant beauty and austere narrative may be read as culturally and cinematically oppositional, they can also alienate the spectators by refusing them entry into the text. As Laura Marks observes, "We are drawn in by the beauty of the images only to be—not repulsed, but deflected, as a stone glances off a wall" (1991, 70).

Close-Up: Mona Hatoum

Hatoum's epistolic *Measures of Distance* (1988) was made under multiple forms of erasure: patriarchal, political, and exilic. In fact, it was made under a dual exile—from Palestine and Lebanon, the filmmaker's previous two homes. Hatoum was born in Beirut, Lebanon, in 1952 to Palestinian parents who had left their home a few years earlier. She attended Beirut University College from 1970 to 1972 and was vacationing in England in 1975 when the Lebanese civil war broke out. Hatoum settled in London, where she studied for six years, graduating from the Slade School of Art in 1981. She began with minimalist sculptures and performance art, and since the mid-1980s has added photography, video, and art installation to her repertoire.

Given Hatoum's own history and that of the Palestinians, it is no wonder that her highly praised artworks insistently probe "the unhealed psychological wounds of lost childhood and of adult displacement" (Cotter 1997, B27). Like many exilic artists, Hatoum is preoccupied with feeling structures of threat, entrapment, and claustrophobia. This was demonstrated in an early performance called *Under Siege* (1982), in which she appeared naked and for seven hours attempted to stand up in a transparent coffinlike container filled with mud. Home for her does not appear to be a refuge or a place of comfort. This is symbolized in her distressing furniture, such as a dysfunctional bed that lacks a bottom, a steel divan that suggests a sarcophagus, and an uncomfortable carpet made of stainless steel pins.

Not all of Hatoum's works are uncomfortable, but all are disturbing. A case in point is her video installation *Corps étranger* (1994), which is disturbingly engulfing. It is in essence a self-portrait of the artist from the literal inside, involving images of her internal organs obtained by medical procedures of endoscopy, colonoscopy, and sonography. These images of moist, pulsating, that soft interior organs and orifices are meshed in with those of the exterior body and projected on the floor of a circular booth that leaves only a few inches of standing room on the edges. The viewers who stand on the edges are hypnotized by the sound of Hatoum's heartbeat and pulsating images, which seem to urge them to give in to the imminent engulfment and plunge in. *Corps étranger* provoked shock and controversy about rape and sexual exploitation in Hatoum's work.

These works of Hatoum are both autobiographical and corporeal, for they involve not only her history but also her body—the height of exilic indexicality. But the body is not at rest or whole; rather, it is agitated and fragmented, and it "fails to cohere" (Morgan 1997, 3). This is a body in exile on which are writ large the traumas of patriarchal and political torture at home and of displacement and disruption in exile.

Hatoum's single-channel videos include *So Much I Want to Say* (1983), *Changing Parts* (1984), and *Measures of Distance*. The latter consists of a series of five letters from Hatoum's mother in Lebanon to her in Canada. Both the visuals and the sound track are richly textured and multilingual. Throughout the video, portions of the mother's handwritten letters (in Arabic) are superimposed on the stills of her nude body, while on the sound track her daughter reads the letters (translated into English). In addition, under the voice-over of the letters, the impromptu conversations and phatic banter of mother and daughter (in Arabic) are heard as they discuss sexuality, family relations, and childhood experiences. Both the mother's nude photographs and the mother-daughter conversations were recorded in Beirut in the father's absence.

A classic form of epistolary prohibition is the one against the transmission of the epistles. In *Measures of Distance* this prohibition is both patriarchal and political. In one letter, Hatoum's mother gives her daughter permission to use in her artwork their taped conversations and photos, but she asks her (twice) not to share them with her father, for fear of upsetting him (these stills and recordings form the documentary, indirect discourse of the film). It is as though, the mother tells her daughter (in direct discourse), by baring her body and soul to her daughter, she has given her something that rightfully belonged only to him. The mother's prohibition serves patriarchal purposes. However, following one of the transgressive impulses of epistolarity, the filmmaker subverts the prohibition and makes her film public. Her boldness becomes more evident if one considers the sociocultural contexts of Middle Eastern, Arab, Palestinian, and Muslim societies, which place a high value on the clear demarcation of gendered spaces and the separation of private and public spaces. Beyond these culture-specific violations, Hatoum's transgression is in line with what Derrida has called the "postcard structure" itself, one that raises questions about what is public or private, inside or outside, real or fictional (1980).

The political prohibition against transmitting the letters is brought on by the chaotic conditions of the civil war and the Israeli occupation of South Lebanon. The last letter, which ends the film, states that a car bomb destroyed the post office, closing off for the foreseeable future the mother-daughter link of letters. Hatoum's mother tells her that from now on they have to be satisfied with an unreliable telephonic link.

To be sure, there are class differences among displaced peoples, and not all of them have access to all the epistolic technologies all the time. And the identities they create with them are neither hermetic nor permanent, as their essential differences threaten to break through, rendering them inappropriate. It is against such a threat that the past and their differences are turned into ethnic objects and nostalgic fetishes. Photo albums, letters, diaries, audio and video recorders, telephones, and computers are some of the ethnic, exilic, and epistolic objects and fetishes that are circulated in exilic music videos and films. People looking through photo albums; watching "home" videos; reading and writing letters; or listening, talking, and crying on the phone are some of the recurring epistolary micronarratives of these videos and films. But these are not simple epistles of diegetic communication or of filmic narration. Epistolary media play a constitutive part in the life-world of displaced people; it is with them that they think and construct their affiliative identities.

Orality and Acousticity

To speak of epistolary films as oral and acoustic texts is to acknowledge the central role in them of sound, voice, and language and to differentiate them from the oral literature. The differentiation is necessary because we cannot assign to them the status of some original orality—that which existed before writing. They are only secondarily oral, in that they partake of a kind of post-oral, postwritten, postprint, post–Third World, postcolonial, and postmodern electronic orality and acousticity. This "postal" orality is driven by such factors as the filmmakers' national origins and current national status and by their films' multilingualism, their specific inscription of human speech and voice, and their epistolary structures and contents.

Although all of the accented filmmakers are postliterate, many have their origin in societies that maintain side by side with print and electronic literacy a residual oral culture that influences the stories they tell and the manner in which they tell them. Residual orality impacts their films' formal, stylistic, and thematic systems, giving them a different accent. This may be evidenced in privileging of oral culture themes and spoken formulas, as in Julie Dash's *Daughters of the Dust* (1991); in emphatically familial and collective relations, as in Mira Nair's *Mississippi Masala* (1992) and *The Perez Family* (1995) and in Gregory Nava's *El Norte* (1983) and *My Family* (1995); in mixing real and magical elements, as in Charles Burnett's *To Sleep with Anger* (1990) and Nava's *El Norte*; in intermixing the past with the present, as in Euzhen Palcey's *Sugar Cane Alley* (*Rue Cases-Nègres*, 1983); and in the presence of translators, storytellers, and griot figures, who retell ancient stories or resituate today's events in the context of ancient stories, as in Jean Rouch's *The Lion Hunters* (*La Chasse au Lion à l'Arc*, 1964) and Haile Gerima's *Harvest, 3000 Years* (1974).[18]

The accent comes about not just from these sources of residual orality but also from the *coexistence* of orality and literacy, colonialism and postcolonialism, nationalism and postnationalism, communism and postcommunism, and premodernism, modernism, and postmodernism. Therefore, the prefix "post" implies "impurity" and "living in tension" with conflicting forces and emergent formations, rather than a clean break with them. The accented style, therefore, is "oral," "postal," and "relational," in the way that Ella Shohat and Robert Stam have described (1994).

The acousticity of accented epistolaries stems from the specific inscription of sound and voice in them. One of the characteristics of sound that distinguishes it from vision is that sound is perishable, evanescent, and unstable. Unlike vision, whose existence can be stabilized, sound exists only when it is dying or coming into being; it cannot be frozen in place like a still frame. Further, if sight is analytical, operating by isolating and distancing the seer from the seen, sound is immersive, functioning to incorporate and unify the sender of the sound with its recipient (Ong 1982, 71–74). While images may exist separately from their producing agency, no voice exists without the force that generates it, the breath (32). Thus there exists a unique relationship between voice, interiority, and identity, and it is perhaps because of this that voice and speech are always associated with potency and magical power.

All societies appear to associate speech and voice with proximity and presence. In film studies, too, speech and voice have been treated, in Charles Affron's words, as the guarantors of "immediacy and presence in the system of absence that is cinema" (1982, 105). However, theories that pose sound as counteracting the cinema's basic lack place a "fetishistic value" on sound (Silverman 1988, 43). Their overemphasis on synchronized sound turns diegetic speech into the "sound analogue of the shot/reverse shot formation" that sutures the viewer/listener to the "safe place of the story" (45). However, the sound track, like the image track, involves mediations and representational practices that push the sound into the realm of ideology, as something that is produced, not as something that simply emanates.

In accented films, particularly the epistolaries, the high value ascribed to synchronous diegetic sound does not entirely hold, and their use of silence and sound misalignment can turn the best of them into counterhegemonic discourses on ideology and cinema. There are long periods of silence in Akerman's *Je Tu Il Elle* or just ambient sound in Suleiman's *Homage by Assassination* and *Chronicle of a Disappearance*. There is no synchronized sound in some films, as in Marker's *Letter from Siberia*, and only sparing use of it in others, as in Mekas's *Lost, Lost, Lost*. Voice-off, voice-over, and image-over narrations often cast doubt on the identity of the speaking subject, the addressee of the epistles, or the voice that is reading them, as in Tabrizian's *Journey of No Return* and Marker's *Sunless*. The misalignment of voice and person can be especially counterhegemonic in the representation of women because it goes against the classical film style, which insists on both synchronization and silencing of women (Silverman 1988; Lawrence 1994). Trinh's *Surname Viet Given Name Nam* is centrally concerned with Vietnamese women as speaking subjects, but they speak in a highly accented English that is out of sync. Although these speeches are subtitled, the subtitling is also deliberately out of sync, lagging behind or running ahead of the subjects' utterance. In addition, the subtitles do not exactly match what the women are saying.

Despite these counterhegemonic sound practices, there is a strong tendency in accented films to preserve the native language as the marker of belonging and authenticity. Its interpellating authority, its bonding effect, its prison house is desired, especially by filmmakers who wish to maintain an organic relationship both with their original culture and with their community of address. There is a particular insistence on language and a complex interplay between language and national identity.[19] Linguistic nationalism is an attribute of both accented films and ethnic television (Naficy 1993a, 1998b).

Calligraphic Texts

Multilinguality, which necessitates extensive titling, turns the film frame into a calligraphic page, contributing to the film's overall accent. In traditional "foreign films," subtitles mediate between a spoken source language and a written target text on the screen (Grillo and Kawin 1981).[20] However, there is no single original, or source, language for many accented films, which are made in the interstices and astride several cultures and languages. Subtitling is thus integral to both the making and the viewing of these films. Out of necessity, subtitles must condense several lines of dialogue into brief textual snippets timed to the flow of the images. This requires a skillful and economic translation of the original spoken words—one of several forms of translation that produces the accent. On many occasions, however, the subtitles either are too long to be read in time or else one set of subtitles partially covers over another set in a different language. And there are the amusing and annoying experiences of having to read incorrectly translated and spelled titles. These problems particularly dog the subtitling of many Third World and accented films, heightening their accentedness.

In some epistolary films, words are superimposed over the images or else the flow of images is interrupted to display intertitles. However, these titles are treated as essential to the narrative, in the tradition of the best silent-era films. In that era, intertitles commented on the action, attested to the accuracy of a setting, identified location, imparted information, explained difficult terms or abstract concepts (such as the passage of time), played on the viewers' emotions, and expressed the characters' feelings and thoughts (Dick 1990, 14–17). In addition, the punctuation, typeface, type size, and layout of the text on the screen were designed to suggest, symbolize, or emphasize the content of the words. With the arrival of sound, the use of intertitles in narrative cinema dwindled, but letters, notes, newspaper headlines, signposts, street signs, highway signs, plaques, and other forms of written and graphic information continued to serve some of the functions of the intertitles. However, alternative cinemas, including the accented cinema, have continued to experiment with on-screen titling as an expressive, narrative, and calligraphic component.

Close-Up: Trinh T. Minh-ha's Surname Viet Given Name Nam (1985)

Trinh's film uses superimposed titles and subtitles extensively, graphically, and critically. Their large numbers and varied contents and layout give this film a truly calligraphic accent. Throughout, subtitles consisting of the translation of the film's dialogue and voice-over and of the Vietnamese poetry and proverbs are displayed, as is customary, in the lower third of the screen. However, on many occasions, what the diegetic women say in Vietnamese or in heavily accented English is superimposed in different layout as blocks of English text on various regions of the film frame, including over the characters' faces. These graphic titles, or what Trinh calls "visualized speech" (1992, 193), act as traditional subtitles by aiding spectator comprehension. However, they also serve other graphic, critical, and deconstructive functions. The film's deconstructive project begins with its title, which plays on, parodies, and critiques attempts at naming a heterogeneous country or nation such as Vietnam, and it ends with listing the various names for Vietnam.

To these text-based complexities must be added Trinh's filming style, which in *Surname* as in her other films, critiques many of the norms of cinematic realism by violating those norms. For example, in some sequences she places the subjects on the margins of the frame or decenters them by panning away from them. Close-up shots that would normally show the subjects full face end up cutting off part of their faces. The film also subverts the accepted practices of lip-synching and title synchronization. Titles of especially long or short duration draw attention to themselves and to the spectatorial readerly

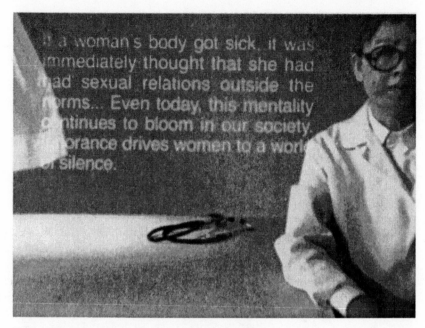

Figure 11. Calligraphic textuality and decentered framing in Trinh T. Minh-ha's *Surname Viet Given Name Nam.* Courtesy Trinh T. Minh-ha.

activities that are encouraged. Finally, on-camera actors speak the words of actual women recorded in off-camera documentary interviews. In these ways the boundary of documentary and fictional films is blurred, and the authenticity and authority of the nonfictional are undermined. Self-reflexive rumination by the women and by Trinh herself about the process of filmmaking further erodes the distinction of the film forms. The sound track is equally complex, consisting of songs, a mixture of real or reenacted first-person narration and interviews (in different Vietnamese dialects and accented English), and multiple voices and voice-over narrations that compete for attention. Consequently, *Surname* enacts both the problems and the problematic of linguistic, cinematic, and exilic translation and displacement. Indeed, it poses translation and displacement as theoretical problems for both diegetic characters and audiences.

These techniques comment on cinema and reality instead of just recording, reporting on, or representing reality. They denaturalize the classical cinema's realist style and posit female subjectivity and spectatorial activity as multiple and shifting (Lawrence 1994). The spectators are forced to engage in several simultaneous activities of watching, listening, reading, translating, and problem solving.[21] However, because these techniques do not necessarily support each other due to their asynchrony and critical juxtaposition, the spectatorial activities do not fuse into an easily coherent interpretation. While such an outcome is Trinh's stated aim in endowing each activity with "a certain degree of autonomy" (Trinh 1992, 207), it is also the source of the film's obscurantism. The film critiques the patriarchal suppression of women in socialist Vietnam and among Vietnamese exiles, but in its emphatic critique of Vietnam, it seems to reproduce cold war binary conceptions of North and South Vietnam.

If Grillo and Kawin are correct in their analysis, subtitles and intertitles encourage two types of reading activities, depending on the side of the brain to which they appeal. According to them, subtitles tend to appeal to the right hemisphere, encouraging syntaxic reading, that is, experiencing the whole film—consisting of dialogue, images, and subtitles—more or less simultaneously. On the other hand, intertitles appeal to the left hemisphere, facilitating parataxic reading, that is, experiencing the whole film in an additive way, by combining the various elements consciously (1981, 27). If the former type of reading is more simultaneous and emotional, the latter is presumably more discrete and intellectual. The accented calligraphic epistolaries that contain both superimposed titles and intertitles may thus involve both types of reading, accounting for their dissonant spectatorial experience.

However efficient the subtitles are, they are unable to convey the subtle differences in the characters' accented speech, which may imply important differences in power and other relations. Michel Khleifi's *Wedding in Galilee* (1987) is a case in point. This film is about the wedding of a Palestinian village chief's son, in an area that is occupied by Israel. The chief must obtain the Israeli military governor's permission for the elaborate traditional wedding. Although the two leaders converse in Arabic, each speaks a different form of it, denoting their profound power differences, as occupied and occupier. The village chief speaks in the colloquial Arabic that ordinary Arabs use, while the governor uses the literary Arabic that is reserved for official and journalistic functions (Alexander 1995, 3). The subtitles fail to render this linguistic power difference. This kind of loss in translation is also characteristic of the accented cinema.

In *History and Memory* (1991), Rea Tajiri uses rolling or static titles that literally question the very images on which they are superimposed. The images consist of clips from Hollywood feature films and newsreels and from U.S. government documentaries made to justify the internment of Japanese-Americans during World War II. In one sequence, a rolling intertitle on a black background, accompanied by a voice-over narration, describes how one day government agents removed Tajiri's family house from its foundations, never to return it, because the family (all of whom were American citizens) had been classified as "enemy aliens." This is followed by a clip from a documentary by the Office of War Information, in which a government official explains to the camera that the Japanese attack on Pearl Harbor has turned the United States' West Coast into a "potential combat zone." He then reminds the audience

Figure 12. Critical titling. Titles in
Rea Tajiri's *History and Memory*
question the "official" story.

that over 100,000 Japanese live in the zone, a third of whom are "aliens" and
considered to be a potential danger in case Japan invades the mainland. As he
is speaking, the following titles appear on his image, slowly, and line by line:
"Who chose what story to tell?"

Tajiri's on-screen question can be applied to *History and Memory* itself, and
to the sequence about the loss of her family home. In that case, the question
would bring under scrutiny not only the politics of the government's official
story but also that of the filmmaker's personal story—an effect perhaps unintended by the filmmaker. As in the case of *Surname Viet Given Name Nam*,
such critical juxtapositions and their intended and unintended dissonant effects
are emblematic of the accented style.

Since in *History and Memory* titles are superimposed on sound film clips,
they compete with existing dialogue, voice-over narration, on-camera narration, and musical passages. This potentially produces an instance of Derridaian
double writing and reading, in which neither the audio nor the visual text has
primacy over the other. However, the government and Hollywood films are
clearly marked as the suspicious source texts that need to be commented upon
by means of deconstructive titling.

There is a tradition in Islamic exegesis in which sacred or authoritative
source texts are commented upon by learned scholars in explanatory texts. Historically, the texts were memorized and recited verbatim to preserve their sa-
credness and authority, while this was not necessary for the commentaries. To
aid memorization, the texts were made extremely compact, their very density
necessitating explanation. When it came to rendering this text/commentary
form into writing, an ingenious method of imbricating the two emerged. On
the page, the text is frequently interrupted by commentary that ranges from
trivial observations to lengthy and important doctrinal elaboration. However,
the two retain their separate identities as color, typeface, and mode of address
differentiated them (Messick 1993, 30–31). The resulting intertextual artifact
is calligraphically very elaborate. Its interpretation is equally complex, for it
involves switching back and forth between the already familiar—because memorized—text and the larger commentary in which it is embedded. This Islamic

form of exegesis appears to have some relevance for the analysis of calligraphically accented epistolary films. Mekas's *Lost, Lost, Lost*, Hatoum's *Measures of Distance*, Suleiman's *Homage by Assassination*, Trinh's *Surname Viet Given Name Nam*, Tajiri's *History and Memory*, and Meena Nanji's *Voices of the Morning* (1992) are filmic examples of such intertextual calligraphic artifacts. Although their visuals generally act as the source text and their titles as secondary or explanatory texts, that is not always the case. Their calligraphic accent lies both in the way the titles comment upon or complement the visuals and in the way in which they and the visuals merge to form one unified text.

Brinkley Messick's study of Yemeni society demonstrates that when the procedures of providing official explanations on core texts are reiterated from childhood on and are dispersed in all private and public domains, they can lead to the creation of a "calligraphic state" (1993). Likewise, the classical cinema's realist style, practiced for decades by mainstream directors who are widely sanctioned by the culture industries of the West, constructs what, following Messick, may be called the "cinematic state." The epistolary films' calligraphic strategies tend to subvert some of the tenets of that state. To that extent, they are part of "resistance cinema."[22]

Daughter-Texts

A more complex relationship between spoken and written language is inscribed in the accented films by women that focus on mother-daughter relations. This type of relationship has produced strong imaginative and scholarly works in both literature and cinema. Made by daughters, their central drama is the daughters' struggle toward self-definition as they come to terms with their mothers (Heung 1993, 598). The daughter's voice tends to dominate, while the voice of the mother, as the daughter's other, is marginalized, even silenced. Recent "postmodern immigration" literature, from Amy Tan's *The Joy Luck Club* to Maxine Hong Kingston's *The Woman Warrior* to Jamaica Kincaid's *Annie John*, has explored the nuances of this dyadic relationship in the context of immigration and generational gap. When they embrace the mothers' voices, these works are multivocal, multilingual, and multigenerational, inscribing female and diaspora consciousness from multiple perspectives.

In both accented literature and cinema, conflict arises because mothers and daughters occupy different generational, cultural, class, linguistic, and imaginative worlds. While mothers tend to be preoccupied with the past and with their far-off homeland, their daughters are more apt to be concerned with the here and now. The mother-daughter relationship is particularly strained when the two protagonists live in different countries. In Ann Hui's exilic film *Song of the Exile* (1990), the mother lives in China but dreams about returning to Japan, the country of her dead husband, while her daughter lives as a foreign student in England and wants to revisit her homeland, China. They meet in a third territory, Hong Kong, where the mother-daughter tensions come to a head. However, even if mother and daughter are not separated geographically, as in Wayne Wang's immigration film *The Joy Luck Club* (1993), they are often so far apart culturally that they feel foreign to one another.

Even if accented daughter-films are produced not in contradiction to but in collaboration with the mothers, they are primarily vehicles of the daughters' self-definition. Ngozi Onwurah's mother cooperated with her fully, and she appears in the film *The Body Beautiful* (1991) as herself and delivers her own voice-over narration. It was apparently the negative British reaction to Onwurah's "harsh" representation of her mother in an earlier film, *Coffee-Colored Children* (1988), that led to their collaboration in this film (Cartwright 1994). Yet *The Body Beautiful* is decidedly from the daughter's perspective. In the opening voice-over, the daughter (played by an actor) sketches the history of Onwurah's family and her exile. We learn that she was born in Nigeria to an English mother and a Nigerian father, that the Nigerian civil war fractured the family forever, sending mother and daughter (age nine) to England. There, her mother gives birth to a second child and undergoes two traumatic events that leave her disfigured: a mastectomy on one breast and rheumatoid arthritis. Onwurah grows up to become a beautiful fashion model. These stories set up the film's central drama and contradiction both between mother and daughter and between bodily disability and exotic beauty.

The film effectively chronicles the daughter's reconciliation with her mother but leaves the contradictions of ethnicity and race submerged. Their reconciliation is most clearly observed by comparing the beginning and the ending of this twenty-three minute video. In the beginning, a young, angry Onwurah cruelly calls her mother a "titless cow." At the film's end, Onwurah, who is now a fashion model, is comfortably sleeping in bed next to her mother (both of them naked), while her voice-over declares with pride: "I am my mother's daughter for the rest of my life." The problematic of bodily disfigurement is resolved partially by recognizing the mastectomy scar as a site of erotic pleasure—graphically demonstrated in a scene of lovemaking between her mother and a black man.

Although the mother does appear as herself in *The Body Beautiful*, delivers her own voice-overs in direct speech, and acts out her own lovemaking fantasy, the daughter never appears in the film and does not deliver her own voice-over narration. An actress functions as her double. This strategic absence, or camouflage, raises questions about the politics of representation and exploitation in daughter-texts, even in a film whose ostensible purpose is to counter such exploitation. Specifically, it poses this question: In making daughter-films, to what extent are the daughters defining themselves against or at the expense of their own mothers, who, in exilic texts at least, are often far away and have less access than their daughters to the media to counter their daughters' representations of them? Although Onwurah's mother had such access, and screened both *Coffee-Colored Children* and *The Body Beautiful* in her educational lecture tours about breast cancer, this question dogs Onwurah's films and, to one degree or another, all accented daughter-films.

In Tajiri's *History and Memory* the filmmaking daughter counters the official U.S. discourse justifying the internment of Japanese-Americans, as represented by government films and Hollywood movies and newsreels, by juxtaposing it against the filmmaker's personal, familial, and ethnic discourse, as represented by her own recollections and those of her family, personal letters and film clips, and deconstructive titles. Unlike many daughter-films, *History and Memory* is centered not on the personal and individual differences between mother and daughter but on the differences between official and privately held histories. While the official history is chiefly visual, governmental, and commercial, and is delivered in indirect speech, the counterdiscourse of memory is chiefly oral, private, and ethnic and is spoken directly.[23] The victims' oral recollections counter the government's visual documentation. The film's focus on collective testimony, transindividual autobiography, and multiple viewpoints turns it into what Gabriel calls the "guardian of popular memory" (1989a), thus saving the film from falling into two of the major traps of daughter-texts: emphasis on hermetic psychic mechanism and on strictly personal relations.

Hatoum's *Measures of Distance* and Akerman's *News from Home* are epistolaries that are also daughter-texts, structured around one-way mother-to-daughter letters. In both cases, the mothers reside at home while their daughters are abroad. Voice, language, and text are woven intricately, producing free indirect discourses that contain various inscriptions and erasures of the daughters and of their mothers. Hatoum's video is structured by letters she has received from her mother in Lebanon. The relationship of the writer, addressee, and reciter of the letters is complex, as is the relationship of spoken and written Arabic with spoken English. Both sets of relations are fraught with exilic erasure and inscription. The mother is visually inscribed by her still pictures in the nude and by her handwritten letters. The voice reading her letters is not hers but that of her daughter, who reads them not in Arabic, which is displayed on the screen, but in English translation. The mother's voice is heard only in the Arabic conversations with her daughter in the background of the letters' voice-over. The daughter, on the other hand, is visually erased from the film, but she is inscribed both by her voice-over and by being the subject of the letters' address. The first letter, written during the Lebanese civil war and reproduced here, provides an example of the dynamics of erasure and inscription, and distancing and intimacy that are at work between mother and daughter (as well as between them and the absent husband/father who is referred to in the letters).

Figure 13. Epistolarity and calligraphic textuality in Mona Hatoum's *Measure of Distance*.

My dear Mona, the apple of my eyes, how I miss you and long to feast my eyes on your beautiful face that brightens up my days. When you were here the whole house was livened up by your presence. Now it feels like the house has lost its soul. I wish this bloody war would be over soon so you and your sisters can return and we will all be together again like the good old days. I enjoyed very much all those intimate conversations we had about women's things and all that. You and I have never talked in this way before. Why don't you come back and live here and we can make all the photographs and tapes you want. You asked me in your last letter if you can use my pictures in your work. Go ahead and use them, but don't mention a thing about it to your father. Do you remember how he was shocked when he caught us taking the pictures in the shower during his afternoon nap? I suppose he was embarrassed to find us both standing there stark naked, and we just carried on and ignored him. We laughed at him when he told us off, but he was seriously angry. He still nags me about it, as if I had given you something that only belongs to him. I actually enjoyed the session because I felt we were like sisters, close together and with nothing to hide from each other. I enjoyed the feeling of intimacy that developed between us. Whatever you do with the pictures, for God's sake don't tell him about it, I will never hear the end of the story.

The conjoining of the mother's words with the daughter's voice in the face of patriarchal challenge binds mother and daughter diegetically and bonds them epistolarily across the oceans, creating a consoling fantasy of maternal symbiosis.[24] This is emphasized further by the untranslated mother-daughter phatic banter in Arabic, which had threatened the husband/father. The mixing of background banter with foreground voice-over creates an overall female consciousness and female solidarity, challenging the hegemony of patriarchal culture and mode of narration.

Akerman's *News from Home* consists of beautifully static tableau shots of New York City streets, subways, and storefronts that express the feel of a foreigner's first impression of a new place. The images are accompanied by emphatic street sounds and passing trains and by Akerman's own voice-over, reading matter-of-factly in her accented English, her mother's concerned letters to her from Belgium. Whereas the letters are intimate and personal, the visuals are public and impersonal (Wakeman 1988, 5). The first letter establishes the pattern for the many letters that follow. Over alienated shots of New York City's desolate streets, where cars occasionally pass and strewn newspapers blow gently in the breeze, the following warm words are heard:

> My dearest little girl:
> I just got your letter and I hope that you'll continue to write to me often. Anyway, I hope that you'll come back to me soon. I hope that you're still well and you're already working. I see that you like New York and you seem to be happy. We're very pleased even though we'd like to see you very soon. Tell us when you're thinking of coming back. At home, it's the same as ever. . . . I am not too well. My blood pressure is up and I am taking medicine and vitamins. Today is my birthday and I already feel a little bit sad. . . . It is very quiet and we're bored. This evening we're going out to a restaurant with friends. That's all for my birthday. Soon it will be yours and I wish you the very best in the world as you can imagine. Write to me about your work and all about New York. I am impatient to hear from you. The three of us send you hugs and kisses and think of you all the time. Your loving mother.

The sound track weaves Akerman's voice reading her mother's letters with the sounds of traffic, subway trains, and street life to create an aural city symphony. The dailiness of the letters' content and the repetitiveness of their form become more apparent with each new letter. As noted in the case of Suleiman's films, dailiness and repetitiveness serve to establish the indexical present of life in exile. They also typify the traditional role of women in patriarchal societies, which forms a critical theme of Akerman's films.

The films of Hatoum and Akerman inscribe not only epistolarity but also orality in their content and form. In *Measures of Distance*, the letters of Hatoum's mother repeatedly address her in culturally formulaic phrases that indicate familiarity and familiality: "My dear Mona, the apple of my eyes," "My dear Mona, the love of my heart." Likewise, Akerman's mother repeatedly addresses her daughter as "my dearest little girl" and bids her farewell with such standard phrases as "your loving mother." In their repetition and variation, these formulaic phrases and patterns of speech emphasize the films' orality.

In *News from Home* and *Measures of Distance*, the mothers' letters tell us much about the filmmakers, countering the daughters' invisibility and silence about themselves.[25] However, in the complex relations of power that are at work here, the filmmaking daughters are victorious, for they are the films' interpretive agents privileged to construct both their own and their mothers' stories.

Telephonic Epistles

The definition of the epistolary mode must be significantly altered to accommodate a host of new communication means that produce social relations and textual effects unlike those produced by film-letters. In today's diasporized and technologized world, letter writing is increasingly being supplemented or replaced by the telephone, answering machine, fax, audio and video recording, audio- and videoconferencing, e-mail, and other types of computer connectivity and interactivity. Accented films inscribe these devices both in their materiality as communication means and in their semiotic dimensions as icons, symbols, themes, and narrative agents.

The psychosocial study of the telephone began soon after its inception in 1876 (Casson 1910). The meaning of a ringing phone and the anxiety of waiting for a phone call were early subjects (Street 1913), and they continue to intrigue scholars and filmmakers:

> Use of the telephone involves personal risk because it involves exposure; for some, to be "hung up on" is among the worst of fears; others dream of a ringing telephone and wake up with a pounding heart. The telephone's actual ring—more, perhaps, than any other sound in our daily lives—evokes hope, fear, anxiety, joy, according to our expectations. The telephone is our nerve-end to society. (Brooks 1976, 8–9)[26]

Psychologically, telephonic contact has a "near but far" character. It can be as intense as face-to-face interaction, and it can create a "psychological neighborhood" for people who are scattered over a wide area (Aronson 1971). The telephone's most profound social consequence has been its "decentralization of relationships" (Ball 1968, 67) and the breakup of the "multigenerational household" (Brooks 1976, 8). The recent ease in transnational travel, the massive fragmentation of nation-states, and the unprecedented scattering of peoples have globalized the psychological neighborhoods and internationalized the decentralized relationships. For many exiles and émigrés, identity is no longer based solely on territorial belonging or on place of residence; it is also based on maintaining a transnational web of group affiliation by means of the epistolary media. Finally, the telephone can be called a gendered technology because women are its most active users and because the meanings of gender are thereby expressed and practiced (Rakow 1992, 33; Ho 1993, 35).

Simultaneity, Multifocality, and Paranoia

There are fundamental differences between recorded epistolary communication by letters, photographs, faxes, and cassettes and the live and interactive epistolary communication by telephone, videoconferencing, and e-mail. Similar to the films that inscribe letters, those that encode the telephone are nostalgic and highly cathected with affect and desire, to the point that the epistolary device itself is turned into a fetish. The telephone is communitarian and, like letters, is subject to various injunctions, prohibitions, and surveillance. On the other hand, because letters are recorded on paper, they have a materiality and permanence that phone conversations lack, and they can be read, reread, and carried close to heart. Letters convey the fragrance of a loved one, and their tattered shape and tear-stained surface bear the marks of the reader's reactions. While writing and receiving letters are characterized by distance, waiting, and delay, telephoning is instantaneous and simultaneous. Its live ontology obliterates spatial and temporal discontinuity.

Exilic telephonic epistolaries encode copresence and bifocality, which can serve critical functions by juxtaposing incompatible and oppositional discourses, times, spaces, and foci in ways that highlight their differences. In addition, while mediated simultaneity is generally regarded positively for its communitarianism, it has the adverse effect of intensifying the rupture of exile. In Suleiman's *Homage by Assassination*, spatiotemporal simultaneity is signaled by two clocks that hang side by side on the filmmaker's wall. One clock shows the time in New York City (his place of residence), the other tells the time in Nazareth, Israel (his place of birth). The filmmaker is painfully aware of both his own simultaneity and his split existence. In fact, he is paralyzed by them. Perhaps that is why he is silent and withdrawn, helplessly observing the milk boil over in his New York apartment and watching television coverage of the Iraqi missile attack on Nazareth.[27]

Close-Up: Fernando Solanas's Tangos: Exile of Gardel *(1985)*

As a charged, almost fetishized, object, the public telephone is endowed with near-supernatural and magical powers of connectivity in this film. In one sequence the exiles' children, upon returning the receiver to its place, are delighted by a shower of coins pouring out of the telephone's coin return slot and by its ability to speak to them. The film contains many scenes in which the Argentine exiles in Paris attempt telephonic contact with the homeland. A humorous, running narrative is the exiles' attempts to rig a public telephone to call their homeland free of charge. One of them, ironically named "Misery," provides good-humored expertise. In one scene, a group lines up outside a telephone booth in freezing weather in an open-air subway station. Misery tries to establish contact by lowering a coin that is attached to a string into the phone's coin slot. As the task takes too long, the shivering exiles huddle together on a nearby bench—a position they quickly abandon to form a line when another potential phone user approaches. In another scene, Misery tries a newer technique that involves applying electric current from a motor scooter to the phone. This sets the phone on fire, filling the booth with smoke and bringing on the police.

In other scenes, the fragmented exiles are made whole by telephonic connection. Juan Dos, the tango-dy writer in exile, is incomplete without his imaginary double, Juan Uno, in Argentina. Periodically, he attempts to reach Uno by phone to receive inspiration. In a night sequence titled "The Singer's Ghost," Juan Dos and Mariana, in their desperate search for an ending for their performance, go to a public phone booth to call Juan Uno. The phone is not working, however, until a mysterious figure in an overcoat (the ghost of Discépolo, a 1930s tango poet) emerges from the foggy darkness and reaches inside. His touch to the phone magically connects them to Juan Uno in Argentina. "Send me an ending," pleads one of the callers. Although the connection is soon cut, all is not lost. The ghost of Gardel, the famous tango singer, steps out of the mysterious car with his musicians and sings one of his famous exile songs, whose refrain is "I am Buenos Aires, anchored in Paris." In a similar sequence, titled "Alone," Juan Dos is in a public booth on the phone to Argentina, where he learns of his mother's death. This motivates a shot in which he imagines his mother transported to Paris, standing in the snow outside the booth. As he tries to reach her, however, she disappears, leaving him alone. In *Tangos*, the phone acts principally as an instrument for connecting and conjuring. It is also an instrument of both narrative emplotment and human embodiment. Not all accented films, however, are as playful or celebratory about the telephone's affiliative possibilities.

Close-Up: Amir Naderi's Manhattan by Numbers *(1993)*

Despite its overoptimistic ending, Naderi's film is pessimistic about the possibility of human contact—epistolary or otherwise. The film is about a laid-off New York journalist, George Murphy, who is desperately searching for his friend Tom Ryan, from whom he wants to borrow enough money ($1,200) to forestall being evicted. The ring of the telephone sets the plot into motion, introducing the protagonist and providing initial exposition. On the phone are Murphy's wife and child, who never appear in the film (except in a photograph). From their conversation we learn that the family is debt-ridden, Murphy has sold or pawned their valuables, his wife and child have moved out to her father's house, and Murphy has only one day to pay his back rent before eviction. In this opening scene, the phone provides all the necessary plot information and acts as an agent of familial affiliation.

The bulk of Murphy's telephonic attempts, however, are marked by a frustrating failure to make connection. During his despairing odyssey through every socioeconomic sector, from Washington Heights by way of Harlem to downtown, with his tattered little phone book in his hands like a fetish object, Murphy stops by several public phones to call mutual friends for a clue to Ryan's whereabouts. In addition, he walks the streets, rides the subway, and visits stores to inquire about his friend. But Ryan is nowhere to be found, as though he has vanished into thin air. The consensus that emerges is that Ryan

Figure 14. Suicide
in a telephone booth
in Sohrab Shahid
Saless's *Roses for Africa*.

has fallen on hard times and, if found, he will be in no position to help Murphy. Gradually, another point becomes clear: what Murphy has confronted is not just Ryan's present homelessness but, very likely, his own imminent homelessness.[28] In that sense, Murphy is a double of Ryan, similar to the way that Murphy is a double for the filmmaker Naderi, who like Ryan is absent from the film but whose experience shapes it. The narrative of desperation of *Manhattan by Numbers* is driven by fear of homelessness and failure of making contact by the phone, which turns this instrument of affiliation into an agent of alienation. As such, it may be called a "black telephone" film.[29] Murphy's desperation and failure reproduce the feeling structure of many exiles.

Unlike genre films, which use the telephone textually to drive the plot and to motivate editing choices, accented films engage the telephone more socially, symbolically, and magically to situate the diegetic characters' relationship to place (homeland, hostland, diaspora), to time (past, present, future), and to reality (real, imagined, remembered). As a result, although accented films do pack a great deal of drama, anxiety, and fear around the telephone as an epistolic instrument, these emotions usually result from or signal the locatedness, the dislocation, or the utter unlocatability of the diegetic figures, their homelands, or the concept of home.

Although the telephone appears only a few times in Sohrab Shahid Saless's *Roses for Africa* (*Rosen für Afrika*, 1991), it plays a signifying role in the dystopic meandering of its homeless protagonist, from despair to death. Made by an Iranian filmmaker in Germany, this nearly three-hour film charts the saga of Paul, a periodically unemployed German, and his wife, Karola, who comes from a bourgeois family. Instead of highlighting nationality or ethnicity, as many accented filmmakers tend to do, Shahid Saless emphasizes class difference. Every time Paul loses his job, his wife suggests that he seek employment from her father, which Paul refuses to do for fear of losing his independence.

Karola's pregnancy worsens matters, as it becomes a wedge that breaks them apart, sending Karola back to her parents' house. All forms of communication, face-to-face or telephonic, become harder, more bizarre, and finally impossible. In one scene, while his wife and her mother are conversing, Paul picks up the phone in their presence, shouts into it, "I don't want the kid," and puts the receiver down. No one is on the line, and he is not addressing those in the room. In another scene, Karola's father prevents Paul from talking to her by hanging up on him. Paul stays on the line, however, and keeps on talking as though she is there (all the while the dial tone is heard). As Paul becomes a totally unemployable and homeless drunk, and as his psychological condition deteriorates, his longing for an exotic elsewhere—Africa (his *fernweh*)—intensifies. He reaches for the phone one last time, calling Karola, who inquires, "Are you calling from Africa?" He responds, "I love you, I love you." As she begins to talk again, the sound of gunfire is heard. A cut from her reveals the dangling receiver of the public phone, with Paul's collapsed body on the booth's floor. The small wound to his temple looks like a red rose. Then, a bloodied teardrop rolls out of one of his wide-open eyes as the loud sound of a jet taking off—perhaps to Africa—is heard. The telephone fails to unify, or heal, or facilitate communication, or to physically transport. However, it succeeds in bitterly expressing the human desire for contact.

Close-Up: *Atom Egoyan's* Calendar *(1993)*

Like Solanas, Egoyan tends to emphasize the magical and connective capabilities of the electronic epistolary media. His heavy use of these media prompted a *New York Times* reviewer to suggest a new title for *Calendar*: "Sex, Lies, Videotape, Film, Telephone and Answering Machine" (Holden 1993b, 18). Although video-within-film is an integral component of almost all of Egoyan's feature films, indeed, of his style, its use in this film—to document a trip to his ancestral homeland—turns the video into not only a narrative agent but also an exilic epistolary agent. This function of the video and the particular way in which the telephone and the answering machine are used to transmit multilingual conversations across time and space make *Calendar* Egoyan's most epistolary film. This is a breakthrough film for Egoyan because up to this point he had avoided making overtly Armenian films. As such, his most epistolary film is also his most ethnic and exilic and, hence, his most accented film.

Calendar charts a trip to Armenia by a photographer (played by Egoyan) whose assignment is to produce twelve stills of ancient churches for a glossy calendar. The time is the post–Soviet Union era, when Armenia has just become an independent nation and is at war with its neighbor, Azerbaijan. The film does not refer to this historical and political context, but the notion of the threatened homeland informs the film's structure of feelings. Accompanying the photographer are his wife (played by Egoyan's wife, Arsinée Khanjian), who acts as a translator, and a driver who gradually assumes the role of a guide, dispensing historical and architectural information. In time, the wife develops a close relationship with her homeland and with the driver, alienating the husband. As he photographs the various sites for the calendar and videotapes his own interactions, behind the camera, with his wife, on camera, his wife videos what she sees. Eventually, the distraught husband leaves his wife in Armenia and returns to Canada alone, where he begins to deal with the videos of the trip, his memories of it, and the many phone calls from his estranged wife to him and from his own female "escorts" to others.

The videos of the trip and the photographer's recollections of the trip are engaged in a complex narrative game of writing, rewriting, and erasure. The film contains much video footage, none of it from the wife's point of view. She is erased as an owner of filmic subjectivity. What is more, the audience is never sure if the video footage represents the photographer's recollection of the trip or the actual footage he has shot during the trip. As a result, throughout, the film raises questions about the nature of memory and its organic or mechanical production, reproduction, and erasure. In some scenes the video image is frozen, slowed down, or shuttled fast forward or backward as though the photographer is searching the footage for some hidden meaning, memory, or incriminating evidence of his wife's affair with the driver. This act of scrutinizing the epistles is common in amorous epistolary literature, in which letter writers and readers search in the turn of each phrase for signs of intimacy, desire, or betrayal.

Voyeuristic desire, which structures amorous epistles, informs the way the husband's camera records the increasingly intimate relationship of his wife, Arsineé (who uses her own first name in the film), with the driver. This voyeuristic structure positions the spectators to feel as though they are engaged in some illicit, secretive, paranoid, or fetishistic activity. What makes the film even more epistolary is its use of eavesdropping—the aural equivalent of voyeurism—by means of the telephone and the answering machine. After his return to Canada from Armenia, the photographer spends months editing the footage he has collected. In this section of the film, the telephone and the answering machine are used extensively. Arsineé calls her husband twelve times from Armenia to repair their relationship, but, unable to reach him, she leaves increasingly desperate messages on his answering machine. The viewers are made privy to her state of emergency by eavesdropping on her messages. Another form of eavesdropping involves both the photographer and the audience listening in on the telephone conversations of nearly a dozen attractive "foreign" women. As though transformed by the instrument, from a polite English-speaking dinner companion to a passionate "foreign seducer," each of the women carries on a sexually charged conversation in a foreign language with an unnamed, unseen, and unheard person. The women's words, spoken in the languages of the people who have hosted Armenian diaspora communities, are not translated or subtitled. The opacity of the language intensifies the viewers' eavesdropping urges—much as the veil heightens voyeuristic desires.

Figure 15. Epistolary video within film. Arsinée Khanjian films the cinematographer who is filming her and the guide in Atom Egoyan's *Calendar*. Courtesy Alliance International.

The photographer attempts repeatedly to write letters to his wife, but he fails. Although his voice-over reads pieces of what he is writing, these letters, like the archetypal love letters with prohibition against their transmission, are never finished and apparently are never sent. All two-way communications are doomed in this film, which is filled with epistolary media and is built on a hermetic, mazelike narrative structure constructed of twelves: twelve months in the year, twelve pictures for the calendar, twelve phone messages from his wife, twelve months of editing the videos, twelve female escorts, and, finally, twelve months in which Egoyan had to complete the film.[30] As James Quandt notes, this structural straitjacket is in the service of the film's central theme, the impossibility of communication:

> The proliferation of foreign languages and the wife's status as a translator, the reiter-
> ated phrases "what are you saying?" "What do you mean?"; the increasingly staticky,
> scrambled phone line between Armenia and Canada; the letters which the photogra-
> pher repeatedly attempts to but cannot write; all reflect Egoyan's concern with the
> increasing difficulty to "connect" because of the inadequate words and seductive,
> insidious images which form a scrim between us and the world. (1993a: 9)[31]

The failure of the epistolary mechanisms to repair the husband and wife's personal relations signals their failure to reconcile the three modalities of Armenian national identity.

One electronic epistle in Egoyan films that fulfills its communitarian promise is videoconferencing in *Speaking Parts* (1989). The film involves a complex series of obsessive affairs and fantasies between a screenplay writer (Clara) and her dead brother (Clarence); between a woman videographer (Lisa), who loves an actor (Lance), who does not return the love; and between Clara and Lance. These relations are mediated by videotape, videoconferencing, voyeurism, and eavesdropping. Although videoconferencing is used in a number of scenes to link the director of the television-within-the-film to his production staff, its most intense and epistolary use is reserved for the sexual relationship of Clara and Lance. Video is integral to the film's structure of deception and guardedness that governs most of the diegetic relations (Naficy 1997a). It instigates unverifiable identities, slippery relations, and absence—all because of the performativity that it encourages and the slippage it induces between self and other, here and there, and now and then. It also fans a crisis of representation by undermining the viewer's confidence in the video's reality effect.[32] On the other hand, the live ontology, the copresence, and the immersive subjectivity of videoconferencing counter these crises of identity and verifiability.

When not acting, Lance is a member of a hotel's housekeeping staff, where he is assigned to sleep with selected guests. Clara is one such guest with whom he establishes an affair. Pretending to be a casting agent for a film, Clara videotapes Lance's audition for a part that she has written. Later, when Clara has left town, this audition tape becomes a cathected souvenir of that encounter, which she plays back several times. The lovers attempt to maintain from a distance their sexual (and other) relationships by "visiting" each other in video conference sessions. Seated in front of a large video projection screen in the ornate but impersonal corporate conference room of the hotel, Lance engages in conversation with Clara's larger-than-life image. Soon, conversation gives way to simultaneous masturbation. Their desire for one another is heightened by the distance that separates them, the deception in which they both engage, and the interactivity of videoconferencing.

Polish filmmaker Krzysztof Kieslowski made several of his films in France, and his three-part film is based on the colors of the French flag and the French Revolution's slogan: liberty (*Blue/Bleu*, 1993), equality (*White/Blanc*, 1994), and fraternity (*Red/Rouge*, 1994). Appropriately, the film that explores fraternity involves the telephone. It begins with an amazingly literal, fast-paced sequence that demonstrates transoceanic phone links: the phone rings in some unspecified room, causing the camera to suddenly swoop down the phone wire to the wall socket, then enter a fiber-optic cable carrying thousands of color-coded lines, plunge into the ocean, diving with it to the bottom, and finally emerge at the other end of the waters in someone else's place, causing the phone to ring. With this high-speed sequence, Kieslowski establishes the literal connective capabilities of the telephone. The rest of the film examines the metaphoric and moral meanings of both the connections and the missed connections, as well as the nature of the communications that the telephone engenders, particularly between a bitter retired judge and a spirited fashion model.

The ringing of the phone motivates narratological camera moves in several scenes, affects character behavior, and dictates editing cuts. The telephone also connects the various diegetic figures, sometimes causing comfort, sometimes suspicion. The reclusive judge lives in a house in the suburbs of Geneva and seems to draw comfort from regularly eavesdropping on his neighbors' telephones. In his living room, the model hears the tapped phone conversations of various people, including a father who is carrying on a sexual dialogue with a male lover. But the judge and the model are not the only eavesdroppers, for the neighbor's young daughter is also listening to her father's conversation on a second phone in the kitchen.

Since telephonic eavesdropping is unethical and potentially damaging and divisive, the film ultimately opts for the communitarian clarity of face-to-face communication, which leads to a deep friendship between the cantankerous judge and the affable model. The film is suffused with a sense of destiny being fulfilled, of enigmatic coincidences bringing people together, of love and compassion growing among the ruins of civilization. The telephone is a magical instrument that weaves together the narratological and philosophical connective tissues of this film, in the process giving a modern interpretation of the French Revolution's concept of fraternity.

Letter-Films

Unlike exilic film-letters that inscribe letters, telephones, and other epistolary media, as well as acts of writing and reading letters and conversing on the telephone, letter-films are themselves epistles that do not necessarily inscribe epistolary media or epistolary production and reception. Letter-films sometimes address diegetic characters, sometimes real or imagined people outside the text. Similar to film-letters, many letter-films have a calligraphic component, consisting of on-screen text and titles. Their mode of address is usually direct, with the filmmaker the speaking subject, primarily by means of voice-over narration. Several letter-films of Jonas Mekas and Chris Marker are examined in the following close-up sections.[33]

Close-Up: Jonas Mekas

Born in Semeniskiai, Lithuania, in 1922, and a resident of the United States since 1949, Mekas is an exemplar of exilic filmmaking. Many of his films not only depict exile, displacement, and longing but also are exilically accented in their visual style, narrative structure, character location, structures of feeling, mode of production, and Mekas's own exilic status as inscribed in the films. Several of his films, among them *Lost, Lost, Lost* and *Reminiscences of a Journey to Lithuania* (1972), have multifaceted epistolary components and thus can be categorized as both film-letters and letter-films. They are episodic and repetitive and have a postcard structure. Each film builds palimpsestically, forming what amounts to a stack of audiovisual postcards or an accented flip-book.

Mekas spent his childhood on his family's farm, working the fields and taking care of animals. This early experience rooted him deeply in his homeland's rural landscape, becoming the wellspring of his exilic longing and suffusing his poetry and films. During World War II, the Soviet Union annexed Lithuania but was driven off by the German occupying army within two years. In this period, Mekas became what P. Adam Sitney calls a "resistance worker" (1990, 565), writing against both Soviet and Nazi occupations. This activity eventually forced him underground. In 1944, Jonas and his younger brother Adolfas boarded a train with false papers heading for Vienna, where they hoped to attend the university. However, in one of the ironic twists of exilic border crossing, the brothers were taken instead to a forced labor camp near Hamburg because their train had been joined to another that was carrying Polish and Russian prisoners there (James 1992, 5). They escaped from the camp some nine months later but spent the next four years in various European displaced persons camps. This was a period of creative homelessness, spent publishing a literary émigré magazine, stories, and poems, and it ended when the brothers arrived in New York City on October 29, 1949, which Jonas described movingly:

Yesterday, about 10 PM the *General Howze* pulled into the Hudson river. We stood on the deck and we stared. 1352 Displaced Persons stared at America. I am still staring at it, in my retinal memory. Neither the feeling nor the image can be described to one who hasn't gone through this. All the wartime, postwar D.P. miseries, desperations and hopelessness, and then suddenly you are faced with a dream. You have to see New York at night, from the Hudson, like this, to see its incredible beauty. . . . Yes, this is America, and this is the twentieth century. Harbor, and piers ablaze with lights and colors. The city lights merged with a sky that looked manmade. (1991, 293)

After this home-founding journey, he and Adolfas settled in Brooklyn among other refugees and immigrants and began working in factories to earn a living. The opening intertitle of *Lost, Lost, Lost* explains that a week after their arrival, the brothers used borrowed money to purchase a 16mm, hand-wound Bolex camera, with which they began their mammoth project of documenting their own life journeys, those of the Lithuanian exiles pining for an independent homeland, and those of the Beat and counterculture figures in the United States.

Of the films that Jonas Mekas put together based on his decades of uncontrolled and unplanned filming, *Walden* (1964–69), *Reminiscences of a Journey to Lithuania* (1972), *Lost, Lost, Lost* (1949–76), *Paradise Not Yet Lost, or Oona's Fifth Year* (1977), *He Stands in a Desert Counting the Seconds of His Life* (1969–85), and *Letters to Friends . . . from Nowhere . . .* (1997), most directly center on the documentation, narrativization, and dramatization of his exile experience.[34] Most of his films are lengthy projects, both in terms of the time he took to assemble them and the time it takes viewers to watch them. For example, it took Mekas five years to film and edit *Walden* and fourteen years to accumulate the footage and to complete *Lost, Lost, Lost*. Several of his films last up to three hours. These forms of time lag, among other factors, contribute to his films' accent.

Mekas became an influential, even "heroic" (James 1992, 16), figure in the rise and cultivation of the American independent and avant-garde cinema, primarily through his tenacity and his skills at building alternative institutions, at networking, and at critical writing. His most enduring institutions, *Film Culture* magazine, Film-Makers' Cooperative, and Anthology Film Archives, continue to provide venues for discussion, promotion, distribution, screening, and archiving of alternative films.[35] Mekas has followed a doggedly low-key, personal, and artisanal mode of production and distribution that is a critique of the dominant cinema and is highly suitable to the exilic and poetic structures of feeling he has cultivated over the years. He is producer, director, writer, editor, actor, cinematographer (with Adolfas), voice-over narrator, and distributor of his films. Throughout the years he has filmed his and other people's daily lives in an unplanned, spontaneous fashion—in essence, living with the camera on. Both the dailiness of the contents and the fragmented and spontaneous filming give his films a tactile sensibility and a performative expression of deterritorialization. He described his method in a lecture on *Reminiscences*:

> I did not come to it by calculation but from desperation. . . . I mean, I didn't have any long stretches of time to prepare a script, then to take months to shoot, then to edit, etc. I had only bits of time which allowed me to shoot only bits of film. All my personal work became like notes. I thought I should do whatever I can today, because if I don't, I may not find any other free time for weeks. If I can film one minute—I film one minute. If I can film ten seconds—I film ten seconds. I take what I can, from desperation. But for a long time I didn't look at the footage I was collecting that way. I thought what I was actually doing was practicing. I was preparing myself, or trying to keep in touch with my camera, so that when the day would come when I'll have time, then I would make a "real" film. (Mekas 1987, 190)

Such a working method accounts for the long time lag between filming and completion of the films. The distinction between filming and filmmaking is crucial. Each squeeze of the camera shutter-release button produced one random epistolary film note, one postcard, to be added to the stack of visual notes and cards that would one day become a film. This mode of production wove the fragmented biographical life of the filmmaker into its cinematic representation, exilically accenting the resulting films, which Mekas characterized as "small films, films that do not force anything upon you" (1970, 319). But these little, unpretentious films are expansive, celebrating the ordinary moments of life by paring them down to such essential simplicity that they achieve poetic eloquence. Unlike many Third Cinema filmmakers of the 1960s, who wanted to use film and the camera as an offensive weapon, a gun, to demolish the status quo, Mekas regarded his cinema and his camera as a defensive weapon, to be used to celebrate life. As he states in Peter Sempel's *Jonas in the Desert* (1994): "I shot all my diaries out of self-defense . . . in order not to be crushed by the blackness of the city, in order to withstand the attacks on all my senses, on my whole being. Yes, out of self-defense. . . . That is why the stress is on celebration, because that's lacking here, today." For the exiles, filmmaking is empowering because it documents, narrativizes, and celebrates their lives, and it gives their chaotic, fragmented existence a narrative order and a performative coherence.

Mekas's diary films are filled with English-language intertitles of various types, typefaces, layout, and lengths, which turn them into calligraphic letter-films.[36] These serve a number of specific functions. In *Lost, Lost, Lost*, for example, the intertitles identify, describe, and comment on people and places (for example, "Gideon," "on 23rd St. pier DP's arrive in America," "Our life on 13th St. goes on"), journeys taken ("A trip to L.I. with Weinbergs"), passage of time ("Later same year," "The long winter"), various activities ("A picnic"),

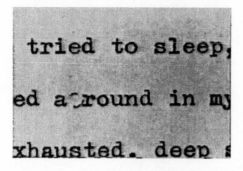

Figure 16. The aesthetics of imperfection. Typographical error in Jonas Mekas's titling in *Lost, Lost, Lost*.

and events ("his first salary," "At the city hall, people gather to protest air raid tests"). Although the titles are usually informational, at times they are emotional, reiterating feelings already expressed by Mekas's own voice-over ("I walked, my heart crying from loneliness"), removing the possibility of narrative suspense.[37]

The printed and typed intertitles have a rough-edged, rough-draft quality (occasionally containing crossed-out words) that reinforces the small, artisanal, improvisational, and "imperfect" aesthetics of the films, emphasizing the notion that we are watching someone's diary in the making.

Most of the intertitles are printed title cards, but some are typewritten. Sometimes intertitles and filmed images alternate in such a way as to create a visual rhythm. An example is a sequence about Mekas's life in Brooklyn in which he alternates shots of the streets with large intertitles typed in capital letters:

WHILE BROOKLYN SLEPT
Camera looks out of a window at a passing elevated train

THRU THE STREETS OF BROOKLYN
Camera pans along the street: people smiling, smoking

THRU THE STREETS OF BROOKLYN
People on the sidewalk talking

THRU THE STREETS OF BROOKLYN I WALKED
Mekas walking along a deserted street

I WALKED MY HEART CRYING FROM LONELINESS

Other calligraphic and rhythmic uses of the intertitles occur during the celebrated "rabbit shit" haiku sequence, in which brief scenes are numbered from one to several dozen in ascending order.

What sutures the silent intertitles and images into a single powerful unit is Mekas's own characteristically sad and sardonic voice-over narration, ambient sounds, and long musical passages. The voice-over's enunciating subject and mode of address in *Lost, Lost, Lost* are complex. Paralleling the complexity and ambiguity of exilic subjectivity, the voice-over shifts between the direct, indirect, and free-indirect discourses. Sometimes the speaking subject is Mekas himself, in first person, while at other times he speaks of himself as "he." This splitting of the pronoun enacts the split subjectivity of the exiles. In addition, Mekas's voice-over often addresses a "you," who can be taken to mean either the diegetic characters, Mekas himself, or the spectators. This extradiegetic address turns the film into more of a letter-film than a film-letter. Despite these complexities, the enunciating source of the calligraphic, epistolary, and voice-over narrations is clearly an empirical individual named Jonas Mekas.

Since, as Mekas told me, he recorded much of his voice-over for *Lost, Lost, Lost* several years after the filming and in reaction to the edited footage, the narration, like the filming, is imbued with intuitiveness, immediacy, and time lag (Naficy 1995b). For example, one intertitle states: "At the city hall people gathered to protest air raid tests." The images that follow show a crowd of demonstrators milling about, speakers addressing them, and the police hauling some of them away. There is an immediacy and present-tenseness both to these documentary shots and to the preceding intertitle; but there is a time lag of years between the filming of the images and the recording of the accompanying voice-over which changes the tense of the film to the past, giving the total work a meditative quality:

> Here I came to this point, to this place. The winds have brought me here and I see you, and I record you. I don't know if I ever understood you, if I ever understood what you stood for, what you went through. But I was there. I was just a passerby from somewhere else, from completely somewhere else, seeing it all with my camera. I recorded it, I recorded it all. I don't know why.

Mekas's halting, sad, and faraway voice addresses the diegetic people philo-sophically from a distance of years, by means of cinema, which itself produces absence. Unlike Marker's nostalgia, which is generally prospective, Mekas's nostalgia is decidedly retrospective. However, Mekas feels nostalgia not just for the referent (the real world, the past, and his homeland) but also for its signifiers and signifieds (the images of the past, the world, and the homeland and what they mean).[38]

There is no strong plot in Mekas's epistolary films, but they do have an evolutionary trajectory that parallels his own life journey as a poet in exile. *Lost, Lost, Lost*, for example, charts the trajectory of his wanderings and evolution in the United States over two decades, beginning with his emigration. The film opens as an exilic odyssey. While the visuals give more or less objective infor-mation about his life in 1949, Mekas's voice-over expresses the feelings of an unwilling journeyman—an exile: "Sing Ulysses, sing your travels. Tell where you have been, tell what you have seen. Tell the story of a man who never wanted to leave his home, who was happy and lived among the people he knew and spoke their language. Sing how then he was thrown out into the world." After this opening, the first two reels concentrate on the Lithuanian exile community in Brooklyn, Mekas's exilic anxieties and utter loneliness, and his move to Manhattan. In reels three and four, he enters New York poetry and film-making communities, and he films the social protest and peace movements of the 1950s and 1960s. Finally, reels five and six chart Mekas's increasing involvement in the avant-garde and independent film and culture movements. The trajectory is chronological and evolutionary. Socially, it chronicles the rise in the United States of political activism and art cinema; personally, it reveals Mekas's decreasing national and ethnic identification with Lithuania and Lithuanian exiles and his increasing identification with America and the avant-garde world. Yet throughout the film he continues to characterize himself as an exile or a displaced person.[39]

In *Walden*, the chronological trajectory continues further. If *Lost, Lost, Lost* presents Mekas as a displaced person who is sad, lonely, and burdened by memories of childhood and homeland, in *Walden* he is a cosmopolitan exile who is freed from them. This suffuses the film with a powerful sense of liberation, experimentation, and exultation. Each of Mekas's epistolary films can be thought of as a stack of postcards, a flip-book, or a letter-film that documents, evokes, and ruminates upon a journey or a road taken that, like the road in the "rabbit shit" haiku poems, has no real end. Exile is nothing if not processual, a never-ending journey. That is why the lack of clear-cut closure is one feature of accented films such as *Lost, Lost, Lost* and *Tangos: Exile of Gardel*.

Close-Up: Chris Marker

Born in 1921 in France, Marker was first a writer and a journalist and then began his film career as an assistant to Alain Renais, who affectionately called him Chris Magic Marker. This characterization acknowledges his fine writing and his highly personal film style. Two key factors seem to have been driving both him and his cine-writing style from early on: his deep interest both in traveling and in "transitional societies," where life is, in his own words, in the "process of becoming history" (quoted in Ellis 1990, 554). He has been a global flaneur for decades, journeying the world and reporting on his observations in a traveling writing style that traverses filmic forms and genres. Without regard for the demands of coherent plot, character psychology, or genre convention, he switches from place to place, from time zone to time zone, from an animated sequence to documentary footage, and from a newsreel to re-created scenes—all the while commenting, in his witty voice-over, on what he sees, creates, and re-creates. His films are unclassifiable, but epistolarity runs through several of them, two of which are discussed here.[40]

Letter from Siberia (*Lettre de Sibérie*, 1958) is both a letter-film and an idiosyncratic, Markerian travelogue so dense, humorous, and intricate as to "defy synopsis" (Durgnat 1985, 1774). Suffice it to say that it contains a collage of poems, folk songs, an animated sequence evoking the discovery of mammoths, an extended tongue-in-cheek television commercial for reindeer products (such as "Horn Flakes"), a sequence deconstructing the expository documentary form, a sequence juxtaposing shots of a raging fire in the Montana mountains with shots of water from a Soviet fire-fighting plane, a song in Russian about Yves Montand, an "imaginary newsreel" on the diversity of Siberian lifestyles and economies, and documentary footage of the diverse cultures, peoples, and animals that inhabit Siberia.

The film poses as a film-letter by Marker from Siberia.[41] It begins with the sound of a typewriter typing the film's opening title, followed by these words on the sound track: "I am writing you this letter from a distant land, its name is Siberia. . . . As I write, my eyes stray along a grove of Russian birch trees. . . ." The typewriter sound and the voice-over narration place the film within the travelogue genre, but the rest of the film deconstructs this traditionally celebratory form.[42] The invocation of a first-person letter writer is repeated several times: "I am writing you this letter from the edge of the world," "I am writing you this letter from the edge of darkness," and the film's ending: "I am writing you this letter from this distant land where charred trees and empty wastelands are as dear to me as her rivers and flowers. Her name is Siberia. . . ." At first, it appears that this autobiographical discourse is authentic, satisfying Lejeun's definition of the autobiographical pact as one in which "the *author*, the *narrator*, and the *protagonist*" are identical (1989, 5). Yet, soon, questions crop up about the authenticity of the film and its author, the identity of its addresser and addressee, and its observance of the autobiographical pact. Who is the film's director, Chris. Marker, whose first name ends with a period? Whatever were the original reasons for Marker to adopt a pseudonym? What are the reasons for its continued use decades later? Does the "I" in the film's voice-over really coincide with Chris Marker, with Christian François Bouche-Villeneuve (his original name), or with some other author?[43] Who is the "you" that is addressed in the film? Do the letters on the sound track predate the film, or were they manufactured specifically for the film?

In an epistolary film it is sometimes impossible, without recourse to extratextual information, to differentiate with certainty between what is forged and what is real. Epistolarity's penchant for creating slippage and doubt must be viewed in the context of the doubling and resistive strategies that many exiles employ in both their lives and their art. For these reasons, epistolarity is structurally a performative genre.

If *Letter from Siberia* were labeled "fiction," some of these questions would not be raised. However, for a "nonfiction" essayistic film that subverts the generic traditions of both fictional and documentary forms, the answer to these questions becomes impossibly convoluted and perhaps even immaterial. One way in which Marker produces these doubling effects is the critical juxtaposition of the documentary footage and voice-over narration, which generate questions about their authenticity. Two examples suffice. The first is the sequence that implies through juxtaposition that the Soviet fire-fighting planes extinguish wilderness fires in the state of Montana. The juxtaposition is critical, partly because of the humor and irony with which it is handled, partly because it raises questions about the ethics of editing together out-of-context documentary footage to achieve narrative flow, and partly because it suggests the kind of cooperation that the cold war hostility between the two "superpowers" would not have allowed at the time. The other example is the celebrated sequence of street traffic and road workers in Iakoutsk, which critiques traditional voice-over documentaries. The visuals are repeated three times, each time with a different voice-over narration that transforms the meaning of the images: the first voice-over is pro-Soviet, the second anti-Soviet, and the third more or less "objective." Lest the spectators think that Marker favors the last version, the voice-over concludes by stating: "But objectivity isn't the answer either."

Marker's films, including *Letter from Siberia*, are so intensely personal and idiosyncratic that, as Ian Cameron put it, "at the end of the film one knows the author as well as the subject" (1962, 14). We learn about the subject, in this case Siberia, not as an objective, factual, or fictional place but as multiple places and cultures experienced, felt, thought about, and signified upon by a specific man, a French man—a man whose pseudonym is Chris Marker. It is only in the way his structures of feeling infuse and his optics defuse his films that one could call them authorial and autobiographical.

Marker's tour de force "travelogue" *Sunless* (*Sans Soleil*, 1982), is ostensibly about a filmmaker's sixteen-year journey (from 1965 to 1981) to a number of exotic and troubled spots in the world (Guinea Bissau, Holland, Iceland, Ile-de-France, Japan, Okinawa, and San Francisco). But this is no ordinary travelogue, for it problematizes the travelogue genre, as well as the authorial and authenticating dimensions of the epistolary form even more intensely than *Letter from Siberia*. The narrator is a woman (Alexandra Stewart), who recounts the travel diary and letters of the globe-trotting filmmaker, a fictional character named Sandor Krasna, who at one point is imagined to be a fictional time traveler from the future (year 4001) visiting our contemporary planet. Since Stewart is reading fictional letters (or are they fictional?) of a fictional filmmaker (or is he?), she herself assumes a fictional identity. All the while, however, there is a perception that the flaneur filmmaker is in some ways Marker himself in disguise. This, in turn, tends to reverse the fictionality of the narrator and the letters. The spectator thus is forced to waver between fictional and nonfictional intelligibility. In this structurally complex and visually beautiful epistolary film, the "I" of Marker's enunciation is at least thrice removed from the text, veiling the author even more than in *Letter from Siberia*. The autobiographical "I" is now hidden in the folds of a woman's voice (Stewart) that reads the words of a male filmmaker (Marker), disguised as a fictional character (Krasna)—neither of whom appears in the film.[44] The ambiguity

Figure 17. Chris Marker's rumination in *Sunless* on voyeurism in the Japanese media and culture.

about the identity of the speaking subject creates within the text and the spectator a profound sense of dislocation. Indeed, this is one accented film whose viewing reproduces the structures of feelings of exilic dislocation itself.

The relationship between narrator and letter writer is even more complex, pushing the intelligibility of the free-indirect style to its limits. Sometimes the narrator summarizes the writer's words; at other times she either tells us that she is reading what he has written or is quoting what he has told her; and at yet other times she comments on what he has said. It is difficult to distinguish her commenting, reading, and quoting one from another. Even when passages are in the first-person singular ("I am writing you this from another world, from a world of appearances"), it is not readily apparent who is meant by the "I."[45] The images, too, are often not sufficiently marked or specified, causing confusion about their geographic location, their diegetic relation with one another, and their enunciating agency. All these elements work together to raise questions about the fictional/nonfictional and narrative/nonnarrative status of the film (Branigan 1992, 211).

Memory provides a key to understanding exile, exilic texts, and Marker's transnational films. *Sunless* is constructed from traces of the filmmaker's memories about the past, the present, and a future yet to come that are synaptically and rhyzomatically recalled and connected. At one point, the narrator quotes the filmmaker as saying: "Think of each memory creating its own legend." Marker's legends are created as each memory trace in his film leads to another trace, resulting in new memories, sights, sites, citations, and insights. These activate "rhyzomatic cuts" from place to place and from image to image. These cuts are driven not by the demands of the plot or by the characters' speech, glance, or desire but by (their) memories. It is as if one is recalling, revisiting, or reworking a place already visited; imagining a place not yet seen; erasing or rewriting what is already experienced; and even reexperiencing Alfred Hitchcock's *Vertigo* and the sites in San Francisco where it was filmed.[46] This is a film primarily of prospective nostalgia, for, as in many postmodern works, the present is looked upon either as a mediated experience or as the past viewed from a future vantage point. At one point, the narrator reformulates Descarte's dictum to say: "I film therefore I am." Later, she adds: "I wonder how people remember things who don't film." The centrality of mediation to remembering points out yet again the difficulty of establishing in postmodernism a real distinction between fact and fiction.

The slippage between writing and reading of epistles and between voice and image tracks, the overlaying of what is experienced with what is remembered or imagined, the peripatetic moves from place to place and from time to time, and the veiling and unveiling of identities beautifully and disturbingly inscribe not only the problems and the problematic in exile of multiple locations and identities and the role of memory in constructing the present but also the modes of exilic expressions and productions—resulting in a textually rich, dazzling, and puzzling film that even more than *Letter from Siberia* questions the various normative regimes of cinema.[47] These strategies transform the epistolary form in *Sunless* from the postcard to the hypercard. If traditional postcards contain limited text and are about known (or at least knowable) locations and identifiable places, the epistolary hypercard contains dense texts that not only point to referents and other texts but also are themselves pointers to other pointers.[48] *Sunless* is a deconstructive film that is not so much about Japan, Guinea Bissau, Iceland, San Francisco, or any other historical places or empirical persons and events (although it is about them also) as it is about itself and its own maker, Marker. This renders the film hermetically self-referential and intersubjectively claustrophobic—yet another feature of the accented style.

The discussion of film-letters, telephonic epistles, and letter-films demonstrates that the epistolary genre of the accented cinema is structurally political, critical, and counterhegemonic. It is so not just because the epistolary films are political, critical, and counterhegemonic in content, which they sometimes are, but also because their structures and narratives defamiliarize in order to retard, impede, or violate both the classical, naturalized styles of mainstream cinemas and the chain of habitual responses and expectations that such cinemas have nurtured in audiences. Defamiliarization involves adopting fragmented, juxtaposed, nonlinear, self-reflexive, repetitive, multivocal, multiauthorial structures and narratives that problematize the dominant ideologies of authority (patriarchy), authenticity (mimesis), and authorship (auteurist parenting). Epistolary defamiliarization blurs the boundaries of gender and genre and emphasizes diegesis instead of mimesis, signification and representation over reflection and presentation, and generic transgression above generic tradition.

5

Chronotopes of Imagined Homeland

THE DIALECTICS of displacement and emplacement are expressed in the space-time configurations of accented films in certain specific ways. Place is a segment of space that people imbue with special meaning and value. It may refer to a country, a region, a town, a village, a particular street, a specific house, or a special nook in a house. It refers not only to a physical entity, however, but also to our relations to it and to our social relations within it. Most of us take for granted our place in the world and come face-to-face with it only when we are threatened with displacement. Thus, placement is tied to its opposite, displacement. Home is bound to horizons of reach and homeland to exile. In addition, since place is also historically situated, displacement and emplacement have a temporal dimension—often linked to the dates of a great homelessness or grand homecoming. For example, the sense of displacement of Palestinians and emplacement of Israelis is strongly tied to the year 1948, in which the state of Israel was created. By marking the onset, or the end, of the exilic trauma, temporal milestones maintain a profound hold on the displaced peoples' psychology and identity. However, such people rarely go from a place of origin directly to a permanent place of exile. Many, particularly refugees and asylees, are forced to stay in intermediary places during their circuitous home-seeking journeys. These transitional places are also part of the idea of place that forms their identities and their chronotopical figuration in accented films.

Mikhail Bakhtin proposed the chronotope (literally, "time-space") both as a "unit of analysis" for studying texts in terms of their representation of spatial and temporal configurations and as an "optic" for analyzing the forces in the culture that produce these configurations. As a unit of textual analysis, cinematic chronotopes refer to certain specific temporal and spatial settings in which stories unfold. Accented films encode, embody, and imagine the home, exile, and transitional sites in certain privileged chronotopes that link the inherited space-time of the homeland to the constructed space-time of the exile and diaspora. One typical initial media response to the rupture of displacement is to create a utopian prelapsarian chronotope of the homeland that is uncontaminated by contemporary facts. This is primarily expressed in the homeland's open chronotopes (its nature, landscape, landmarks, and ancient monuments) and in certain privileged renditions of house and home (see later discussion). The rendition of life in exile, too, initially tends to be just as cathected with dislocatory affect, but it is manifested in dystopian and dysphoric imagining of the contemporary times.[1] This is expressed chiefly in the closed chronotopes of imprisonment and panic (see chapter 6). Finally, the exiles' various journeys, transitions, and meanderings are inscribed in thirdspaces and border chronotopes (see chapter 7). These chronotopes are not just visual but also, and more important, synaesthetic, involving the entire human sensorium and memory.

These chronotopes are the "organizing centers" of the accented films, the places where "the knots of narrative are tied and untied" (Bakhtin 1981, 250). Each film may contain a primary chronotope or multiple "mutually inclusive" chronotopes, which may reinforce, coexist with, or contradict one another. These configurations provide the optics with which we may understand both the films and the historical conditions of displacement that give rise to them. However, as Bakhtin himself warned, we must not confuse the chronotopically represented world with the world outside the text (253). Robert Stam, too, in his study of Bakhtin and cinema, notes that although chronotopes are "correlatable" with historical reality, they are "not equatable" with it because they are always mediated by art (1989: 11). It is in these acts of artistic mediation and transformation that the accent that signifies, and signifies upon, exile and diaspora may be detected.

In their chronotopic inscription of utopia and dystopia, accented films embody both "open" and "closed" cinematic forms. Stylistically, these forms are encoded in the mise-en-scène, filming, and narrative structure. And each form has both a spatial and a temporal dimension. Spatially, the open form is represented in a mise-en-scène that favors external locations and open settings and landscapes, bright natural lighting, and mobile and wandering diegetic characters. In terms of filming, openness is suggested by long shots, mobile framing, and long takes that situate the characters within their open settings, preserving their spatiotemporal integrity. The spatial aspects of the closed form in the mise-en-scène consist of interior locations and closed settings, such as prisons and tight living quarters, a dark lighting scheme that creates a mood of constriction and claustrophobia, and characters who are restricted in their movements and perspective by spatial, bodily, or other barriers. Tight shot composition, static framing, and barriers within the mise-en-scène and in the shots' foreground suggest closedness.

Temporally, the open films are imbued with structures of feeling that favor continuity, introspection, and retrospection. The present is often experienced retroactively by means of a nostalgically reconstructed past or a lost Eden. This is in line with Fredric Jameson's assertion that massive displacement and globalization have forced us to experience and express time as loss (1989). It is as though the experiences of here and now are not sufficient or real enough by themselves unless they are somehow projected as loss or are mediated by memory and nostalgia. The closed temporal form is driven by panic and fear narratives, in essence, a form of temporal claustrophobia, in which the plot centers on pursuit, entrapment, and escape. In most accented films, mise-en-scène carries a heavier narrative burden than editing, for it conveys and embodies displacement and placement in its configuration of space and in the manner in which characters occupy the space or are occupied by it.

These open and closed characterizations are relative and mutually inclusive, as many of the films contain both forms. Each form may be distinguished not only by its distinct utopian and dystopian feeling structures but also by its specific relationship to style. According to Louis Giannetti, the open form is in general recessive, appears to be spontaneous and accidental, and can be associated with realism. On the other hand, the closed form is conspicuous, appears to be self-conscious and deliberate, and may be associated with formalism. In closed forms, mise-en-scène gives the impression that space and time are predetermined by an agency external to the diegesis. As a result, the closed form tends to emphasize control, distance, and unfamiliarity, while the open form tends to connote immediacy, intimacy, and familiarity. Philosophically, open forms tend to suggest freedom of choice, while closed forms imply destiny and the futility of the will (1990, 67–71).

The thirdspace chronotope involves transitional and transnational sites, such as borders, airports, and train stations, and transportation vehicles, such as buses, ships, and trains. Border crossing and journeying are narratives that prominently engage these sites and vehicles. Epistolarity also partakes of this form, as it facilitates human interaction across spatiotemporal zones. It must be emphasized, however, that the connotations of the open, closed, and transitional forms do not reside inherently or permanently in these forms; their significance and meaning must be derived from the contexts in which they are deployed. That is why in the sections to follow it will be seen that closed spatiality (such as imprisonment or housebondage) sometimes is interpreted by the accented films as entrapment and other times as safety and liberation.

Film genres are often spatially overdetermined by gender and sexuality. Traditionally, melodrama is associated with women, the feminine, the domestic space, and with "emotion, immobility, enclosed space, and confinement." Such a configuration is postulated in opposition to a masculine space that is outside and characterized by "adventure, movement, and cathartic action" (Mulvey 1992, 55). If in the classical Hollywood cinema the feminine space is encoded mostly in the melodrama genre, the masculine space is found primarily in the American Western. Every social formation, such as exile and diaspora, creates its own space in its imaginative productions. The space that exile creates in the accented cinema is gendered, but not in the binary fashion of the classical cinema. And if gender is coded dyadically, the poles may be reversed. For example, the outside, public spaces of the homeland's nature and landscape are largely represented as feminine and maternal. The—inside, enclosed spaces—particularly those in the domestic sphere—are also predominantly coded as feminine. In that sense, all accented films, regardless of the gender of their directors or protagonists, are feminine texts. These films destabilize the traditional binary schema of gender and spatiality because, in the liminality of deterritorialization, the boundaries of gender, genre, and sexuality are blurred and continually negotiated. Moreover, spatial configuration in these films is driven not only by gender and by structures of identification and alienation but also by eruptions of memory, nostalgia, and the longing to return and by the politics and poetics of acculturation and resistance.

If the emotional high and low points of many classic Hollywood melodramas are staged against the vertical axis of the staircase, where the staircase becomes the site for not only the presentation but also the representation of emotional extremes (Elsaesser 1992, 528), in accented films it is the open, closed, and border chronotopes that express and encode the (melo)drama of (dis)placement, liminal subjectivity, and hybridized identity.

Homeland's Utopian Chronotopes: Boundlessness, Timelessness

Exilic deterritorialization necessitates an enhanced stress on territoriality, often in the form of emphasis on nature and the natural order—what Mikhail Bakhtin called the "idyllic chronotope," consisting of the love idyll, family idyll, and agricultural idyll. All of these appeal to the unity of an ancient complex and a folkloric time, which is expressed in the special relationship that space and time have within the idyll. This relationship is

> an organic fastening-down, a grafting of life and its events to a place, to familiar territory with all its nooks and crannies, its familiar mountains, valleys, fields, rivers and forests, and one's own home. Idyllic life and its events are inseparable from this concrete, spatial corner of the world where the fathers and grandfathers lived and where one's children and their children will live. This little spatial world is limited and sufficient unto itself, not linked in any intrinsic way with other places, with the rest of the world. But in this little spatially limited world a sequence of generations is localized that is potentially without limit. (Bakhtin 1981, 225)

In the chronotopes of the idyll, all temporal boundaries are blurred thanks to the unity of place. The idyllic chronotopes of homeland take a number of forms in the accented cinema.

Nature

In the postcolonial and post–cold war periods under study here, in many parts of the world the ownership of land and of national territory was an object of frequent and ferocious dispute among warring groups, nations, and superpowers. In fact, such disputes were key instigators of the displacement and emigration of massive numbers of peoples, including many filmmakers. It is no wonder, then, that accented films are preoccupied with the chronotopic construction of both nature and nation. Faced with the destruction of the homeland, the erosion of former structures and authorities of home (such as language and culture), and the impossibility of return, many exiles seem to turn to the structural authority and certainty that only nature seems capable of providing: timelessness, boundlessness, reliability, stability, and universality.

Traditionally, people have considered nature and wilderness to be the sacred space-time of uncontaminated spirituality, contrasting it with the profane space-time of culture and civilization. Nature, however, also connotes a place of adventure and danger. This complex relationship may stem from the rise of agriculture that tamed the wilderness. While the defeat of wilderness was a mark of human progress, wilderness "became a symbol of an earthly paradise, the place of before the fall where people lived in close harmony and deep sympathy with nature" (Shorts 1991, 10). Since then, various phenomena of modernity and late modernity have compounded that originary disruption, intensifying the desire to "return" and to become whole again. Third World civilizations, which are closer to that primordial agricultural epoch—and from which many accented filmmakers hail—maintained until recently a fundamentally organic and direct relationship to nature, land, and tradition. This relationship is informed not only by the collective memory of the land and nature long lost to wars, modernity, urban sprawl, environmental degradation, and exile but also by their own phenomenological experiences of it as former villagers, farmers, and tribespeople.[2] What is substituted for the impossibility of return and reunion is the staging of a metaphoric reunion with nature and a return to imaginatively constructed categories that represent prelapsarian wholeness, such as imagined communities (Anderson 1983), invented traditions (Hobsbawm and Ranger 1983), or foundational myths of a pure, original people, or folk (Hall 1996).

Close-Up: Gregory Nava's El Norte (1983)

This film was directed by Gregory Nava, a Chicano filmmaker of Mexican-Basque ancestry, and produced by his partner and wife, Anna Thomas, whom he met at the UCLA film school. It is about a Mayan Indian brother and sister (Enrique and Rosa) who escape government terror in Guatemala to reach the United States (El Norte). The story takes place during the Guatemalan civil war, which came to an end in December 1996 after thirty-six years of fighting between "an American-armed military and leftist guerrillas that killed more than 100,000 people and forced a million more into exile or out of their homes" (Rohter 1997, 6). The film's three acts are identified by on-screen titles and distinguished by their mise-en-scène and filming style. The first act, "Arturo Xuncax," begins with the chronotopes of the Guatemalan nature and agricultural idyll, consisting of verdant mountains and valleys shrouded in timeless fog and mystery that nurture the Mayan Indians of San Pedro who work the coffee fields. This primordial chronotope becomes a cathected image, a fetish, that Enrique and Rosa, in the course of their increasingly difficult journey north and settlement in the United States, fondly remember to solace themselves.[3] What is cathected to it is not just their memories of their homeland's nature but also that of their culture: their Mayan traditions, rural way of life, family gatherings, labor in coffee fields, and antigovernment resistance. Nava's insistence on such associations with nature gives the film an "exotic strangeness," as though Indians are "from another time and space" (Fregoso 1993, 106).

After thus establishing the agriculture idyll, *El Norte* concentrates on the close-knit Xuncax family, talking naively around the dinner table about the good life in the United States, as gleaned from *Good Housekeeping* magazine ads and tourist tales. This family idyll is soon disrupted, however, when one night soldiers attack a secret land-rights political meeting, which results in the death of some peasants, including Arturo, the disappearance of others, including his wife, and the eventual escape into exile of Enrique and Rosa. Throughout the film, Rosa situates herself by acts of imagination and remembrance: she dreams about or remembers the Guatemalan nature and the Mayan culture, and in "dream realist" scenes she recalls her father in a lush garden and her mother with fluttering butterflies.[4] These scenes, which are glorified by diffused lighting and aestheticized cinematography, interrupt the realist flow of the narrative, forcing viewers to experience time, space, and causality in a nonlinear fashion. In some ways, this narrative style replicates the bifocality of displaced people, who live in empirically and symbolically different spaces simultaneously.

Rosa's poetic recollections disavow the violence of her homeland and the disruption of exile, suturing her nostalgically to timeless nature, immemorial Mayan traditions, and deep family roots. However, by attaching female subjectivity to poetic imagination and male subjectivity to realism, the film reproduces the conservative politics of gender, which associates women with nature and culture and men with action and adventure.

The film's second act, "El Coyote," charts the siblings' passage through Mexico and the process by which they obtain help to cross the border through an abandoned sewer tunnel. If the first act is marked primarily by openness and immensity, the second is characterized by closedness and claustrophobia, condensed in the powerful episode of the crawl through the dark, rat-infested tunnel (see chapter 6). The third act, "El Norte," is devoted to the life and times of Enrique and Rosa as illegal immigrants, working in Los Angeles restaurants and garment factories, respectively. With the exception of the dream realist scenes, the mise-en-scène and filming style of the third act follow the realist conventions of the classical cinema, charting the transformation of the couple's dream into nightmare. Toward the end, Rosa is hospitalized with incurable typhus, contracted from the rats in the sewer. Rosa's deathbed musings point up the profound homelessness with which many exiles live: "In our own land, we have no home. They want to kill us. There's no home for us there. In Mexico there's only poverty—we can't make a home there either. And, here, in the north, we aren't accepted. When will we find a home, Enrique? Maybe when we die we'll find a home." The family unit, large and extended at the film's beginning, is now reduced to just one member. And he is left for now without a house, a home, or a homeland. This is reinforced by the film's shocking last image: against a background of the idyllic Guatemalan landscape, Arturo's severed head dangles from a tree, closing the possibility of return for Enrique. The swinging severed head revises the harmonious meaning of the background landscape and tradition that the film had initially posited. These two bookend scenes of harmony and horror, utopia and dystopia, together form the nature chronotopes of the homeland in *El Norte*.

The film is politically conservative not only because of its gender politics but also because it posits the Indians only as victims. By couching their story in the "emotional cliché's of melodrama," the film essentially urges toleration, not confrontation and change (List 1989, 30). However, political conservatism and ambivalence are not limited to this film, for these characterize the hybridity of the accented cinema.

Armenian filmmakers Artavazd Pelechian and Don Askarian also tap into the chronotope of the homeland as a primordial nature idyll. Pelechian's *Seasons* (*Les Saisons*, 1982) is a fluid and lyrical agricultural idyll, a genre that conjoins "the human life with the life of nature" (Bakhtin 1981, 226). Born in Leninakan in 1938, Pelechian studied mise-en-scène at the All-Union State Institute of Cinematography (VGIK) in Moscow and began his filmmaking career by making documentaries. He developed a theory of "counterpoint montage," involving both sound and image, which he practiced in his films, including *Seasons*. Made before the breakup of the Soviet Union and the independence of Armenia, the film associates Armenia entirely with nature, landscape, water, and the traditions of peasants, shepherds, and cowherds.[5] In endlessly repeated slow-motion shots, exquisitely photographed, huge bales of hay are pulled down the steep hills by men who run in front of them as fast as they can to avoid being run over by the speeding cargo. Elsewhere, man after man slides down narrow, snowy, mountain chutes, each carrying a sheep in his lap, trying to protect it. Sometimes men and animals roll over each other, crash into one another, and pile up at the bottom like carefree children at play. In other slow-motion sequences, men and sheep are rolled over, crashed into one another, and carried away by tumultuous, powerful river rapids. Our first impression is that they are drowning. But as they bob up and down, disappear and reappear, it becomes clear that we are witnessing the intimate conjoining of the lives of peasants, animals, and nature in the relentless tide of history.

There are also moments of human intimacy during a lengthy traditional wedding that are aestheticized by slow-motion and close-up cinematography: raised hands waving in the air, jubilant faces of dancers, people hugging and kissing, a white bow being tied to the bride's hair, a wedding ring being placed on her finger, bride and bridegroom dancing. These features of the family idyll, together with those of the agricultural idyll, bring us as near as possible to achieving on film the traditional antiquity and folkloric time. The film has no dialogue or narration, as though fearing that words may violate such antiquarian imagining, contaminating the unsullied homeland and rendering it contemporary. Only orchestral music accompanies the visuals, which are themselves organized and repeated like musical movements.

Pelechian's "counterpoint" style, like musical composition, develops themes, variations, leitmotifs, and tempos of various kinds (Niney 1993, 87–88). By orchestrating the music and by orchestrating the musical uses of visuals, he recreates the rhythm of the lived world of his homeland. In so doing, he creates from it an aestheticized chronotope, an exilic opera about a prelapsarian rural utopia.

A dominant chronotope in Don Askarian's haunting and enigmatic *Avetik* (1992) is that of Armenia as a ruin and as a rural and natural landscape. Born in 1949 in Stepanakert, Nagornoy-Karabagh, Askarian studied art and history in Moscow and worked as assistant director and film critic in the early 1970s. After he was released from a two-year stint in a Soviet prison, he emigrated in 1977 to Germany, where he has been making documentary and fiction films. Like a storyteller, he relates how he came to make *Avetik*:

> One day my doorbell rang. I opened the door. A jovial young man introduced himself: Otto Namman, Homicide Squad of the Berlin Police. He gave me a black notebook with red corners (made in China). It belonged to an Armenian emigrant N.N., who had recently been murdered in Berlin with seven unusually precise ax blows. It turned out that he had bequeathed his diary to me. After reading it I decided to shoot *Avetik*. We hardly knew each other. (quoted in *Avetik*'s press kit)

Askarian filmed *Avetik* during the Armenian civil war in the late 1980s, at huge personal and financial risk. By making the film's protagonist an Armenian documentary filmmaker named Avetik who lives in German exile, Askarian integrated himself and his own exile into that of the owner of the diary— becoming the subject of the film. The film contains Avetik's reaction to the devastation of his homeland and his reflections on Armenian history, his childhood, and his coming to terms with love and with anti-Armenian racism in Germany. These descriptions do not do justice to the experience of watching the film, however, as *Avetik* is a visual poem that contains a massive amount of silence during which viewers are drawn into the diegesis by the mesmerizing images of landscape and destruction.

As in the work of many accented filmmakers, nature is feminized and maternalized, a nationalist project in whose support women's bodies are pressed into service: naked women walking in the orchards, a girl's naked body seems to have sprouted plantlike limbs, a woman tenderly suckles a motherless lamb that is lost in a church. The Edenic symbiosis is interrupted by human and natural disasters, such as the Turkish genocide of Armenians in 1915, the Azerbaijanis' killing of Armenians in the 1980s, and the devastating earthquakes of 1989.

While Armenia is represented as feminized nature, the German exile is defined by the close quarters of Avetik's Berlin apartment, whose psychological space is reduced even further by the sudden shaking and roaring of passing trains. Like many exiles, he is bifurcated: physically in exile, he is mentally and emotionally in the homeland—even if it is a ruin. This makes for a very limited life in exile. As Askarian notes: "Avetik himself would not use the word 'live,' he would say: 'I have an address in Berlin'" (quoted in *Avetik*'s press kit). Although both Avetik the diegetic director and Avetik the real life filmmaker are homeless, they are both emplaced by the narrative home away from the homeland, which they create.

Mountain, Monument

In accented films, certain aspects of nature and culture, such as mountains, ancient monuments, and ruins, are used as such powerfully cathected collective chronotopes that they condense the entire idea of nation—particularly if the nation's status is in dispute, as with Palestinians, Kurds, and Armenians. In this configuration, the mountain stands not as a barrier but as a bridge that consolidates the national idea and heals the ruptures of exile. In Hanna Elias's *The Mountain* (*Aljabal*, 1991), it serves to bring two lovers together. Made by a young Palestinian filmmaker trained at UCLA, *The Mountain* is about a teenage girl named Insaff, who is being pressed by her debauched father to marry a London-educated lawyer she does not want. She prefers a local boy who, like her, works the fields nearby and sells the produce in the street markets. She is caught between dependence and independence, dread and desire. Her grandmother becomes the catalyst for her decision to elope, and the mountain becomes the site on whose slopes the drama of elopement and its deadly punishment unfolds. What makes this mountain the film's emotional centerpieces is the memory of Insaff's mother, who years earlier had eloped and had been shot dead on it by her own relatives as punishment. The film intercuts Insaff's escape into the mountain with the grandmother's pleas to it: "Let her reach her love safely, only you have the power to unite them." To appease the mountain, she offers herself as a sacrifice: "Take me instead, my mountain, take me instead and set her free."[6]

The mountain also expresses nostalgia for an authentic "world before" and the desire to return to that world. In the exilically accented films, the mountain is usually posited as feminine and maternal, and the return to it as reunion with homeland, motherland, and mother. The nostalgia for the monument, on the other hand, is posited as masculine and heroic, making the return to it less enveloping and nurturing. The popularity of the "mountain film" genre in Germany (*bergfilm*) in the Weimar period and its continued reverberation in the works of such contemporary cinéastes as Werner Herzog may partly be attributed to this enduring nostalgia for the times and places of before—before civilization ruptured humankind's intimate and direct relation to nature.[7] The accented films that inscribe mountains are not mountain films as such, but both types tap into the tactile dimensions of identity and longing by means of the mountain. In this sense, Eric Rentschler's analysis of the appeal of the German mountain films resonates with the accented films. According to him, the mountain films' appeal "lay in primal nature explored with advanced technology, in pre-modern longings mediated by modern machines. This is a genre where visceral and visual pleasure meet, where the haptic and the optic are of a piece" (1990, 152). Accented films, like mountain films, mobilize ancient sentiments and collective longings around the mountains, as will be seen in the following case studies. Mountains historically have been linked to spirituality; indeed, they are the sites of religious sight and insight. As Simon Schama notes, from Chinese paintings to Christian narratives and from Mount Eden to Mount Sinai to Mount Ararat, sacred mountains equate altitude with beatitude, mediating between the terrestrial and the celestial (1995, 411–17). Indeed, all major world religions and ancient civilizations associate their inception with a sacred mountain—Mount Sinai in Lebanon, Zion in Israel, Hira in Saudi Arabia, Elborz in Iran, Ararat in Turkey, Olympus in Greece, Fuji in Japan, Kailas in Tibet, and T'ai Shan in China (Bernbaum 1990). These associations serve not only religious but also nationalistic and exilic discourses and politics. Mountains and monuments, like nature, are chronotopes not only of an external geographic landscape but also of inner psychological and spiritual landscapes.

Close-Up: Nizamettin Ariç's A Song for Beko
(Klamek ji bo Beko/Ein Lied für Beko, *1992*)

Mountains play a significant part in this film by a Kurdish filmmaker from Turkey who lives in Germany, where about half a million Kurds live (Kinzer 1998). According to Ariç, this is the first Kurdish-language feature fiction film ever by a Kurd. Born in 1956 in Agri (a town at the foot of Mount Ararat) in Turkey, Ariç began his career in the entertainment business, first as a singer and actor for radio and television, then as a leading film actor. In the early 1980s, during a live musical concert in Agri, attended by town officials, he was arrested for performing a popular Kurdish love song requested by the audience (public speaking and performing in Kurdish were illegal). He was released two days later, pending the civil court's decision on charges of fomenting Communist propaganda, Kurdish separatism, and anti-Ataturk ideas. In the meantime, a military coup toppled the civilian government, and Ariç's case was forwarded to a military court. At this point, he was advised to leave the country, which he did. Since 1981 he has been living in exile in Berlin, where he was granted political asylum in 1984.[8] Unable to return to his homeland, Ariç filmed all of the scenes that occur in Turkey (some 90 percent of the film) across the border in Armenia, against the same mountain range that had formed the backdrop of his childhood world.

The film is told retrospectively, from the viewpoint of a Beko, a Kurd (played by the filmmaker) who lives in exile in a concrete- and steel-choked Berlin. Homesick for his family, he begins a letter home that transports us to the Kurdish areas of Turkey before Beko's exile. His exilic saga is set into motion when his younger brother, Çemal, escapes the draft by joining the Kurdish *peshmerg* guerrillas fighting for an independent homeland. Beko's search for his brother takes him across the Euphrates River into Syria and across the mountains into Iraq, where he camps out for some time with a group of displaced Kurds.

However, this is no ordinary squalid, overcrowded refugee camp; rather, it is a nurturing, pastoral idyll of green meadows surrounded by protective mountains—a veritable authentic world before for the exilic Kurds. Here Beko befriends a group of strong women and determined children, including a smart girl named Zinê, with whom he forms a strong bond. Life unfolds against the magnificent backdrop of mountain ranges that are lovingly filmed in early or late daylight to give them a warm glow. On a dark, cloudy day, the voice of an old woman singing a Kurdish lullaby echoes against the mountains, interweaving Kurdish landscape and language. In ethnographically rich sequences, women, men, and children shear sheep, make wool, bake bread, gather firewood, haul water, build walls, and learn to read and write the banned Kurdish language. Periodically, the sound of gunshots beyond the hills or of fighter jets flying overhead disturbs the pastoral idyll, reminding the Kurds of the cause of their displacement. The slow pacing and the long shots of these camp scenes that integrate the characters into their natural landscape and daily routine, and the characters' unpretentious acting and dialogue (most of them are amateurs), reproduce both a Kurdish structure of feelings and the rhythm of their rural and seminomadic life. Audiences may become impatient with the film's pace, but it is here, in the daily routines of a displaced persons camp, that Beko's eyes open up to the full force of his culture and identity.

In a pivotal scene, he and the children flee from the Iraqi fighters into a cave, where Ariç learns about the children's past. Emboldened by the security of the enclosed mountain space, each child, in quick succession, tells Beko his or her family history of victimhood and resistance against their oppressors.[9] Because of his camp experience, Beko's search for his brother becomes less important than helping the displaced Kurds return to their valley-nested village. This leads to a harrowing sequence that re-creates the real-life chemical gassing of the Iraqi Kurds in 1987–88 by Saddam Hussein's ruthless military.[10]

Figure 18. Kurdish rebel (played by Nizamettin Ariç) rescues Zinê from Iraqi chemical attack in his *A Song for Beko*. Courtesy Nizamettin Ariç.

From a position high above the village, Beko watches helplessly as Iraqi helicopters spew an orange cloud of poison gas that envelops the valley below. Horrified, he rushes down. As the camera hurries along with him in a silent, long, handheld sequence, everywhere he turns he encounters the dead bodies of the women and children he has gotten to know. Silence is used effectively in this and several other key scenes to emphasize gravity. Conveniently, only Zinê appears to be alive. Beko swoops down, sweeps her up, and runs out into the mountains. In the next scene in a Berlin hospital, Zinê is alive but is suffering from eye damage. In the film's closing scenes, Beko learns that his brother was captured, forced into serving in the Turkish army against his own people, and killed by a young Kurd defending his village. Beko's home village is wiped out, leaving him with nothing to go back to but the sweet memories of the mountains and the Kurdish life they nurtured. Despite the sharp contrast between the impersonal urban cityscape of Germany and the intimate natural landscape of Kurdish homeland, *A Song for Beko* is not dystopic like other Turkish exile films, for Beko must now fulfill his newfound responsibility to care for the injured and orphaned Zinê in an inhospitable foreign land.

Like many exilic directors, Ariç performed multiple functions in his film: director, lead actor, composer and player of the film's score, set designer, prop man, and cowriter of the screenplay with Christine Kernich, his partner and wife. Funded by commercial, civic, and state agencies in Germany, the film's budget was 1.2 million deutsche marks (some $650,000). Ariç complained that, lacking an indigenous film industry and film culture, the Kurds expect too much from a single Kurdish film: "They want it to be documentary, fictional, tender, and action-packed all at the same time" (Naficy 1997b). Such an exaggerated expectation is not so much a Kurdish proclivity as it is an exilic tendency.

Rural landscapes and mountains, particularly Mount Ararat, figure large in Armenian accented films. Atom Egoyan's *Calendar* (1993) uses the chronotopes of Mount Ararat, ancient church monuments, and rural landscape as privileged markers of Armenian national and spiritual identity (there is only one urban scene in the entire film). The film opens on a long shot of a car slowly pulling up a steep hill crowned by a church, framed against a majestic blue sky. The visual is accompanied by an ancient plowing song and the tolling of the church bells reverberating in the valleys beyond. The plowing song, the bells, the mountain, and the ancient church—so old as to have become a natural phenomenon—mark Armenia as natural, rural, spiritual, and in the past tense, close to folkloric time.

Despite Egoyan's postmodernist ironic attempts to undermine all authentic formations in the film (including love, family, and nation), such shots of nature, mountain, and monument express a deep nostalgia for the prelapsarian unity of nature and nation and an underlying sadness at the separation of the signs from their referents. More, because almost all the ancient churches in the film—that date back some ten centuries—are in ruins, there is a profound sense of loss. All these are powerful reminders of the exilic gap that never closes. It is to disavow this gap that the images of ruins are turned into sacred icons, fetishes, and commodities that are circulated not only in the film *Calendar* but also in the Armenian wall calendars, pop music, music videos, and television made in diaspora. Other exilic groups also engage in such practices of semiotic healing.

In a following sequence, *Calendar* brings up Mount Ararat, as seen through the windows of the cab that is taking the photographer, his wife, and their guide to the sacred sites. Ararat is an enduring emblem of Armenian national identity, to the point that even during the Soviet era—when icons of national consciousness were generally removed from official insignias of the Soviet republics—Ararat remained on the flag of Soviet Armenia.[11] To my question "If you were to think of Armenia, what landscape comes to mind?" Egoyan answered:

Well, the most obvious one, the most fetishized symbol is Mount Ararat. It's incredible because Ararat is not even within the Armenian territory (it is located across the border in Turkey). . . . And yet if you go up to Yerevan, on a clear day, it has an almost surreal presence. It is quite strange. It's as though it's pasted to the city. It's so large. And yet it's in the forbidden territory. (Naficy 1997a, 219)

The shot of the snowcapped Ararat is brief, but the mountain peak, this fetishistic marker of lost paradise, is unmistakably there in the center of the frame as trees and branches streak by the speeding car. The occupants of the taxi appear oblivious to the mountain's presence outside their window, but the filmmaker is vigilant and keeps Ararat centered, holding the shot long enough for us to notice it.[12] The film further emphasizes the psychologically redemptive identification of Armenia with the agricultural idyll by repeatedly lingering on a flock of sheep. In the same way that the churches were built only on sacred ground, the photographer is very careful about the placement of his camera tripod, as if that will ensure the transfer of the earth's sacred energy to the shot and thereby to the calendars that will grace the Armenian homes in diaspora.

The fascination with the Ararat chronotope is encoded in Ara Madzounian's twenty-minute film *The Pink Elephant* (*Vartakuyn Peegh*, 1988). Under the fierce shelling of the Lebanese civil war, an Armenian troupe in Beirut rehearses a play in the basement of a theater. Periodically, the film returns above ground, showing news photographs of gutted buildings and mangled bodies. Meanwhile, as the bombs fall nearer the rehearsal hall, the troupe is forced into a dark shelter below, where members play chess, read newspapers, and argue about the meaning(lessness) of life, artistic creation, and Armenian "neutrality" in the civil war—a war that does not directly involve them but engulfs them nonetheless. A giant painting of an idyllic Mount Ararat on the wall shows a river flowing from the mountain that nourishes the cypress trees downstream. The debate intensifies, and a nearby bomb shakes the shelter, opening a leak in a water pipe above the painting. As the actors rise from the ground, a sight transfixes them—ending the film: the dark liquid that is dripping on the painting (water? blood?) is gradually washing it away.

With this image, Madzounian poses the possibility of Ararat losing its hold on the Armenians in diaspora as a unifying chronotope. When he was growing up in Lebanon and the United States, the image of Ararat was found on nearly every wall in every Armenian home. His postindependence visit to Armenia, however, showed the falseness of that unified construction:

I have gone to Armenia since its independence three times, but it does not feel like home to me. My home is Lebanon. When I went to Lebanon, after the civil war and after a nine-year absence, I felt strange for only a couple of days. Soon, I felt comfortable and at home again. My culture is a hybrid of Lebanese and Armenian diaspora cultures which is very different from the culture of the Armenians in Armenia. But we were raised with the notion of getting back home, and that was a very emotional notion for me. In my first visit to Armenia, I realized that diaspora Arme-

nians are very different and I cut my umbilical cord from Armenia. I felt very free. I
am not a nationalist with attachment to any particular country; my attachment to
Lebanon is based on my childhood memories there. (Naficy 1997d)

The Pink Elephant's story may be regarded as an allegorical reworking of its
maker's life and career. Madzounian was born in 1953 to an Armenian family
in Beirut, where he began acting in theater as a teenager. With the start of the
civil war, he emigrated to the United States to pursue filmmaking, enrolling
at UCLA, where he made *The Pink Elephant*. Like many accented filmmakers,
he performed multiple functions in this $11,000 film: he produced, cowrote,
directed, and edited. He made *Land without Graves* (1990), a fifty-five-minute
documentary, for his master's thesis. Filmed in Armenia and underwritten by
Czech television, this film is essentially a history of the Armenian people that
emphasizes their massacre in Turkey in 1915 and in Nagarno-Karabagh in the
1980s. It also recounts the Armenian armed struggles for self-determination,
focusing on the importance of heroic martyrdom, religious traditions, and historical monuments—such as churches and "cross-stones" (crosses made of
stone), which hold considerable symbolic value for Armenians.

Home Land

Contemporary historical and political factors other than exile have made the
issues of land and territory important. In the Middle East, for example, territorial ownership is the key issue in the Palestinian-Israeli dispute, which has
been kept in the forefront of both sides' consciousness by various wars and
mutual atrocities. These have resulted in the displacement of nearly half of the
5.2 million Palestinians as refugees, exiles, guest workers, and émigrés, often
to inhospitable lands near and far. Lebanon has been home to some 350,000
refugees who live in some fifteen camps.[13] These camps are often bounded
places designed to "contain, manage and re-invent the identities of refugees."
At the same time, they are important sites of refugee resistance (Peteet 1996,
3); The shared suffering experienced there promoted solidarity among refugees
from diverse places.

Not all Palestinians were dispersed into external exile. Many remained in
Israel or in the Occupied Territories under Israeli control (these are called
the "remnant"). Barbara Parmenter has identified three symbolic landscapes in
Palestinian exilic literature, which are also inscribed in Palestinian films: desert,
city, and refugee camp (1994, chap. 4). A number of films, especially much of
the work of the documentary team of Mai Masri and Jean Chamoun, center
on the Palestinian and Arab refugees in Lebanon. Rashid Mashrawi's nonfiction films, particularly *Waiting* (*Intizaar*, 1995) and *Curfew* (1993), forcefully
deal with Palestinian life in the Gaza refugee camps.[14] An increasing number

of Palestinian exiles in Europe and North America, Michel Khleifi among them, are making films that center on Palestinian life in Israel, in the Occupied Territories, and in the Palestinian diaspora. These are all part of the corpus that forms what might be called the Palestinian "national cinema"—one that is uniquely driven by exile.

Despite the scattering of Palestinians to different places, the Palestinian identity is often constructed vis-à-vis an original place, that is, Palestine before the creation of Israel. Thus, as Edward Said has noted, for the refugees and the exiles, Palestinian identity has meant both the idea of return to a previous place from which they were evicted and the birth of a new pluralistic place (a new Palestine side by side with Israel). On the other hand, for the remnant it has meant staying in place while fighting for independence, freedom, and self-government (1979, 125–26). The generally inhospitable environments in which the refugees and the remnant have lived contrast sharply with the prosperous land, orchards, and fields that many Palestinians, particularly those from Galilée and the West Bank, remember. Because of this idyllic memory, these places have become important symbolic sites in the Palestinian cinema's rhetoric of the land, home, and identity. A lengthy key sequence of Khleifi's film is a case in point.[15]

Close-Up: Michel Khleifi's Wedding in Galilée (Urs bil Galil *1987*)

The film is about the wedding of the son of a Palestinian village headman in Galilée (named Abu Adel) whose village is under Israeli military occupation.[16] Since curfew rules do not allow the wedding to extend into the night, Abu Adel seeks permission for an extension. The military governor agrees on the condition that he and his entourage be invited to the wedding as guests. The process of obtaining wedding permission allegorizes the process that Khleifi himself went through to gain filming authorization from Israeli local municipalities in Nazareth and the West Bank. Apparently, the casting of several well-known actors served to protect the project (Hoberman 1988: 84).

In the course of the elaborate wedding ceremony, conducted under the governor's watchful eyes and resented by young Palestinian radicals, Abu Adel's favorite thoroughbred mare escapes from its stable. The image of the mare galloping across the surrounding fields and hills expresses the Palestinians' wish for freedom from occupation. The two boys who had let the mare loose discover that she has wandered into an area mined by the Israeli military. One of them hurries back to the village to fetch Abu Adel.

As the boy runs through the hills, cultivated lands, orchards, and yards and into Abu Adel's house, where the wedding ceremony is in process in its traditional fullness, another configuration of space is rendered. If the Zionists' project historically was to deny the existence of a Palestinian people, *Wedding in Galilée's* thick description and documentation of Palestinian culture and agriculture provide a counternarrative. It forcefully posits that Palestinian Arabs are

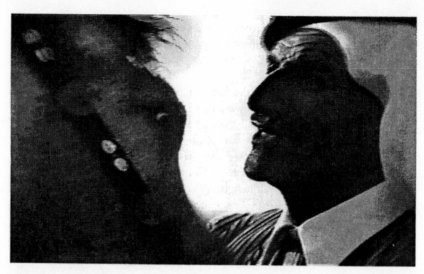

Figure 19. Masculine space of the nation. Abu Adel greets the mare that has been rescued from the Israeli minefield in Michel Khleifi's *Wedding in Galilée*.

there on the ground, and that like the Israelis they are capable of making the desert bloom. By so integrally linking the Palestinians to the land and to its cultivation, the film creates an agricultural idyll before occupation and expulsion. This kind of representation has correctly been criticized as "painterly, quasi-Orientalist idealization of a pre-industrial village" (Shohat 1988, 46).

So far I have defined the Palestinian-Israeli predicament of the homeland in terms of two spatial configurations: those of militarization and cultivation. By proposing a solution to the problem of the escaped mare, Khleifi adds a third spatial configuration—that of cooperation. Using the information provided by the Israelis, who had mined the land in the first place, Abu Adel is able to guide the animal to safety. As the mare gingerly steps through the minefield, she becomes a powerful symbol of the multiple minefields of the Israeli-Palestinian politics and the hair-trigger dangers that await any effort at creating a homeland. By collaborating, enemies succeed in demilitarizing their spaces.

While the exterior fields in *Wedding* are male spaces of militarization and eventually of masculine reconciliation, the home interiors are coded as feminine spaces of culture and of female reconciliation. During the wedding, an Israeli female soldier becomes ill. She is brought indoors, where Palestinian women tend to her and, in an erotically charged sequence, undress and massage her. By experiencing the synaesthetic world of Palestinian women—involving Arabic language, flowers, colors, perfume, water, and sensuous touching—the soldier undergoes a transformation, which is signaled when she exchanges her uniform for a Palestinian dress. The film establishes a parallel between the saving of the mare and the transformation of the female soldier, both of which involved demilitarization as a result of cooperation of the opponents. It posits that the Palestinian national identity is dependent not only on securing land but also on creating a thirdspace of cooperation.

House

For the exiles, the house is a site of both deep harmony and hatred. Two instances of harmony and a case study of Amos Gitai's *House* (1980), which embodies disharmony, are presented. In her fascinating ethnography, Joëlle Bahloul examined a multifamily house in Sétif, Algeria, in which her maternal Jewish grandfather's family had lived harmoniously with their Muslim neighbors. With the Algerian war of independence, the Jews moved away to France, leaving the Muslims behind. By interviewing former housemates, Bahloul discovered that they used "semantics of memory" to fondly re-create the harmonious environment they had once shared: "The remembered house is a small-scale cosmology symbolically restoring the integrity of a shattered geography" (1996, 28). Significantly, the discourse of memory feminized the house as an enclosure of femininity and domesticity, associated with motherhood and reproduction. This is how many exiles feminize the homeland.

Sometimes a small object taken from the house into exile becomes a potent synecdoche for house, home, or even the homeland, feeding the memories and narratives of placement and displacement. Historian Patricia Seed (1999) relates the story of many Jews and Muslims, driven into exile by the Spanish Inquisition, and of many Palestinians, pushed out of Palestine in the mid–twentieth century, who kept above the front door of their homes in exile the keys to their former houses in their homelands. It appears that the key to a lost house is the physical expression of the house and a symbol with which Jews, Muslims, and Palestinians remember and memorialize their former homes and their past harmonious relations. The keys also serve to construct them as exilic or diasporic subjects, for as long as all they have of their homes are the keys, they remain homeless.

In the accented cinema, the house is an intensely charged place and a signifying trope. As a trope, it signifies deterritorialization more than reterritorialization, for displaced filmmakers are fully aware that in today's age of "ethnic cleansing," possessing a house, a home, or a homeland seems to require first the expulsion of its current residents.[17] Instances of harmony in their films are few, and they are usually created only retrospectively.[18]

Close-Up: *Amos Gitai's* House (Bait, *1980*)

The house can neither be taken for granted nor be taken to be just a site of memory, for it is a threatened physical place that may experience successive possessions, dispossessions, and repossessions. Nowhere is this cycle demon-

Figure 20. Palestinian Muslim workers in the Hebron quarries taking a prayer break in Amos Gitai's *House*. Courtesy Agav Films.

strated more graphically and forcefully than in Gitai's *House*. Born in Haifa, Israel, in 1950 to Jewish parents who came from Poland and Russia, Gitai received a doctorate in architecture from the University of California, Berkeley. Back in Israel, he was wounded during the Yom Kippur War of 1973, when Syrian forces shot down his helicopter (Kronish 1996, 128). His first works were documentaries for Israeli TV, including *House*, which was not aired because of its "sympathetic attitude towards Palestinians" (Willemen 1993, 107). However, the controversy that it aroused in private screenings in the kibbutzim apparently prompted Gitai to take up filmmaking as a profession. Since then he has made a number of documentaries, some of them dealing with architectural issues, and several fiction films. In both film categories, he has developed an experimental style that includes the fragmentation of both linear narrative and space-time representations. After his *Field Diary* (1982), a lyrical journal about the Occupied Territories and south Lebanon, which criticized policies of the Begin government, Gitai could not find backing for his films at home. He relocated to Paris, where for nine years he made films. For this and other reasons, many of his works are centrally concerned with exilic and diasporic subjects, even though he is not in exile.

House is a fifty-one-minute, black-and-white documentary. The house of the title is located in Jerusalem and is under major renovation. The film begins with close-up shots of Arab and Palestinian laborers in Mount Hebron quarries breaking off pieces of limestone with hammers and chisels (they are not trusted with explosives). The film, which sets out to document the reconstruction of the house, soon becomes a historical excavation. As the quarries are mined to rebuild the house physically stone by stone, the film mines the memories of the current and former owners and the thoughts of laborers and masons to rebuild it discursively layer by layer. In the process, the film reveals the complex social and political history not only of this house but also of the house of Israel.

The house predates the state of Israel, and it has changed hands several times. In 1948 it belonged to a Palestinian, but in 1967, when Israel won the war with the Arabs and occupied the West Bank, it became the property of the state of Israel. The government first rented it to an Algerian Jewish couple and a few years later sold it to its current owner, an Israeli professor. The history of the laborers and masons is no less complicated. All of them are Arab or Palestinian, most of whom come from lands that Israel has occupied since its inception, and they have been hired for the job by a Jewish Iraqi contractor. The bitter irony of Palestinians rebuilding a house for a Jew at the same time that Palestinians are fighting Israel for a homeland is not lost on the laborers, who resent their jobs but appear to have no other source of employment. A mason named Walaji says that because the Israelis razed his house, he hates them, but he has no choice but to work for them: "We work to earn our living as prisoners of Israel. It breaks my heart."

The old Algerian couple and the original Arab owner, a physician, walk through the ruined structure and the courtyard, pointing nostalgically to rooms that once existed but are now either gone or incorporated into the new house. Ruins, like monuments, are powerful metaphors for creating individual and collective identity. Understandably, their rebuilding also acquires gravity, especially in such cases as this house, in which possession and renovation function as metaphors for the ownership and occupation of the homeland.

House documents three reconstruction projects: those of a physical house, a house of memory (for the former occupants), and a celluloid house. We see how the same structure can bear different, competing histories and meanings for differently situated people. With its dialogue spoken in three languages (Arabic, Hebrew, and English) and its subtitles in French, the *House* that Gitai builds fits the double meaning of the film's title in Hebrew, *bait*—meaning both house (the physical structure) and home (the value that habitation and memory bestow upon it). In addition, *bait* for the Israelis stands for the land, the state, and the homeland of Israel (Klein 1993, 29). The conflation of all these meanings makes the house of stones and Gitai's house of celluloid a potent structure, indeed, too potent for Israeli television, as Gitai notes: "The Israeli Television did not want to admit that Palestinians have memories, attachments and rights in this part of the country. Such a recognition would mean, on a political level, that a political solution must be found for the Palestinians, not just as individuals but as people" (quoted in Willemen 1993, 82). The film never shows the completed house; it posits it as a ruin of a house, a powerful symbol of the multiplicity of histories that have converged at this particular site without congealing them into a single History. In so doing, Gitai creates, in Teshome Gabriel's formulation of the ruin, a poem that contains many ellipses and fragments of narratives but not a totalizing, coherent story (1993, 217).

Almost two decades later, Gitai returned to the house, which resulted in the feature color documentary *House in Jerusalem* (*Une maison à Jerusalem*, 1998). In it he revisited the house, its current owner, the previous owners, and residents and their descendants, as well as the issue of owning not only this particular house but that of the Israeli and Palestinian homelands. By all accounts, the Israeli-Palestinian divide has widened; what has remained constant is the suffering of the expropriated Palestinian family, the Dejanis. No reconciliation seems possible.

Many of these housing issues are documented from a Palestinian perspective in *Jerusalem: An Occupation Set in Stone?* (1995), which was photographed, edited, and directed by Marty Rosenbluth for the Palestine Housing Rights Movement. It begins with the expulsion of Muhammmed Al Hafizah Obeid and his family from their house in a village in East Jerusalem that has been occupied by Israel since 1967. A large contingent of soldiers and police forcibly remove the family, scuffle with the Palestinians gathered to protest the eviction, fire guns into them, injuring a number of people, and finally bulldoze the house flat. The film includes touching testimonials by Arab and Palestinian residents of East Jerusalem whose homes have been destroyed to make room for Jewish settlements.[19] Several of the evicted, as a sign of their continued claim to the land, opt to live in makeshift structures within sight of their former homes, such as in an old bus or in shipping crates. Interviews with the Jews who live in the confiscated properties show a disingenuous disinterest in these homeless Palestinians. Maps and statistics, as well as interviews with Israeli and Palestinian city planners, geographers, professors, and lawyers, serve to demonstrate that these are not just isolated instances but part of a calculated governmental policy to transform East Jerusalem's character from Arab to Jewish.[20] The film shows that by erecting checkpoints, roadblocks, and other security measures, Israeli authorities restrict the Palestinians' movement in and out of East Jerusalem, hampering their employment, family reunification, and pilgrimage to holy sites. Under these regimes of erasure, the two capitals, East and West Jerusalem, are becoming unified as a single capital of Israel, turning the divided house into an Israeli *bait*.

Clearly, these physical and discursive battles are not only for the house but also for the home. bell hooks fused the physical and discursive aspects into the single term "homeplace" (1990). In her formulation, in the context of African-

American culture, homeplace could be a slave hut, a wooden shack, or a house, which, however fragile or humble, has a "radical political dimension." She discovered this dimension in the women-centered household's care and nurturance in the face of racist oppression and sexist domination. In the idealized black homeplace, women taught critical consciousness, subversive values, alternative structures of meaning, and ways of remembering, healing, and self-recovery.[21] The Israeli tactics spelled out in *House* and *Jerusalem: An Occupation Set in Stone?* were designed to deprive the Palestinians of such radical political homeplaces, and the Palestinians' vehemence for the house is driven by their understanding of its larger political import for their struggle for homeplace and homeland.

Close-Up: Andrei Tarkovsky

If Palestinian and Israeli films focus on the dispute about the physical house and its bearing on the idea of a national home, Tarkovsky's films deal with the house and its significance for the family. However, as both a physical and a family structure, the house is in ruins in his films, echoing Tarkovsky's own biography. He was born in Zavrazhie on the Volga in 1932. Even though he lived in Moscow most of his life, the dacha (wooden house in a rural and forested setting) in which he spent his childhood constituted for him the ideal vision of a family home, and variations of it appear in *Solaris, Mirror, Nostalgia,* and *The Sacrifice*. When he was young, his distinguished poet father, Arseniy Tarkovsky, abandoned the family. This biographical model of the fractured family reverberates both in Andrei's own family life and in the life of his diegetic families (Mitchell 1986–87; Green 1984–85). The father's absence haunts the films, particularly those that cite his poetry. His mother appears as a maternal/lover double in several of his films, including *Mirror*.[22]

After studying filmmaking at VGIK in Moscow, Tarkovsky made six features for Mosfilm in two dozen years. In July 1984, while abroad, he defected to the West, where he was able to make *Nostalgia* (*Nostalghia*, 1983) and *The Sacrifice* (*Offret Sacrificatio*, 1986) before succumbing to lung cancer in Paris in December 1986. Circumstances surrounding his self-imposed exile are not simple or completely clear. Although a number of his films were held back by the Soviet censors, in particular *Andrei Rublev* (1966), which was withheld until 1971, all of Tarkovsky's films were released domestically and internationally. He made all of them under the Soviet state-driven mode of production, which sometimes afforded him great luxury.[23] Because of this and because he had not been repressed, tried, or imprisoned like others, including Sergeï Paradjanov, some of his peers called him "the darling of the Goskino" (State Committee on Cinema) (Johnson and Petrie 1994b, 4). That Tarkovsky was able to operate in this manner points not only to his high-quality films and high status in the Soviet Union but also to several favorable conditions there, among them the following: Soviet totalitarianism was not as homogeneous and monolithic as its critics claimed; artists and intellectuals were persecuted differently, with writers suffering much harsher treatment than filmmakers; Stalin's death and the Twentieth Party Congress brought about a cultural "thaw"; and Tarkovsky's films were not overtly political, since they did not on the whole engage with present-day Soviet public life (Le Fanu 1990, 1–5). Given these circumstances, the question of why Tarkovsky exiled himself must be raised.

Tarkovsky's disengagement with the contemporary Soviet state ideology and public sphere and his dystopic vision of the future, empty of the kind of positivism that the state demanded, were read by hermeneutically sophisticated Soviet people as a criticism of the regime. This did not endear him to the authorities, who nonetheless funded his projects, but it made his life difficult and the pace of his filmmaking slow. In a fateful letter to Goskino (dated June 15, 1983), in which he requested an extension of his stay in Europe, he listed a series of complaints: that his films had not received any Soviet recognition or prize, their distribution was hampered by official unfavorable classification, their press reviews were curtailed or politicized, and if they were entered in film festivals, "official conspiracy" prevented them from winning prizes (Wakeman 1988, 1085).[24] Paranoia, one of the diseases of exilic existence that can distort vision, befell Tarkovsky, who became "almost paranoid about the lengths to which the Soviet authorities might go in persecuting him, even fearing forced expatriation" (Johnson and Petrie 1994b, 46).

All these were "push factors," conditions within the homeland that drove him out. There were also a number of "pull factors" that attracted him to the West. By this time, Tarkovsky had become internationally recognized as an uncompromising artist; his *Nostalgia* was a coproduction involving the Soviet Union, Italy, and France; he had directed a successful opera in London; and he was busy negotiating with Swedish, French, and British film concerns for his next film project, *The Sacrifice*. In short, he was terrified by the prohibitions that awaited him at home and tantalized by the possibilities that the West offered. Tarkovsky admitted that he was not a political dissident and that his reasons for asking for an extension of stay were artistic freedom and economic necessity. In the end, however, claiming that Soviet authorities had ignored his application to extend his stay abroad and that they would not permit him to make films should he return home, he sought political asylum in Italy, where he and his second wife, Larissa, were given an apartment by the city of Florence.

While professionally promising, his exile was tinged with personal tragedy: that of forced separation from his son and from his stepdaughter and mother, all of whom had been kept in the Soviet Union by the government to ensure Tarkovsky's return. This personal loss and some of the factors noted earlier fed into the myth of Tarkovsky as the suffering genius, auteur, martyr, and prophet—a myth that was shaped, to some extent, by his own "messianic tendencies and persecution complex" (Johnson and Petrie 1994b, 2).

Nostalgia's mode of production in Italy was exilic in many respects, despite the promise of professional advancement, bigger budget, and access to modern technical facilities and to ten times more raw stock than he had used in his previous film, *Stalker* (1979). For one thing, Tarkovsky made the film in exile without the benefit of his usual "family" of longtime collaborators both behind and in front of the camera. For another, his command of Italian was rudimentary, forcing him to communicate with most of the actors and crew through an interpreter. His intense and demanding style of work also magnified the communication difficulties, leading to frustration and tension on the set (Johnson and Petrie 1994b, 33). In addition, Tarkovsky, who was used to the Soviet mode of production, which gave him the luxury of a slow work pace and an individually designed shooting schedule, had a hard time adjusting to a capitalist mode of production that emphasized strict time and financial management. All these and more made the making of the film, the status of the director, and the content of the film more exilic than anticipated.

The house-as-a-ruin is a key site and metaphor in Tarkovsky's cinema, bearing both the mark and the stigma of exilic longing. Since this metaphor long predates his actual exile, some of his Soviet films may be regarded as protoexilic. His exilic structure of feelings is driven not only by his deterritorialization but also by the various philosophical, spiritual, and personal falls that bedeviled him throughout his life—the fall from the state of grace and harmony with God and nature, from the prelapsarian world of childhood, and from the presymbolic union with mother.[25] As a metaphor for a time before these multiple falls, therefore, the house always already necessitates nostalgia for its coming into being. This means the house is subject to continual metamorphosis, as a result of which in Tarkovsky's films houses can be neither complete nor permanent. Sometimes they are leaky ruins, inhabited by isolated individuals or alienated families (*Nostalgia*, *Stalker*). If the house of the past is remembered as a setting for joyful childhood (*Mirror* and *Solaris*), the present house is either wanting and cold (*The Steamroller and the Violin/Katok i skripka*, 1960), a veritable prison (*Nostalgia*), a decaying ruin (*Nostalgia*), or a home that must be destroyed (*The Sacrifice*).

The various configurations of the house are examined in more detail in *Nostalgia*, Tarkovsky's most exilic film. The protagonist, Tarkovsky's namesake and alter ego, is a musicologist who has come to Italy in search of information about an eighteenth-century Russian serf composer, who once lived there. Although Andrei, like many exiles, including Tarkovsky himself, is physically in exile, emotionally he is at home. Russia is associated, by means of Andrei's remembering and dreaming, with earth, spirituality, and home, and the house is tied to family, femininity, and the maternal. In many of Tarkovsky's films, the dacha is identified closely with the mother and the maternal, whose icons are lace curtains, embroidered clothing, indoor plants, household objects, wrought-iron beds, and fluffy pillows. Some of these objects migrate from film

Figure 21. Imagined home (dacha) in the homeland in Andrei Tarkovsky's *Nostalgia*.

to film and are found in *Nostalgia* as well (Johnson and Petrie 1994a,: 227–28). In addition, an image that is repeated in this film is Andrei's dream or daydream of his wife standing outside the dacha with their children, near a pond. The prevalence of dreaming and daydreaming and the film's oneiric structure gives *Nostalgia* a trancelike haptic feel.

Haunted by home, Andrei pays little attention to the Italian landscape's beauty or to its people. Almost all signs of Italian specificity and contemporaneity are removed from the film: "Few have been able to 'de-Italianize' Italy as effectively as Tarkovsky" (Turovskaya 1989, 120). Indeed, as much as Russia is associated with home, family, and spirituality Italy is associated with exile, ruin, and decay—the force behind all of which is nature and its primordial elements, particularly water. Graffy's description of the pervasiveness of water imagery in Tarkovsky's films is apt: "Water is ubiquitous and palpable, falling as rain and snow, flowing as streams and rivers, dripping from taps and showers, lying in puddles and pools, often clean and purifying, sometimes stagnant and polluted" (1997, 20). Andrei forms an instinctive bond with Domenico, a man of faith, and an outsider like himself, whom others call a "mad man." He has imprisoned his wife and children in his dilapidated house for seven years while waiting for the world to end. In an amazing scene, it suddenly rains hard inside the house, forming puddles everywhere, and a dog lies in one. The rain brings the outside in, as though the house has been turned inside out like a coat. In many scenes, the sound of dripping water accompanies the painterly visuals that denote the passage of time. In one virtuoso scene, Andrei is sleeping in his hotel room. As the camera moves ever so slowly in on him, his shift from waking to dreaming is signaled by the almost imperceptible changes in the room's lighting—all while rain falls noisily outside the window whose reflection dances on the wall inside and whose sounds soothe the sleeping man.

In a way, what we witness in *Nostalgia*, the most waterlogged of Tarkovsky films, is the action of water and time on the physical world as they gradually decay, erode, and transform it from a structure into a ruin, from culture into nature. In this sense, the film creates a "time monument," in Michael Snow's formulation in a different context, or a "sculpture in time," in Tarkovsky's own term (Tarkovsky 1987, 63). Both the state of incipient collapse and ruin that seem to be everywhere and the long-take shots (many of them lasting over one minute, and some as long as eight minutes), encourage the reading of what the film is doing as the sculpting of time. When ruin and time are processed through nostalgia and childhood memory—both at inscription by Tarkovsky and at reception by viewers—his films in general, and *Mirror* and *Nostalgia* in particular, acquire a tactile and haptic structure of feeling. Audiences can almost feel and smell the rotting wood, the pouring rain, or the raw earth. This overemphasis on ruins and ruination in exile and on nostalgically produced idealized Russian nature is not only a function of exilic longing but also a critique of the high cost of modernity.

A strong autobiographical inscription and a motif of doubling runs throughout *Nostalgia*. Like the eighteenth-century musician whose life he is researching, Andrei the character and, by extension, Andrei the director are caught in the agonistic bind of exilic liminality, unable to free themselves from either the world of home or exile.[26] The two spiritual journeymen, Andrei and Domineco, exchange places at the eerie sulfuric thermal baths of Vigononi, where Andrei performs the ritual crossing of St. Catherine Pool as an act of faith, while Domenico tries to save the world by self-immolation.

The film ends with a breathtaking scene in which Andrei's Russian home is incorporated into the ruins of an Italian cathedral (San Galgano), suturing home and exile. Rain falls in the foreground, then snow falls in the background, and then snow falls in the foreground. This composite shot is held for quite some time, encouraging philosophical contemplation and haptic comprehension of the time sculpture that Tarkovsky has created of exile. On one level, it can be said that the house and the cathedral as ruins have both been reclaimed by nature. On another level, the house inside the cathedral begins to resemble the house inside a paperweight globe that upon shaking is blurred by a flurry of snow. Having made this connection, it is possible to make another between this globe and that which falls from the hand of a dying Charles Foster Kane in *Citizen Kane* (1941). The Tarkovskian and Wellesian globes both fuse home and childhood into one powerful monolith of terminal loss and permanent homelessness in the world.

The quest for what Michael Dempsey calls "a lost harmony" (1981)—a physical, natural, and spiritual home—is a key theme in Tarkovsky's films, even in the futuristic ones such as *Stalker*, in which the "Zone" and the "Room" may be read as homeplaces of sorts. However, since this harmonious place always harbors dangers and fears, return is impossible, intensifying the nostalgia for it, which is expressed in the staging of return, either to nature or to homeland. In *Nostalgia*, this restaging takes the form of the merging of the Russian home into the Italian cathedral. The nostalgia for a lost harmony is influenced not only by Tarkovsky's own philosophical and physical exile but also by a peculiar "Russian nostalgia," which he describes as "the fatal attachment of Russians to their national roots, their past, their culture, their native places, their families and friends; an attachment which they carry with them all their lives, regardless of where destiny may fling them" (1987, 202). Then, realizing the parallels between his film and his own exile, he wonders, not with irony but with profound sadness, the kind that feeds into his myth of the exilic auteur as martyr: "How could I have imagined as I was making *Nostalgia* that the stifling sense of longing that fills the screen space of that film was to become my lot for the rest of my life; that from now until the end of my days I would bear the painful malady within myself?" (202).

This discussion of house and home in the accented cinema has followed a trajectory of increasing abstraction. In Gitai's *House*, there is a physical house, but it is under renovation and its ownership has been in dispute; in *Nostalgia*, the house exists either in memory, as an ideal place in the homeland and in the past tense, or in the present tense in exile, but as a ruin. In the discussion of Egoyan's *The Adjuster*, the idea of the house is pushed up another level on the scale of ruination and abstraction.

Close-Up: Atom Egoyan's The Adjuster *(1991)*

House and home in Egoyan's cinema are troubled places where the drama of traumatized and dysfunctional nuclear families unfolds. Even in his *Calendar*, which is about a real homeland, no house or home is in sight, and the photographer's relationship with his wife is in tatters. In *The Adjuster*, the house as a solid, stable, or "real" structure disappears, to be replaced by either a cheap motel or an ersatz "model home." Likewise, the family structure undergoes a transformation from being based on descent and blood to one that is almost entirely derived from consent and contract.

At the manifest level, the film is about two adjusters: Noah, an insurance adjuster, and his wife, Hera, a film censor. They live in their model "dream house" with Hera's sister and her daughter, who are recent Armenian immi-

Figure 22. Film censor Arsinée Khanjian secretly records porno films in Atom Egoyan's *The Adjuster*. Courtesy Alliance International.

grants from Lebanon. Working nights, Noah appears at the site of burned-down houses to help their owners process their insurance claims. He interviews them, completes lists of objects and properties lost, collects photographs of those items, and places the victims in a motel, where they stay awaiting new housing. He further helps both the male and the female guests adjust to their transitional condition by engaging in sexual relations with them in their hotel rooms. Hera is a censor for a bureaucratized film board for which she views hours of pornographic films. Using a hidden video camera during the films' projection, she secretly tapes the most illicit sequences to take to her émigré sister at home. These scenes are not shown to us, but we know about them by their explicit sound track. By censoring films, Hera adjusts them to fit the official codes and the public taste, and by screening them for her sister, she helps to undermine them.

From the film's last shot we learn that the Noah-Hera nuclear family itself is not a biologically constituted unit; rather, it is a "pseudofamily" composed of people who had lost their homes in previous fires. However, it is not only the family that is constructed and fake. Their house is a demonstration model, and everything inside is for show and ersatz, including the prop books. In a funny scene, Bubba, a maker of pornographic films, tours the house as a location for his upcoming movie, during which the prop books fall out of the shelves without causing any surprise. Indeed, the family's life in the dream house seems to be just a show, designed to demonstrate to prospective customers what an occupied house would look like. There is no warm relationship among the family members, for as in most of Egoyan's films, all the main characters in *The Adjuster* harbor secrets and secret desires. The house is thus not a home. It appears that Noah is more at home in the motel, moving nomadically from client to client.[27]

Although there are no affectionate or sexual relations between Noah and Hera, the house itself is highly sexualized—even though in a perverse way. For example, one night, a man from outside the house voyeuristically peers through the window, where Hera's sister is viewing a porno film, and masturbates openly. In another sequence, the pornographer Bubba prepares the interior of the house for filming a group of children (he ends up burning the house down). Pressed on the linkage between home and transgressive sexuality, Egoyan told me "There is something about the house that has this incredible illicit sexual energy. What is it based on? To me, anything that's unreal, that's heightened, that's figurative has a sexual power because it means that we have to relate to it through our imagination" (Naficy 1997a, 212). This creates a tension between the audience and the image, and between the image and its referent, eroticizing both relations—a characteristic of haptic cinema. The fakeness of the house and of the family intensifies the sexuality of the house, turning most goings-on in it into pornography because they are based on simulating something real. The sexual and haptic pleasure that the difference between image and referent creates speaks to why Egoyan's films are so concerned with images, imaging technologies, and mediation. In a scene in *Calendar*, while the cameraman is filming a ruined monument, the translator asks him to touch and feel the monument. He responds with puzzlement, saying something like, "What do you want me to do, caress it?" Then the photographer reaches into the shot, touching the image of the monument on the viewfinder, not the real thing. It appears that for him the image is more powerful than its referent. This overcathexis of the image implies that there is nostalgia for a world, which exists entirely as image, which has itself as referent. In that world, the sexual charge that is based on the difference of image and referent will theoretically be absent. For the exiles whose referent (homeland) exists but is out of reach, this sexual charge does not cease. However, the visual fetishization of the homeland and the exiles' immersion in its haptic aura provide a temporary solace. As Egoyan notes, "You can always go back to an image. But you can't go back to a land" (215).

In Egoyan's cinema, houses are not real or stable, and there is little struggle over them as personal, familial, or national territory. In *The Adjuster*, for example, houses are either snapshots of burned houses (that Noah collects from his clients), photographs (of the sister's house in Lebanon, which she burns), real houses (which burn down), fake houses (in which Noah's pseudofamily lives, which also burns), or transient motel rooms (in which Noah services his clients). A network of mediations, adjustments, and exchange relations replaces both house and home. The referent has disappeared. No house, home, or homeland exists. All that remains is the play of signifiers and significtion.

Homeland as Prison

In the accented cinema, the nation is not always imagined as a timeless, boundless, and primordial home, synonymous with nature and associated with the rural or the monumental. Sometimes it is imagined in an opposite space-time configuration, particularly by filmmakers who have escaped authoritarian regimes and societies. As Kofi Anyidoho notes, "Prison and exile are two sides of the experience of oppression . . . considering that intellectuals and creative artists who insist on fighting oppression often end up in prison, that those who manage to survive prison often end up in exile" (1997, 3). However, even those who manage to escape to exile are haunted by the prison house of their homelands. They tend to construct their homeland as a present-tense place and as a chronotope of modernity, surveillance, claustrophobia, and control. Such places and chronotopes fit both Foucault's notion of the "panopticon" (1977) and Deleuze's concept of "societies of control" (1992). For the Turkish exile filmmaker Yilmaz Güney, the key chronotope of homeland is that of prison.

Close-up: Yilmaz Güney

According to Turkish film critics, no film has damaged Turkey's public image more than Alan Parker's powerful but hysterical and ethnocentric prison movie, *Midnight Express* (1978).[28] And yet it is the image of the prison that Güney deployed in his protoexilic film, *Yol* (*The Way*, 1982) to critique his own society. Born Yilmaz Putun in a village near Adana in southern Turkey in 1937, Güney had a long history of involvement with the Turkish prison system and political exile. Educated in law and economics, he began working with director Atif Yilamz in 1958. Three years later he was sentenced to eighteen months in prison and six months of exile for publishing a "communist" novel. After his release he wrote for and acted in commercial films, popularizing a rough-hewn mythic antihero character known as *cirkin kral* (the ugly king). In the late 1960s he formed his own production company and began directing films, which were at first commercial and traditional. Soon, however, he changed to a radical, socially conscious ethos, in part due to the banning of his milestone realist film, *Umut* (*The Hope*, 1971), and several bouts of incarceration. In 1972 he was charged with sheltering wanted anarchist students and was condemned to twenty-six months of jail (commuted by a general amnesty in 1974). After that, he was charged with the shooting death of a judge in a restaurant, for which he was sentenced to twenty-four years hard labor (later reduced to eighteen years). Interestingly, during his incarceration he maintained his contact with the outside world and continued to write screenplays (Thomas 1990, 357–60).

In fact, from his prison cell, Güney obtained permission to direct *Yol* by proxy, under the pretext of combating the negative images of *Midnight Express*, by focusing on the liberal Turkish prison policies, including a furlough program (Wakeman 1988, 407). His associate Serif Goren shot the film on his behalf and under his supervision. After serving seven years of his sentence, Güney escaped from prison (and the country) using the very furlough program depicted in *Yol*. He edited and completed the film in Switzerland. This is a "protoexilic" film, for it anticipates the filmmakers' own external exile before it occurs. Upon their release, protoexilic films often cause further trouble for their makers, expediting their eventual exile or contributing to their continued stay in exile.

Yol tracks the harrowing stories of five male prisoners released on a five-day leave from their small jail cells into the larger prison of the Turkish society, where both the modern military and bureaucratic apparatuses and the traditional feudal patriarchy keep a relentless check on all citizens. The chronotope of the nation is extremely claustrophobic, turning Turkey into both a national panopticon (per Foucault) and a rhizomatic society of control (per Deleuze). If the disciplinary society is characterized by modern central institutions such as prisons that mold "individuals," the new societies of control are driven by dispersed networks of domination that serve to modulate "dividuals." In them schools are replaced with perpetual training, watchwords by passwords, discipline with control, and factories with corporations—all in the interest of "universal modulation" (Deleuze 1992, 7). The film charts the personal and emotional journeys of the five convicts as they fan out in different directions by train and bus to their towns and villages, illustrating both the diversity of Turkish society and its widespread draconian system of control and modulation. The army and police exercise control over the population by their constant presence and relentless surveillance, questioning, body searches, harassment, and detention (one of the convicts, Yusuf, is detained and prevented from visiting his wife because he has lost his papers). As the convicts' travels continue, these militarized scenes are intercut with scenes of their arrival and reception at their homes, where the traditional Islamic patriarchy and honor system exercise additional control over the lives of the four remaining travelers and their women. Every move of the convicts and their wives is watched and judged by relatives, in-laws, children, elders, neighbors, and the police.

These military and patriarchal mechanisms of social control are augmented by the film's cinematic regime of control: its closed and crowded mise-en-scène (trains and buses filled with passengers), closed shot composition, and dark

Don't forget the dishonor she brought upon us. No pity.

Figure 23. Patriarchy perpetuates itself through honor and shame. Seyit is reminded of his wife's infidelity in Yilmaz Güney's *Yol.*

lighting scheme—all of which work to produce a decidedly claustrophobic diegesis and a gloomy structure of feeling.

By emphasizing the stories of several wives of the convicts, Güney genderizes his claustrophobic chronotopes and emphasizes the double oppression of women. When Mehmet was imprisoned, his wife, Eminê, left him to return with her children to her father's house because the family considered him a coward and responsible for the death of her brother. Mehmet must now face his wife and her irate family and endure humiliation in front of his own children. However, Eminê braves the condemnation of her parental family by spending time with her convicted husband. On the train, Mehmet and Eminê are caught in a sexual embrace in the bathroom; they are saved from a terrible mob justice only by the presence of their children. In the end, however, both are gunned down by Eminê's vengeful brother.

Seyit, on the other hand, must engage in a different patriarchal drama of family disgrace, caused by the infidelity of his wife, Zinê, during his absence. Awaiting final punishment by her husband, she has been held for eight months in chains by Seyit's family in a dark, damp barn, where she is left unkempt and fed only water and bread. To reach his family, Mehmet braves a treacherous snowy peak, where his horse collapses, forcing him to put it out of its misery and to finish the journey on foot. Similar to Mehmet's situation, Seyit's reactions to the family crisis are watched intensely—not only by the elders but also, and more important, by his children, who will learn a lesson about manhood and the role of women's sacrifice and punishment in its proper construction. Seyit is torn between pity and hatred for Zinê, however, and he does not want to murder her as custom dictates. Instead, he decides to return her to her parents by the same treacherous snow pass (with their son tagging along). The return journey in deep snow proves impossible for Zinê, who is ill clad, without snowshoes, and weak from undernourishment. In a tragic and powerful sequence, when she collapses by the horse's carcass, father and son beat her mercilessly to prevent her from losing consciousness. The film is darkly ironic, for it does not resolve the question of whether Zinê dies from the cold or from the beating she receives out of belated kindness.

In this film, unlike in the nostalgia-tinged films of Elias (*The Mountain*), Madzounian (*The Pink Elephant*), Egoyan (*Calendar*), Ariç (*A Song for Beko*), and Nava (*El Norte*), the mountain is not a bridge to a state of before, to a nurturing nation, or to an idyllic homeland; rather, it is an imposing barrier and a formidable foe.[29] The only nostalgic space of nature in *Yol* is the verdant hills around the Kurdish village near the Syrian border whose earth the convict named Ömer kneels down to kiss, and whose openness and beauty the film emphasizes. This nostalgia is driven by the Kurdish (and Güney's) desire for an independent Kurdish homeland yet to come. It is thus a prospective form of nostalgia.

The women's physical confinement and social isolation are reinforced by their general silence and lack of voice and agency in the film. If the men are subjected to oppressive state apparatuses, they are also granted agency, that is, the opportunity to articulate and to engage in resistance and subversion of those apparatuses (by their exchange of views about their oppression, their narrative transformation, and Ömer's involvement in pro-Kurdish struggle). Their treatment thus gives the film an optimistic turn. However, with the exception of Eminê, none of *Yol's* women undergo any transformation; instead, they remain static and devoid of "a voice and consciousness of their own" (Suner 1998, 17–19). Viewed from a feminist perspective, therefore, the film acquires a pessimistic and oppressive structure of feeling—even though it treats women sympathetically. The "way" of the film's title is open only to the men, not to the women.

Accordingly, if the most confining metaphors are reserved for women, the most liberatory one is offered the Kurdish convict, Ömer. Kurds form a significant minority in Turkey and have been battling the central government for decades in their violent push for an independent state.[30] By focusing on the story of one of them, Güney ethnicizes his national chronotope and points to the double oppression of ethnic minorities as well. Ethnicization extends to the film's use of the banned Kurdish language and the screen caption "Kurdistan," which identifies the region that Ömer visits. According to Güney, *Yol* is the first Turkish film that contains Kurdish dialogue and folk songs (quoted in Suner 1998, 11). Himself a Kurd, Güney identified with Ömer and with the Kurdish separatist cause. He graphically portrays the Turkish army's ruthless massacre of the Kurdish rebels, who are under siege in their walled village homes and alleys.[31] In one battle, Ömer's brother is gunned down, and his body is brought into the village circle for identification. Ironically, however, no one dares to identify him for fear of reprisal. The brother's death brings another irony: it is now Ömer's duty to marry his brother's widow, as tradition requires, even though he likes another village girl with whom he exchanges intense looks of desire. In the midst of the claustrophobic and militarized spaces of the village, Güney introduces a new space of immensity and freedom, which he encodes as the open and longed-for Kurdish homeland that can be created only from exile. This is underscored by the film's ending, in which Ömer, wooed by his love for the Kurdish girl and by his passion for a Kurdish nation, joins the rebels in the hills beyond Turkey's borders. His fast-trotting horse becomes, like the mare in Khleifi's *Wedding in Galilée*, a symbol of freedom. However, both the horse and the landscape are symbols of male liberation, a point that becomes clear when Ömer's horse, trotting into freedom, is compared with the rotting carcass of the horse on the snow-covered mountain by which Zinê dies her terrible death.

Upon its release, this scathing and profoundly sad film invoked two diametrically opposed reactions from outsiders and insiders. The 1982 Cannes International Film Festival awarded *Yol*, along with Constantin Costa-Gavras's *Missing* (1982), the Palme d'Or Grand Prize. The military government in Turkey, on the other hand, sentenced Güney in absentia to twenty additional years in prison, revoked his citizenship, and confiscated and banned all his films, including those he had directed and scripted and those in which he had acted (Ilal 1987, 125). This unavailability of his films has hampered their serious study, but it has helped to mythologize Güney, a process given momentum by his refusal to return home.[32]

A year after *Yol*, with financial aid from the French Ministry of Culture and French Television, he directed his last film, *The Wall* (*Duvar*, 1983), before succumbing to stomach cancer in France in 1984 at the age of forty-seven. About a prison in Turkey, *The Wall* is shot almost entirely within the walls of a single prison, itself divided into smaller walled prisons housing women, boys, and anarchists. The film was shot in an old abbey forty miles north of Paris, which was converted into a prison by the collective efforts of the film's exilic crew, musicians, director, and large cast. As Güney states:

> Our set was a meeting place where the French, Algerians, Argentineans, Uruguayans, Venezuelans, Chileans, Tunisians, Turks, Kurds, Armenians, Iranians and so many other nationalities worked for a common goal. . . . For me, the fundamental reason for this exceptional mobilization, was our conviction that this film, would also be a slap in the face of the fascist military dictatorship. It is that which gave us such incredible energy.[33]

A central theme of the film is the sadistic mistreatment of children: their torture, beating, rape, hard labor, and an ill-fated uprising—one that is based on a real children's revolt in the Fourth Dormitory of the Ankara prison in March 1976, which was brutally crushed. In a more insightful and nuanced manner than *Midnight Express*, but in a manner that is relentlessly pessimistic, *The Wall* demonstrates the Foucaultian structures of vision and division so necessary for coercion and control. Claustrophobic spatiality and human degradation are emphasized not only by the confining settings but also by the continual close-up photography, often through bars and cracks in the walls. However, perhaps because of the specific microeconomics of control and the cultural characteristics and diversity of Turkish society, the prisoners are not totally atomized and neutralized. There is much life and happiness, even though these moments are brief and tinged with irony and tragedy. A male and a female prisoner awaiting execution are prepared by other prisoners for an elaborate wedding. They are married, but they are also executed in their wedding clothes, with the palm print of the bride's hennaed hand on the prison wall the only reminder of their moment of joy. There is an uprising by the anarchists, ironically, not to be freed but to be transferred to another prison, which turns out to be no better than the one they left. Although there is reference to the Kurdish aspiration for political independence, this theme is muffled in the interest of presenting Turkey as a total phobic space.

The only alternative to submitting to the brutal rules of the prison guards is uprising—an alternative ruled out because it may at best result in moving prisoners from one prison to another. And when an escaped prisoner returns to the prison, he volunteers this desolate discovery: "There is no life for us anywhere." Consequently, the various metaphoric and physical walls remain immovable and unalterable. The meticulous portrayal of life's routines (including a birth), the wide spectrum of social strata that are incarcerated, and the high-angle shots that dramatically capture the entire prison system with its subdivisions—all these work to turn the diegetic prison into a metaphor for confinement as a fundamental condition of life.

As is true of all key symbols, Güney's relation to prison was complex and evolutionary. When Turkish-born Greek-American film director Elia Kazan interviewed Güney in prison in 1979, jail was not just a brutal place of confinement for him. It was also a place of security, where he was given a study from which he ran his successful production company, directing by proxy at least three features. At the time, the prison rules were so lax that Güney could have escaped, but, as he told Kazan, he felt safer where he was (Kazan 1979). However, the military takeover at home and exile seem to have hardened this mild view into a totally pessimistic one, disallowing any possibility of escape or change. This is borne out by Güney's brief on-camera statement, at the beginning of the print of *Yol* in distribution in the United States, in which he says: "The people in this film are Turkish, but these very same people are everywhere. . . . Some are prisoners of their own minds, but all are prisoners of the state."

In Güney's case we can observe the dynamics of the accented style at work, where the filmmaker's own memories and biographical experiences at home, his liminal subjectivity in exile, and his filmic spatial chronotopes intersect. For Güney the prison was partly an allegorical rumination on the stifling social conditions of his homeland, especially under military rule. The inscription of prison in *Yol* and *The Wall* also expresses and reworks Güney's own life experiences before exile, so much of it spent in jail: of the twenty years he had been active in cinema, he spent twelve years in jail, two years in the military service, and three years in exile (Armes 1987, 271). In much of the Third World, incarceration for political reasons confers social status and moral authority upon the prisoners and ex-prisoners. As a result, intellectuals, including filmmakers such as Güney, take pride in publicizing their prison experience—unlike criminals. Moreover, creating phobic spaces and safe zones of prisons may have been Güney's attempt at stemming the tide of exilic chaos and uncertainty. Finally, an inflexible vision of the homeland as a total prison is appealing when one is caught in the flux of exile and when one is not there in the belly of the beast, so to speak, where one may be forced to consider other tainted options, involving compromise.

Accented filmmakers imagine their country of origin in certain ways that are driven by national, historical, political, and personal differences, experiences, and desires. The homeland's chronotopical representation tends to emphasize its boundlessness and timelessness by cathecting it to the privileged sites of natural landscape, mountain, monument, and home and the retrospective narratives of longing, nostalgia, fetishism, and return—all of which emphasize continuity and descent. Such chronotopes and narratives are inscribed not only in the exilic films, TV programs, and music videos but also in the other performing arts, and by both straight and queer artists working in exile.[34] Political exiles, such as Güney, on the other hand, tend to represent the homeland using closed spatial and narrative forms. In configuring exile as prison (discussed in the following chapter) imprisonment becomes a two-sided metaphor, at once implying confinement and security.

6

Chronotopes of Life in Exile: Claustrophobia, Contemporaneity

IF THE UNCERTAIN and fluid conditions of deterritorialization liberate some filmmakers, they cause others, particularly political filmmakers, to seek the "security of dogma," in the form of political opposition and commitment (M. Robinson 1994, xvi). In their art this is expressed in their preference for the closed form, particularly in the chronotopical representation of life in exile and diaspora, which is generally the opposite of that of the homeland, as it stresses claustrophobia and temporality, cathected to sites of confinement and to narratives of panic and pursuit. These dogmatic and paranoid structures emphasize discontinuity and rupture. However, they also serve the comforting and critical functions of embodying the exiles' protest against the hostile social conditions in which they find themselves. While acting as safe havens, these very critical structures of protest can become potential traps. To explore their dynamics, it is helpful to bring in the concepts of agoraphobia and claustrophobia.

In 1871, a Berlin neurologist, Carl F. O. Westphal, described three male patients who shared common symptoms, which he termed "agoraphobia" (Crump 1991). All three men became extremely anxious when crossing empty streets or wide-open spaces. Today agoraphobia is understood to be a complex complaint, involving fear and avoidance of public places whether they are mobile, such as trains, elevators, buses, and subways, or stationary, such as streets, tunnels, movie houses, and restaurants. It is also associated with "panic attacks," consisting of breathlessness, air hunger, heart palpitation, and fear of going insane or of dying (Chambless 1982, 2; Marks 1987, 323–24). Light aggravates agoraphobics, as does social interaction. Finally, agoraphobia also usually involves claustrophobia, or dread of enclosed places, which most of these public places are.

The onset of agoraphobia is often preceded not by a single trauma but by "excessive adverse life events," among them relationship disruptions, loss, bereavement, and separation anxiety (Marks 1987, 360; Chambless 1982; 3; Garbowsky 1989, 58). To gain control over these clusters of fearful symptoms, agoraphobes withdraw to "safe zones," confining themselves to their place of residence or sometimes to a single room or even to bed. They draw comfort from "housebondage" and from "phobic partners," such as a trusted person or an object, perhaps an umbrella or a suitcase. They prefer dark places and, when they venture outside, tend to wear dark glasses. This voluntary narrowing of the living and bodily spaces has psychological, political, and symbolic meanings.

Although Westphal's first agoraphobic patients were men, the majority of agoraphobes today are women. However, agoraphobia, like other so-called women's disorders such as anorexia and hysteria, are not only individual conditions and responses but also social control mechanisms by which dominant ideology recruits the willing participation of its subjects. As Susan Bordo notes,

> Anorexia, hysteria, and agoraphobia may provide a paradigm of one way in which potential resistance is not merely undercut but *utilized* in the maintenance and reproduction of existing power relations. The central mechanism . . . involves a transformation (or, if you wish, duality) of meaning, through which conditions that are objectively (and, on one level, experientially) constraining, enslaving, and even murderous, come to be experienced as liberating, transforming, and life-giving. (1993, 168).

A similar mechanism is at work among the exiles. Women and exiles may willingly whittle down the space that they occupy in order to fit the normalizing gaze of society about gender, sexuality, and citizenship ideals—a way of "behaving themselves" by overcompensation. By so doing, they also send a signal of "embodied protest" against the dominance of those repressive ideals. These disorders have historically been influenced not only by gender but also by class differences and racial and ethnic oppression. However, as a strategy of resistance, pathology is an "unconscious, inchoate, and counterproductive protest without an effective language, voice, or politics" (Bordo 1993, 175). This is because the same embodied or confined space of protest and safety can become its opposite: a trap that intensifies yet another related pathology, claustrophobia. Thus, the subjects may oscillate between agoraphobia and claustrophobia, between feeling secure and feeling trapped. Erica Jordan and Shirin Etessam's film *Walls of Sand* (1994) provides a thorough examination of the cluster of phobias from which female agoraphobes suffer and the strategies of coping which they employ (see later discussion).

For many exiles, the separation from the homeland, the loss of status, language, culture, and family, and the fear of the hostile host society may constitute sufficiently "excessive adverse life events" to lead us to expect to see in their lives and their films agoraphobic and claustrophobic spatiality. A particularly moving account of such exilic events and the resultant panic attacks is provided by the American director Joseph Losey, who emigrated to England after he was blacklisted as a communist in the early 1950s.[1]

> I was petrified. And I had physical attacks. I thought that I was going to die. I thought that I had a heart problem. I used to have to leave the theatre because I was suffocating. I had to sit down in the middle of London traffic on the kerb because I couldn't breathe. I went to various doctors—kind doctors who charged me little. I had no heart problem. And it was just sheer, absolute panic, because I had nothing.

I had no family: my wife had left me, my child was living in the United States in a boarding school, I had no lover, I had no money, I had no work. I was 44. So I was at a point when most people begin to coast in their lives and everything that I had accomplished meant nothing. It was a terrifying period and probably terribly valuable for me. I had absolutely no preparation for being a pariah. I had no preparation for being a "Jew," for being a minority person! (quoted in Ciment 1985, 134–35)

Exilic ruptures and the phobic states they engender are also structurally linked to paranoia, defined as a "feeling of persecution unjustified in reality," characterized by fragmentation, decentering, and loss of subject-object boundaries (Burgin 1994, 232). As liminal exiles and interstitial filmmakers, accented directors are less apt to follow the conventions of established genres or the styles of dominant cinema than to inscribe in their films their own torqued and tortured experiences. While liminality encourages rule breaking, it can also encourage its opposite and become a "paranoid structure." Such a structure has many sources at home and abroad, including fear of persecution by the police, secret agents, interrogators, torturers, border guards, immigration officers, human smugglers (coyotes), and intolerant and hostile citizens. A paranoid structure may involve forms of dissociation, that is, the perception of fragmentation or multiplication of the self and of reality. For the politically exiled and refugee filmmakers, such structures are in part justified because they are based on legitimate fears.

These structures may also result from a collective siege mentality that is motivated by real or imagined historical and political threats. For example, according to Nitzan Ben-Shaul, "there is a pervasive mythical belief held by many Israelis that they are a besieged nation and that the whole world is against them. This notion of siege influences the ways in which Israelis evaluate fundamental socio-political concerns" (1997, 1). This is dubbed the "Massada syndrome," which refers to the ancient mountaintop fortress in southeast Israel, in which the Jews in A.D. 66–73 made a last stand against the Romans. This syndrome is intensified by the national aspiration of the Palestinians, which many Israelis and diaspora Jews consider to be a threat to the existence of the Israeli state. Such a threat finds its expression, on the one hand, in the Israeli right-wingers' expansionist policies of annexing and settling the Occupied Territories and, on the other hand, in the siege and paranoid mise-en-scène, filming, and narrative structures of many liberal Israeli films that deal with Palestinians. Ben-Shaul describes their phobic textual strategies, which are uncannily similar to the closed-form strategies of the accented films:

Claustrophobia and violent environments presented through labyrinthine deployments of shadowy spaces, usually in places where people lack freedom such as jails, mental institutions and army barracks; abrupt camera movements and editing patterns; temporal circularity; tragically bounded narrative structures; and the depiction of a society under a constant threat, whose members are motivated by suspicion and lack of trust among themselves and towards outsiders, conducting themselves through conspiracies and plots for which all means are legitimate. It is this formal structure that turns the vague ideas for resolving the conflict which motivate the protagonists into hopeless protest. (1997, 69)[2]

The closed and phobic structures are also associated with the space-time of modernity and late modernity, their concomitant discontinuities and ruptures, and the panoptic and rhizomatic disciplinary powers that have bureaucratized, militarized, and commercialized the public and private spheres of the Western world, to which accented filmmakers have predominantly relocated.[3] These phobic chronotopes and paranoid structures take the form in the accented films of closed mise-en-scène and filming style and a receding structure of feelings. Small, dingy, and overcrowded immigrant apartments, prison cells, hotel rooms, buses, tunnels, and confining symbolic spaces such as the suitcase are favored. The claustrophobia of these settings is intensified by a dark lighting scheme that limits sight, by barriers in the shot that impede vision, and by tight shot composition, immobile framing, and a stationary camera. The characters' physical disability or immobility deepens recessive feeling structures. These phobic spaces and structures, along with panic-ridden plots, which create a sense of psychic narrowing, may serve therapeutic, strategic, and pathological purposes. By expressing the psychic tensions of displacement and by embodying the security of closed spaces, they are therapeutic. By giving the exiles an iconography both to critique the home and host societies and to construct new identities, they are strategic. By becoming traps that immobilize the exiles and close their horizons, they are pathological.

Exile as Prison

Turkish Films in Germany

Unlike Güney's exilic films, which dealt with Turkish society, and whose narratives of siege occurred at home, the films of many Turkish filmmakers in Germany focus on Turkish immigrants living in Europe. Despite the shift in location, prison remains a key chronotope, and phobia and panic prominent feeling structures. However, this time they express anxiety and fear about life in exile, particularly in the Europe of the 1980s and 1990s, which has been increasingly intolerant of its guest workers and immigrants, even though many of them are born and bred there. These filmmakers include Tunç Okan, Erden Kiral, Tuncel Kurtiz, Yilmaz Arslan, Enis Gunay, Rasim Konyar, and Tevfik Baser, and the Kurdish filmmakers from Turkey Nizamettin Ariç and Ismet Elci. There are also a number of women documentary filmmakers, among them Janine Meerapfel, Serap Berrakkarasu, and Merlyn Solakhan. Their collective output has created a "Turkish cinema in exile." These filmmakers belong to the large Turkish population in Germany, which is over 2 million currently. Their heaviest concentration is in Berlin, which has more Turks than any city in the world outside Turkey (Kinzer 1997c, 3). However, this population is demographically diverse in terms of ethnicity, religiosity, nationality, and nationalist politics. Among them, for example, are an estimated 500,000 Kurds from Turkey, Iran, Iraq, and Syria who form the largest population outside these traditional Kurdish regions (Kinzer 1998, A9). This has created a classic case of exilic reversal in which ethnicity initially wins over nationality: many immigrant Turks of Kurdish descent in Germany have become nationalist Kurds not Germans, as part of their acculturation process (Leggewie 1996). As filmmaker Ariç told me in an interview:

> I really started learning my mother tongue in Berlin. In Turkey, Kurds do not know much about their own language and history because studying these subjects is forbidden there. Even though Kurdish children could speak Kurdish at home until they went to school, we did not, because in our area a Kurdish uprising in years past had been beaten down so violently and Kurdish families so frightened that no one dared speak Kurdish, even in the privacy of our homes. Because of their harsh treatment of us, we called the Turkish elementary schools "torture chambers for Kurdish children." For example, when I could not pronounce a Turkish word properly, my teacher grabbed my ear, twisted it, and pulled it up really hard. For weeks after, I heard noises in my ear. I was very frightened of my teacher. As a result, we Kurds have learned to be better Turks than the Turks themselves. I was an assimilated Turk when I went into exile in Berlin. (Naficy 1997b)

No longer faced with the suppression of their identity in Germany, the Kurds found a historic opportunity to become more deeply educated about themselves. It was in the Western liberal democracies like Germany that members of the Kurdish diaspora could come together to form a pan-Kurdish national identity.[4] Finally, the anti-Turkish neo-Nazi racism and criminality, as well as the Kurdish violence against the Turks, which flared up periodically during the 1990s, forced both Kurdish and Turkish immigrants into a kind of circling of the ethnonational wagons to produce and protect a specific Kurdish or Turkish identity.[5]

Even though the Turks (including the Kurds from Turkey) represent only about 2.5 percent of the total German population, they form the largest single group of "foreigners" (*ausländers*), and as such they exert significant influence on both German and Turkish politics (Chapin 1996). They are part of the phenomenon of labor migration called "guest workers" (*gästarbeiter*), which is no longer an accurate designation, for it implies a temporary stay for the immigrants and a favorable reception by the host society—neither of which is true. Many of the Turks are in Germany permanently, and many others are born and bred there, yet they are treated neither as full Germans nor as welcomed guests. On the other hand, many Turks have themselves resisted assimilation in order to vote in Turkish elections and own property in Turkey by maintaining their original language, culture, religion, and nationality. This complex social history of emigration, division, and reception informs the claustrophobic and dystopic structures of feeling of Turkish accented films made in Germany.

Close-Up: *Tevfik Baser*

In Baser's films, the claustrophobic chronotope of home is relocated to the host society, isolating and confining primarily women. Born in 1951 in Cankiri, Turkey, Baser received his training in photography, graphic design, and cinematography in England, Turkey, and Germany in the 1970s and 1980s. He began making documentary and award-winning feature films in Germany, where he became a citizen in 1989 (Pflaum and Prinzler 1993, 236). His two features of the 1980s, *40 m² Germany* (*40 m² Deutschland*, 1986) and *Farewell to a False Paradise* (*Abscheed vom Falschen Paradies*, 1988), are both shot in confining locations (in a one-bedroom apartment and in a prison, respectively), and they are characterized by closed mise-en-scène and closed-form filming. His *40 m² Germany* portrays a young wife (Turna) who is literally locked by her possessive guest worker husband (an older man, Dursun) inside their apartment every morning that he goes to work. She discovers this fact dramatically, in the course of housecleaning and confronts her husband when he return home that night:

> TURNA [*washing clothes in a pan on the floor*]: Why did you lock me in? Am I an animal?
>
> DURSUN [*seated at the table, eating*]: Listen up! Don't get on my nerves. This is not like home, we are in Germany. You don't know how sly the German men are. How did you know that you were locked in in the first place? Do you want to leave? Then, go on, leave. Perhaps you'll find a pile of shit.
>
> TURNA: I don't want to leave or quit. I just wanted to clean the floor in front of the door.
>
> DURSUN [*eyeing her with lust*]: Come, girl, come to me. I can see that you are also exhausted.
>
> [*the husband forces himself on her from behind, but with each of his thrusts, she lowers her head farther in the frame until it disappears below it*][6]

The film's criticism of the Turkish patriarchy is embedded in the framing of the last shot of this sequence, which shows both Turna's sexual violation and her shame about it. Throughout the film, she unwillingly acquiesces to her husband's sexual demands, grimacing with pain, shame, or disgust. She also fights him by withdrawing from him emotionally and psychologically: she unwillingly reduces her conversations with him and refuses even to look at him directly. In the meantime, she works hard, washing clothes, cooking, and cleaning. These strategies of denial and aversion and her constant labor reduce her space considerably. By so doing, she is both "behaving herself" by overcompensation and embodying her protest against her husband's oppression. The result is that she is trapped and powerless. She possesses neither forty square meters

Figure 24. Claustro-
phobia and withdrawal.
Turna whittles her
bodily space and turns
away from her husband
in Tefik Baser's *40
m² Germany.*

of Germany nor forty square meters *in* Germany. All she owns is the space of
her own body, her warm memories of her childhood home, and the suitcase
and the ethnic niche in the apartment that contain Turkish clothing, objects,
and souvenirs. Her access to these private spaces, which are not claimed or
violated either by her husband or by Germany, expands her psychic space,
turning spatial confinement into moments of liberation.

Many exiles leave their homelands because of social and political oppression,
yet they obsess about it and create oppressive chronotopes in their imaginative
works. As Aijaz Ahmad has noted, émigré writers and artists, such as Henry
James, Joseph Conrad, Ezra Pound, T. S. Eliot, Pablo Picasso, Salvador Dali,
James Joyce, Gertrude Stein, and Salman Rushdie, experienced suffocation
and claustrophobia

> in their own spaces of this globe, and were subsequently to leave behind immense
> resources of genre and vocabulary for delineating the predominant image of the mod-
> ern artist who lives as a *literal* stranger in a foreign and impersonal city and who, on
> the one hand, uses the condition of exile as the basic metaphor for modernity and
> even for the human condition itself, while, on the other hand, writing obsessively,
> copiously, of that very land which had been declared "suffocating." (1994, 134)

This self-created claustrophobia is a proactive strategy of embodied criticism,
resistance, and temporary liberation, which is fundamentally different from
either the oppression the filmmakers would face in the homeland or the hostility they encounter in the host society—both of which are imposed upon them
from without and are, therefore, stifling.

One day Turna discovers that the apartment door is left unlocked; she gingerly steps out into the dark stairwell for a few moments, only to return inside.
The reasons for her withdrawal may be her fear of the German society, her
awareness of her own inadequacy to survive outside as a single female and a
foreigner without language and profession, and her fear of severe reprisal from

her husband. Confinement thus reveals its Janus face, that is, its ability to generate a sense of (false) comfort. Compression and expansion, together, constitute the dual chronotopes of the accented cinema. In the end, when Dursun dies of a violent heart attack in the shower, Turna has no choice but to finally step into the light and the uncertainties of the German day.

In his second feature, *Farewell to a False Paradise,* Baser continued his examination of émigré Turkish women but associated the spaces of confinement with an enhanced sense of security. In most of the exilic films studied, closed forms are coded negatively, as prisons that trap individuals. In this film, Baser reverses the coding, turning the prison into a haven. It begins with the film's female protagonist (Elif) recovering from a suicide attempt in prison. She is serving a four-year jail sentence in Germany for killing her abusive husband, but as her release date nears, the fear of what freedom means begins to gnaw at her. Imprisonment means escape from German and Turkish societies, each of which poses a different threat to her, as an immigrant and as a woman, respectively. It provides her with a safe haven from the German neo-Nazi attacks and from patriarchal retributions of her Turkish relatives. It also provides her with much-needed normalcy and continuity, as seen in the daily routines and scheduled events.

But this safe haven does not turn out to be a heaven. It is a false paradise in which Elif is alienated from both German and Turkish cultures: she is alone, isolated, and silent throughout much of the film. She receives threatening letters from male relatives at home and threatening visits from those in Germany, since they are imperiled by her bold action against her abusive husband. She is caught between very difficult options: she can neither go home to Turkey, nor continue to stay in jail, nor allow herself to be released. Home for her is in a state of crisis—one that is exacerbated when her petition to remain in Germany as a refugee is denied and her release date is advanced due to her good conduct. Panic sets in. She is left with only one way out: she attempts suicide but fails.

The film cuts back to the beginning, showing Elif's recovery from her suicide attempt. This circular structure helps drive home the dystopian point that for exiles in the societies of control there is no outside anymore. What a frightening prospect: a world from which no escape, or exile, is possible! However, letters from her mother, a love interest in an inmate, and a renewed hope in the possibility of acculturation into German society revive her. The prison becomes not only a place of security but also one of transformation, symbolized by her departure from prison in the end dressed not in Turkish clothing, with long hair, but in men's clothing, with a short haircut. Despite their claustrophobic chronotopicality, *40 m² Germany* and *Farewell to a False Paradise* do not give in to cynicism, for they validate women's individual initiative to counter collective and patriarchal values.

The closed-form films, such as Baser's, which contain the chronotopes of modernity, contemporaneity, and exile, tend to critique traditional values, while the open-form films, which emphasize the chronotopes of nature and retrospection, seem to embrace those values. That the accented films that critique the homeland's traditions seem to get funded and distributed more readily raises the troubling specter of politically motivated film funding—even by organizations that are sympathetic to minoritarian values and practices. For example, it can be argued that while Baser's representation of Muslim women as victims and of Muslim men as patriarchal overlords in these two films reflects and critiques the real gender relations among Turkish émigrés, it also corroborates the West's jaundiced view of Islam and of Muslims. By funding films that primarily highlight the negative aspects of Turkish society, funding agencies help to control the repertoire of available images of Turks and Muslims. By accepting those funds, accented filmmakers become complicit with their own self-othering, thus confirming the dominant prejudices against themselves.

In Baser's third feature *Farewell, Stranger* (*Lebewohl, Fremde*, 1991), there is a shift of location, from closed, interior, urban places to open, exterior, rural spaces of a spectacular island in the North Sea called Halig. This shift is not only from the inside to the outside but also from the ethnic (Turkish) to the national (German). There is also a shift in the diegetic characters, from strictly Turkish to German-Turkish, and to a multiethnic configuration. These shifts might be related to a significant change in Baser's own status: his becoming a German citizen just before making this film. Despite these changes that favor assimilation, Turkish émigrés and Turkish prisons are among the film's key issues and chronotopes.

The land in this coastal region is flat, and it is flooded for part of the year. Each house is built far from the others and on a rise, so that when floodwaters cover the flat lands, the houses stand above water like islands in the midst of a vast ocean. However, the vastness of the ocean and the natural surroundings are not coded as open or as symbols of a utopian homeland or communion with nature, as is the case with Palestinian and Armenian accented films. In fact, they are very oppressive. Most of the time the atmosphere is dark, the ocean waves rough, and the sky brooding and raining. As the film progresses, the storms gain strength until, at the film's end, all the inhabitants are evacuated, leaving isolated little island-houses in the rising tide. In addition, a great portion of the film's plot takes place in the closed interiors of the home of Karin, a beautiful, middle-aged German who has left her unfaithful husband in Hamburg to reassess her life in the solitude of her childhood house, which she has inherited. However, like the other women in Baser's films, she discovers that she is now a foreigner in her own childhood village. From Karin's point of view, the film is one of inner exile.

Life in her small village nearby is disturbed by the arrival of a number of male political refugees from the Third World—Pakistan, Africa, and Turkey—

who are brought there by a local pastor. Their presence injects the external exile perspective into the film's discourse of homelessness. Several of the refugees live in a one-room trailer without much privacy. During a heavy storm, each takes a turn inside with a prostitute while the others wait outside in the pouring rain. The villagers deeply resent these "undesirables"—a resentment they demonstrate by boycotting the pastor, drowning one of the refugees who had befriended a local woman, and setting fire to their trailer. As the social climate becomes more intolerant, the natural climate also worsens. The sense of panic and claustrophobia gradually builds up.

In the meantime, however, Karin's relationship with Deniz, a Turkish refugee and poet, moves toward the intimate immensity of a passionate love affair, despite their inability to speak or understand each other's language. Karin's house becomes both a safe refuge from the threatening environmental and social worlds outside and a prison that isolates them. For a long time the lack of a shared language does not pose a barrier: they share meals, drink, smoke, laugh, write, paint, cook, touch, dance a slow tango, and make love.

However, this synaesthetic sharing of difference comes to an end when the floods force their evacuation, bringing Deniz to the attention of the authorities, who arrest him. A year later, Karin receives a package containing Deniz's book of poetry, *Farewell, Stranger*, which is dedicated to her. The biographical blurb on the book's jacket reveals what Deniz could not tell her without verbal communication: condemned to a 128-year prison term in Turkey for his writings, Deniz had fled the country to seek political asylum in Germany. Upon his arrest, his asylum request was denied, and he was deported to Turkey, where he died in prison. Thus prison again looms large in this Baser film.

Close-Up: *Yilmaz Arslan's* Passages (Langer Gang, *1992*)

This is a disturbingly confining black-and-white film with moments of operatic freedom, made by a young Turkish filmmaker. Born in 1968, Arslan left Turkey for Germany in 1975 with his parents to receive treatment for his polio. He spent much of his youth in a rehabilitation center in Neckarmünd, near Heidelberg, where he founded the theater troupe Sommer-Winter, consisting largely of handicapped actors, which has since performed in Germany and abroad. The film is about a rehabilitation center for disabled youth, many of whom are of Turkish or other foreign origins. Almost the entire film occurs in the center's prisonlike, industrial spaces, such as in empty hallways, ramps, staircases, and elevators, or inside the small rooms of the inmates. Since much of the film "looks as if it were shot from a motorized wheelchair, the center has the scary oppressive feel of a large, well-kept prison as experienced by a child" (Holden 1993a, B2).

The claustrophobia of these institutional settings and the style of filming are intensified by the severe disability of the center's inhabitants, which reduces their mobility and human interaction to an unimaginable degree. A boy and a girl want to have sex; with difficulty they take off their clothes, but their bodies, which are badly contorted, cannot meet in the right places (even to kiss) despite their excruciating efforts. Another boy walks down an empty hallway for only a few steps before collapsing with a loud thud onto the floor. He does not give up, however. As the camera holds the shot, he gets up a number of times, walks a few steps, and collapses again and again, somewhat reminiscent of Hatoum's efforts in her film *Under Siege*, in which she tried for hours to stand up in a container of mud. The neck muscles of a boy in a wheelchair are so weak that he is unable to lift his head from his chest without assistance.

Arslan does not dwell on victimhood or shy away from disability. Instead, he presents his diegetic world, which is a microcosm of the "able" society outside, from the perspective of the disabled people. One key protagonist in a wheelchair is a Turkish girl named Nesrin, who with her boyfriend Didi looks after a young German boy, forming a family. The family is short-lived, however. Nesrin gets pregnant and, instead of facing her parents, commits suicide by jumping from a window. The paraplegic Martin is humiliated and raped after he rapes his own girlfriend. A group of boys in a corner drink alcohol, smoke marijuana, exchange sick jokes about thalidomide babies, and fantasize about moving to Venezuela to cultivate pot. There are also artists in this minisociety. Dieter is a talented painter who mixes the paint with the tapered ends of his shoulders and applies the brush by holding it between his toes. An African-American girl, who is about to be taken back home by her soldier father, sings the blues for her friends in a staircase. These scenes demonstrate disability and ability, corporeal confinement and psychological expansion.

These human stories are told with the kind of point-of-view filming and camera positioning that encourage audience identification with the disabled. Unlike a majority of the films that deal with the disabled, *Passages* neither objectifies nor isolates them. As a result, viewing it also discourages the usual reactions: self-loathing, alienation, and anger among the disabled audiences and pity among the rest.[7]

However, the feeling structure of *Passages* is dark, dystopic, and sardonic, and it provides a savage critique of German society from the vantage point of its outsiders and foreigners. A key scene is the film's opening, which shows the administrator giving visitors a tour of his institution, including a visit to the rooftop from where one of them takes a snapshot of one of the giant establishment's buildings. The official proudly explains that the center's aims are to "fully rehabilitate our children and young people" through education and vocational training so that they can "live a full, independent life." The next shot literally tears that claim to pieces. It shows the visitor's photograph, which now fills the frame, and on which the film's title is superimposed. Two feet reach into the frame; the toes grab the edges of the photograph and tear it into several pieces. Then, as the opening credits are superimposed over the scene, the same two feet in extreme close-up roll a cigarette with magical dexterity and take it to a mouth off-camera. It is only in the next shot, in which a foot brings a candle to the cigarette, that we realize we have been witnessing the actions of an armless dwarf. The critique in *Passages* is impassioned, not senti-mental. The institutional neglect throughout the film (no attendant, nurse, or caregiver is seen after the opening sequence) makes a mockery of the pride and compassion that the German administrator expresses in the beginning. No effort at training or rehabilitation is apparent. The film ultimately suggests that there is no real home anywhere; even that most intimate and primary of all homes, the body, is not safe or nurturing.

As the influx of new émigrés into Germany increased and multiculturalism became a reality, the country's citizenship laws were changed in 1999 to permit any child born in Germany with at least one parent who has lived in the country for eight years to become a citizen (Cohen 1999, A3). Perhaps in response to this changing situation, filmmakers have recently been paying more attention to the plight of the hyphenated youth and their lifestyle. A strong entry is Kutlug Ataman's third feature film, *Lola and Billy the Kid* (*Lola & Bilidikid*, 1999), which focuses on the claustrophobic underworld of gay Turkish youth in Berlin. It centers on Murat, a German-born Turkish boy, and his growing awareness of his homosexuality that has alienated him from his family, headed by a ruthless brother who himself turns out to be gay. Murat's identity is doubly convoluted, for it is caught in the crosscurrents of an ethnic drama and a sexual orientation trauma. The mise-en-scène and filming of tawdry public bath-rooms, dingy apartments, and threatening streets at night are highly claustro-phobic, as are the exploitative and explosive social relations of Turkish (and German) men, who, having come out of the ethnic enclave and the closet, must now contend with psychological hostility and physical violence from all sides. Ataman, who is himself gay and lives in Istanbul, does not pull any punches in choosing his targets; he criticizes the German and Turkish societies, both gay and straight, for their intolerance of people who are different.

Iranian Filmmakers in Europe and the United States

Close-Up: Sohrab Shahid Saless

In insisting on the security and freedom that confined spaces can offer, *40 m²Germany* and *Farewell to a False Paradise* echo Shahid Saless's powerful film *Utopia* (1982), about a confining house of prostitution in Germany. Born in Tehran, Iran, in 1944, Shahid Saless received training in film production in Austria and France and began making films in Iran in the late 1960s. While employed by the Ministry of Culture and Arts, he made twenty-two documenta-ries and short films. He directed his first feature, *A Simple Event* (*Yek Ettefaq-e Sadeh*, 1973), under the guise of working on a short film. It brought Shahid Saless to national attention. His compelling, award-winning *Still Life* (*Tabi'at-e*

Bijan, 1974) put him on the international map of cinéastes, garnering him high praise, including the top directing award, the Silver Bear, from the Berlin Film Festival. He left Iran in 1974 for Germany because of the stifling conditions governing the film industry, which had put a stop to his production of *Quarantine* (*Qarantin-eh*), a film he never completed. In the course of his twenty-three years of German exile, he made fifteen uncompromising, lengthy films for cinema and television. Many of his features are over two hours long and have won international recognition. After several fallow years, he terminated his German exile by relocating first to Canada and then to the United States in the mid-1990s, where he died in 1998 at the age of fifty-four.

In a series of interviews with me a year before his death, Shahid Saless preferred to speak of his lengthy sojourn abroad as a kind of "long vacation," not exile.[8]

> I do not belong to the Iranian diaspora cinema. I left the country in 1974 because of certain difficulties that had been placed in my filmmaking path and because I was very interested in filmmaking, like any young person. I left the country voluntarily and worked for twenty-three years in Germany without returning home, despite encouragement by the regimes of both the Shah and Khomeini to do so. I must admit with extreme sadness that I have no nostalgic longing for Iran. When each morning I set foot outside my house, whether it was in Germany, France, Venice, or the Soviet Union—the places where I have lived and made films—I would feel at home, because I had no difficulties. I am essentially not a patriot. . . . I think one's homeland is not one's place of birth, but the country that gives one a place to stay, to work, and to make a living. . . . Germany was my home for a long time. (Naficy 1997f)

Yet Shahid Saless's critically dystopic films, his successful but marginalized career as a filmmaker in Germany, and his reasons for finally leaving his adopted homeland for yet another exile all point to a deep undercurrent of exilism in his life and oeuvre. The German house of prostitution, which in his subversively titled film *Utopia* is a microcosm of German society, is far from a home (*heimat*); it is more like a dystopia. The film centers on the lives of five female prostitutes and their ruthless male pimp (Heinz) and their exploitative relationships inside the brothel named Club Arena. The women, who come from different walks of life, are hoping to improve their own lives and support their families by working in the brothel. Similar to the exilic films of Güney, Baser, and Arslan, in *Utopia* the external world of the host society is a threatening presence that is shunned. The women leave the house only once, when the pimp drives them to a medical clinic for their periodic examination. While indoors, they are always behind the closed doors of Club Arena's various rooms. Every door that opens must be closed, all the windows are shut, and all the curtains are drawn (except the one in the kitchen). Frequent long shots of the corridor with closed doors on both sides give the impression of a prison. The walls are bare and austere, lacking any decoration.

This spatial claustrophobia and severity are intensified by a temporal claustrophobia caused by the slow pace of the film, the slow movement of the diegetic characters, the slow camera movements, and the women's frequent questions to each other about the time of day. Time passes slowly as they await their infrequent customers. There are long pauses when each woman is in thought, staring into the distance or looking at herself in the mirror. Their averted eyes and limp arms, their silence, and their general suppression of feelings during sex emphasize both the film's closed form and the prostitutes' withdrawal into themselves. Like Turna in *40 m² Germany*, they have whittled their living and bodily spaces to a minimum. Midway through the film, the student named Susi, who is the most outspoken of the prostitutes, demands her back pay from Heinz so she can leave her abject circumstances. Heinz brutalizes her physically, and she leaves without her money. Surprisingly, she returns after a few days. It seems that the financial rewards and psychological security that the enclosed brothel provided—even though violent, sadistic, and degrading—outweighed the threat that choice and freedom outside offered. This is a damning critique by an exile of the German homeland.

Heinz's frequent threats and abuse and the women's lack of retaliation, or their instant punishment when they mildly question his authority, build a tremendous amount of tension, turning Club Arena into a battle arena in which the unequal power relations of the male master and his female slaves must be settled. At first, the women deal individually with the attractions and abuses with which Heinz manipulates them. One of them attempts suicide, another temporarily leaves the club, while a third confesses her love to him during sex. However, as his arbitrary and abusive behavior gradually encompasses all of them and they realize that there is no outside and no escape, they unite against him. One day, Renata, the ranking prostitute, finds the opportunity she has been waiting for and stabs Heinz in the heart with a pair of scissors, injuring him badly. The others gather enough collective courage to finish him off. The film ends with each prostitute expressing her desire to leave the brothel. A customer's ringing of the doorbell brings them out of their fantasizing. Business goes on as usual but without a slavemaster. Their exile, too, continues, but it is likely to change to voluntary banishment.

Over three hours long (198 minutes), *Utopia* exhibits Shahid Saless's Chekhovian naturalism and his characteristic minimalist style, consisting of a slow pace, slow acting style, and a slow line delivery; a rather static and observational camera that is prone to long takes, long shots, and slow pans; and a concern for the life of ordinary people and the routine practices of their everyday existence, rendered with an ironic distance. Although he usually shuns symbolism, this film has a metaphorical and political import. Shahid Saless himself has pointed out that both the prostitutes and their master are symbols: the former, of the citizens who dream of liberty; the latter, of their exploitative rulers whom they

Figure 25. Oppressive
spatiality. The prosti-
tutes after stabbing
their pimp to death
in Shahid Saless's
Utopia. The subtitle
reads "We are free."

wish to overthrow. In his pessimistic view of humanity, once they have over-
thrown their masters, subject people often turn on each other (Shahid Saless
1993, 63). *Utopia*, however, leaves open the possibility that the masterless prostitutes may work cooperatively as independent sex workers, much like the interstitial filmmakers working in the capitalist postindustrial cinema—a cinema
Shahid Saless condemned as a "whore's milieu."

One of Shahid Saless's many accomplishments in *Utopia* is that the concrete
and the symbolic do not clash with one another. As *L.A. Reader* reviewer Dan
Sallitt observed, "The concrete behavior keeps the film from floating off into
metaphysical realms, and the abstraction of style gives the story an odd sense
of universality without straining the demands of realism."[9] The play of the
concrete and the abstract is also inscribed powerfully in his first feature film
made in Germany, *Far from Home* (*In der Fremde* 1975), which portrays the
life of Turkish guest workers, who are not being treated very much like guests.
The protagonist, Hussein, is a factory worker who maintains a crushingly routinized work life as an earnest prisoner of the factory's monstrously noisy machines. As Silvia Kratzer-Juilfs notes: "Work gives his life a much wanted
structure, but its structured rules are also prison bars. At work he feels comfortable, safe and useful—all of which are important aspects of the notion of
"home." At the same time this is also the place of the ultimate alienation since
no individual expressions are allowed or even possible here" (1996, 238). Hussein's austere life outside the factory is no less confining and crushing, as his
attempts to enter German society fail. What few German words he has learned
from an audiotape lead to more misunderstanding than understanding. He
lives an isolated life, even though he shares an overcrowded communal apartment with other guest workers.[10] Hussein's only contact here is with a younger
man named Kalim, who claims to have a prized connection to German society:
a German girlfriend. He borrows money from Hussein to sustain this relationship—money that he gambles away and never returns. The girlfriend turns out
to have been a forgery on the part of both men, a figure of desire with which

they emplaced themselves in the midst of their total displacement. An urgent letter forces Kalim to return to Turkey—a return that is unwanted and dreaded and which permanently forecloses his dream of freedom and connection to Germany, even though what he has experienced of Germany is far from that idyllic German dream of an elsewhere (*fernweh*). In this dystopic figuration of the exilic return, *Far from Home* runs counter to many accented films, which inscribe and celebrate actual or imaginary returns longingly and nostalgically.

Shahid Saless's *Order* (*Ordung*, 1980) also offers a critically dystopic vision of German society, which seems to be suffering from a coma. Precise but deadly routines rule the life and work of the diegetic society, including those of Herbert, a middle-aged engineer, and his wife. This routinized life is interrupted when Herbert loses his job, an event that sends him, like Paul in *Roses for Africa*, into a tailspin, characterized by increasingly erratic behavior. The most startling are his repeated shouts of "Wake up!" in the streets in the early morning hours. Despite the pleas of his wife and annoyed neighbors to desist, he continues with his noisy wake-up calls. This passive-aggressive behavior appears to be Herbert's (and Shahid Saless's) critique of the German condition, which is so routinized and impersonal that no emotional connection or spontaneity is possible. When he cannot be subdued, Herbert is placed in a mental institution, where by means of drug therapy he is again normalized into a passive, comatose "good citizen" like the rest of his compatriots.

In *Diary of a Lover* (*Tagebuch eines Liebenden*, 1976), a butcher waits during the entire film for his fiancée, whose body is discovered under his bed at the film's end. The sound track contains excerpts of the man's diary. For much of the film, he is isolated and confined to his small, dark apartment in a nondescript, high-rise building—a confinement that is excruciatingly emphasized by Shahid Saless's filming strategy. One of these consists of very slow zoom-ins from the outside onto the man's window, and slow zoom-outs from the reverse angle from the inside, showing him waiting by the window. As Mehrnaz Saeed Vafa notes in her documentary *Sohrab Shahid Saless: Far from Home* (1998), "We get a sense that all those people living behind those windows are prisoners of the system. And that behind each window is a man like him who is waiting."

Like the work of many accented filmmakers, Shahid Saless's films resonate autobiographically, their despondency both reflecting and constituting his exilic structures of feeling. They contain a nostalgia for a lost or absent mother, while father figures are rare. These figurations have strong personal sources, for Shahid Saless lost his own mother, who abandoned the family before he was two years old, and he was not particularly close to his father.[11] His most autobiographical film made in Iran was his first feature, *Still Life*, while his most autobiographical exilic film was his last film, *Roses for Africa* (*Rosen für Afrika*, 1991). As he told me, *Roses* "is all about myself, even though it is an adaptation of a novel. I have changed the story a lot and, at any rate, Paul's attitude and behavior is exactly like mine. Whatever he does, I do. I wanted to see myself on the screen as I am" (Naficy 1997f). What is this most autobiographical film about? It is not about escaping the trap of here and now by *returning* to an earlier home (*heimat*); rather, it is about the unfulfilled desire to escape this trap by *departing* for an idealized elsewhere (*fernweh*) named "Africa." As such, it is about a home-founding journey—one that fails, like Shahid Saless's own. Despite their manifest differences, all his films ruminate about a common dilemma: that of pervasive homelessness and unbelonging. Their collective vision constitutes one of the most sustained critiques by an exilic filmmaker of his adopted homeland. In *Far from Home* he offers undesired return home; in *Utopia*, a form of internal exile; in *Order*, amnesia; and in *Roses for Africa*, suicide.

In a sardonic, short write-up, Shahid Saless called cinema a "whore's milieu," one that does not do "much for one's potency" (1988, 56). The designation of filmmakers as impotent whores working in societies to which they do not fully belong and from which they cannot truly escape (like the prostitutes in *Utopia*) is both a pessimistic and a realistic assessment of the interstitial conditions under which they operate.

Sadly, this characterization of impotence hangs ominously over his own life and times in Germany, for Shahid Saless's career there reveals the attractions and the pitfalls of this whore's milieu, as well as the very high cost to him of his uncompromising individualism and auteurist integrity. While in Germany, he regularly received national, multinational, and television funding for his films, whose budgets were not particularly small for interstitial filmmakers, ranging from 150,000 marks for his documentary *Lotte H. Eisner's Long Vacation* to 1.5 million marks for his last fiction film, *Roses for Africa*. However, obtaining sufficient funding was never easy. For example, he spent three years pursuing five multinational TV and film funding sources in order to film, in the Soviet Union, *Anton Chekhov: A Life* (*Anton Pavlovlo Cechov: Ein Leben*, 1981), his loving tribute to the person he called "my master." "I had chased after the 450,000 mark film's budget so much that I felt like an exhausted, panting poodle" (Naficy 1997f).

Despite these difficulties, Shahid Saless was prolific until the early 1990s, making more than one film every two years, an output that exceeds that of most exilic filmmakers. In addition, his award-winning films were shown repeatedly on ZDF German television and on the Arté European channel, and some were screened commercially in major German cities. Half a dozen retrospectives in Europe and America, from London to Paris to Chicago, honored his career achievements. For each film, he received a salary for directing and for writing the screenplay, and he continued to receive residuals when they were aired on television.[12] His filming method was fast and furious: *Utopia* was shot in under three weeks, and *Roses for Africa* was shot in twenty-nine days, three days ahead of schedule. Such speed (given the length of his films) necessitated not only preplanning but also faithfulness to the plans. He rarely veered away from his screenplays during either filming or editing.

Despite his accomplishments, Shahid Saless remained an outsider in the German cinema, chiefly because of his uncompromising attitude, his difficult and demanding work habits (requiring working through an attorney since *Utopia* [Dehbashi 1992, 205]),[13] his minimalist style, his critical dystopia, and his bitter feeling structure (one sympathetic critic called his films "dark as tar" [Ruhani 1992, 229]).[14] Although there are numerous journalistic reviews of his films in various languages, Eurocentric scholars in Europe and North America have paid little attention to him, treating him as more of a guest than a contender.[15]

Given the dystopic trajectory of his films, it is no wonder that the metaphor of filmmakers as impotent whores became a reality for Shahid Saless in the mid-1990s. Up to the early 1990s, the state-subsidized funding involving loans, advances, guarantees, prizes, and awards helped to partially shield alternative filmmakers (including accented filmmakers) from the vagaries of the market. As Anton Kaes notes, this economic dependence on the state meant that these filmmakers "never gained a mass following" because government subsidy ensured that they "never needed to gain one" (1989, 21). However, after Germany's unification and the intensified privatization of the media, which profoundly transformed both Germany and its film industry, Shahid Saless was no longer able to make the type of "art films" he had been making for two decades. The transformation had in fact worsened the whorish competitiveness he had critiqued. Unwilling to compromise, he was now not only an outsider but also a true stranger in a strange land, because of which he became increasingly despondent and darker in outlook. Interstitial authorship takes a high toll:

> After *Roses for Africa*, for six years I could not make a single film. I had three great screenplays, which people in the know thought could be made into successful films. Unfortunately, one by one they were rejected by the producers who wanted films with happy endings—the type of films I'd never made before. When all three screenplays were rejected, I began drinking all alone from the crack of dawn until five in the afternoon. At five o'clock I would fix myself a meal, eat it, and then make numerous phone calls to friends in different parts of the world. All of them would admonish me for drinking. After hanging up the phone, I would fall into a state of stupor until the next morning. I did this for three years. Without any films to make, I was totally undermined and vanquished; while when I was making films, nothing in the world mattered to me. (Naficy 1997f)

His refusals to continue to play along meant that there was no place for him in Germany, even in its interstices. Unlike his alter ego, Paul, in *Roses for Africa*, who commits suicide when he is unable to leave for his idealized elsewhere, Shahid Saless succeeded in leaving for the United States, where he settled in 1995 with the hope of making his first American feature.[16] But this proved not to be an ideal place, for he was unable to finance any film projects; in addition, he had to battle a series of long-standing illnesses, including tuberculosis, pneumonia, and an ulcer, to which he finally succumbed in a sad, lonely death in Chicago. If for two decades he had felt at home in Germany—albeit marginalized—he was not comfortable in the United States, largely because of its history of interventionist foreign policy in Iran and other Third World countries: "I do not feel at home here for I have an open account with America that cannot be closed" (Naficy 1997f). The place of comfort was not outside; as in *Utopia*, it was inside, in a nondescript apartment.

Shahid Saless's profound homelessness and exile—despite his denial—comes through in his elegiacally dystopic films and in the snippets of my interviews with him. What more than anything else turned him into an exilic figure, causing his successive departures from previous homelands, was not national unbelonging but obstacles in his filmmaking path:

> From the time that I went after film and became a filmmaker until today, I have not felt for a moment that I am Iranian. But that which gave me everything and was my home, my wife, my father, my mother, my children, my life was filmmaking. If one day they tack a red ribbon on my lapel, that says "Filmmaking Forbidden," I won't commit suicide because I hate people who do so, but I think I will die within two years' time. (Naficy 1997f)

While such obsessive passion for cinema is peculiar to only a few exilic filmmakers, such as Shahid Saless and Buñuel, the empowering function of filmmaking, which helps the exiles cope with deterritorialization by creating new narrative homes, motivates all accented filmmakers.

This discussion of Turkish and Iranian filmmakers in Germany sheds light on another issue that is central to accented films: the relationship of the accented cinema to the national cinema. As noted in chapter 2 on the mode of production, the accented cinema cannot be examined separately from the ruling national cinema, as these cinemas influence one another. In the case of Germany, the New German Cinema of the 1980s, recognized as a national cinema, shares many elements with the German exilic cinema that I have been describing. These include a preoccupation with homeland (*heimat*) both hated and loved, a utopian yearning for faraway utopian places (*fernweh*), a homesick nostalgia for the past (*heimweh*), a schizoid perception of the present, loss of identity and belonging, and a desire for social others and foreigner (*fremde*) (Kratzer-Juilfs 1996, 225–36). While the New German Cinema and the German accented cinema are similar in these themes, they differ in the optic with which they treat them. If the New German Cinema (now defunct) escaped its own internal exile by giving in to nostalgia for a past or yearning for an idyllic place and time elsewhere, the accented cinema centers on contemporary tensions and fragmentations as inflected by the dystopic optic and structures of feelings of external exile, and the exclusion of accented filmmakers from the category of the New German cinema.

Close-Up: Houchang Allahyari's Fear of Heights (Höhenangst, *1994*)

An Iranian psychiatrist in Austria, Allahyari began his filmmaking career while counseling young criminals in prison. Born in Tehran in 1941, he went to Austria to study psychiatry, theater, and film. He received his medical training from professional schools, but he learned filmmaking on his own. Filming prisoners was initially part of his therapeutic procedure, from which he assembled some fifty short 16mm films in the 1970s. Since the mid-1980s, in addition to continuing with the short film format, he has made feature films, some of which have won high praise. Allahyari's medical training and his work in prisons directly or indirectly influenced his film work. Several of them, such as *Borderline* (1989) and *Meat Grinder* (*Fleischwolf,* 1990), center on the problems of sentencing criminals, their life in prison, and their execution. His *Fear of Heights* shows this influence more indirectly.

Winner of the Max Öphuls Prize in 1995, *Fear of Heights* is about homelessness and belonging and is driven by fear. However, this fear takes the form of acrophobia rather than agoraphobia and claustrophobia. A young criminal named Mario is freed from jail in Vienna, but he refuses to return to his parents' home because of an Oedipal conflict with his father (who in childhood had handcuffed him to a bed to force him to watch his sexual affairs). Freed from traditional authority figures, Mario goes into a kind of social free fall that lands him among a group of criminals. Eventually, however, he flees Vienna for rural Austria to escape their influence. There he is taken in as a field hand by an old farmer and his middle-aged acrophobic daughter, who are themselves outsiders to their small farming community. He gains the farmers' acceptance when he spearheads their fight against a new road that threatens their fields.

As he gets to know his hosts more, especially the daughter, and begins to look at life anew, Mario's idyllic situation is shaken by the threat of his past catching up with him. Fear is inscribed in layers, in the fear of the past, fear of society, fear of the police, fear of prison, fear of father, sexual anxiety, and existential angst. Like many prisoners, exiles, and refugees, Mario is haunted by the past and wants to forget or escape it. Some of the film is shot from high-angle cameras, such as from a roving helicopter, that strengthen the impression of being trapped or of free-falling. This slow-paced psychological film ends dramatically on top of a very tall factory smokestack where Mario and the farm girl are finally able to name and to face their fears, thereby freeing themselves. Both *Fear of Heights* and *Walls of Sand* (discussed below) offer human companionship and the taking of individual initiative as the twin solutions to fear and anxiety and as the women's countermeasures to their previous complicity with their own subjugation.

Close-Up: Erica Jordan and Shirin Etessam's Walls of Sand *(1994)*

Gender and confinement are intimately intertwined in the aforementioned Turkish and Iranian accented films, but all of them are presented from the male perspective. One film that centers on this particular relationship and is made by women is *Walls of Sand*, a crisp black-and-white feature whose mode of production was artisanal and collaborative. The film was directed by Jordan and Stars Etessam; they coproduced and cowrote it. Made in the United States for the rather small sum of $80,000, it was one of the first films to be entirely webcast by The Sync in 1998.[17] The filmmakers received "fiscal sponsorship" from Women Make Movies, which allowed them to claim nonprofit status, raise funds, and accept donations. They financed the film mostly through small donations, and, as Etessam stated in an interview, by the filmmakers charging to the limit on some twelve credit cards, borrowing from one to pay the other—a situation that is all too familiar to alternative and accented filmmakers.

The two filmmakers met in the film production program of San Francisco State University, where they collaborated on small class projects and then branched out into feature production. Etessam was born in 1966 in Iran and immigrated with her parents to the United States when she was ten years old. She grew up chiefly in Seattle and now works as a filmmaker and television producer in San Francisco. Jordan was born in the United States in 1964 and was raised in a Jewish family. What distinguishes their film from other films about confinement and panic is not only its collaborative production mode and the filmmakers' gender but also the manner in which it posits a direct, not an allegorized, relationship between women's agoraphobia and claustrophobia and their confinement. As Etessam told me:

> We wanted to make a film about women and we wanted it to be bicultural, but we did not want to create a binary good woman/bad woman situation. We decided to reverse the traditional position of the women by giving the Iranian émigré woman the freedom to roam in society and by trapping the American woman in the house. After some research we decided that what would keep her housebound would be her agoraphobia. (Naficy 1997c)

The Anglo woman (Ellen) has a son (Alex) over whose custody she is fighting with her ex-husband. Because of her clinical agoraphobia, Ellen hires an Iranian émigré au pair (Soraya, played by Etessam) who does not have a permanent residency "green card." Soraya's job is to take care of the house, Alex, and all the outside chores that Ellen is unable to perform because of her house-bondage. At first, the women's relationship is strictly businesslike and compartmentalized. Very few words are exchanged between them, and Alex is almost mute. Ellen stays in her bedroom but makes periodic forays into the kitchen for her meals, which consist of a box of candy from the neatly stacked boxes in the cabinet. When Soraya opens the curtains, Ellen pulls them shut. All

Figure 26. Female entrapment and agoraphobia. Ellen (on right) and Soraya (Shirin Etessam) in Erica Jordan's *Walls of Sand.*

objects and furniture are meticulously placed in symmetrical arrangements. The desire for spatial, social, and linguistic control and the concomitant claustrophobia are palpable. Tight shot composition, the framing of characters against strong horizontal and vertical lines of windowpanes, mirrors, and walls, and other filming techniques intensify the sense of female entrapment and isolation, particularly in Ellen's case.

On the other hand, Soraya, who begins the film in first-person voice-over, is physically free to socialize with her émigré family and friends during gatherings, funerals, and parties. Gradually, though, she becomes alienated from them. Ironically, they accuse her of having become too Americanized at the same time that she has lost her legal right to remain in America. By rejecting them, she becomes a liminal figure who belongs nowhere. Fearing anti-Iranian hostility, she conceals her country of descent. She has no place to go, since her boyfriend refuses to marry her, forcing her to sleep in her car. Although these miseries pile up too neatly and become predictable, they are nonetheless real issues for new immigrants. Because of the fear and flux of the outside world, the various regimes of control in Ellen's household appeal to Soraya. Her precarious legal status, however, forces her to make a deal with Ellen's estranged husband to spy on her (to gather evidence for his custody case) in return for his promise of employment and a green card.

The film's central drama, however, is the evolving relationship of these physically and socially entrapped women. The gulf that had initially isolated them is bridged in a pivotal sequence that intercuts Soraya's surreptitious reading of Ellen's diary and letters with Ellen's taking of a bath. As Soraya reads Ellen's writings, Ellen's voice recites them on the sound track. In one passage, she explains that Soraya's voice brings to the heaviness of her house "sweetness and warmth." All the while the film alternates between extreme close-up shots of Soraya's face and flowing curly hair engulfed in the diary and shots of Ellen luxuriating in the steaming bathtub. The intercutting between the two women, one voicing what the other is reading, unites them, creating a charged homoerotic bond—although they are not in the same physical space. A lovely musical score that mixes Eastern and Western motifs symbolizes the coming together of the two women from different cultures. In the next scene, with knowing smiles, as though they have just shared a secret, they prepare a meal together for the first time and, like a couple, tend to various household chores and repairs. The lesbian eroticism is unmistakable but subtle. The baring of Ellen's thoughts and body, which brings the two women closer, removes many other barriers between them. It is precisely because they are trapped together that they are able to cut through their individual psychic, social, and sexual barriers and fears to initiate a new empowering relationship. Ellen no longer locks herself in her bathroom or bedroom. She now comes to the living room, where the two women talk, share meals with Alex, play backgammon, look through Ellen's photo album, and dance to Persian music. The heterosexual family unit that was fractured at the beginning appears to be reconstituted with a new twist. Together, they devise a plan to demonstrate that Ellen is not incapacitated by agoraphobia and should continue to have custody of her child, and Soraya chooses friendship with Ellen over a dubious promise of a green card. Confinement seems to have acted like a chrysalis, inside whose cocoon the women have developed into new creatures, ready to burst free.

An iconographic motif that accentuates this move to freedom is a shot of three unidentified women, clad in dark head-to-toe chadors (veils), walking on a deserted California beach, reminiscent of Shirin Neshat's films, including *Rapture* (*Owj*, 1999). The film cuts to this metanarrative image several times without any explanation or context. Out of place, the image is a challenging enigma to viewers. Traditionally, the chador is considered a patriarchal device imposed upon women to demarcate and subjugate them. However, veiling and its multilayered power relations are complex, involving women's own complicity and resistance (Naficy 1994). *Walls of Sand* playfully inscribes these veiling and unveiling complexities, culminating in the film's last shot, in which the chador suddenly slips off one of the women to reveal a completely bare body underneath. Unfazed, the three women continue their cheerful beachside march without a hitch. The veil also acts as a symbol of the transformation of Ellen and Soraya, from trapped to freed. The chador, thus functions as a chrysalis, inside whose confines magical transformations can take place. The veiling and the unveiling also symbolize the initial restraint and the subsequent openness of the two women toward each other. The film's criticism is not limited to Muslims, as director Erica Jordan noted in her interview with me. In its inscription of closed spaces, the film offers a feminist critique not only of women's confinement in Islamic societies but also of the freedom that American society promises but often fails to deliver to women (Naficy 1996c).

Close-Up: *Jonas Mekas's* The Brig *(1964)*

This is a black-and-white cinema verité film of Kenneth H. Brown's uncompromising play, staged by the Living Theatre in New York City, photographed by Jonas, and edited by his brother Adolfas Mekas. It is an impassioned rumination on male authoritarian uses of space to exert control and to modulate power and identity. Jonas Mekas characterized the film as "not an adaptation of a play" but "a film play, . . . a record of my eye and my temperament lost in the play" (1972, 194). In fact, the film does not reveal that it is a record of a play until the end, thus creating the illusion of being a cinema verité documentary or a highly structured and stylized fictional film. This illusion is created because Mekas set out to film the play as though it was a live news event, without rehearsal or prior exposure to it. He likened his role to that of a "newsreel reporter" who throws himself into the action and reacts to it as it unfolds.

The play re-creates the life of a brig on March 7, 1957, at the U.S. Marine Corps' Camp Fuji in Japan. It begins at 4:30 A.M. and continues for a twenty-four-hour period. This indexical information about place and time is given in titles at the film's opening. Like all indexicals, the information points to the specificity of this particular brig, at this particular time, with these groups of guards and prisoners, doing these very specific things. But since no one is identified by name or singled out, the indexical present, the here and now, becomes the timeless universal that comments upon and critiques man's inhumanity toward men.

Spatially, the brig is nothing but a large, claustrophobic, boxlike cage made of heavy-duty fence wiring with certain interlocking spaces that act as halls and walkways. The guards are stationed outside the cage, from where they keep the prisoners under constant surveillance and threaten them with disciplinary action. Claustrophobia is inscribed not only in the particulars of the brig's closed setting but also in the film's high-contrast lighting, which obscures full view of things, in the dehumanizing and violent physical and psychological treatment of the prisoners, and in the tight, nervous camera work.

Mekas's camera—a bulky, single-system Auricon—is restless and mobile, anxiously reacting and searching. It pans and tilts, it stands, sits, walks, and almost runs in order to stay with the action. This immediate and direct reaction to the profilmic events, a hallmark of Mekas's style, tends to emphasize the film's indexical present, its live ontology. This is evident also in Mekas's own account of his filming, while single-handedly carrying some eighty pounds of camera, microphone, and batteries:

My intention wasn't to show the play in its entirety but to catch as much of the action as my "reporter" eyes could. This kind of shooting required an exhausting concentration of body and eye. I had to operate the camera; I had to keep out of the cast's way; I had to look for what was going on and listen for what was said; I had to make instantaneous decisions about my movements and the camera movements, knowing that there was no time for thinking or reflecting; there was no time for reshooting, no time for mistakes: I was a circus man on a tightrope high in the air. All my senses were stretched to the point of breaking. . . . I became so possessed by what I was doing that it literally took me weeks to get my body and all my senses back to normal. (1972, 191)

This direct and synaesthetic engagement with the here and now turns the camera into another prisoner in the brig whose bewilderment, nervousness, stolen glances, and jerky movements replicate the prisoners' reactions and dramatize the dehumanization of the brig's inhabitants—guards and prisoners alike.

The action of the filmed play, to use Mekas's own characterization, is a "ballet of horror" (1972, 192). It consists of various repeated routines in one day in the life of the prisoners, such as sleeping, waking, washing and scrubbing of floors, dressing, making beds, reading, smoking, coming, going, and drilling. The prisoners are required to ask permission or receive a specific order to perform any of these routines; if they disobey or fail to follow the minutest of instructions, they are severely punished. In scene after kafkaesque scene, the marines approach a white line drawn on the floor, requesting permission to cross it. Repeated over and over by prisoners whose identity is only their assigned numbers or a degrading appellation such as "maggot" or "worm," the shouted request transforms the status of the white line. It is no longer just a line on the floor but a barrier more real and forbidding than the high fence walls that cage them. Unlike the panoptic regime of control proposed by Bentham and theorized by Foucault, vision is bidirectional, as prison guards and prisoners are visible to and in direct contact with each other. As a result, both sides are equally dehumanized, and control is not internalized by the prisoners. They must constantly and violently be reminded of the hierarchy and the rules and of the punishment they will receive should they fail to abide by them (and sometimes they receive it even when they do obey).

Mekas's exhaustion may have been due less to physical exertion than to the emotional and psychological toll that exposure to such regimes of control must have exacted of him, reviving the memories of his own four-year experience in European displaced persons camps, and of the totalitarian communist regime that took over in Lithuania—both of which drove him into exile. With this inexpensive "cinema of hunger" film, costing a mere $1,200, Mekas created a powerful document and a searing critique of social control and injustice.

Thirdspace Play of Open and Closed Chronotopes

Many accented films contain both closed and open spatiotemporal topoi and forms. These inscriptions express the exilic tensions of liminality, interstitiality, and hybridity. Whereas the tensions regarding the homeland result in primarily open chronotopes, those regarding exile produce chiefly closed chronotopes. At the intersection of these two is the slipzone of thirdspace chronotopicality that is most characteristic of exile. As Edward Soja states, thirdspace is distinguished by an "all-inclusive simultaneity": "Everything comes together in Thirdspace: subjectivity and objectivity, the abstract and the concrete, the real and the imagined, the knowable and the unimaginable, the repetitive and the differential, structure and agency, mind and body, consciousness and the unconscious, the disciplined and the transdisciplinary, everyday life and unending history" (1996, 56–57). In this slipzone of simultaneity and intertextuality, original cultures are no longer fixed. They are presented not discretely but in a structure of play of sameness and difference, of authenticity and translation.

While the pervasive space in Egoyan's earlier films was one of claustrophobia, driven by closed urban locations, enclosed mise-en-scène, voyeuristic camera gaze, obsessive character relations, stilted acting style, entrapping narrative, and nonlinear structure, his *Calendar* simultaneously encodes both open and closed chronotopes. It inscribes the open form in its natural locations (mountains and valleys) and its motivated objects (monuments and churches), and it encodes the closed form in its filming style, character relations, and the maze-like structure that is based on the number 12. While the open form is made identical with a historical homeland (Armenia), the closed form is not identified with any particular place, but it may be taken for Canada or for the general space of postmodernity. The simultaneous expression of these spatiotemporalities in a single film constitutes most fully the thirdspace chronotopicality of the accented cinema.

Michael Snow's celebrated *Wavelength* (1967) embodies thirdspatiality in its very formal structure. It begins as a high-angle establishing shot that encompasses an eighty-foot loft in New York City, and it ends, after a forty-five-minute slow, halting, and relentless zoom-in, on a small picture of ocean waves, on the opposite wall, on which it eventually goes out of focus. During this journey, the camera registers four human events (including an apparent death), but it does not make any concession to them, for they are incidental to the film's real plot, which is the inexorable formal trajectory of the zoom and the rising pitch of an electronically generated sine wave on the sound track.

The audiovisual grinding down of space and time becomes so strong that it is hard not to gasp from air hunger and claustrophobia. Yet the film counters its own compressive properties in several ways. For one, it stretches the zoom, which is usually quick, into many minutes (MacDonald 1992, 3). For another, it hurls the audience into the oceanic space of the photograph when both the zoom and the sine wave suddenly come to a stop on it. This is because the spectators' forward-moving trajectory, internalized over the previous forty-plus minutes, continues apace, turning the flat photograph into a three-dimensional illusory seascape of immense depth. Another form of expansion occurs cognitively during the long forward zoom, when the mind wanders in the loft, inhabiting it, even imagining and remembering the portions of it that have fallen off the frame edges and into the past tense. Finally, the long zoom transforms the optical space of the loft into the haptic space of spectatorship, forcing viewers to go beyond visual perception to achieve a tactile and phenomenological apprehension of their own spectating.[18]

By forcing us to experience space as time, Snow creates what he called a "time monument" (quoted in Michelson 1987, 173). In doing this, his film poses a further relationship between space and time: the longer the zoom time lasts, the smaller the space contained by it becomes. Denotatively, after forty-five minutes, a large, three-dimensional loft has been reduced to a small, two-dimensional photograph on a wall; connotatively, we have moved from the enclosed indexical space of a specific loft here and now into the boundless, timeless abstract and universal space of the ocean beyond.

Close-Up: Nina Menkes's The Great Sadness of Zohara *(1983)*

Menkes's major avant-garde films invoke in one way or another the play of oppressive and open spaces, especially involving women. Menkes's mode of production is fiercely artisanal, involving the following practices: independent, grant-driven, low-budget financing (she spent a mere $7,000 for *The Great Sadness of Zohara* and $125,000 for *Queen of Diamonds*); collaborative production (her sister, Tinka, is the lead in all her films and coedits them); and performing multiple functions in all her films (as producer, writer, cinematographer, and coeditor). She describes her collaboration with her sister as a "profound partnership" and her artisanal mode of production as a "political choice" (Willis 1992, 10–11). Her opposition to Hollywood cinema comes from both political and aesthetic criticism of it, and it is so profound that one can say that her films embody oppositionality per se. Like many accented and avant-garde filmmakers, her films are intensely personal and auteurist, coming from what she calls an "intuitive place," not filtered by genre category, classical narrative paradigms, or even feminist discourses. "I film stuff the way I feel, so I let the camera run until I sense that the shot is over" (10).

Only Menkes's forty-minute film *The Great Sadness of Zohara* is discussed here, since it depicts internal exile and an exilic quest journey, and it engages with diasporic sensibilities and thirdspatiality more than her other films. Menkes was born in 1956 in the United States to Jewish parents who fought in the Israeli war of independence, got married, and emigrated to the United States to pursue their higher education and professional careers (she became a psychologist, he a mathematician). As a first-generation Jewish-American, whose parents were displaced by the Holocaust (her father's family was decimated by the Nazis, and her mother's family emigrated to Palestine at the start of the Nazis' rise to power), Menkes has a deep sense of homelessness and rootlessness, which she explained in an interview:

> My father's family was murdered. My parents' first language was German, then Hebrew and English, in that order. My immediate family is very small, and I did not grow up with a sense of a community, an extended family, or a network of relations. Since childhood, I have tried to claim myself as an American, but I have not succeeded. I never felt fully or completely American. I have tried to find a home somewhere but without success. (Naficy 1997e)

Figure 27. Fetal position in public places. Tinka Menkes leans against an alley wall in Nina Menkes's *The Great Sadness of Zohara*.

Made as a student project at UCLA, *The Great Sadness of Zohara* is a lament about alienation, desolation, and homelessness, especially by and from a female and a Jewish point of view. It focuses on the physical and psychological journeys that a young Orthodox Jew undertakes in her search for identity.

The film begins with Zohara (played by Tinka), a lonely, isolated woman ensconced in a small room in Jerusalem. She spends much of her time under the bedcovers or curled up in a fetal position in various private and public places, in the classic iconography of fear and withdrawal. From that position, she is a lonely observer of the world that passes her by. She also wanders in the streets and alleys and visits synagogues, cafés, and bazaars, but she has no effect on anything and does not interact with anyone. At the same time, she is objectified by the gaze of others, who clearly consider her an anomaly, an alien being, a foreigner.

This objectification and Zohara's own withdrawal and silence signify her profound alienation from Jewish Orthodoxy and life in general. Such a feeling structure is also expressed by the film's closed form, consisting of claustrophobic settings, static framing, long takes, and repetitious editing, which have since become characteristic of Menkes's style.[19] She explains the impact of long static takes and repeated shots in imparting women's constricted possibilities and alienation in *Queen of Diamonds*:

> To me these are two important aspects of alienation. In the long shot, you're sort of trapped and suffocated in this claustrophobic thing that doesn't move. It's as if she's imprisoned in the frame. And then, the other manifestation of the same thing is the endless intercutting, as if you're cut off from some nurturing source, say, your self. So the length of the shots and the way the shots are fragmented is an evocation of emotion. (quoted in Brooks 1992, 7)

Zohara's increasing alienation drives her into action: she adopts a new red punk hairstyle and colorful clothing and sets off on a spiritual journey to the Moroccan deserts in search of some sort of mystic transcendence. At this point, the sound track, which previously had consisted of chants, Bible quotations, whispering voices, ringing bells, and bits of music, suddenly shifts into what amounts to a powerful externalization of Zohara's claustrophobia in the audio register. As she walks the alleys of a Moroccan town, and the children's gazes follow and question her every move, the voice of a woman on the sound track struggles agonizingly to utter words. But she produces only a series of incomprehensible half words and forced whimpering, wailing, and stuttering, creating a sense of air hunger and panic that potently reinforces the film's visual claustrophobia. Then the film gives way to open spatiality and quietness, as Zohara washes herself in an indigo river topped by an azure sky, after which she walks toward a Moroccan ruin and lies down in a cane field. There she disappears as if swallowed up by the earth. This scene resonates with a passage from the Book of Job (7:12), quoted at the film's beginning: "Shortly I will lie down in the dust / And when you look for me, I will be gone." Stifled by life with humans in Jewish and Arab places alike, Zohara finds the solace and redemption she is seeking only through communion with nature or death.

Unlike traditional male quest journeys and return narratives, which are usually transformative and triumphal, Zohara's quest and return home are neither. She is a type of modern-day wandering Jew, who is "unfulfilled in orthodox traditions" and is "shiftless, uprooted, and aimless outside them" (Fernandez 1984, 12). This inability to find a homeplace resonates with Menkes's own search for one, which animates all her films. Considering her collective output, however, one notices a progression of self-discovery in them, which represents Menkes's gradual liberation from dependence on place-bound identity to a discursively created thirdspace in her art.

Close-Up: Joris Ivens's A Tale of the Wind *(Une histoire de vende, 1988)*

In his final contribution to world cinema, the great wandering cinéaste created, with help from his longtime companion and collaborator Marceline Loridan-Ivens, a thirdspace ode of joy to the natural world, to China, and to cinema. Born in 1898 in Holland, Ivens died in France in 1989.[20] Between his first film, a short Western called *The Burning Arrow* (*De Brandende Straal Or Wigwam*, 1911), made at age thirteen, and his last, *A Tale of the Wind*, made at age ninety, he made over fifty documentary films in nearly two dozen countries. Because in Holland he felt like "an emigrant whose country is too small" for him (CAPI Films n.d., 7), he traveled nomadically from one troubled spot of the world to another to document what he saw. Perhaps no other filmmaker, with the exception of Peter Watkins for his massive film *The Journey* (1987), has traveled so widely and made so many socially conscious films in so many different places. Influenced by Pudovkin and Eisenstein and committed to a socialist point of view, Ivens's films document and forcefully espouse social change in colonizing and colonized countries alike. He paid dearly for his views: the Nazis burned a number of his films, France banned his *New Earth* (1934), the American military prevented him from finishing *Know Your Enemy: Japan*, and his country of birth declared him treasonous and revoked

Figure 28. Joris Ivens is overjoyed by the Gobi Desert's winds in his *A Tale of the Wind*.

his passport for making *Indonesia Calling* (1946).[21] His social activism and internationalism extended to working with multinational film crews on a number of films, making a single film in more than one country, making several films in a single country, and working on films collaboratively and collectively. These crossings of geographic, authorial, national, linguistic, and cinematic boundaries are characteristic of accented filmmakers.

Unlike the bulk of his oeuvre, *A Tale of the Wind* deals less with political movements than with nature's movements. The film represents multiple returns for Ivens: return to some of the abstract concepts that had shaped his earliest films, to the lyrical style that had been suppressed somewhat in his socially conscious filmmaking, to the filmmaker's childhood, and to a topic that had fascinated him all his life, and about which he had made an earlier film, the wind.

Like many accented films, *A Tale of the Wind* is autobiographically accented: Ivens appears on camera, playing himself as the speaking and enunciating subject of the film. In so doing, he shifts his position from the one who is doing the documenting to the one who is the subject of the documentary. However, this is no ordinary documentary, for it is a hybrid, thirdspace film that bridges the cinemas of Méliès and Lumière. In it Ivens plays a real character, himself, but the film's plot revolves around fictional encounters, and its narrative moves freely between imaginative and realist renderings of the world.

Immediately after its opening, the film sets out to demonstrate the presence of the wind—this universal but invisible force. A shot of the blue sky is disrupted by a sudden whoosh of the massive blades of a windmill whose tip diagonally slashes the frame upward. As the camera pulls back and slowly travels around the windmill, the rapidly turning blades and their sound set up a powerful rhythm. The next few scenes, seen through the turning blades from a high angle, show horses in a bucolic landscape and a verdant backyard nearby, where the clothes on the line are violently blown about. A boy, representing Ivens, approaches a large toy plane, gets in it, and shouts, "Mummy, I am going to fly to China!" The next cut shows Ivens, now nearly ninety years old, sitting alone on a chair on the ochre sand dunes of the Gobi Desert, his intense, watering eyes looking ahead and his long, white hair blowing in the wind. These and many other aestheticized shots of the dunes under various conditions of light, wind, and color establish the intimate immensity of the desert that opens the heart.

Soon a film crew arrives and sets into motion the film's plot of capturing China and the wind on celluloid. The crew members roam the deserts, climb mountains, bivouac here and there, and just wait for the arrival of this invisible visitor. During their wanderings, they visit Chinese villages and towns, interacting warmly with the people they find. In these encounters, the film carries a "very specific look—one that could only belong to an aged man—affectionate and detached at the same time" (Doraiswamy 1992–93, 93).[22]

In time, the film reveals its claustrophobic spatiality as well, in Ivens's labored breathing. Born in a windy country, Ivens ironically has suffered since childhood from a lack of breath due to asthma. He has come to China to replenish his failing breath with the immense reservoir of the Chinese winds. His breathlessness is dramatically juxtaposed against the free-flowing winds of nature, and the claustrophobia of his air hunger is set against the immensity of the land. Once, when he is waiting atop a sand dune for the wind, his breathing becomes difficult, air hunger sets in, he begins to sweat and hallucinate visually and aurally, and he finally collapses to the ground. He is taken to a hospital, where he is visited by a circus monkey-man who had befriended him previously. In one of the film's fanciful sequences, through magic, Ivens dreams or imagines that he has landed on the moon in the rocket ship that Georges Méliès had used in his film *A Trip to the Moon* (1903). He also re-creates and whimsically explains a number of Chinese proverbs, and he mocks with gentle and somewhat detached humor the contemporary official Communist Chinese culture.

Tired of waiting and searching for the wind, Ivens resorts to magic performed by a woman and to his own angry demands for the wind, even a destructive one. Soon a rapidly intensifying wind blows sheets of brown sand everywhere, wrecking the tents, darkening the sky, and hampering visibility. With his white mane blowing violently above his head, Ivens delightedly shouts into the wind, "Wait a moment, I'll give you back my asthma!" Gradually, the wind calms down, leaving Ivens freed from his lifelong illness.

Chronotopically, the film is not only about the boundless space of nature and the bounded space of human lungs but also about time, for the natural world of the dunes and mountains in which the winds reside is both timeless and boundless. By acting as carriers of human voices, thoughts, aspirations, and memories, from ancient times to the present, the winds are agents of human history and memory. Although at times it is long-winded, sentimental, and condescending toward the Chinese, *A Tale of the Wind* has charmed audiences "wherever magical filmmaking is appreciated" (Yung. 1988). It did just that at the 1988 Venice Film Festival, where it won a Golden Lion and Ivens himself received a fifteen-minute standing ovation.

Ivens's film is imbued with whimsical playfulness and a sense of possibility that are characteristic of thirdspace hybridity. However, these are absent from the films of many political exiles, such as Güney, Sayyad, and Allamehzadeh, and from the films of dystopic exiles, such as Baser and Shahid Saless, whose works favor binarism or closed spatiality, phobia, and panic. They are also absent from the films of nostalgic exiles, such as Pelechian and Ariç, who tend toward open chronotopicality. As a peripatetic and nomadic Western subject, Ivens, like Luis Buñuel, had the freedom—despite many obstacles—to roam the world, touching down here and there like the wind, and make films. On the other hand, exilic, Third World, and postcolonial filmmakers, whose original countries have a lower international status than those of the First World filmmakers, usually do not enjoy the same transnational freedom of movement. They are often forced out of one place and forced to stay in another—a type of choiceless deterritorialization and reterritorialization that breed pessimism and paranoia. And once emplaced in the new society, they often have to put up with xenophobia and racism—usually colored by a history of imperial, colonial, or neocolonial relations between the original and host countries. Because of these deep-seated differences, Third World accented filmmakers in the First World sometimes do not feel welcome and thus may be suspicious of the freedoms and possibilities that either exilic interstitiality or full integration promises.[23] This in turn intensifies their critical dystopia and outsiderism, as evidenced by the inscription of phobic spaces and liminal panics in their films.

In today's unipolar, globalized, late-modern world, fragmentation and uncertainty are immanent and imminent. Under these centripetal conditions, nations and communities (not just individual filmmakers) have become involved in last-stand battles and seminal sieges and in creating outsiders and others against whom they can (re)define themselves. The ideologies and practices of the European Union, the American militia movement, Serbian ethnic cleansing, Islamic, Christian, Hindu, and Jewish religious fundamentalism, and what we might in general call "heimatism," following David Morley and Kevin Robins's formulation (1995), are instances both of creating actual, material borders and of drawing new discursive boundaries between the self and its others. The result is not thirdspace or hybrid cultures but "citadel cultures" (Werckmeister 1991). Exiles living in liberal democracies must constantly redefine themselves not only against these forms of militarization of the public sphere but also against the militant privatization and commercialization of all spheres and the resulting abstraction and semiotic manipulation, which the reduction of all of life's spheres to commodified sign systems promises. Under such circumstances, space becomes untrustworthy. Place, on the other hand, becomes attractive and emplacement a viable resistive option. The emphasis on the utopian, liberating spaces of the homeland's landscape and on the dystopian, confining phobic spaces of the exile is part of the transnationals' attempt to turn the abstraction of space in their diasporized lives into the concreteness of place in their cinematic representation.

This favoring of the concrete is similar to the privileging of what in philosophy are called indexicals (for example, "I," "here," and "now"), demonstratives (for example, "this" and "that"), and proper names—all of which refer to the properties of being identical only with a particular time, place, or person (Austin 1990). Expanded and compressed locations, mise-en-scène, and shot composition in the accented cinema are spatiotemporal propositions about displacement and emplacement. Every open and closed location, mise-en-scène, or shot provides spatiotemporal indexicals and demonstratives that situate the diegetic characters (sometimes using their own proper names, as in *Calendar*) in time and place, while providing a commentary about or allegorizing displacement and emplacement. With some exceptions (such as with Güney), the open spatiotemporal configurations tend to express the thereness and thenness of the homeland, while the closed-form films favor the inscription of the presentness and the hereness of the exile.

By indexically specifying unique times and places, both open-form and closed-form films inscribe ontological security and place-bound identity. When in place, the space is mine—even if it is only forty square meters. By insisting on their particularity and their thisness and hereness, accented filmmakers critique the dominant society and reterritorialize themselves as "exiles" and "refuseniks." As a result, they may temporarily avoid becoming either the society's others, against whom its overarching identity is formed, or its full citizens, who are pressed into servicing its values. In this sense, these films are structurally political, even if they are not manifestly about politics.

As demonstrated in this chapter, on the other hand, refusal and emplacement may become forms of either entrapment or camouflage, limiting them to ethnic or binarist identity or hiding their potentially massive transformation not only from outsiders but also from themselves. The liminal exiles have an opportunity to introduce a critical "other-than" choice or "thirding" within culture. As an exilic strategy, thirding goes beyond the sum of its binary antecedents of homeland and host society, for it involves reconstituting "an open alternative that is both similar and strikingly different" (Soja 1996, 61). Soja's phrase "similar and strikingly different" must now be added to Derrida's "both and neither," Rushdie's "at once plural and partial," Anzaldúa's "*mestizaje,*" Bhabha's "hybridity," Naficy's "haggling" and "interstitiality," Robertson's "glocal," and Gillian Rose's "at once inside and outside" (1993, 154) as key paradoxical terms of psychology, geography, ideology, and social formation that describe the doubling, performative, and translational processes that occur inside the exilic chrysalis.

By acting thirdly and interstitially, subjects can resist both absolute essen-tialism and total integration to produce, instead, partiality and positionality. This means that they will have to become moving targets, strategically adopt-ing not only marginality and interstitiality but also at times centrality. As Gaya-tri Spivak, in speaking about herself, stated: "Certain peoples have always been asked to cathect the margins so others can be defined as central. . . . In that kind of situation the only strategic thing to do is to absolutely present oneself as the centre" (1990, 40–41). However, the micropolitics of transnational posi-tioning is much more complex and contingent than that of national position-ing. The Third World or postcolonial filmmakers discussed here, who live in First World exile, are often regarded as belonging neither to the margins nor to the center of their original cultures. Sometimes they are marginalized there because they are thought to have become part of the center of the First World. Conversely, at times they are considered central in their original countries pre-cisely because they have entered the halls of discursive power in the First World. In the First World, on the other hand, they are often pushed to the margins against which the First World defines itself. However, sometimes, and in certain circles of the First World, they are thought to be central to the very definition of the First World. What they think of themselves and what posi-tions they take or project affect their intercultural haggling for position. There is a price for strategic micropositioning, however, which is eternal vigilance of the kind that may force the interstitial exiles into compulsive defensiveness and reactionary agency, both of which arouse hostility. Besides, few individuals can successfully and continually deal with the psychological, social, and practical burdens of such vigilance, which can turn them into bitter and paranoid people.

7

Journeying, Border Crossing, and Identity Crossing

THE GLOBALIZATION of capital and media also globalized the local, and the fragmentation of nation-states and the massive scattering of people transformed the meaning of the global. Therefore, contemporary exiles and diasporas are structurally "glocal," at once global and local (Robertson 1995). Those benefiting from higher class affiliation are no longer obliged to confine themselves to claustrophobic, if comforting, ethnic niches and ghettos because they travel frequently and are in constant contact with compatriot communities. Poised at the intersection and in the interstices of other cultures, they are subject to historical dynamism and evolution, as well as to national longings for form that are unprecedented in degree, variety, and speed. Their deterritorializing and reterritorializing journeys take a number of forms, and they cross many borders—not only physical and geographic but also psychological, metaphorical, social, and cultural borders.

Journey and Journeying

Journey narratives tend to dominate in certain literary and cinematic traditions. It is not surprising that the literary tradition of an émigré-created country like the United States is characterized to a "remarkable and peculiar degree" by "narratives and images of journeys" (Stout 1983, 3). Likewise, in certain American film genres, such as Westerns and road movies, the themes and narratives of travel predominate. Understandably, journey and journeying are also key features of accented films. There is a pattern to journey narratives, based on the "direction of journey, motivation for journeying, and reference to actual historical precedence." In addition, each journey pattern "displays recurrent elements of form such as characteristic incidents, images, and tone" (Stout 1983, x–xi). Depending on their motivation, journeys may take the form of exploration, pilgrimage, escape, emigration, or return—the latter three more precisely qualify as exilic and diasporic journeys. However, journeys are rarely simple or homogeneous. Most often, they are composite and evolutionary. Exploration, for example, may involve quest, wandering, search, homelessness, or even conquest and colonization. Once initiated, journeys often change character: begun as escape, for example, a journey may become one of exile, emigration, exploration, or return. The journey of the Kurdish rebel in Ariç's *A Song for Beko* (1992) begins in Turkey as a search for his brother. Soon, however, the search evolves into escape from Turkey into Syria, a period of homelessness in a Kurdish camp, and finally a forlorn exile in Germany, from where he fondly recollects his home, to which he longs to return.

Textual journeys may refer to actual historical or biographical journeys or tap into mythical, epic, or metaphoric travels. Whether documentary or fictional, accented filmmakers consistently feature journey of some sort in their films, for their own journeys set them off from their homes, profoundly shaping both their experiences and their identities henceforward. Allamehzadeh's *The Guests of Hotel Astoria* (1989), Nguyen's *Cyclo* (1995), and Hui's *Song of the Exile* (1990) are all based partially on the escape, emigration, and return stories of their makers. Cinematic travels may also mobilize certain universalist or particularistic mythical and epic journeys, such as the expulsion of humans from Eden or the Exodus of the Jews from Egypt and their search for the promised land. Menkes's *The Great Sadness of Zohara* (1983) charts the spiritual quest as well the physical journey of an Orthodox Jewish woman for her roots, religious fulfillment, and identity. In *Lost, Lost, Lost* (1949–76) Mekas analogizes his own journey out of Lithuania, his years of wandering through European displaced person camps, and his arrival in the United States to the decade-long wandering of Ulysses, who left his homeland but returned triumphantly. The return home for this Lithuanian Ulysses, as recorded in *Reminiscences of a Return to Lithuania* (1971–72), was cathartic but not triumphant.[1]

Güney's *Yol* (1982), Naderi's *Manhattan by Numbers* (1993), and Tarkovsky's *Nostalgia* (1983) are not only about physical journeys but also about psychological journeys into deep despair. Armenian filmmakers Paradjanov and Askarian also favor the use of the journey as a metaphor for psychological and spiritual transformation. Some journeys assume additional import by symbolizing philosophical travels, as in the "night journey," or by metaphorizing the passage of time, as in the "journey of life" and "journey of seasons," or by inscribing passage of history, as in the "journey of history." Solanas's *The Journey* is an example of an inward journey into the individual psyche and the national and regional history. Since each journey has both direction and duration, journeys transform space into time. Because of this, they are exemplars of the Bakhtinian chronotopes. In terms of direction, three main types of exilic journeys stand out: outward journeys of escape, home seeking, and home founding; journeys of quest, homelessness, and lostness; and inward, homecoming journeys.

Home-Seeking Journey

The direction of the journey has profound empirical and symbolic values that shape not only the travel but also the traveler. This is because significant journeys tend to be meliorative and redemptive experiences. In the United States, the home-founding settler journey is typically thought of as the triumphalist, progressive, and melioristic westward movement—from known to unknown, civilization to wilderness, and restriction to freedom—emblematized in the manifest destiny doctrine and in the Western film genre. On the other hand, there has been a smaller countermove, involving return journeys eastward by discouraged pioneers and travel eastward to European roots by disaffected intellectuals (Stout 1983, 4–5). For Chicanos and Chicanas the directional value, as inscribed in Navas's *El Norte* (1983) is south to north, even though once the travelers arrive there, the North is found to be wanting. Cheech Marin's comedy *Born in East L.A.* (1987) provides a reverse north-to-south trip, engendered by the deportation to Mexico of a third-generation Chicano, that endorses the North as the place of value.

Understandably, for African-Americans, for whom the original westering journey was one of enslavement, westerly travel does not hold the liberatory and triumphalist potential that it offered to white European settlers and slave owners. Instead, positive directional value is bestowed upon the south-to-north movement to freedom, as inscribed in many films, including Oscar Micheaux's *The Exiles* (1932) and Julie Dash's *Daughters of the Dust* (1991), and later on in south-to-west movement, as in Charles Burnett's *To Sleep with Anger* (1990). These northward and westward displacements open up opportunities not available to African-Americans in the South, but the South is not an empty place, particularly in the films by Dash and Burnett, which evaluate the South differently. In *To Sleep with Anger*, the South, as represented by Harry, is primarily a source of evil and threat for the middle-class urban African-Americans in Los Angeles. In *Daughters of the Dust*, however, the South, as represented by Nana and the Unborn Child, is a link to a life, particularly for women, that was rich with ritual, culture, and memory rooted in an original home, Africa. Their differing treatment of the South marks them politically: *To Sleep with Anger* is assimilationist, while *Daughters of the Dust* is resistive. Since the American South is represented as a fecund place, the northward (and to some extent westward) journeys are structured as loss in the same way that the Westward journeys of the Third World populations in accented films are structured by loss. On the other hand, positive value is placed on the eastering homecoming journeys to Africa by which the loss and injury of slavery and displacement are recovered and healed. Haile Gerima's *Sankofa* (1993), for example, offers the eastering return journey to Africa as a return to roots and as a way of gaining strength to go forward.[2]

These directional values are motivated by the historical experiences and imaginative acts of travel of the displaced people who were brought, or who came, to the Americas; but they are not permanent or unambiguous because rejection, failure, and disillusionment, which accompany life-making journeys, almost always mar the clarity and certainty of each direction's values.

In accented films, the westering journey dominates because it reflects the trajectory of the movement of a majority of the filmmakers and displaced populations. Whether of escape, emigration, or exile, this journey is embedded in a number of films, among them Koller's *Journey of Hope* (1990), Ariç's *A Song for Beko*, Allamehzadeh's *The Guests of Hotel Astoria*, Ebrahimian's *The Suitors* (1989), and Tarkovsky's *Nostalgia*.

Journey of Homelessness

Journeys of homelessness and wandering take different forms and sometimes are transformative. *Johanna d'Arc in Mongolia* (1989), made by German filmmaker Ulrick Ottinger, charts the wandering of European and Mongolian nomad women in the expansive steppes of Inner Mongolia that transforms both sets of women. The journey in Nair's *Salaam Bombay!* (1988), on the other hand, is less transformative. It centers on the travels and travails, from childhood to premature adulthood, of a young circus boy named Krishna. His travel begins as a simple errand for the circus master to Bombay. When Krishna returns to discover that the circus is gone, however, it becomes a journey of homelessness. He is left to fend for himself in a city teeming with users, abusers, prostitutes, outcasts, and coyotes of all types. Although the children and women are portrayed sympathetically and Krishna kills a manipulative pimp, the characters are not transformed by their experiences. The film posits no way out for them; the best they can do is learn to survive. Jalal Fatemi's futuristic video *The Nuclear Baby* (*Nozad-e Atomi*, 1989) emphasizes the wandering and aimless aspects of the journey, involving two protagonists whose names signal their nomadic status. Hitcher, a burly mustachioed old-world Persian wearing a fedora hat, is on his way to a small desert village called Caspiana, while Passer, a blond pregnant woman, is escaping by car from deadly nuclear clouds. The only apparent survivors of a nuclear holocaust, they are both lost in an unrelenting desert, where missiles routinely fly overhead and insects dominate the land. Hitcher wants to hitch a ride to Caspiana from Passer, but car trouble stalls their progress. In an elegiac slow-motion scene against the setting sun, Passer gives birth to a "nuclear baby" on the desert floor. In the course of her labor she enters a surreal world of technological disasters (nuclear and biological warfare), social strife (labor strikes, revolutions, surveillance), and personal nightmare (created by the Ministry of Nightmare). Although plodding and incoherent at times, the video creates both a dystopian vision of a future yet to come and a parodic critique of media representations in today's America. Hitcher and Passer do not get to where they were going, and neither one is transformed by their wandering experience.

Close-Up: Emir Kusturica's Time of the Gypsies (Dom za Vesanje, *1989*)

Born in 1955 to a Muslim family in Sarajevo (in the former Yugoslavia), Emir Kusturica is regarded as one of the most innovative filmmakers of his generation in Europe, where his features have consistently won top awards in major film festivals (Riding 1995b, B3). Since the breakup of his country and the subsequent nationalist wars of ethnic cleansing there, this Bosnian Muslim-Jewish filmmaker has lived in France, where he has sought French nationality. His films deal centrally with national and nationalist aspirations (what might be called discourses of emplacement) and with the uncertainties of deterritorialization and homelessness (discourses of displacement). Some of them have been highly controversial, which stems less from his flashy film style or dark vision of human beings than from his politics of emplacement and displacement.

This is particularly true of his *Underground* (1995), whose original title translates as "Once Upon a Time There Was a Country." This is a film of lament about the destruction of a united Yugoslavia, but it was roundly criticized by French and Bosnian intellectuals as Serbian apologist propaganda that is in part financed by Bosnian Serb television (which purchased the film's broadcast rights). Kusturica was also accused of treason by the Bosnians from Sarajevo for his relocation to France and for his refusal to back the wartime government of Alia Izetbegovic (Yarovskaya 1997–98; Riding 1995b). This sort of criticism from all sides is part and parcel of accented filmmaking in today's fragmented, factionalized world, but it was so biting that Kusturica reedited the film a number of times and finally declared that henceforth he would stop making films. Fortunately, he later retracted the declaration and nullified it definitively with his latest phantasmagoric film, *White Cat, Black Cat* (*Chat noir, chat blanc,* 1998).

His *Time of the Gypsies* is about the Gypsy, or Romany, populations that lead a more or less nomadic existence in the interstices of European societies, to which they do not fully belong. As a result, they are exemplary exiles and outcasts, who in this film live a rather hermetic life of petty thievery and crime. The central drama concerns the journey of self-discovery, or rite of passage, of a young Balkan Romany boy named Perhan, who is being raised by his grandmother. His demeanor and behavior are accurately and colorfully described by a reviewer: "Scrawny, hunched, fabulously ugly, radiating a goofy innocence, Perhan drifts through the eccentric and distrustful world of the Gypsies like an angelfish through a school of sharks, playing the accordion, stoking his grandmother's lime kiln, taking his pet turkey to the movies on a string" (Phillips 1990, 77). He falls for a young girl named Azra, whose mother refuses their marriage until he has demonstrated his ability to earn a living. To do that he throws his lot in with a corrupt uncle named Ahmed, a godfather figure, a pimp, and a user of Gypsy children as beggars. Perhan leaves the shelter of his grandmother's home for a journey with Ahmed that takes him to Milan, Italy. In the course of this physical journey and Perhan's psychological evolution, his relationship with Ahmed sours, leading to a deadly revenge against his mentor, involving magical powers of telekinesis.

The film is based on a newspaper article about the arrest of a group of Gypsy children who had illegally crossed the Yugoslav-Italian border. Dissatisfied with a straight realistic treatment of their story, Kusturica told himself, "If you're going to make a structure based on Gypsy life, you have to change your form and explore with nonprofessionals the substance of that life" (Insdorf 1990a, H18). Accordingly, he used a nonprofessional Gypsy cast for most of the principal parts, who speak almost entirely in the Romany language instead of in Serbo-Croatian. And in a move that both expresses the Romany worldview and exilically accents his film, Kusturica mixes the realistic treatment of Romany life with frequent interjections of the characters' flights of fantasy, dreams, and magical ability to move objects and themselves by telekinesis. Reflecting the oral traditions of the Gypsies, many of whom were illiterate, the film is highly cacophonous, imbued with talk and music—indeed, with what Kusturica calls "an overproduction of speech and music" (Insdorf 1990s, H25).

Time of the Gypsies is filled with both sad and tragic and comic and exuberant aspects of the Gypsy life, rendering an unforgettable portrait of an interstitial people perpetually on the move. However, like Perhan's journey of self-discovery and homelessness, the film itself is rather roundabout and meandering (Maslin 1990).

In *Paris, Texas* (1984), German filmmaker Wim Wenders, who has had an affinity with the road movie genre (his production company is named Road Movie) and with American culture and cinema, presents a rumination on wandering and homelessness. The American Southwest desert and icons of mobility are the film's shaping presences. Into this landscape, made archetypal by American Westerns, walks a disheveled, disoriented man in a tattered, dusty suit and a red baseball hat. His name is Travis, and he is variously but aptly described by reviewers as a "prairie dog" and a "vagabond" (Ansen 1984, 132), a "mysterious drifter" (Smith 1995, 35), and a "shell-shocked mute" (Dieckmann 1984–85, 3). He has literally been "lost" for four years, having abandoned his son and wife for unclear reasons. What is clear is that he is profoundly traumatized: he is disoriented, does not speak for quite some time, does not eat, and has a poor memory (for example, he does not remember how long he has been away). It is also clear that he is suffering from a deep sense of homelessness. He carries with him a tattered postcard showing the place where he was conceived: Paris, Texas. Pointing to it, he proudly tells his baffled brother: "That's where I began." The irony is that his birthplace is now an empty lot that bears a "For Sale" sign. Despite the fact that he purchases the empty lot, he cannot restore his last home by possessing either the photograph or the land.

Paris, Texas is an angst-ridden modern road movie about an American road by a German director, which is written by a quintessentially American playwright, Sam Shepard. However, the film also expresses something quintessentially German called *fernweh*, or the longing to escape the homeland for another place. This other place is the United States, to which Wenders was attracted as a child by means of rock and roll music broadcast by the American armed forces radio. In this road movie, vehicles and sites of journeying, mobility, and rootlessness abound: cars and roads, trains and railroad tracks, planes and airports, and road cafés and motels. The film also contains many themes of journeying: wandering, search, return, and reunion (with his brother, son, and wife). These are recurring themes and tropes of Wenders's films, which collectively bespeak his preoccupation with human homelessness. *Paris, Texas* is his most heartfelt and eloquent, if meandering, expression.

Andrei Tarkovsky's preoccupation with house, home, and homeland are examined elsewhere. Here I will deal briefly with *Stalker* (1979), one of Tarkovsky's Soviet-era films, which best expresses his idea of a journey to nowhere. Three characters, a "writer," a science "professor," and a "stalker," set off on a journey through bleak, dark, damp, and barren industrial plants, nuclear power stations, guard posts, and human-created wastelands. Their destination is the Zone, a forbidden and deserted but alluring place in which wishes are supposed magically to come true. The Stalker is an unauthorized guide, a coyote, who smuggles his charge to the Zone. The three travelers (none of whom has a proper name) represent art, science, and faith, but they talk little about such matters, and when they do, their talk is elliptical. Once they brave on foot and on rail the urban and industrial horrors and the countryside that is no less horrible—with its odorless flowers, leaking drainage tunnels, abandoned railroad tracks, destroyed buses, crooked telephone poles, and ghostly and silent passersby—and they arrive at the Zone and at the Room, they discover that the unknown remains unknown: they are unable to make a wish, and the Room is incapable of granting it. Within the bowels of the Zone, exilic epistolarity exerts itself in the form of a mysterious telephone, which rings a number of times and which the scientist uses once to conduct an enigmatic conversation. As this journey of loss unfolds, the three disillusioned explorers (whom the writer analogizes to the "wandering Jews") become increasingly fearful, anxious, and disoriented.

Unlike in *Solaris*, *The Mirror*, and even *Nostalgia*, the journey in *Stalker* seems to yield nothing; no home is found (despite the Stalker's declaration, once in the Zone, that "We're home!"), and no salvation, liberation, or new insight is produced. What appears important here is the journey itself and not the goal, but the various frustrations which the characters encounter give the film a claustrophobic structure of feeling. These, along with long takes that last for over four minutes, stationary shots, shots in which characters stare ahead (particularly at the film's end in the Zone), and the film's changing color scheme, are components of what has been called Tarkovsky's "trance" style (Dempsey 1981, 16) or "cinematic oneirism" (Petric 1989–90, 30). Time itself appears frozen, "sculpted," in Tarkovsky's own term, and the characters seem mesmerized by the invisible mystery of the Zone. Despite the failure of the travelers and the film's overwhelming dystopia (an allegory for the Soviet Union), *Stalker* is not pessimistic. In the end, Stalker returns home—reconstituting the Tarkovskian family comprising man, woman, child, and dog—and his disabled daughter succeeds in moving water glasses across a table by telekinesis. As Vida Johnson and Graham Petrie note, "The subdued beauty of the images and the grave intensity of the child's gaze" provide an epiphany that "compensates for the sense of failure and despair that might otherwise permeate the film" (1994b, 29).

Homecoming Journey

Because the accented filmmakers studied here are generally located in the West, any easterly journey in their films tends to be one of return. Every journey entails a return, or the thought of return. Therefore, home and travel, placement and displacement are always already intertwined. Return occupies a primary place in the minds of the exiles and a disproportionate amount of space in their films, for it is the dream of a glorious homecoming that structures exile. Without that dream, the exiles would be émigrés, expatriates, refugees, and ethnic subjects. Because of this, more attention is paid to homecoming journeys than to home-seeking or homelessness journeys. Mekas acknowledges the enduring circularity of escape and homing in his voice-over to *Reminiscences of a Return to Lithuania*: "The minute we left [Lithuania], we started going home and we are still going home. I am still on my journey home." The film begins with Mekas's accommodation in the 1950s to his new American home, continues with his return journey to his homeland, marked by the intertitle "100 Glimpses of Lithuania, August 1971," and ends with his visit to filmmaker Peter Kubelka in Vienna on his way back to the United States.

Forming the bulk of the film, the hundred glimpses—which vary from brief shots to a long sequence—chart the Mekas brothers' return to their ancestral village of Semeniskiai after decades of exile. Each "glimpse" is separated from the next by a large intertitle number—from one to hundred—that fills the screen, giving the film a calligraphic accent and a staccato rhythm. Shot in Mekas's characteristic diarist style of handheld, random bursts of filming of daily events, and accompanied by his postfilming faraway narrator's voice and by emotional music, these glimpses document his brief visit to a Sovietized Lithuania, particularly his sentimental stay with his aged mother, who continues to milk cows, make fires in her outdoor kitchen, prepare meals, haul water from the well, and observe the clowning around, dancing, and singing of Mekas and his childhood friends. Homecoming, however, involves not only documenting the return but also retracing the past with the camera-pen, as Mekas's voice-over states: "I am a displaced person on my way home, in search for my home, retracing bits of my past, looking for some recognizable traces of my past." What he retraces are the daily farming and fishing routines and significant places (monastery, friends' homes, Elmshorn concentration camp, and Gebrüner Neunert factory). He reexperiences and savors these details as he documents them on film. His reactions range widely, from sadness to exhilaration, and while they signal the meliorative properties of nostalgia and memory, they show that the return to the homeland for the exiles does not necessarily create closure or a home. In Vienna, Mekas's voice-over about Kubelka, which states, "I envied his peace, his being at home," points out that Mekas's return had failed to provide him with a home. His homeland is Lithuania, but his home is elsewhere, and it is not a place; it is Western high culture and art (poetry, alternative cinema, and film criticism).[3]

Close-Up: *Fernando Solanas's* South (Sur, *1988*) *and*
The Journey (El Viaje, *1992*)

Return to the homeland is a structuring sentiment in Solanas's *Tangos: Exile of Gardel* (1985). During its production, the military dictatorship ended in Argentina, to which Solanas returned to complete the film. Despite his own return and the film's deep nostalgia for return, the narrative concentrates less on return than on the process of exchange between home and exile—with the former nourishing the latter through visitors and epistolary transactions. On the other hand, his subsequent film *South*, shot and edited in Argentina, is primarily about return from exile; like its predecessor, it is driven by the tango. For these reasons, *Tangos* and *South* are companion films, but there are significant differences between them. The most salient in this context is that exile in *South* is internal, involving imprisonment, and return from it involves release into the home society. During Argentina's military rule (1976–83), which involved a military coup and a "dirty war," some nine thousand people were "disappeared" and many citizens were incarcerated and tortured. Indeed, the nation itself was deterritorialized in place, or internally exiled: "The abstract guarantee of protection of life for citizens within their own national boundaries was revoked and citizenship was redefined" (Newman 1993, 244). The film centers on the return home one dark night of Floreal, a pro-union slaughterhouse worker, who had been incarcerated in the south of Argentina as a political prisoner for five years. His release/return coincides with the end of military rule; like many returns, it is filled with hope and fraught with anxiety about what he will find at home and what will be the consequences of his return. As Solanas states, it is a return "full of hope, but also full of mistrust" (quoted in Mizrahi 1988, 10).

The entire film takes place in one night, between Floreal's release from prison and his arrival home and reunion with his wife, Rosi. As such, this is a "night journey" film of mythical duration in which profound realizations and reorientations take place under the mysterious, contemplative guise of darkness. The night is long and dark, and the deserted streets, as in key scenes in *Tangos*, are filled with billowing smoke and scattered papers that blow about in the wind. While loose papers in *Tangos* bear a primarily exilic charge, in *South* they carry a political meaning by referring to political campaigns and to electioneering leafleting that became possible and popular after the military dictatorship. Periodically, Floreal encounters figures from the past who tell him of, or reenact, events that occurred in his absence. These are punctuated by his own recollections and by tango songs about love and loss. The interjection of memory and the past into the present, which gives *South* a fragmented, surreal structure, and of tango numbers, which give it the structure of a musical, continually postpone the lovers' reunion until both the film and the night have come to a close. The film contains not only Floreal's recollections and adventures but also those of Rosi, who gives up her French lover upon Floreal's return. In the course of these, both Floreal and Rosi undergo their night journeys, what Solanas calls "an analytical journey of understanding" (Mizrahi 1988, 10), whereby they realize that it is not the country alone that has changed; they, too, have changed. They also discover that reconciliation is necessary to heal the personal and national wounds of internal and external exile.

The film's last shot, which brings Floreal and Rosi together for the first time, seals this dual reconciliation. Floreal, who is in the street, approaches the windows of Rosi's house, behind which she is observing him. As he nears, his reflection in the window matches Rosi's image inside, forming a single composite image. While this scene powerfully embodies such reconciliation, it borders on being too facile, effacing the specificity of different forms of exiles and the deep rupture that they create between those who leave and those who stay. As Newman observes, this is precisely what Solanas does by conflating the return from exile with Perónist democratization (1993, 249). However, Solanas signals his awareness of the basic incommensurability of things exilic by staging the lovers' reunion not in person but in the coincidence of their reflected and refracted images.

The film's title is highly cathected, resonating with the multiple meanings and values of Argentina's journey of identity. At one level, "South" refers to a key tango by that name, about loss and regret, which begins and ends the film. At another level, South represents directional value, as it is favored over the colonizing North and its local despotic agents. Finally, it refers to the place of the southern plateau in the Argentine imagination, which is perhaps as potent as the West is in the American imagination. The film posits the south as the beating heart of Argentina.

In Solanas's *The Journey* (*El Viaje*, 1992), the South is not the place of return but the point of departure for a boy's northward quest by bicycle in search of his missing father. The journey takes Martin vertically into maturity and horizontally across five Latin American countries, from Tierra del Fuego to Mexico. Like the best of journey films, it interweaves multiple journeys. It fuses Martin's personal journey of self-discovery with a "journey of history," that is, with the Argentine national and the Latin American regional journeys over the centuries of conquest, colonialism, imperialism, and independence. This is how Solanas himself describes the journey theme in the film: "Using the most basic transportation system Martin will come into contact with the American peoples, the most humble and humbled. The half-breeds, the Creoles, the blacks, the Indians, the outcasts: 'brown' America. There he finds tracks and vestiges of other mythic journeys, the journeys of memory, of evolution." (from *El Viaje*'s publicity booklet, p. 12) This is a film of travel and traveling not only in its theme of the journey but also in its production history. Like Solanas's *Tangos* and *South*, *The Journey* is an Argentine and French co-production. However, this is made considerably more complex by the film's journey theme that necessitated travel to several countries, its use of multinational and multilingual production companies, crews, and cast, and its multinational financing, distribution, and broadcasting. Similar to most accented filmmakers, Solanas performed multiple functions in the film: as producer, director, screenplay writer, production designer, and writer of lyrics and musical numbers. *The Journey* also traverses several film genres, including grotesque, comedy, fantasy, poetic, and epic, and it features a number of fascinating amphibolic and traveling characters, including Tito the Hope-Giver, Someone Rows, Americo Inconcluso, and Libertario the Oriental. For these reasons, it can be considered a border film.

The anxiety about return that is inscribed in *South* is present in many accented films, for increasingly the exiles' longing for return is tempered by their worries about what they will, or will not, find once they get back. Indeed, return is rarely the grand homecoming that many of them desire, for both the exiles and the homelands have in the meantime undergone unexpected or unwanted transformations. Consequently, the return home sometimes requires as profound an adjustment as the exilic relocation in the first place, thereby extending the exile into yet another realm. Both the worries and the adjustments that return engenders are delineated in Ann Hui's *Song of the Exile* (1990), which is based partly on her own biography.

Close-Up: Ann Hui's Song of the Exile (Ketu Qiuhen, *1990*)

Before making this film, Hui had had a successful career directing film and TV programs for Hong Kong television stations. Her feature films placed her in the forefront of Hong Kong New Wave cinema in the 1980s, but she periodically returned to her professional home, television, where she made another film about return, a "fictional documentary" called *The Prodigal's Return* (1992). Like many exilic films, *Song of the Exile* is partially autobiographical in that Hui's mother was Japanese and much of the film's story line was lifted from Hui's own experiences. However, as she stated, "a lot of the facts have been reorganized, sublimated, or even changed for the sake of the drama" (Hui 1991, 56). The film is concerned with several reconciliations: that of the diegetic mother-daughter, that of Hui and her own mother, and that of Hong Kong residents with China after the 1997 handover. The diegetic, personal, and national reconciliations are all structured by the discourse of return.

Filmed in Japan, London, Hong Kong, and China, *Song of the Exile* is a daughter-text. The engine for the various reconciliations is the return journey of the daughter to Hong Kong and of her mother to Japan. The daughter, Hueyin, is a twenty-five-year-old Chinese who in 1973 has just graduated from film school in London. Her mother, Aiko, is a Japanese native who during the Chinese-Japanese war had married a Chinese nationalist soldier and stayed in China. When Hueyin's application for a job at the BBC is turned down, disappointedly she returns to Hong Kong for her sister's wedding. Instead of healing, however, her return exacerbates the old wounds. She encounters her mother's stern attempts to transform her back into an Asian woman, motivating many flashbacks on Hueyin's part, which create the film's binary structure by juxtaposing the present against the past and by comparing life in China, Hong Kong, and Japan. As forms of symbolic return, flashbacks overdetermine the structure of return in the film. They also function to shift the film's viewpoint, from daughter to mother. Until the first flashback, the film encourages the audience to favor the daughter's point of view. However, as they show how years ago Aiko's Chinese in-laws mistreated her and spoiled her daughter, eventually separating the two, the flashbacks help change the audience's allegiance to the mother. Only years later does she discover the surprising reason behind her grandparents' ill treatment of her mother as a lowly outcast: her Japanese birth.

The mother stages her own return journey to her original home, Japan, with similar profound consequences—a journey in which Hueyin accompanies her. The initial response of Aiko's family in Japan turns her arrival into a grand homecoming; but all is not well, for her return, like that of her daughter's, is fraught with discord. In the meantime, Hueyin's inability to understand Japanese turns her into a bumbling foreigner, which provides her with insight into her mother's foreignness in China. It is only when she achieves such an empathic understanding that her mother reveals to her the full story of how she and her father met during the war. Appropriately, this cathartic scene of confession occurs at a border, by the sea. Told against the background of an ocean liner docked nearby and a night sky that gradually turns into the dawn of a new day, this scene finally ameliorates the mother-daughter rupture. The homecoming journey thus becomes a home-founding one. And home is found not only in a geographic place—by their decision to stay in Hong Kong—but also in the newly formed mother-daughter relationship.

It appears that return is more conciliatory and meliorative in the films of women filmmakers than in those of men, for not only Asian filmmakers M. Trinh Nguyen in *Cyclo* (1995) and Hui in *Song of the Exile* but also Middle Eastern filmmakers Frida Ben Lyazid, Persheng Sadeq Vaziri, and Mai Masri configure return in this manner. Ben Lyazid's *A Door to the Sky* (*Bab Ilsama' Maftouh/Une Porte sur le Ciel*, 1989), the first fictional feature directed by a woman from Morocco, centers on the return from Paris to Fez of a young woman (Nadia) to visit her ailing father. Wearing a red and blue punk hairstyle and a black minidress on arrival, she is gradually transformed by the family mansion, familial memories, and the Islamic spirituality and female solidarity that she encounters inside. Guided by an older woman, Nadia undergoes a crisis of faith and gains a deeper understanding of Islam. The film evokes a powerfully tactile experience of the mansion's beautiful courtyard, verdant garden, water fountains, colorful tile works, and arches and passageways—thus turning it from a place into a felicitous space. The film's cinematography and pacing in these scenes, which are intercut with the father-daughter relationship and childhood memories, favor spirituality and contemplation and create a sense of intimacy with the whole of Arab culture and history beyond the walls. Despite her relatives' objection, Nadia fuses a Western feminist activism with the Islamic tradition of women activism and turns the house into a shelter for battered and abused women. In this manner, the feminized house becomes the site not only of women's spirituality but also of social empowerment (Shohat and Stam 1994, 165). The weak link of the film is the love relation Nadia develops with a man.

Vaziri's documentary *A Place Called Home* (1998) is a touching, sensitive homecoming film, which like all homecomings kicks up more dust than it settles. It is about the filmmaker's return to Iran after a long stay in the United States, higher education, and an unsuccessful marriage. She rejoins her father, whose wife has been living apart from him for years, and visits her birthplace in the Kurdish regions of Iran. These visits and the memories they evoke are rendered with poetic delicacy and deeply reattach her to her family and homeplace. However, the film shies away from exploring the troubled undercurrent of her parents' relationship and the life of her sister, who seems to be well adjusted in the United States but actually is on the verge of a breakdown.

Mai Masri's *Children of Fire* (1991) documents her return in 1989 to her hometown of Nablus to make a film about the Palestinian *intifadah* (uprising) against the Israeli occupation of the West Bank. Like Vaziri's *A Place Called Home*, this film is fully autobiographical in that the filmmaker, the narrator, and the subject of the film are all the same person. Masri was seventeen when she left Nablus; now, fourteen years later, she enters it illegally under foreign occupation and finds it partially ruined. For eleven days the Israeli army's curfew confines Masri and the residents to their homes; but, ironically, when the curfew is lifted, the shopkeepers go on strike to demonstrate their opposition to the occupation.

Masri, a Palestinian-American filmmaker trained at San Francisco State University, and her Maronite Lebanese husband, Jean Chamoun, have made a number of films about Lebanese and Palestinian issues. Many of them were filmed in the Middle East and completed in Europe. During their forced housebondage, Masri records the daily activities of her uncle's household and the testimonials of a number of precocious children who are pushed by circumstances into early maturity and adolescent bravura. A five-year-old boy, Fadi, relates how every day when he returns home from school, he washes his hands, eats his lunch, does his homework, and then goes outside to throw stones at the Israelis. He also keeps watch from an upper-story window to warn the children in the streets below of the arrival of the soldiers. Hanna, a mature eleven-year-old girl, comments soberly on the children's involvement in stone throwing and their cat-and-mouse game with the Israeli soldiers. Her keen observation that the uprising broke the tradition of unequal treatment of girls and boys points to the gender empowerment of the uprising.

At one point, Masri's voice-over intones: "I feel a deep sense of belonging as if I have never been away," indicating that although she returned to a war at home and to a ruined hometown, her return was meliorating. As in most exilic films, however, her return is temporary.

A frequent narrative device in the accented films is return by means of flashbacks, inscribing recollection or reimagination of the experiences of childhood and of homeland. While the documented historical past is often static and stable, the remembered past is fluid and malleable, empowering the remembering subjects. Women are the dominant agents of such returns-by-memory and of their narratives of empowerment, for example, in Baser's *40 m² Germany* (1986) and *Farewell to a False Paradise* (1988) and in Tabrizian's *The Third Woman* (1991).

Elia Suleiman's *Chronicle of a Disappearance* (*Sigil Ikhtifa'aa*, 1996) is about the return of a Palestinian filmmaker known as E.S. (Suleiman's initials) to his homeland, Nazareth, and then to Jerusalem. Nazareth is Suleiman's birthplace, and he plays the part of the filmmaker himself; his parents also play themselves.

Despite these and other autobiographical and authenticating elements, the film is neither truly autobiographical, nor documentary, nor fictional, as it contains elements of each type without specifying which is which. The San Francisco Jewish Film Festival labeled it a "work of autobiographical fiction," while Jay Hoberman characterized it as "part documentary, part psychodrama, part structuralist investigation, and part absurd comedy" (1997, 65). The crossing of textual boundaries is a characteristic of border films. *Chronicle of a Disappearance* is divided into two parts: "Nazareth personal diary" and "Jerusalem political diary." In line with its ironic postmodern aesthetics and ideology, however, the filmmaker's return to these places results in neither an emotionally fulfilling homecoming to an originary homeland nor a dystopian vision of total rejection of the old country. Instead, an ironic split subjectivity is developed, which juxtaposes critically and often with incisive humor aspects of Palestinian and Israeli histories, cultures, and identities. Home turns out to be the critical distance, the third discursive space, which Suleiman creates and inhabits in the film.[4]

Sometimes, the desired return is postponed not out of anxiety about its possible disappointing outcome but because of timing, which may lead to a long-lasting deferral that further intensifies the desire for return. At the end of Solanas's *Tangos: Exile of Gardel*, Maria, the film's young narrator, reports in a direct address to the camera that all the elders in her performing troupe have returned to Argentina, but that she and the other "children of exile" will not follow them until they have first found themselves. Such a journey of self-discovery may defer their return forever, or for long enough that it may no longer matter whether they return.

For many political exiles, return is impossible, making a metaphoric, imaginative, or filmic staging of it a viable option. The single African mother in Maureen Blackwood's *Home Away from Home* (1994) is not at home in her house in England and cannot return home. Consequently, she frequents an airport, where she longingly watches the planes take off. This tenuous connection, however, does not assuage her, causing her to build a small replica of her African home in her backyard. This miniature home away from home appears to comfort her until it is destroyed by a racist neighbor. In a music video about longing for the homeplace, the Iranian exile singer Sattar, who was forbidden to return home, staged his return by inserting his own image from exile into a family photograph taken in his absence in the homeland. Returning to the family photograph was the only safe return and reunion for him.

Like exile itself, return is not always voluntary or desired. Sometimes it is forced, taking the form of deportation; at other times, the exiles are tricked or lured into returning home. Turkish émigré filmmakers in Germany, who have fewer return problems than exiled filmmakers, have made a number of films on this theme. Kurdish filmmaker Ismet Elci made *Sinan, without a Country* (*Sinan, Ohne Land*), a three-part television series that is partly based on his own life story. In the series, a young Sinan is forcibly brought to Germany to work by his tyrannical father. Years later, when Sinan has made a home in Germany, his father again attempts to compel his relocation, back to Turkey. But this time the son resists his father and refuses to return. In Elci's subsequent feature film *The Wedding* (*Dueguen*, 1989), the protagonist is tricked into returning to Turkey by a letter that claims his mother is dying.[5] Once he arrives in his native village, however, he encounters an orchestrated attempt by his family to marry him off to a local girl, although he has a German fiancée. Entrapped, he agrees to marry the girl but runs away on his wedding night, causing shame for the bride, who shoots herself. In *The Journey* (*Die Heimreise*, 1988), filmmakers Enis Günay and Rasim Konyar examine the issue of return in a lighthearted manner. Given the general dysphoria of Turkish exilic cinema in Germany, this is a fresh approach.

In the accented films neither the home-seeking journey nor the homecoming journey is fully meliorating. The wandering quests, too, are often tempered by their failure to produce self-discovery or salvation. However, by invoking other places and other times by means of their journey structures, epistolarity, liminal subjectivity, border aesthetics, and memory- and nostalgia-driven narratives, every accented film, even those that do not inscribe actual or metaphoric journeys, are about human desire for traveling and homing.

Borders and Border Crossings

Journeys are not limited to those that take exilic and diasporic subjects physically, psychologically, or metaphorically out of home countries and deliver them elsewhere or return them to their points of origin. There are also "journeys of identity" that displaced people inevitably undergo once they arrive in the new lands. Like other journeys, these internal journeys are composite and serial, since most exilic conditions involve multiple motivations and evolutions. Displaced individuals and uprooted communities may enter the host country with one status—as exiles, refugees, asylees, émigrés, students, or illegal aliens—but they do not remain in that status for long, especially if they arrive with significant cultural, racial, educational, class, and other capitals. They undergo transformation, or their transformation is hindered, by the legal status with which they enter the new country and by the work they do there, the activities they undertake, the associations they form, and the media they produce and consume, as well as by the host society's historical perception and current reception of them. Many accented films deal with these status shifts, the desire embedded in them, and their cost to the travelers. After the brother and sister in *El Norte* arrive in the United States, the film focuses on their drama of adjustment and on their unrequited desire to become legal residents. The narrative of *Walls of Sand* centers on two protagonists, one of whom is attempting to break free from her agoraphobia, while the other is trying to change her status from illegal alien to legal resident. Both of them have to make compromises and take risks to achieve their goals. Like exile itself, the journey of identity in accented films is processual and endless. Such a journey can also take the form of the performance of identity, whereby exilic subjects travel strategically across a range of identities, as in many of Egoyan's films.

For exilic transnationals, some of their key moments of border crossing occur in certain empirical border places that are cathected with affect, such as airports, seaports, and railway stations, and which act as portals to other places and times. Depending on the nature of the journey and the crossing—whether it is legal or illegal, accomplished openly or clandestinely, with false papers or valid documents, and undertaken voluntarily or involuntarily—these portal places are charged with intense emotions, involving fearful escapes, tearful departures, sudden entrapments, devastating rejections, joyful arrivals, and a euphoric sense of liberation that cannot be recuperated easily.[6]

Border and Chicano Films

Ellis Island was the chief border entry point in the United States, through which some 12 million immigrants passed from 1892 to 1954. Indeed, the ancestors of some 40 percent of the current population used that gateway in their journey to the new land (Greenhouse 1998). It was there that undesirable immigrants were weeded out. Brutality and corruption occurred frequently, and many hopefuls were deported because of extreme poverty, diseases such as trachoma, or anarchist tendencies. A German-language daily in New York called Ellis Island "hell on earth," and a municipal reformer, Frederic C. Howe, characterized it as "a storehouse of sob stories for the press," where "deportation, dismembered families, unnecessary cruelties made it one of the tragic places of the world" (quoted in Brownlow 1990, 303). The Jewish novelist Isaac Bashevis Singer remembers that Polish immigrants called it the "Island of Tears" (quoted in Coan 1997, 169). Many of these conditions were dramatized in the early films.

Although these fictional films were not exilic, many of them contained elements of the border films, such as documentary "arrival" footage of actual immigrants on ships, their processing at Ellis Island, and their ride on a ferry to the mainland. Some of them also spoke of the fears and wishes of the newly arrived.[7] Films about immigrants were made not only in the receiving country the United States but also in the countries of origin, and not all of them lauded the promises of America. For example, the outflow of Swedes to the United

States was so high in the early 1900s that some Swedish companies made films that discouraged emigration.[8]

Perhaps the border that has resulted in more feature films than any other is the two-thousand-mile United States–Mexico border, which has generated scores of films in the United States and, according to Norma Iglesias, 147 films in Mexico in a single decade, between 1979 and 1989 (quoted in Fregoso 1999, 189–90).[9] The following features characterize "border films":

- The plot involves significant journeying and border crossing and use of border settings.
- The story deals with characters from the borderland regions, regardless of the setting.
- The story deals with border subjects who live on the border.
- The film is shot on location in the borderlands, regardless of the plot.
- The story makes significant reference to the borderlands or to the problems of ethnic or national identity.
- Border subjects make the film themselves.
- The film crosses generic and narrative boundaries.[10]

To be a border film, more than one of these characteristics must be present.

One type of border films that highlights the border subjectivity of the filmmakers is the Chicano/a cinema, produced by Mexican-Americans in the United States. Recognized as a film movement since the release of Luis Valdez's *I Am Joaquin* (1969), its first exemplar, Chicano cinema has undergone rapid evolutionary changes. It began in opposition to both Hollywood cinema and the dominant culture that it represented. This critique is evident in the artisanal mode of production of Valdez's film (based on a slide tape and using a Mexican oratorical poetic narration) and in the strict binary opposition that it posited between American and Spanish "imperialist" cultures and Mexican and Indian "authentic" native cultures. Chicano cinema also began in support of the politics of Mexican farmworkers and Chicano student and civil rights movements. These politics are inscribed in Jesús Treviño's early films, *The New People* (*La Raza Nuevo*, 1969), a super-8 film with sound and narration on separate tape, *Enough Already!* (*Ya Basta!* 1969), a 16mm film, and *I Am Chicano* (*Yo Soy Chicano*, 1972), a TV documentary.

Despite these "cinema of imperfection" beginnings, Chicano cinema moved away from straight inscription of politics toward a "politics of professionalism within the industry and the independent sector" (Noriega 1996, 16–17). It also moved away from a cinema by, about, and for Chicanos to a cinema by and about Chicanos, but made to appeal to crossover audiences. At the same time, it continued to develop alliances with the New Latin American and Spanish-language cinemas outside the United States. The result is a varied menu of border films, including Gregory Nava's films, Ramón Menéndez's *Stand and Deliver* (1987), Cheech Marin's *Born in East L.A.* (1987), Salmoé España's *Spitfire* (1991), Edward James Olmos's *American Me* (1992), and Robert Rodriguez's *El Mariachi* (1993).

Along with this evolution of the Chicano cinema, terms such as "border" and "border crossing," which originally referred to the experience of undocumented and bracero Mexican farmworkers who crossed into the United States for seasonal work, expanded to become metaphors for borders and border crossings of all kinds. This centrifugal expansion was embodied and critiqued in Guillermo Gómez-Peña's early performance and video *Border Brujo* (directed by Issac Artenstein, 1990), in which he transformed himself into and parodied more than a dozen personae, including some shifters, and he spoke not only in English and Spanish but also in tongues.

The metaphorization, multiplication, and shifting of borders are often made productive in postcolonial and multicultural discourses by safely abstracting the borders and by ignoring the unequal power relations there. However, for many accented filmmakers, the site-specific, physical borders are both real and formidable barriers, and crossing them is fraught with much risk and high anxiety. Consequently, while some of them inscribe metaphorized borders and border crossings, many of them deal centrally with the empirical borders, and the emotions and wounds they inflict. Judged by the aforementioned criteria, some of the accented films are border films. They are grouped by the cathected borders and means of border crossing.

Tunnel

By providing access to adjacent countries and cultures, borders are places not only of transition but also of translation and transgression. Sister border cities, such as Tijuana and San Diego, Nogales and Nogales, Brownsville and Matamoros, and El Paso and Ciudad Juarez, which connect Mexico to the United States, are sites of intensive intermeshing of politics, cultures, economics, media, and identities. They are also sites of struggle over both immigration issues and human traffic. Some of them are so well guarded and militarized that they force border crossers to take desperate measures, as a result of which hundreds of Mexican and Central American border crossers turn up dead annually (Verhovek 1997).[11] Such border towns and border crossings have figured in many mainstream and independent films by Chicano and other filmmakers.[12]

Close-Up: Gregory Nava's El Norte *(1983)*

Made by Chicano filmmaker Gregory Nava, *El Norte* inscribes one such desperate measure and its disastrous consequences for the border crossers. The second part of the film, "El Coyote," is devoted to the efforts of the Mayan

Figure 29. Sewer tunnel as "middle passage." Brother and sister (with their "coyote") about to enter the tunnel that connects Tijuana to San Diego in Gregory Nava's *El Norte*.

Indian brother and sister from Guatemala, Rosa and Enrique, to journey through Mexico and cross into the United States at the Tijuana–San Diego border. In their Mexican journey, they attempt to cross cultural borders by passing as Mexicans. But their inappropriate use of Mexican slang and swear words, their accent, and their clothing give them away. During this physical crossing and cultural passing, they are truly in a liminal slipzone: caught in the vise of their longing for the Guatemalan homeland (which is mixed with fear) and their desire for El Norte beyond. The border town of Tijuana has the appeal of neither—a view that is inflected by the director's own biography and childhood experiences: "I am from San Diego, but I come from a border family. I have relatives in Tijuana. As a kid, I crossed the border several times a week, often wondering who lived in all those cardboard shacks on the Mexican side. The border is unique—the only place in the world where an industrialized first-world nation shares the border with a third-world country" (quoted in Insdorf 1984, 17). Having discovered that overland passage is too dangerous, Enrique and Rosa decide, with help from a friendly coyote, to illegally cross the border through a narrow, abandoned sewer tunnel.[13]

This long sequence, lasting some ten minutes, is claustrophobic and frightening for the two travelers. As they creep and crawl on all fours against the tunnel's tight metal walls, rats attack them and bite Rosa—an incident they do not take seriously until at the film's end, when she dies of typhus contracted from the rats. At the same time, the United States border patrol searches for them aggressively from a roving helicopter, which buzzes the tunnel and shines its powerful searchlight on it. The scenes of rats attacking from the inside are intercut with those of the buzzing helicopter from the outside to intensify Enrique and Rosa's sense of siege. The travelers pant, sweat, and cover their mouths and noses to protect themselves. Finally, they emerge from the tunnel on the United States' side, where their loyal coyote meets them and offers them sandwiches.

This sequence, which began in the daylight squalor of Tijuana, ends with a luminescent San Diego cityscape glittering in the night. However, this view sets up a false hope for a new beginning for the migrants—false because the negative legacy of the crossing, the "border effect," will continue to haunt them until the film's end. The most prominent border effects are Rosa's death by typhus and Enrique's decision to stay with her in the hospital instead of grabbing his big chance—a job as a factory foreman in Chicago and legal residency. This decision forecloses his possibilities in the North.

In depicting the epic journey of the Mayans, *El Norte* is highly didactic and earnest, and the two protagonists do not achieve real psychological depth. They remain only types: good-hearted, hardworking, naive Third World peasants, victimized by oppressive but faceless military and commercial structures. The film is epic in another way. As Pauline Kael noted, it is "an epic of the independent and underfinanced film movement, which means that moviegoers have to be willing to settle for humanistic aims and considerable amateurishness" (1985, 130). For accented films, however, amateurishness is not a liability but a distinguishing feature. The film's artisanal mode of production forced the filmmakers to re-create the Guatemalan scenes in Mexico (in Chiapas, bordering Guatemala), hire non-Guatemalan actors for their leads (both of whom are Mexican), and use Guatemalan nonactors for smaller parts. But if necessity and underfinancing drove them to film in Mexico, the political turmoil of the Chiapas, which according to the filmmakers "was ready to blow," offered them some insight into the oppression that the Mayans were experiencing in Guatemala. Indeed, the difficulties they encountered in Mexico turned the film's mode of production from the artisanal to the guerrilla. Mexican government secret agents, apparently bent on stopping the filming, visited the set while carrying weapons. They kidnapped the production manager and chased the cinematographer in a car, finally running him down and taking away the exposed negatives at gunpoint. Frightened, Nava and his producer-wife, Ana Thomas, checked out of their hotel and found residence elsewhere using assumed names. After much negotiation with the kidnappers, they agreed on a cash ransom for their hostage and the exposed film and designated a Mexico City parking lot as their rendezvous point. Thomas explains what happened there next: "Two cars pulled up, with guys who had submachine guns and sunglasses, at night. It sounds almost comic but it was very scary. We paid around 1.3 million pesos, around $17,000 at the time. They threw down a metal box and drove away. Although we had another week of shooting left there, we had to get out of Mexico within 24 hours" (quoted in Insdorf 1984, 26). Filming had to be completed in California.

Despite the flaws stemming from its production mode, *El Norte* demonstrates that border crossing—despite its celebration in much of the border literature—leaves both physical and psychic scars that may never heal. In some accented films, the border is terminal; in others it is a festering wound. Every successful cultural translation and transition exacts a price. There is no painless crossing and no free passage! By being historically situated and culturally specific, and by paying attention to the inequality of power relations at the borders, the best of border films avoid being recuperated into the hegemonizing and homogenizing celebratory discourses of border crossing and globalization.

Seaport and Airport

Borders and border spaces tend to fire up the human imagination, for they represent and allegorize wanderlust, flight, and freedom. This idea is eloquently expressed in the dialogue of Frank Capra's quintessentially American film *It's a Wonderful Life* (1946). George Bailey, who has had to put aside his own wanderlust and dream of individual achievement for the sake of protecting his small community of Bedford Falls, asks his uncle: "Do you know what the three most exciting sounds in the world are? . . . Anchor chains, plane motors, and train whistles." Sadly for George, he is never able to answer the call of these border vehicles that beckon him to other places and possibilities. The call of the wild, the desire for foreign places, remains a powerful attraction throughout this film and in many accented films.

Close-Up: Amir Naderi's The Runner (Davandeh, 1985)

This protoexilic film presents one of the most graphic inscriptions of the desire to escape to foreign lands. It also foreshadows its maker's own actual exodus from his homeland. The film's visually stunning narrative is almost entirely driven by the love of Amiro, an eleven-year-old boy, for airports and seaports, and by his longing to be taken away to freedom elsewhere. Amiro does not cross any actual borders, but he inhabits a psychic and a metaphoric border where the allure of escape and the pull of the permanent rub against each other. In several long scenes, the liminal Amiro (aged between a boy and an adult) stands in the liminal space of the seaport (between land and sea) during the liminal time of day (at dusk), hailing the giant tankers and ships anchored in the distance, shouting, "Take me, take me, take me."

Figure 30. Longing to escape. Amiro (Majid Niroumand) calling a tanker to carry him away in Amir Naderi's *The Runner*.

Amiro is an illiterate orphan who earns his keep by polishing shoes for foreign sailors, selling ice and cold drinking water to dockworkers, and collecting discarded bottles from the sea for resale. He is enamored not only of ships and seaports but also of airplanes and airports. He spends much of his earnings on purchasing English-language flight magazines, which he cannot read but whose visuals he studies carefully. In addition, he frequents a local airport, where he climbs the fence to get close to the prop planes. There he caresses them with awe and pleasure and chases them as they take off and land, all the while shouting at them and jumping up and down with joy.

Amiro lives alone in an abandoned ship hulk that he has turned into a pleasant, self-sufficient home; but life is hard for him and for a large group of homeless street urchins. Running and racing are their main activities and the film's key metaphors for transcendent effort. Amiro races against his friends and against trains; he also races against himself, trying to best himself at running and at memorizing the alphabet that he has belatedly begun to learn (the latter in a dynamically edited sequence that intercuts scenes of students in a classroom sounding out the alphabet with bored disinterest and Amiro's staccato shouting of the alphabet into the pounding surf). And yet this little, independent, scrappy boy-man is vulnerable and humane, as revealed in the film's powerful finale, which pits the children against each other and against a block of ice that is fast melting away from the heat of a blazing oil field.

In its loving, respectful, and unsentimental treatment of Amiro and the other children, *The Runner* has been compared favorably with Buñuel's *Los Olvidados*, Hector Babenco's *Pixote* (1981), and Mira Nair's *Salaam Bombay!* (1988). It has also been called "a work of astonishing power and simplicity, reminiscent of the finest Italian neo-realist films" (Thomas 1987a).

Much of the film's story and its allegorical inscription of wanderlust and escape resonate with Naderi's own biography. Born in 1945 in the Persian Gulf city of Abadan, Iran, Naderi lost both his parents before he was six years old.

Orphaned like Amiro, he spent his childhood, like Amiro, in the Gulf seaports, where *The Runner* was filmed.[14] The representation of seaports as a "montage culture," which critically juxtaposes native and foreign elements, and some of the film's key stories (including Amiro's fascination with foreign magazines) are all based on Naderi's own childhood observations and recollections: "At age twelve, I became aware of periodicals. It was in the cargo ships anchored in the Abadan port that for the first time I encountered film periodicals and at that very moment I decided that I would go to the United States. Most of the films that I used to see in Abadan in those days were in English and this attracted me to English-speaking people" (quoted in Haidari 1991, 19). For Naderi, the border was not a wound, and the border effect was not one of defeat. Instead, the border was a place of imaginative possibilities. Fascinated with cinema, young Naderi began loitering around movie houses, doing odd jobs, selling concessions and tickets, and eventually projecting films. His attraction to the pictures in foreign magazines pulled him toward an early career in photography in Tehran, where he took publicity pictures on film sets. This eventually led to his second career, filmmaking. Naderi's thirteen features and short films since the early 1970s can be divided into two groups: social realist action films, which form the output of his early career, and lyrical, highly visual minimalist films, which constitute the bulk of his later effort.[15] The films of the latter category have brought him the lion's share of his international reputation. *The Runner* was his penultimate film before his permanent and voluntary exile to the United States in the mid-1980s. Naderi, like Shahid Saless, does not want to be considered an exiled filmmaker. As he told me, "I want to make a complete break, destroy all the bridges. I want to have nothing to do with Iran, my family, Iranian cinema, or being an Iranian exile filmmaker. I want to be a great filmmaker, period" (Naficy 1996d). The desire of postcolonial and Third World filmmakers—such as the Iranian Shahid Saless and Naderi, the Algerian Charef and Allouache, and the Romany Gatlif—not to be associated with their homelands, which are sometimes labeled "pariah" or "rogue" nations, and their desire not to be ghettoized as "ethnic" artists in the host society are certainly understandable. However, this disavowal of their origin can rob them not only of their precious sources of ethnic funding and pride and of their collective audience but also of the stories in which they have a deep and abiding personal investment. In the Iranian exilic cinema, the universalism of Naderi and Shahid Saless is the other face of the localism of Sayyad and Allamehzadeh. In both cases, it is easier to be polar and categorical, to create hard-and-fast borders between self and other, here and there. The real challenge and reward lie in fighting for a hybridized thirdspace of being and working, which is neither orderly nor secure.

Border spaces such as airports not only fire the imagination of people who are caught in repressive societies (such as Amiro) but also fuel the longing of the exiles for home, particularly of those who cannot return. Maureen Blackwood of the Sankofa Film and Video Collective made *Home away from Home* (1994), a prizewinning short (eleven minutes long) about an African émigré mother and her children who live in the cramped spaces of a dreary house near an airport in England. The film begins with a touching shot that powerfully condenses the bittersweet structures of longing for home that airports evoke. As a jumbo jet lands on the tarmac, the camera pans with the plane to reveal the back of the mother, who is observing the landing. The camera continues to track around her in close-up and comes to rest on her face as tears stream down her cheeks. As much as her house in England is physically confining, the arrival and departure of the planes are psychologically expanding, for they symbolically carry her to her faraway rural home.

In addition to offering representations, symbols, and allegories of elsewhere and of home, borders are actual physical locations in which exilic narratives are enacted. For many exiles and refugees, airports are not just rhizomatic points of linkage to other points in an abstract network of relation and commerce, as they may be for transnationals and cosmopolitans. These are nodal sites of high intensity in which their belonging and unbelonging are juxtaposed in often cruel, sometimes humorous ways. If for some upper-class, cosmopolitan transnationals, planes are where they feel most at home, for many exiles airports and planes are places of dread and dissemination, where safety and identity are at stake.

Race, ethnicity, religious affiliation, politics, and national origin are the criteria by which airport personnel usually filter passengers. In the United States, antiterrorist filtering has involved a secretive but widespread "profiling" system that in the late 1990s unfairly targeted people of Middle Eastern origin or people with Middle Eastern names (Lewis 1997, A10). Such filtering, profiling, and subsequent questioning and detention at airports turn the simple arrival and departure of the exiles, particularly those moving between the Third World and the First World, into highly uncertain and anxiety-ridden political affairs.

Close-Up: Ghasem Ebrahimian's The Suitors *(Khastegaran, 1989)*

Ebrahimian's first feature in the United States opens on a group of Islamic men driving to a farm in upstate New York to purchase a sheep to ceremonially slaughter (in the bathtub of their apartment) to celebrate the arrival of Haji and his new bride, Maryam, from Iran. This scene is intercut with the newcomers' arrival at Kennedy Airport, where several borders are crossed simultaneously—national, cultural, religious, and gender—and which highlights the complexities of the arrival scenes of the Third World travelers to the West. Arriving at the immigration counter, Haji is wearing the traditional Muslim stubble beard and knit skullcap, and Maryam wears a black chador that covers her from head to toe, leaving only her eyes exposed. As is customary for traditional Muslim women, she stands at an angle to the unrelated male immigration agent and maintains averted eye contact with him. In this way, not only her body but also her uncovered eyes are veiled.[16]

Yet, to ascertain her identity, the agent demands that she "take off the veil," a demand that he repeats a number of times in a game of veiling and unveiling that, although somewhat heavy-handed, is nonetheless insightful about the unequal power and knowledge negotiations at national borders. Acting as a translator for an act of unveiling that is offensive to traditional Muslims like him, Haji reluctantly tells his wife to abide by the request and open her chador for the stranger. She complies by inching the veil open just enough to reveal more of her eyes and nose. Subsequent demands by the agent lead to a series of graduated unveilings that expose her eyes, nose, mouth, face, right ear, and some of her hair. What we discover at the end of this miniature striptease is no elderly, traditional-looking woman but a striking, modernly dressed, slender young woman. Satisfied, the agent returns their joint passport with a sly "Wonderful!"

Loaded down with their unwieldy suitcase and bulging plastic bags, Haji hurriedly leads the way across the busy airport terminal, leaving Maryam stranded. Completely lost and frantic, she finally reaches the terminal's main hall. Here, in a high-angle shot in whose foreground looms a large United States flag, Maryam's black chador slips off to the floor, exposing her completely (wearing a black dress underneath). She quickly recovers her chador and her composure, but the literal unveiling has been accomplished, producing several metaphoric readings: it allegorizes the power of the host society to strip away not only the physical veil but also the autochthonous identity of the newcomers; it symbolizes the complex historical, semiotic, and political relationship of Iran and the United States, including the American government's interference in Iranian politics; and it foreshadows Maryam's own voluntary unveiling and independence later in the film, after her husband is killed by a SWAT team.

Having found Maryam, Haji and the greeting party drive off into the city in a car scene that, in terms of its mise-en-scène and editing, duplicates the scene in which the sheep was driven to the city for slaughter. With such a parallel between woman and sheep, *The Suitors* initially posits Maryam as a victim of patriarchy—a parallel that is reemphasized when a Persian cat, in an airline carrying cage, is compared with Maryam, who is trapped by persistent suitors. However, both exile and loss of husband empower her to take charge, eventually resulting in her stabbing one of her suitors to death. Having committed murder, she decides to escape the country without a passport (inside a suitcase, as described later). The film's departure scene, like its arrival scene, occurs at an airport and is just as conflicted emotionally as the former.

Born in Mashhad, Iran, in 1953, Ebrahimian came to the United States in 1974 to study filmmaking. He earned his bachelor of fine arts degree in 1979 from the State University of New York, College of Purchase. His short film *Willie* (1981), about an African-American boy in Harlem, received the Best Student Film Academy Award in the dramatic category. He and his partner-wife, Coleen Higgins, established Ebra Films in the early 1980s, through which they made *The Suitors*, as well as several documentaries for European television. Ebrahimian is also responsible for the crisp cinematography of Shirin Neshat's film and video installations.

The mode of production for *The Suitors* was independent and artisanal. The film had a relatively low budget of $250,000, which Ebrahimian and Higgins obtained from various local, state, and national arts agencies in the United States and from Channel 4 television in England. Ebrahimian performed multiple functions as director, coproducer (with Higgins), writer, and coeditor (with Amir Naderi). He shot the film in only 6½ weeks, on 16mm stock (later blown up to 35mm), and at an extremely low shooting ratio (using only forty film rolls). Most of the scenes were "one take situations" (Muscarella 1989, 42). Although some of the cast members had acted in theater, none had acted in films before. Despite its mode of production and its somewhat uneven narrative, the film was selected as the official United States entry for the Directors' Fortnight at the 1988 Cannes International Film Festival. And it is perhaps the first Iranian film made abroad to have received commercial, if limited, distribution in the United States. Understandably, for a film that deals with the clash of cultures, its reception was controversial (see chapter 3).

Hotels and Motels

Hotels have served as places of residence for the urban poor and homeless populations in Europe and North America, as well as for well-to-do cosmopolitan exiles and transnationals, such as for Russian novelist Vladimir Nabokov and Iranian-American futurist FM-2030.[17] For ordinary postcolonial and Third World exiles, hotels and motels often serve only as transitional places of residence. Sometimes these structures are located in a third country, where uprooted people anxiously await money, family members, visas, and tickets to their desired destinations. These anxieties are compounded by the fear that failure to obtain passage may lead to their deportation and severe punishment at home, including death. For thousands of Iranian exiles, Turkey was such a third country of transit in the 1980s, while Italy served as such a place for Kurdish refugees from Turkey in the 1990s. Third-country or transitional hotels and motels both shelter immigrants and refugees and nurture manipulative shifters, loan sharks, corrupt officials, and coyotes of all sorts who prey on their uncertain status and apprehensions. Allamehzadeh's film provides an example.

Close-Up: Reza Allamehzadeh's The Guests of Hotel Astoria (Mehmanan-e Hotel-e Astoria, *1989*)

This film is about a group of Iranian would-be refugees on their way to Europe and North America who are trapped in a dingy hotel in Istanbul, Turkey. Shot on location in Turkey, Holland, and the United States in 1987–88, the film brought together a large cast and crew of Iranian artists in exile (with the notable exception of the African-American filmmaker Charles Burnett, who was the film's director of photography). Because the director's autobiography strongly accents the film, it is pertinent to review briefly his filmic and political background.

Born in Iran in 1943, Allamehzadeh began his film career in 1969. He made a number of short children's films and socially conscious documentaries until 1973, when he was arrested along with a group of leftist intellectuals, among them Keramat Daneshian and Khosrow Golsorkhi. Daneshian and Golsorkhi, the most outspoken members, were executed after an infamous nationally televised military show trial, which backfired against the Shah's government.[18] Allamehzadeh, who was in the show trial, was sentenced to a long prison term, but he spent only five years in jail. He was freed with the start of the anti-Shah revolution, at which time he joined the Marxist guerrilla organization known as Peoples' Guerrillas (Fadaian-e Khalq). Soon he headed the organization's national film production and distribution system.[19]

To supply it with appropriate material, he and others edited, dubbed, and retitled some fifty foreign films, including films about revolutionary struggles in Nicaragua and Vietnam and documentaries made in the Soviet Union. The Peoples' Guerrillas made several agitprop films of their own, which were shown along with others in mosques, colleges, universities, and other educational institutions throughout the country.[20] Allamehzadeh himself directed several hard-hitting documentaries, including *Speak Up Turkoman* (*Harfbezan Torkaman*, 1979) and *The Wise Little Black Fish* (*Mahi-ye Siah-e Kuchulu-ye Dana*, 1980), the latter about Samad Behrangi, a famous leftist schoolteacher. The former film was screened, but the latter was banned by a government censor who, according to Allamehzadeh, was actually blind!

When the Islamist government closed down all higher education institutions in the early 1980s to Islamicize them, Allamehzadeh and his cohorts changed course by dubbing East European feature films for distribution to television and public cinemas. However, because of government terror and internal division, the Fadaian organization split into factions. Allamehzadeh escaped to Turkey, where he spent some time in a hotel that was similar to the Hotel Astoria of his film. Unlike the protagonists of his film, however, he was able to obtain political asylum in Holland, where he has been living and making films since 1983, primarily shorts and documentaries.

His first feature fiction film, *The Guests of Hotel Astoria* is an exemplar of the exilic hotel-films, even though it is flawed by slow pacing, underdeveloped characters, and uneven technical quality. The film's publicity booklet provides a full description of the world that these hotels represent:

> Hotel Astoria is a small guesthouse in Istanbul where Iranians who have fled their homeland are residing while waiting to find refuge somewhere in Europe or America. This entrepot is used by an Iranian smuggler for stockpiling his human merchandise until it is dispatched to its final destination. It is the focal point of the shortlived hopes and the endless cares of people who are prepared to face any form of hardship and alienation. These travelers have packed their bags and set out without knowing who will be their host in the end. They have left behind the inferno of "Khomeini" while before them lies a foreign world about which they are completely uninformed.

While anxiously waiting in the drab hotel, the exiles engage in talk, games, drinking, making phone calls, writing and receiving letters, listening to the homeland's music, and watching television. The roar of passing cars outside and the arrivals and departures of "guests" underscore the transitoriness of their lives on the run.

The chief protagonists are a young couple (Puri and Karim) who, after losing their teaching jobs in Iran, have escaped the country in hopes of emigrating to Holland to join Karim's brother. Unfortunately, they fail to obtain a visa, and when they sneak into Holland and ask for political asylum, they are sent back to Turkey. Meanwhile, Puri hears through the refugee grapevine that if a pregnant woman gives birth in the United States, the child's parents automatically become American citizens. This erroneous information sets her on a desperate but disastrous course. She sleeps with an attractive leftist denizen of the hotel, unbeknownst to her husband, and becomes pregnant by him. Gladdened by this turn of events, Puri and Karim sell all their jewelry to raise the needed funds for her trip to New York City. However, all is not well when she gets there. She learns that the leftist lover has been deported to Iran and executed. She rents a small, dark, tomblike room in which she broods alone. As her delivery date nears, her failure to obtain prenatal medical care lands her in a hospital's emergency ward, where she dies giving birth to a healthy boy. A lawyer tells her friend with some irony that with the mother's death, the road is now cleared for the husband to obtain a visa, as the child's legal guardian. No one tells Karim of his wife's death, and the film ends during a celebration in Hotel Astoria, where various guests congratulate him both on his son's birth and on his own imminent departure to the States.

Claustrophobic spaces and narratives are dominant. In a letter home, one of the residents refers to Hotel Astoria as "this ruin that has become our prison." Fear and anxiety for their loved ones at home and for their own safety are rampant. The corrupt police raid the hotel several times, but they are paid off each time. There are two Iranian coyotes: one is a smuggler of refugees from Iran; the other is a translator for the Turkish police who informs on the refugees

Figure 31. Puri (Shohreh Aghdashlou) suffers from fear and anxiety in Turkey, but she dies in the United States during childbirth (inset) in Reza Allamehzadeh's *The Guests of Hotel Astoria*. Courtesy Take 7 Productions.

and procures sexual favors for the police. Money sharks charge exorbitant prices to provide papers, passports, and tickets. Caught in the physical vise of the hotel and the confining web of exploitative and fearful relationships, the refugees have little breathing room. Concerned about the difficulties and dangers of crossing real borders, they have little ease of mind to think about other metaphoric or transgressive border crossings.

Two women protagonists take independent action, for which they are punished severely. Puri pays for it with her life, and a sixteen-year-old girl who defies her father pays for it by becoming a prostitute. Despite the women's prominent presence, *The Guests of Hotel Astoria* is not a feminist film, for it represents the women primarily as victims.

The film was shown in a number of festivals and theaters, but, according to Allamehzadeh, it suffered from such inadequate distribution that it did not make any profit (Allamehzadeh 1991, 222). The film's failure, however, must also be attributed to its uneven, flawed narrative. Thanks to private and public funding in the Netherlands, Allamehzadeh has continued to make documentaries and short films, which are his forte.

Close-Up: Atom Egoyan's Speaking Parts *(1989)*

In Egoyan's *The Adjuster* and *Speaking Parts,* hotels and motels figure prominently (the former is discussed in chapter 6). As for the latter, much of the story
occurs in a hotel, where protagonists Lisa and Lance work in the housekeeping
department. Lisa is enamored of Lance, a part-time, androgynous movie extra,
who shuns her despite her insistent and imaginative efforts to seduce him,
including placing a bouquet of red roses in the clothes dryer for him to find.
In addition, she obsessively watches videos of the films in which Lance has
acted (and only the scenes in which he appears), and she becomes involved
with a video shop owner who videotapes weddings.

Meanwhile, the housekeeping manager brings Lance into a prostitution ring
for the hotel's high-toned clientele. He develops a steamy sexual relationship
with Clara, a casting-agent-cum-screenplay-writer, who frequents a video
mausoleum to repeatedly view a videotape of her younger dead brother, Clarence, who resembles both her and Lance. It appears that for Clara, Lance is a
double for Clarence, who died after donating a lung to her—thus causing her
guilt. When Clara is absent from the hotel due to travel, she and Lance continue their romantic and sexual encounters via satellite videoconferencing.

Lance, Lisa, Clara, and Clarence interweave in multiple ways: in the similarity of their names, bodily resemblance, the lung transplant, and their sexual
relations with one another, including a strong suggestion of incest. One character appears to be a partial double of another or in some uncanny way an echo
or a shadow of the other. Thus there is a multiplying effect of identity at the
same time that each character is less than whole.

Identity is also ensnared in a web of vision and revision. The hotel as a site
of exchange relations and video as an instrument of voyeurism, recording, and
remembering drive the characters' deceitful behaviors and transgressive crossings of identity and sexuality. However, these performative strategies—unlike
what is suggested in much of the literature on hybridity and border crossing—
do not free the participants. In fact, they make the participants extremely self-
conscious and uncomfortable. As Egoyan told me:

> In the case of *Speaking Parts,* people are basically lying to each other all of the time,
> setting up stratagems all based on deceit. When people are being deceitful, I think,
> they're a lot more guarded. There's not a lot of room for spontaneity. They're very
> aware of what comes out of their mouths and how it's interpreted or distorted in
> some way in order to fulfill someone else's motivations. (Naficy 1997a: 205)

Hotels and motels are signifying sites in Egoyan's films as a result of his own
experience working in a hotel for five years—where, like Lisa and Lance, he
was on the housekeeping staff. As he stated, "I was fascinated by the process
of preparing a room for someone to come into, so that the guest would believe
it was virgin territory. When I began to make films, I became aware of parallels:

Figure 32. Multiplying effect of identity. Lance (Michael McManus) in the hotel room, videoconferencing with Clara (off camera); his audition tape plays throughout in Atom Egoyan's *Speaking Parts*. Courtesy Atom Film Arts.

both professions have systems to support illusion" (quoted in Insdorf 1990b, H25). The prominence of locations of exchange and illusion in his films is also based on his criticism of the way late modernity's capitalist relations are threatening to colonize all spheres of human activity. In these dislocatory sites, rooms can be rented, anonymous access to the usual amenities and comforts of home obtained, and forbidden desires fulfilled—all for a fee and without the messy and complicated human relations that characterize life at home. Consequently, *Speaking Parts* and *The Adjuster* both pander to the ethos of postindustrial capitalist relations of exchange and protest their distorting consequences. Finally, as places that "symbolize a way of life in transit rather than in residence" (Wall 1993, 133), motels and hotels allegorize exilic and diasporic transitionality.

Close-Up: Caveh Zahedi's I Don't Hate Las Vegas Anymore *(1994)*

The Iranian-American filmmaker Caveh Zahedi creates in this film an angst-ridden minimalist comedy that takes place almost entirely in two transitional locations: in a traveling car and in a Las Vegas hotel. Dubbed the "Iranian Woody Allen" (Skyler 1994, 8) or a "Woody Allen type" (Daws. 1991, 3),

Zahedi was born in 1960 to Iranian parents in Washington, D.C. While completing his undergraduate degree in philosophy at Yale, he began making experimental films on his own. Subsequently, for three years he lived in France, trying to make films and write film criticism. Disappointed but undeterred, he moved to California for formal film training in the M.F.A. program at UCLA, which he completed summa cum laude in 1990. He has made a number of "admittedly pretentious and painfully arty" shorts (Burgeson 1994) and two ambitious black-and-white feature films, *A Little Stiff* (1991) and *I Don't Hate Las Vegas Anymore*, both of which were critically acclaimed and shown on national and international festival circuits. However, as is the case with many alternative films, both of his films, particularly the latter, failed at the box office.

I Don't Hate Las Vegas Anymore, which Zahedi characterizes in his résumé as an "experimental documentary," is exilically accented: it inscribes the filmmaker's autobiography, uses the claustrophobic and transitional spaces of car and hotel, and deals with issues of ethnic shame and guilt in its narrative. It also critiques the New Hollywood mode of production and its dominant mode of realist narration. These criticisms are embodied in the film's independent, artisanal production mode, consisting of personal stories, "nonprofessional" close friends who worked as crew and cast, and its meager budget of some $26,000, obtained as grants. It is also embodied in Zahedi's auteurist style: self-referential inscription of himself as the film's lead, self-reflexive incorporation of the filming process that blurs the boundary separating the documentary from fictional cinema, and a minimalist filming style that involves long takes and, with some exceptions, static camera and framing.

This mode of production and narration also operates in his film *A Little Stiff*, in which Zahedi played himself and re-created his own unrequited crush on a fellow student. He has characterized both films as "autobiographical, first-person diary films" (Yari 1994, 55). That his use of biography is a criticism of Hollywood is gleaned from the following statement about *A Little Stiff*: "I really wanted to make films about ordinary things and show them in such a way that people could appreciate them. I guess what I don't like about Hollywood is that it invalidates your life" (Skyler 1994, 8).

I Don't Hate Las Vegas Anymore begins with Zahedi's on-camera confession delivered by his singular on-screen persona, which a reviewer aptly described as "a meeting of unquenchable philosophical inquisitiveness and mesmerizing, anxiety-ridden verbosity" (Rooney 1994). He nervously speaks about how he wants to prove the existence of God by undertaking an unplanned and unscripted film journey to Las Vegas—a journey his parents used to take him on when he was a youngster, which he hated. What follows is a three-day trip from Los Angeles to Las Vegas on Christmas eve with his divorced and remarried sixty-two-year-old father George/Ali, his fifteen-year-old half brother, Amin, and a crew of three. He hopes that this journey will bear out his faith not only by producing a compelling film but also by healing his relationship with his real-life father and brother. Like many accented film-makers, Zahedi harbors deep feelings of shame and ambivalence concerning his origin and his parents. As he told me in an interview: "My mother was from a well-to-do family who was very Europeanized and looked down upon Iranians. I picked that up from her and distanced myself from my parents' culture as though I was better. I was prejudiced and did not learn about my past and my culture. Now I realize that that attitude was detrimental to my own growth" (Naficy 1997g) His mother is totally elided from the film, but Zahedi expresses his feelings toward his father with rare candor.[21] As the travelers approach their destination after hours of contentious driving, Zahedi takes advantage of the absence of his father and brother during a brief pit stop to confide to the camera:

> We're about twenty minutes from Vegas, and I am kind of depressed. I keep wanting to say things but I can't because my father is here and Amin is here. The thing is I don't know what to say, I can't say it in front of them. It is a kind of, you know, thorny issue. All my life I've been ashamed of my parents, more of my father than my mother. He is Iranian and he has an accent and he does things that to me seem stupid. I am trying to embrace that and I am ashamed of myself, ashamed of a lot of things about myself, that I try to hide. Part of the reason I wanted to make this film was because I wanted to deal with that shame thing. I don't know how you see it, but it is embarrassing for me, because I don't know how to be with it. I feel like it is a freak show, or something. I kind of want to show how weird my dad is and I also want to accept [him] and to feel like [he] is not.

As he takes the camera into his confidence, speaking to it in a soft, private voice, Zahedi implicates the audience both in his ethnic and familial power games and in his cinematic manipulations. On two other key occasions, he crosses the classic documentary's ethical line to heighten the drama. In one scene he insists that his brother and father (who has a heart condition) take the drug ecstasy, which he offers them as a Christmas gift, while in the other scene he reveals both the sexual preference of his soundwoman and her alcoholism.

Despite these manipulations, the film contains authenticating elements: Zahedi, his father, his brother, and the film crew all play themselves, use their own names and nicknames, and cross the fourth wall as they walk in and out of the shot and perform for and speak to the camera. The filmmaker's on-camera negotiation with his annoying teenage brother Amin about their agreed-upon, and now disputed, acting fee ($300 or $500) is hilarious; so are Amin's snide comments at the film's end about his brother's film. However, these authenticating elements are continually undermined by the film's self-reflexivity and postmodern irony, which create a slippage between self and identity and between reality and its representation. Zahedi frequently slates the camera by hand clapping and nervously inquiring if the camera is rolling. In several scenes, he expresses his panic at the way the unscripted film appears

Figure 33. Authenticating elements in a "postmodern" documentary. Filmmaker Caveh Zahedi (left) with his own father and brother in an off-guard moment in his *I Don't Hate Las Vegas Anymore*. Courtesy Caveh Zahedi.

to be going nowhere and at his sense of an incipient doom. The many technical glitches, including no sound recorded, no picture recorded, and double-exposed footage, are all incorporated into the film, creating a highly ironic and slippery text.[22] There is a roadside discussion between him and his crew about abandoning documentary filmmaking in favor of reenactment. However, the sections of verité and the reenacted footage are so seamlessly integrated that it is impossible to distinguish the real from the fictional or to trust the truthfulness of Zahedi, his film's characters, and ultimately his film. Zahedi is fully aware of these tensions:

> The film is extremely honest and extremely dishonest at the same time. It's actually an honest film about a guy who's trying to make drama despite his desire to also be honest. It's about that weird tension. If anything, I come off looking like a jerk in the film. But I think there's value to representing my character defects honestly. To do that, I need to cut out the stuff where I look better. (Mordler 1994, 41–42)

Filmmaking is a performance for him, but one that has an inherently therapeutic and empowering effect, for it integrates his life into his work; in his words, it makes "my life a work of art" (quoted in Burgeson 1994). He did just that by making a film named *I Was Possessed by God* (1999), which showed him drinking on his birthday (April 29, 1998) a brew containing an unusually large dose (five grams) of hallucinogenic mushrooms. The ensuing three-hour "possession" was edited into a twenty-five-minute film, warts and all.

That the crew and the talent of *I Don't Hate Las Vegas Anymore* were thrown together into the small spaces of a car and a hotel room for long periods may have contributed to the film's therapeutic result. In addition, the film journey seems to have acted as an agent of family reconciliation and ethnic realignment for Zahedi.[23]

Trains and Buses

Exilic border spaces and border crossings are inscribed not only in fixed transitional sites, such as airports, seaports, tunnels, hotels, and motels, but also in mobile spaces such as vehicles and suitcases. Claustrophobia pervades the mise-en-scène, shot composition, and often the narratives of films that feature buses and trains as vehicles and symbols of displacement. And since these vehicles travel through countryside and wide-open spaces and between countries, there is always a dialectical relationship in the accented films between the inside closed spaces of the vehicles and the outside open spaces of nature and nation. Inexorably, vehicles provide not only empirical links to geographic places and social groupings but also metaphoric reworkings of notions of traveling, homing, and identity.

The Bus (*Otobüs*, 1977), directed by Turkish filmmaker Tunç Okan, deals with a group of Turkish migrant workers who, swindled by a Turkish con man, are abandoned without passport, food, or money in their battered bus in the middle of a square in Stockholm. Although the film is comic at times, the metaphor of a mobile prison is grimly multilayered here. At one layer, the bus (a means of mobility, freedom, and safety for the migrants) is transformed into its opposite (an immobile and confining edifice). At another level, those who venture out of the bus discover that the host society they had feared is not always hostile; more often, it is just indifferent to their presence. The bus (and its inhabitants) represents an encysted ethnic organism, a "foreign body," inserted under the skin of the Swedish body politic, that must be expelled, which is symbolized when it is destroyed at the film's end.

Buses and trains are also heavily used in Güney's *Yol*, as they carry the five convicts who are on furlough to different parts of the country for a brief visit with their families. These vehicles establish both the wide horizontal expanse of the country and the deeply vertical system of control in a patriarchal and militarized Turkey of the 1980s.

Close-Up: Parviz Sayyad's Checkpoint (Sarhad, *1987*)

Much of *Checkpoint's* story, made in the United States, takes place in a bus during the so-called Iranian hostage crisis (1979–81) when Americans were held hostage for 444 days in their own embassy in Tehran. Although the specific circumstances of this Iranian bus are different from that of Okan's Turkish bus, as a symbol of exilic confinement and liminality they are nearly identical. Born in 1937 in Lahijan, Iran, Sayyad was raised in a religious family, headed by a polygamous father who was a poet and an actor in Islamic passion plays known as *taziyeh.* He was not close to his father, and from early on he discovered a discrepancy between pious belief and practice: "I watched my father be very cruel to his wives—my stepmothers—and right from the beginning I thought there was something wrong with his ideas of what it means to be religious" (quoted in Feeney 1983, 27). Despite his early discovery of religious hypocrisy, the boy began singing in these dramas by the time he was four. This early love-hate relationship with Islam and its cultural manifestations and with authority figures would become a lasting pattern in his works, including those made in exile.

Sayyad left his home at twelve to live with relatives, and throughout his youth he helped support himself by working. He received a bachelor of arts degree in economics from Tehran University in 1968 and began a fast-rising career writing, directing, and acting in plays, television shows, and movies. According to one critic, he is "one of the most prolific artists in modern Iranian theater, television, and cinema" (Dabashi 1993, xii). In 1974, he, along with a number of prominent directors, formed the New Film Group, whose aim was to assist Iranian "new wave" filmmakers in producing quality films, including Shahid Saless's *Still Life* (1974). By the time of his exile, he had participated in twenty-one films, including thirteen that he had written and directed under the Shah, many of them light comedies (Stone 1983, np). His protoexilic film *Dead-End* (*Bonbast*, 1979), which won a top award from the Moscow Film Festival, was his most serious and politically nuanced work that apparently was banned by both the Pahlavi and the Islamist regimes.[24]

Given Sayyad's biography and social history, it is not surprising that the contradictions between religious piety and hypocritical practice and between "authentic" rural and "worldly" urban lifestyles would become key themes of his films. These themes were condensed in the figure of a country bumpkin named Samad, played by Sayyad himself in a plethora of television shows and movies, who with a combination of country wiliness and naïveté consistently outwits his sophisticated but corrupt urban counterparts. In the process, like the comic figures of the Iranian traditional theater (called *ruhozi*), Samad critiqued the official culture, particularly government figures, clerical leaders, and fathers. Sayyad transplanted these themes and the Samad character into his exilic theatrical and televisual productions.

Sayyad was in Germany in 1979, apparently exploring a coproduction deal, when the revolution disposed the Shah and the revolutionary forces took over his theater in Tehran. He decided not to go back, instead moving to the United States, where he applied for political asylum and was joined by his family four years later. After his family's safe departure from Iran, Sayyad became highly and publicly politicized against the Islamist government and began to direct, write, and act in satirical political plays (some involving Samad), in polemical, antigovernment television shows (among them *Parsian TV* and *Jam-e Jam TV*), and in two feature films (*The Mission/Ma'muriat* [1983] and *Checkpoint*). In addition, he undertook a dogmatic campaign that condemned cultural exchange between Iranian diaspora communities and the homeland, including calling for the boycott of films made in Iran. With these actions, he cut a figure for himself of a political exile in its most polar and traditional sense. In fact, his polemical politics became such a consuming preoccupation that they increasingly distorted much of his exilic works, reducing their complexity and artistic merit. This can be seen in the differing critical and public reactions to *The Mission* and *Checkpoint*. Both films are political, but while the former dealt with the Iranian politics in a dramatic narrative with universal appeal, the latter handled the politics in a polemical narrative that was only locally attractive. *The Mission* received both critical acclaim and audience appreciation; *Checkpoint* received neither.

Checkpoint's principal story is based on a real event that occurred in April 1980, involving a number of Iranian and American students from Detroit's Wayne State University who upon returning to the United States from an outing to nearby Windsor, in Ontario, were detained at the border. Apparently, while they were in Canada, President Carter, in retaliation for the Iranian government's hostage taking, had suspended the student visas of Iranians in the United States, as a result of which the bus and its passengers were caught in a spatial and legal no-man's-land. They could neither return to Canada nor pass into the United States (the Americans refused to abandon their fellow students). The liminal place of the border and the claustrophobic space of the bus produce a tremendous emotional and political flare-up among the passengers, during which the various parties exchange long-winded hostile accusations and assign blame for the anti-Shah revolution. These reflect Sayyad's own polarized view, which, according to a reviewer for *Variety*, rejects "everything taking place in his home country lately. . . . For him, everybody, whether the religious or the political one, is immediately labeled a villain" (August 19, 1987, 20). The film lapses into "repetitive ideological debate," and the actors, whose ability "ranges from the impressive to the embarrassingly amateurish" (Thomas 1987a, 32), appear to mouth positions without much psychological depth.

The border space in *Checkpoint* is interstitial in that the bus is caught between and astride two intersecting liminal zones: the physical Canadian-American border and the discursive politics of Iran, the United States, and the

Iranian exiles. In this location, the phobic space of the bus provides neither security nor comfort. Such conditions are obtained only when the bus is finally allowed to return to the United States and the students gather at the home of one of the passengers, an Iranian-American electrical engineer (played by Sayyad himself), who seems to have all the answers.[25]

In his debut film, *Who's That Singing over There* (*Ko to tamo peva*, 1980), Slobodan Sijan offers an important and entertaining but ultimately sad and dystopic intervention in the use of the bus as a vehicle of racial, ethnic, and national understanding. It is a nuanced, universal, and prophetic film. Like Bosnian filmmaker Kusturica in *Underground*, Sijan, a Serbian, creates a lament about humankind's capacity for evil and intolerance. The film involves a two-day, hundred-kilometer bus journey from the former Yugoslavia's countryside to Belgrade. It begins on Sunday, April 6, 1941, the day Nazi Germany launched its savage bombing of Belgrade. That the passengers are not aware of the attack on the city of their destination adds to the film's poignancy. As it travels through the rough country roads toward its fateful end, the rickety bus brings together the comic and smoldering differences of people of varied ethnic and national origins, including two Gypsies. In the 1990s, those differences would blow apart Yugoslavia and indelibly carve the term "ethnic cleansing" into the annals of the world's politics of intolerance. At their destination, the bus and its occupants are destroyed in a shelling, leaving the Gypsies as witnesses and as the only survivors who stand in the rubble to sing of the terrors yet to come.

Allamehzadeh's award-winning short film *A Few Simple Sentences* (*Die Paar Zinnetjes*, 1986) explores Dutch xenophobia, particularly regarding the Third World émigrés and refugees who in recent years have flocked to Holland. The vehicle for this exploration is a long bus ride in the city that takes up twelve of the nineteen minutes' running time. On his way to school, a young Iranian boy, who seems to be carrying something under his coat, catches a city bus. The lap dog of an elderly woman barks at him, initiating a lengthy discussion about the émigrés. One passenger complains of their large numbers, while another advocates their expulsion. A group of rowdy boys tease the Iranian, demanding to see what he is hiding in his coat. In the ensuing scuffle, an injured pigeon is freed and begins to fly frantically around the bus, hitting into passengers and windows. The boy is accused of having hurt the bird with a slingshot. Because of his rudimentary command of Dutch, however, his attempt at explaining that he had saved the pigeon from a dog in the park causes only more confusion. Finally, he is kicked off the bus for not having a ticket.

Although Allamehzadeh's film is less pedantic that Sayyad's *Checkpoint*, both filmmakers use the bus as an arena to present a debate about the issues that are important to political exiles: the politics of the homeland in *Checkpoint* and the politics of the host society in *A Few Simple Sentences*. If Sayyad generates an irreconcilable polarity between supporters and attackers of the Islamist

regime in Iran, Allamehzadeh posits an unbridgeable barrier between prejudiced First Worlders and their victimized Third World others. However, *A
Few Simple Sentences* is more honest with itself because it does not provide a
facile closure. The pigeon, a symbol of freedom, is injured, and a foreigner
who is himself psychologically hurt nurtures it. Yet what happens to the boy
and to the pigeon is not revealed.

Bus rides and train rides can also make for quiet occasions during which
displaced passengers can sleep, dream, recall, and reflect upon their lives, or
displaced filmmakers can reflect upon exilic issues. Chris Marker's *Sunless*
(1982) contains long scenes in which Japanese passengers sleep and dream in
their express trains. Indeed, the entire film can be taken as Marker's own self-
reflexive dreamwork. Enrique in *El Norte* falls asleep during the long bus ride
that takes him and Rosa from southern Mexico to Tijuana. He dreams of a
man cutting his throat with a forceful stroke of a giant knife, declaring, "You
can't escape this time, you bastard!" He is woken up as a passenger tells him,
"We're here in Tijuana, the shithole of the world." The dream seems to have
been engendered both by the "day's residue," that is, the violence in Guatemala
that pushed the brother and sister out of the country, and by the fear of what
lies ahead for them in El Norte. In a sequence of Solanas's *Tangos: Exile of
Gardel* called "Absences," a train ride is used as an occasion for a poignant
reflection on the meaning of exile and the multiple absences and losses that
constitute it. Marianna sadly reflects upon her forced exile to France when her
husband Herman was "disappeared" in the Buenos Aires streets. The downcast
sky and the wet landscape that pass by the windows of the speeding train match
her sadness at the loss of home, career, husband, and country.

Naderi's *Manhattan by Numbers* contains many scenes in which the unemployed journalist George Murphy rides the subway in his futile search for his
elusive friend, Tom Ryan. As his desperation mounts, his train rides also become more distressing. This is signaled visually by the way that train cars are
either compressed spatially by long-focus photography from the outside or
compressed temporally by shots taken from the inside of the cars speeding
through the tunnels. These visual distortions are intensified by Murphy's isolation from the passengers, his pensive and defeated look, and his audio flashbacks to phone conversations with mutual friends that fail to lead him to Ryan.

Suitcase

The suitcase is a contradictory and multilayered key symbol of exilic subjectivity: it contains souvenirs from the homeland; it connotes wanderlust, freedom
to roam, and a provisional life; and it symbolizes profound deprivation and
diminution of one's possibilities in the world. In recent years, it has been used
in its various meanings in art, advertising, cinema, journalism, and pro-immi-

grant social protests.[26] And it has influenced the lives and art of exile directors, as in the case of Milos Forman. When Forman was ten years old, the Nazi gestapo visited his home in Cáslav, Czechoslovakia, and arrested his mother, who was not seen again. This event set into motion a thirty-five-year odyssey of exile and homelessness for Forman that entailed living out of a suitcase. His travels eventually brought him to the United States. As he relates in his memoir *Turnaround*, this protracted period of living with and out of a suitcase influenced his definition of home ("Home lay under the roof that sheltered my suitcase"; 1994: 289) and sensitized him to the plight of others who were in similar situations ("I guess I'll always be moved by the sight of a young person with a suitcase seeking a connection in a strange city"; 147). However, living out of a suitcase also made him aware of the nuances of interstitiality and of the value of provisionality, both of which are keys to the survival and success of accented filmmakers:

> Living out of a suitcase in households where they secretly felt sorry for me, passing from one kind of relative to another, I quickly realized that it helps in life to make yourself liked and it helps if you don't give people unnecessary trouble. . . . I found out that being a rebel and raising hell is a huge existential luxury, and I suppose that I grew up to be more of a diplomat than anything else. I learned to read people's moods and to understand what they felt even if they didn't fully understand it themselves. I noticed that people don't always believe in doing the things they do, that there often is a gap between who they think they are and who they really are. I didn't know it at the time, but I see now that living out of a suitcase gave me a very good training for my future trade as a director (35).

If the suitcase does not figure prominently in Forman's films, it appears from his autobiographical account that the lessons it taught him shaped his perception of the world and his improvisational directorial working style. The provisionality that the suitcase imposes, the improvisation it encourages, and the displacement it symbolizes may all become sources of new rootedness and identity.

Close-Up: Atom Egoyan's Next of Kin (1984)

In Egoyan's cinematic universe, identity is not so much a biological or preordained fact as a construction or a performance that involves choices, mimicry, doubling, and transgression more than obligation and responsibility. As a result, identity in his films is not stable or unitary but mobile and multiple—for which the suitcase serves as an apt symbol. In his first film, *Next of Kin*, which is about a young man named Peter who is dissatisfied with his own biological family, the suitcase takes on the symbolic function of both travel and traveling identity. It begins with an airport scene, filmed from the low-angle point of view of the suitcases that are going around on a luggage carousel. These suitcase point-of-view shots are intercut with objective views of the suitcases being taken away by their owners.

The airport scenes are intercut with scenes of Peter in his home environment (hiding under his bedcovers from his feuding parents, swimming in the pool, and celebrating his twenty-third birthday) and with scenes showing him and his family at a therapy session with a role-playing psychiatrist who videotapes their sessions and asks them to study the tapes for insight into their own behavior. The sound track throughout these scenes consists of passages from a minimalist music score, character dialogue, and Peter's voice-over diary, which tells of his unhappiness with his overcontrolling parents, particularly his mother. He rejects them and his identity as their son and begins, as he states, to "spend a lot of my time pretending." The intercutting of the airport and home scenes reinforces the provisionality and performativity of identity that each scene implies individually.

While looking at the tapes of his own family's therapy session, Peter comes across the tapes of an Armenian family, headed by a volatile rug merchant named George, who upon immigration to Canada long ago had put up his son for adoption out of desperation. This has created a gaping hole in the family structure and in the psyche of its members. Dissatisfied with his own vacuous Waspish family and intrigued by the possibilities that this ethnic family offers, Peter decides to fill the hole by pretending to be that family's long-lost son. He takes a vacation from his biological family, ironically named Foster, and joins the Armenian foster family, called Deryan.

The rest of the film focuses on the deepening relationship between Peter (now called Pedros) and his newly found parents and sister (named Aza). Embraced by them, he has found a home, an ethnic home; there is no more need to continue searching for one. This point is underscored as the film cuts to the airport baggage carousel for the last time, when Peter picks up his suitcase upon arriving in the Deryans' town. However, if there is no longer any need for physical traveling, psychological traveling remains essential. This is brought on by Peter/Pedros's discovery that in his new homeplace his presence and pretense function to heal both the Deryan family's scar and his own wounded identity. As he states in his voice-over, it is easier to pretend, to be two people at once: "One part of you would always be the same like an audience and the other part would take on different roles, kind of like an actor." Here Egoyan posits that traveling between multiple identities, or being a shifter, is comforting and empowering, not unethical and debilitating.

Next of Kin forcefully proposes the suitcase as a metaphor for both the constructedness and the mobility of identity. As a metaphor, it tells us that identity never fully maps out onto biology, that it is always provisional and traveling, that there is a slippage between descent relations and consent relations, and that routes are freeing while roots can be stifling. The portable suitcase is preferred to the house—and, for that matter, to the home and the homeland (a theme that is elaborated upon more centrally in *The Adjuster*).

While the film celebrates the crossing of identity boundaries, it fails to deal with the high ethical cost and the responsibilities of such crossings, which can transform doubling into duplicity. At one point, Peter tells Aza, "There's nothing wrong in pretending as long as you know that's what you're doing." That may be true from the pretender's viewpoint, but what about the pretender's responsibility for those who may believe him? Peter's pretense comforts him and gives him the self-confidence he has been lacking; but his Armenian family does not know about his game of pretense, and they genuinely believe him to be their biological kin. Because of this, the threat of exposure continually mars the clarity of Peter's relations.

Indeed, as the films of Zahedi and Egoyan demonstrate, all pretense structures carry with them the potential not only for exposure and betrayal but also for unethical manipulation of innocent people. The insincerity in Noah's relations with the homeless victims of the fires in *The Adjuster* and in Peter's involvement with his Armenian surrogate family in *Next of Kin* stems from these characters' games of pretense. Although Noah spouts to his clients such lines as "I can help you, this is what I am here for," one senses that these are formula phrases he delivers to everyone. And when Peter lies down on the kitchen table to be hugged and comforted by Sonja, his surrogate mother, a very uncomfortable moment is created, for the audience knows both Sonja's sincerity and Peter's pretense. This latter knowledge is chillingly driven home when Peter secretly looks up from Sonja's arms and peeks at the camera, at once acknowledging both the constructedness of his relationship with her and the voyeuristic relationship of the audience with the film. Both techniques are characteristics of Egoyan's accented style.

The structures of pretense and insincerity in both *The Adjuster* and *Next of Kin* result from what might be called a split or detached self. Egoyan cleverly embodies such detachment and possible reattachment in the very filming of *Next of Kin*. Detachment is embodied by the many high-angle, fixed shots that appear to have been taken from the viewpoint of surveillance cameras at Peter's home, in his family therapy session, and in an elevator. The camera becomes active, implying attachment and engagement, only during the therapy session with the Armenian family and when Peter finally joins them to become Pedros.

If Egoyan celebrates the liberating and utopian possibilities of the suitcase and of traveling identity, Iranian exiles are attracted to its opposite possibilities. The suitcase became a multifaceted symbol of both patriarchal oppression and exilic dystopia as a result of a tragic event in the early 1980s in which a newlywed woman, who was being smuggled inside a suitcase into the United States from Europe by her husband, was crushed to death in transit. Devastated by his wife's terrible end, the husband committed suicide a few days later. This story became a cause célèbre in the Iranian exile media and was restaged, albeit in a different manner and with a more hopeful outcome, in Ebrahimian's *The Suitors*.

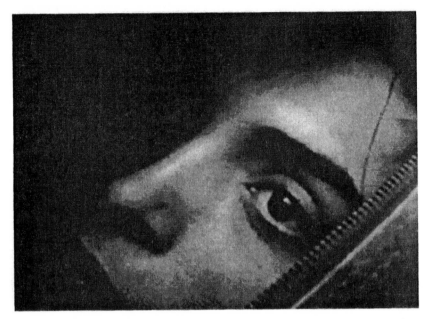

Figure 34. Maryam (Pouran Esrafily) inside the suitcase just before being checked in as luggage in Ghasem Ebrahimian's *The Suitors*.

After stabbing a persistent suitor to death, the young widow, Maryam, decides to leave the United States to avoid arrest; however, she learns that she cannot do so without a passport. Entrapped, she enlists the help of another suitor, who packs her in a large suitcase and checks her in as his luggage to Europe. As the conveyor belt, in its slow, inevitable journey toward the aircraft, carries the suitcase away, the screen goes black. We are inside the suitcase and can hear Maryam's troubled breathing and her quiet desperation, which builds into a panic. At that point, few exiles would fail to grasp the connotations of constriction and diminution that exile spawns and that the suitcase symbolizes. Counter to the original news story, however, just before being loaded onto the plane's cargo bay, Maryam unzips the suitcase and steps out onto the tarmac. With this act she abandons her helper, who takes off, thinking she is in the suitcase aboard the plane. The film's last shot shows Maryam outside the terminal flagging a cab, heading not toward a potentially constricting relationship but toward the full immensity of American society, with its choices and uncertainties, including possible punishment for committing murder. It is only when she abandons the suitcase that Maryam can be said to finally have left both the physical and the psychological liminality of exile.

Journey of Hope (*Reise de Hoffnung*, 1990), by Swiss filmmaker Xavier Koller, is about Kurdish and Turkish refugees fleeing Turkey on foot across treacherous snow peaks toward the Swiss border. At one point in their journey, the suitcases and bundles that the would-be refugees are carrying become forbidding burdens that threaten their safe and timely passage. Consequently, in a remarkable but brief scene, they hurl them into the valleys below. As some of the suitcases burst open, releasing their contents into the air, we, as well as the refugees, realize that with that seemingly simple act of unburdening, they have also discarded some of their past and frayed some of their connections to their culture and homeland.

Many accented films, including Baser's *40 m² Germany,* have brief or extended suitcase scenes, where homesick refugees and exiles—especially women—go through suitcases while lovingly caressing, selecting, examining, and reading their contents and remembering the people and places they have left behind. In Solanas's *Tangos: Exile of Gardel,* the suitcase is the bearer of Juan Uno's epistles, which provide inspiration to the Argentine exiles. In these iterations, the suitcase is more a vehicle of connection and expansion than of separation and constriction.

Close-Up: Mitra Tabrizian's The Third Woman *(1991)*

Tabrizian's short black-and-white film explores the intersection of exilic politics, gender, and sexuality. Although the reference to the suitcase is brief, it serves as a multifaceted metaphor of the mobility of identity. Made in England with a 22,000-pound grant from the British Film Institute, *The Third Woman* focuses on a female protagonist who assassinates the antidemocratic and antifeminist leader of a "progressive" Islamist guerrilla organization, which is fighting the Islamist Iranian government. Told from her perspective, the film begins with her arrival in London to meet with Ali, the organization's leader who is operating from exile. While she has not met him before, she has secretly admired, even desired, him.

In the film's opening sequence, after arriving in London, the woman enters a dingy hotel room, carrying a suitcase, which she places on the bed. The suitcase becomes a motivated prop that inspires a childhood flashback: her grandmother has packed her a suitcase to send her off to live with her father, saying, "You don't want your father to forget you, do you?" She is taught to hate her mother who had apparently left her family for a lover and to respect her father who had raised her. A cut brings us from the girl's home in the past in Iran back into the London hotel room. The suitcase before her contains neither the personal items of the childhood suitcase nor the ethnic objects that exilic suitcases generally carry. Instead, it contains her papers, her organization's literature, a photo of her father, a gun, and three passports. Two of the passports carry the Islamic names of Fatimah and Zaynab, two women who were the prophet Mohammad's next of kin and who constitute the quintessential official role models for women in Islamic Iran. The third passport bears no name, implying neither an Islamic nor a Western identity but a third identity, which must be constructed by the woman herself. She selects the blank passport, which according to Tabrizian is "a metaphor for the woman's identity as a masquerade"—a masquerade that prevents her from aligning her identity with her role.[27] Tabrizian notes that the film is about "de-idealization of Islam from a woman's point of view" without offering any "solutions." However, by selecting the blank passport, the female protagonist does opt for the thirdspace of identity as the proper solution—even if it might be temporary and ambiguous like all masquerades.

By juxtaposing the two suitcase scenes, Tabrizian deftly suggests the woman's sociopolitical evolution, from childhood innocence to adolescent radicalism, and her physical displacement, from homeland into exile. Additionally, she critiques (deidealizes) not only the sectarian politics of the male-dominated Islamist guerrilla organizations, which have "rediscovered" Islam as a new form of identity, independent of both the capitalist West and the Marxist East, but also their sexual politics.

From Ali's reading of her file, we have come to know that the "third" woman is unattached, without friends or husband, and that she has been involved in several of the organization's previous operations, performing decisively, discreetly, unemotionally, and loyally. In other words, she has been a good soldier. Because of this record, he has summoned her to London to give her an important new operational assignment—the assassination of a high-ranking official in Iran. During her interview with Ali, however, she realizes the extent of the antidemocratic and antifeminist sexual politics of both the leader and his organization. Again she acts decisively and immediately, but this time by turning the gun on the leader (or on his reflection in a mirror). By so doing, she deidealizes the leader and transforms herself from a soldier into a leader.

The Third Woman produces an activist, if somewhat programmatic, vision of empowered and decisive women and a timely critique of the instrumentalist uses of Islamic ideologies and practices by both the Left and the Right. Without saying so directly, the sharp edge of Tabrizian's critique is toward groups like the People's Mojahedin Organization—a guerrilla group fighting the Islamic Republic from Iraq, with a mixture of Islamist and socialist tendencies. The organization has generated much propaganda in recent years about its promotion of women to its highest offices, including the office of the "president-elect" in exile. But such "promotions" are regarded by many people as suspiciously self-serving for the organization's male leaders and demeaning for its female members.

Tabrizian is an Iranian-British photographer and university professor with a doctorate in psychoanalytic theory and photography from the University of Westminster, London. The role of the father, the father-daughter relations, and the relation of women to male authority are themes that run through her two films, *The Third Woman* and *Journey of No Return* (1993). *Journey of No Return* is an epistolary film that, unlike the mother-daughter epistolaries dis-

Figure 35. "The Leader" interviews "The Third Woman" in Mitra Tabrizian's *The Third Woman*. Courtesy Mitra Tabrizian.

cussed here, centers on father-daughter relations. It contains despondent letters from an exiled Third World photographer-filmmaker in England to her father, who lives in an unidentified country. Despite parallels between the protagonist's story and Tabrizian's own life, she denied in an interview that the film is autobiographical: "My father is more important to me than my mother, but this is not an autobiographical film. I am not trying to work out my relationship with my father. I was sick and tired of mother-daughter films then prevalent and wanted to upset that paradigm. Fathers can also be feminine" (Naficy 1998a). Because the filmmaker does not mail her "Dear Father" letters, they serve to communicate with the spectators more than with the father. From them we learn that she was sent abroad as a child. Now, years later, she wonders why she is here and complains of forgetting the language she knew and not knowing the language she was supposed to learn. What is worse, her film script is rejected because, as the voice on the answering machine tells her, "History is not what we are looking for just now." In a world in which history seems to have been replaced by surface images, she is in a state of crisis and paralysis, unable either to write or to photograph.

Her deep anomie is illustrated by a haunting image that opens and closes the film. In the opening, attracted by the sound of running water, the filmmaker walks into her steamed-up bathroom, where a woman's long black hair is hanging over the bathtub. In the end, the same shot is repeated, but it goes further: the filmmaker reaches into the tub and lifts up the immersed body to reveal that it is she in the tub, looking vacantly at herself. Whether these scenes imply exilic dissociation, doubling, or suicide is not made clear. What is clear is that the woman's home-founding journey abroad has not produced a home, and she has no place or no one to turn to or to return to. A photograph of her father, or, as the voice-over says, "the father who mothered me," is on her desk. But, she is not close to him as indicated by the inhibition against mailing the letters; consequently, returning to him is not an option. Both of Tabrizian's films problematize patriarchal structures at the same time that they are fascinated by these structures. Ironically, like the mother-daughter texts that Tabrizian abhors, this film is a daughter-text in that it provides only the daughter's perspective on her life and on the parent-daughter relationship. In Akerman's *News from Home* and Hatoum's *Measures of Distance*, the spectators learn a lot about the filmmaking daughters from their mothers' letters; but in Tabrizian's *Journey of No Return*, the father is absent and silent, never reading or writing letters. And as the sole enunciative figure, the diegetic filmmaker—like her real-life double, Tabrizian—supplies little substantive information about herself, preferring to remain an enigma: a masquerade, a third woman.

The Ethics and Politics of Performed Identity

An issue that I have discussed a number of times, particularly regarding the films of late-modernist accented filmmakers such as Egoyan and Zahedi, is the ethical questions raised by concepts such as traveling, multiple, hybridized, crossed, and performed identities. The various global transformations in the last four decades have problematized the received models of belonging and the predetermined notions of self and nation. With the blurring of these boundaries have come new fears and freedoms, leading, on the one hand, to new kinds of narrow-minded essentialism and utopian heimatism and, on the other hand, to new forms of dystopian cosmopolitanism and opportunistic identity politics.

Loosened from the biological moorings of blood and descent, identity is now recognized as socially produced. The hereditary kinship is being relaxed in favor of new collective formations based on constructed paradigms. Because in exile the familiar becomes unfamiliar and the natural denaturalized, one is forced to face, perhaps more than at any other time, the essential constructedness of one's own structures of belonging. Distanced from familial and familiar structures, the exiles are in an enviable position of being able to remake themselves. If it can be constructed, identity can also be reconstructed, deconstructed—even performed.

In recent cultural theory much has been made of minorities' uses of certain defensive, resistive, and pleasurable performance strategies as creative means of fashioning new and empowered identities that counter their sociopolitical subalternity and cultural marginalization.[28] Of these, mimicry, passing, posing, camp, drag, sly civility, doubling, and masquerade depend on the existence of an original something that is turned into something else, a copy of the original. Put another way, they depend on repeating an original as the same with a difference—a difference that often implies criticism of that which is being imitated. In this process, identity becomes, in Judith Butler's words, an "effect" of discursive practice, not an original so idealized as to be unmatchable (1990a, 18). That kind of "ur-original" (or "uriginal") is either outside the discourse, in which case it assumes an unrealizable materiality *and* an abstraction of its own (a fetish of sorts such as the homeland), or within discourse, in which case it becomes itself another "effect" of discursive practices. All discursive practices are regulated by the culture at large, by the dominant paradigms of law, sexuality, patriarchy, ethnicity, nationality, race, and others and by the resistive and pleasurable strategies of individuals and groups interacting with the regulating mechanisms. However, all these forms of doubling that critique or mock the authority of the original are not necessarily, or equally, subversive or resistive. For one thing, they may not be read as being subversive or, worse, they may be entirely misread as pure identification and imitation. For another, as Chris Holmlund has noted in her discussion of masculinity and femininity as masquerade, these strategies might serve to reinforce hegemonic power relations by suggesting that "there may be something underneath which is 'real,' and/or 'normal.' As Lacan has shown, masquerade is inherently nostalgic, an appearance which gestures toward a lack perceived as originary" (Holmlund 1993, 224–25). Moreover, the exilic nostalgia for a real and originary homeland prevents the exilic performance of identity from becoming either totally unmoored or totally subversive. In fact, nostalgia tends to drive the exiles' conservative tendencies (in the sense of keeping them rooted). Finally, because these subversive and defensive strategies—many of which have historically been deployed productively by colonial, postcolonial, subaltern, Third World, and exilic subjects—depend on splitting and multiplication, they produce subjectivities and identities that are often more anxious and phobic than at-ease and pleased.

These performative strategies are dependent on twoness. The power of two has had a surprising and enduring hold on the arts, mythology, literature, and cinema. Many modernist and exilic writers have investigated doubled, divided, and crossed selves in their novels by means of doppelgänger figures.[29] In these works, human consciousness is posited as inherently disunified, subject to division and multiplication under certain conditions. Postmodernist authors such as Salman Rushdie multiply the doppelgänger effect severalfold to obtain highly complex and mobile identities that are fissured and mongrelized and are in a continual state of slippage and overlap. In the literature of the double (and the multiple), the double is sometimes a projection of the self, the externalization of the unconscious, the internalization of an outsider, or the twin of the other; sometimes the doubles are friends, sometimes foe; and sometimes they are real, sometimes imaginary.

Accented filmmakers who live in various modes of transnational otherness inscribe and (re)enact in their films the fears, freedoms, and possibilities of split subjectivity and multiple identities. These take the form of fragmented narratives, consisting of ellipses, ruptures, and generic juxtapositions and admixtures; self-reflexive interweaving of the filmmaker's own biography, person, and persona in the diegesis; and an emphasis both on a performing self and on a performance structure. Some of these cinematic strategies create distance among diegetic characters, between camera and diegetic subjects, and between screen and spectators. They also take the form of doppelgänger characters, who depend on the existence of a split or a distance between the self and its others, observer and observed, original and copy, home and exile. They can also take hybridized forms, which depend on both multiplicity of identity and multifocality.

Distance is the engine of all exilic identities; in the case of the split identity, it works reductively and by introjecting difference, while in the case of multiple or hybrid identity, it operates additively and by projecting similarity or difference. Distance also motivates the doppelgänger characters and activates the films' narratives of desire, nostalgia, and memory for other people, places, and times. Moreover, distance propels the films' self-reflexive aesthetics, which mediate the acts of seeing and being seen, exhibitionism and voyeurism, and presence and absence. In short, exilic distance allows, even necessitates, a variety of mediated and performative strategies in accented films, particularly in those that are influenced by late-modernist discourses. These take several forms.

Diegetic Staging

The staging of an event, a presentation, or a performance within the diegesis constitutes one of the forms of performativity and mediation in the accented cinema. Solanas's *Tangos: Exile of Gardel* is about a group of Argentine exiles in Paris who are rehearsing a "tango-dy" performance that is a hybrid of tango, comedy, and tragedy. The hybridization itself is a performative act of signifying on the original, which is driven by the tango-dy's exilic location. It is not a straight performance of the tango but a parodic take on it, since it mimics and comments on this existing and deeply held national culture and dance form from a position of exile. While the film emphasizes the exilic context of the tango-dy, it demonstrates that, although this particular exile makes the tango somewhat different from the original in Argentina, the tango as a form remains intact. Its elasticity and continued expressivity deepen its hold on the Argentines and validates their Argentineness. The tango-dy's exilic context, which drives the film's fragmented narrative and its doubled and split characters, revolves around receiving inspiration from the homeland, numerous rehearsals of the tango-dy numbers, the nostalgia-driven exilic lives of the performers, and the difficulty they encounter in obtaining French commercial sponsorship of their project. In the dogged pursuit of staging the tango-dy and of finding an appropriate ending for it, the film reiterates the power of this Argentine national longing for form.

In addition, as a musical *Tangos* is very self-aware. The actors are not acting for the camera alone but also for the tango-dy performance within the film. The spectators, too, are placed in a split position. By mixing presentational and representational modes that solicit spectatorial duality, the film simultaneously thwarts and encourages audience identification. In its presentational mode, the narrative is suspended, and the audience can appreciate the tango-dy performances as spectacle, admiring the beauty of the dancers, the elegance and sensuality of their movements, and the poignancy of the songs' exilic lyrics. In its representational mode, on the other hand, the film's character-driven narrative and editing strategy encourage identification with both the characters and their exilic concerns, suturing the viewers into the diegesis.

In Nair's *Salaam Bombay!* Krishna and other street children quote the dancing and the singing of the stars of Hindi films, in the process demonstrating their competence not only at imitating but also at mimicking their look, posture, gestures, and singing style. These competences are pleasurable and empowering. However, the film contains other instances of colonial performance that are demeaning. In one particularly nasty episode, Baba, the chief pimp and drug dealer bent on proving his superiority and masculine sexuality to a Western female reporter, demands that Chillum, a small-time dealer, serve her tea while dancing. To make sure that Chillum follows his order, Baba humiliates him further by whipping his feet while he is holding the tea tray, causing him to jump up and down. Indian insiders have accused Nair of another form of performance, that of "performing poverty." This is not uncommon. Third World insiders frequently lodge this sort of accusation against their own filmmakers who deal with their society's poverty and marginalia, even though the same films win plaudits from Western critics as exemplars of realism.

Doppelgängers, Doubling, Duplicity

Accented films embody the constructedness of identity by inscribing characters who are partial, double, or split, or who perform their identities by means of the strategies already mentioned. By so engaging in the politics and poetics of identity, they cover up or manipulate their essential incompletion, fragmentation, and instability. Solanas's *Tangos: Exile of Gardel*, which dramatizes these identities in the form of divided and double characters, has three leading characters who because of artistic rejection and exilic tension literally disintegrate. After the French officials refuse to sponsor the commercial staging of the tango-dy on grounds that it lacks an ending and is "too Argentine," one arm of Angel (played by Solanas) literally separates from his shoulder and dangles from his waist. In another situation, Juan Dos, who is seated in a chair, deflates rapidly like a balloon whose air has been let out. In a third situation, after the rehearsal of the "Crazy Tango," an exhausted Pierre snaps under pressure: he twirls and falls into a chair, and he suddenly pops open to expose a boxlike chest full of electronic gear and wires. In a gesture that self-reflexively parodies the film itself, a gurney is brought in and attendants administer oil to Pierre's mechanical chest with an oversized oilcan. Each instance of visual disintegration is preceded and accompanied by an eerie extradiegetic musical track. Such corporeal literalization of the effect of exilic splitting and evisceration gives the film an air of comic surrealism and performativity, but it also embodies the kind of shattering tensions that many exiles, particularly creative people, undergo.

Solanas also uses doppelgängers to embody exilic division and multiplication. Juan Dos is the tango-dy's composer and lyricist in Parisian exile who seeks inspiration for the show from Juan Uno, his never-seen-or-heard counterpart in Argentina. In all likelihood, Juan Dos has conjured up Juan Uno to feed his own imagination and to maintain his linkage to the homeland. The two characters, continents apart, symbolize the splitting of identity that occurs in exile. What makes the film exilic is the binary and unequal power relation between these two, which favors the "original" self at home as the authentic, authoring agent.[30] Without the original, an exile is incomplete. Juan Uno and Juan Dos attempt to complete one another by the epistolic means of phone calls, letters, and snippets of papers hidden in a tattered suitcase. Since the epistolary chain is never complete or without interruption, however, the two do not map out onto one another, and they never make up a whole person.

Accented films inscribe the filmmakers not only authorially and autobiographically but also diegetically. Sometimes they take the form of diegetic characters who are the filmmakers' alter egos. Juan Dos is the closest character in *Tangos* to Solanas's alter ego. Like Solanas, who tried for years to make a living in France by making films about exile, Juan Dos struggles to create a tango-dy on exile. The problematic of a hybridized tango-dy that has no ending and Juan Dos's search for a language that is appropriate for expressing exilic conditions parallel Solanas's own predicament in his film. The relationship of Solanas to his diegetic alter ego (Juan Dos) is similar to that of Juan Uno to his alter ego (Juan Dos). Consequently, Juan Uno is Solanas's own double once removed, and each is necessary for the authenticity and authority of the other. In yet another iteration of this repetitive structure of doubling, one can speculate that Juan Uno, who is never seen or heard in the film, is a double for Juan Perón, dead since 1974, and a heroic figure in Solanas's Perónist politics (de las Carreras 1995, 327).

The film also inscribes machines and mannequins as human doubles to symbolize both exilic multiplication and dehumanization. The younger Argentines perform a comic dance in Paris streets in which they move in incremental jerks like robotic people and animals. Here the film criticizes the dehumanization of the exiles at the same time that it mocks it. Mannequins accompany the exiles frequently, on the dance floor, in cars, and when climbing stairs. These can be interpreted as stand-ins for those who feel split, multiplied, absented, or dehumanized by exilic trauma. Alternatively, the mannequins with missing limbs may represent those who were mutilated by torture and were disappeared in the military's "dirty war" against civilians. These readings are in line with one of the main topics of the film, the poetics of absence and loss. *Tangos* is a film of absent people.

Another reading of exilic doubling may be obtained by noting that in the early liminal phases of exile, the liminars are haunted by a profound dissonance between inside and outside. Their insides may feel ambivalent and unstable as they shift and waver between multiple self-perceptions, identities, and cultures, while on the outside their bodies may give the impression of self-containment, stability, and cohesiveness. The double, the fragmented, and the robotized bodies in *Tangos* symbolically externalize this internal fracturing and doubt.

While the strategies of multiplication and doubling are put in the service of expressing exilic fragmentation and angst in *Tangos*, their adoption by Egoyan characters and by Zahedi characters leads to behaviors and situations that blur the line between doubling and duplicity.[31] The case of Zahedi has already been discussed. In Egoyan's films, as noted in the earlier discussion of *Next of Kin* and *Speaking Parts*, doubling makes for the dis-ease and the guardedness of the characters, since many of them harbor secrets they want to protect.[32] Many marginalized people, including exiles and gays, use the stratagems of concealment and doubling in subversive ways to critique the dominant culture and to empower themselves creatively. As Morris Dickstein notes,

> The strategies of concealment many gay people used in their lives were turned into richly layered artistic strategies by gifted writers, choreographers, directors, and set designers. For the writers, wit and paradox became more important than sincerity, since sincerity meant self-acceptance (which could be difficult) and self-exposure (which could be dangerous); style, baroque fantasy and sensuous detail were disguises that suited them far better than verisimilitude or realism. (1995, 6)

Although straight exiles do not adopt the same specific strategies of concealment and doubling, both exiles and queers share a penchant for turning naturalized reality into reality-effect and normative identity into identity-effect. In so doing, identity is turned into what Amy Robinson calls the "theater of identity," in which the politics of prior substance and essence is replaced by the politics of optics (1994, 716).

In addition to divided, double, and crossed characters, accented films contain certain other character types that are informed by the tensions and ambivalence of exilic liminality. Understandably, travelers on their home-founding or home-coming journeys are rampant, while tourists are rare in these films. Some of the films also contain lost figures and wanderers, people who have no fixed home or cannot settle. Because of their subject matter, accented films frequently contain foreigners who attempt to pass as natives, with their success dependent on the knowledge by both foreigners and natives of what constitutes "foreign" and "native" and on the accuracy and deftness with which these codes are reproduced and signified upon. In *Walls of Sand*, the Iranian au pair who is an illegal immigrant successfully avoids the pitfalls of her despised native identity in the United States by passing as a Latina or, if she is mistaken for a Greek, by playing along with the mistake. This causes her compatriots to criticize her as a "sellout." In *El Norte*, both Enrique and Rosa, the Mayan Indians, learn how to dress, walk, talk, swear, and behave in order to pass first as Mexicans in Mexico and later as Chicano and Chicana in the United States. But they are not successful because their knowledge of the optics of performed identity is rudimentary. On the other hand, in a humorous episode in *Born in East L.A.*, Cheech Marin's character shows his deft awareness of this optics when he tutors a group of illegal Asians in Mexico in how to pass as street-smart Chicanos in the United States. The performative skills of passing by the exiles and émigrés and the hermeneutic procedures of discovering the pass are not just part of the accented filmmaker's diegeses but also of their own lives and identities. The discussion throughout about insider-outsider positionality is precisely based on determining not only the authentic original and the phony copy but also the mechanisms of passing, slipping, and doubling.

Absent figures in the accented films serve varied ideological and narrative functions. Sometimes, like Juan Uno, they are imaginary figures necessitated by exile. At other times, they are real figures who serve as archetypes with which to think about exile. *Tangos* has three such real-life exiles to whom the film pays homage. One of these is General San Martín, liberator of South America from Spain, who spent the last twenty-five years of his life in French exile, where he died in 1850. The second is the famed tango singer Carlos Gardel, who was born in France but spent most of his life in Argentina and other countries, and died in a plane crash in 1935. The third is the Turkish filmmaker Güney, who also died in Parisian exile, to whom the film is dedicated.

There are also other more abstract character types, such as Hitcher, Passer, and Dream Terrorist in Fatemi's *The Nuclear Baby*, or Stalker, Scientist, and Writer in Tarkovsky's *Stalker*. These function less as characters with subjectivity than as characters who represent certain types. The figure of the terrorist appears frequently in the films of political exiles, among them Iranian exiles who oppose the Islamist regime. These filmmakers create stability out of the anxiety and chaos of displacement by internalizing the dominant views of themselves, even those that go counter to their self-perception, self-interest, or self-preservation. In this regard, Third World and postcolonial filmmakers are similar to the émigré German directors escaping the Nazis, who reproduced in their films and embodied in their lives the national stereotypes of Europe then prevalent in the United States. They are also similar to Jewish actors escaping Nazi Germany who portrayed Nazi characters and SS men in Hollywood films in order to survive. Whatever the justification, however, by engaging in this doubling optic, the filmmakers advance their own personal careers by reaping the professional rewards of their national self-othering.[33]

Self-Reflexivity

Self-reflexivity as a performative strategy, exemplified by most of Egoyan's films, involves mediation within the diegesis and the narrative. This often includes using audiovisual, electronic, and other mediating technologies as narrative agents to view, record, or play back already recorded scenes. Such mediations create distance and doubt between diegetic characters and between them and the audience, which are further modulated by epistolarity, voyeurism, surveillance, exhibitionism, and other forms of sexual and visual power relations. There is considerable ambiguity regarding who is gaining or losing sight, hearing, or power.

Self-reflexivity also involves making visible what the invisible style of the classical realist cinema has traditionally concealed: the filmmaking process, the filmmaking product, the filmmakers, and film audiences (Ruby 1988). Self-reflexive films tend to incorporate in various degrees one or all of these "nonrealist" components into their narratives. Like the mediating and epistolary technologies, these self-reflexive strategies create and inscribe distance, or bridge the distance, between diegetic characters who are in different temporal and spatial zones due to their displacement. They also function to create slippery situations where identity and narrative agency are multiplied, camouflaged, or obfuscated, as in Akerman's News from Home, Hatoum's Measures of Distance, Tabrizian's Journey of No Return, and Marker's Sunless. In addition, self-reflexive techniques distance the audience from the film, undermining full identification with the diegesis and with its characters. Egoyan's films, Zahedi's I Don't Hate Las Vegas Anymore, Marilou Mallete's Unfinished Diary (1986), and several of Jonas Mekas's films fall within this category of self-reflexive cinema. Of the four modes of self-reflexivity in which the filmmaking process is made visible, the most germane to the accented cinema is the inscription of the filmmaker.

Self-Inscription

In this modality of performativity and doubling the filmmakers appear in their own films, visually or on the sound track only, either as themselves or as fictional characters. Neither Akerman nor Hatoum appears visually in their films *News from Home* and *Measures of Distance*; however, each is inscribed by her voice-over narration, reading her mother's letters addressed to her. In both cases, there is ambiguity about who is reading the letters, simply because she is not identified. Egoyan, on the other hand, does appear in *Calendar* but as a fictional photographer, not as himself. What complicates his inscription is that his real-life wife appears opposite him as the photographer's wife, using her own name, Arsinée. The similarity between the empirical and the onscreen husband and wife was so strong that their friends wondered if the breakup of the diegetic couple meant the breakup of Atom Egoyan and Arsinée Khanjian. For them, the doubles had matched the originals.

Naderi, on the other hand, does not appear in *Manhattan by Numbers* visually or orally, but from interviews he has given and the similarities between protagonist George Murphy's despondent roaming and Naderi's own exilic wandering in New York City, one may deduce that Murphy is a camouflaged double for the filmmaker. Similarly, Shahid Saless does not appear in his *Roses for Africa*, but based on contextual information and on my interview with him, the lead character, Paul, is a stand-in for the director, duplicating his bleak and despairing structures of feeling. Tabrizian denies that the diegetic filmmaker in *Journey of No Return* is her double, but there are parallels that suggest the contrary. In another strategy of camouflage, Sayyad appears as a fictional leading character in both of his exile-made films *The Mission* and *Checkpoint*, but because they speak from a position that represents the director's own point of view and politics, the characters become somewhat autobiographical and nonfictional.

Autobiography is a strong motif of the accented cinema. It is woven into the idea of film as performance, but few exilic filmmakers appear as themselves in their films. There are exceptions, however, such as Caveh Zahedi, Jonas Mekas, and Miguel Littín, who employ autobiography with varying levels of ambiguity and complexity. Zahedi appears as himself in both of his features, using his own name and enacting his own life. In *A Little Stiff*, he plays himself and re-creates his real-life crush on a fellow UCLA art student. Both the girl and her boyfriend also play themselves. Likewise, in *I Don't Hate Las Vegas Anymore*, Zahedi, his father, his brother, and his crew members all appear on camera as themselves, using their own names. However, both films (which Zahedi calls "experimental documentaries") are far from being straight documentaries, for the inscription of real people as themselves is designed less to enhance the film's authenticity or its mimetic truth value than to problematize them. By seamlessly combining re-created and documentary scenes and auto-biographical and fictional accounts, Zahedi's films problematize cinematic authenticity, truthfulness, and autobiography. Ultimately, his films, like those of Marker, are performances of the documentary form, not documentaries themselves.

Phillip Lejeune's "autobiographical pact" (1989) operates more fully in Mekas's "diary films," including *Lost, Lost, Lost* (1949–75), *Walden* (1964–69), and *Reminiscences of a Journey to Lithuania* (1971–72), in which the filmmaker, the lead character, and the narrator coincide. In these films, Lithuanian exiles, Mekas himself, his family, his brother, and his various New York avant-garde friends and colleagues appear as themselves, in scenes that are filmed in a cinema verité, home-movie documentary style. The fact that much of the footage is shot, edited, and narrated in first-person singular by Mekas himself consolidates the exact mapping of the three terms of the autobiographical pact onto one another. Although the exilic films of both Naderi and Mekas are autobiographical, a key difference between them is the manner in which auto-biography is inscribed. While Naderi allegorizes his autobiography in *The Runner* and *Manhattan by Numbers* by hiding behind doubles whose stories are largely based on his own, Mekas inscribes himself in his films as himself manifestly, fully, and indexically. Their films of self-inscription may have something to do with their deep differences in feeling structures, which are pessimistic and nostalgic, respectively.

Parody has become a major performative strategy in our age, dubbed the "age of irony." As Richard Poirier notes, until recently, parody was predominantly other-directed (1992, 27). In cinema, filmmakers have parodied each other, or they have parodied specific film genres, styles, characters, story lines, and periods. Self-parody is a newer strategy, which Marker and Zahedi have used effectively. In Marker's epistolary films, from *Letters from Siberia* to *Sunless*, parodic signifying is multifaceted and is aimed at the conventions of travelogue and documentary films, at tourists and travelers, at government and business officials, at political campaigns and advertising, and at Marker himself as a parodically self-reflexive presence in the films. Zahedi's *I Don't Hate Las Vegas Anymore* inscribes the filmmaker as a parodic on-camera personality who constantly and self-reflexively worries about his unscripted film in progress.

What irony and ironic self-inscription tell us is that nothing, including reality, is inherent, of value, or can be taken for granted; that heroes and heroism are to be deconstructed and deflated; that plots emanate not so much from the interplay of individuals as from an author who is outside and prior to the text (Poirier 1992, 36). All these ironic effects prevent any standardized reality from becoming either stabilized or authoritative. This is both the advantage and the risk of irony—advantage, for it acts subversively against hegemonic powers and narratives; risk, because it can lead to the impression that irony can replace acting politically. Another risk of irony is self-indulgence or overindulgence in formal displays of repetitive elements. A further risk is that irony, as discussed in the case of Egoyan, may not be read as subversive or it may intentionally or inadvertently be misread altogether. Several of these issues are brought out in the following case study, which also deals with a homecoming journey.

Close-Up: *Miguel Littín's* General Statement on Chile
(Acta General de Chile, *1986*)

This film encodes the onscreen appearance of the filmmaker in a highly complex combination of his own biography, authorial filmic enunciation, and politically motivated performance of identity involving parody. Littín was born in the small village of Palmilla, Chile, in 1942 to a Palestinian father and a Greek mother. His grandparents were the first immigrants to settle in that area at the turn of the twentieth century (Marquez 1988, 97). He was trained at the Theatre School of the University of Chile, after which he embarked on a multifaceted and increasingly political media career that involved directing and producing for TV, directing and acting for the stage, working as assistant director (for Joris Ivens), founding (with others) the Committee of the Popular Unity Filmmakers, and, for a brief time, directing the national production company Chile Films, for which he made weekly newsreels (Thomas 1990, 519–20). During this period, he also directed a number of important films, including *On Foreign Land* (*Por la Tierra Ajena*, 1968) and *The Jackal of Nahueltoro* (*El Chacal de Nahueltoro*, 1969), which catapulted him to the forefront of the New Latin American cinema. Salvador Allende appointed him to his position at Chile Films, a political and artistic position that, despite its brevity, became a liability in 1973 when General Augusto Pinochet staged a coup d'état that toppled Allende, forcing Littín (and his family) into exile, first to Mexico and later to Spain.

He was not alone, as the coup scattered many Chilean filmmakers to Europe and the Americas, who used the wealth of films and film footage that had been smuggled out of Chile after the coup, to mount campaigns against Pinochet and the military junta (Pick 1987, 40). Chilean filmmakers made over 250 feature films and documentaries in exile—far more than were produced in Chile itself up to 1973 (Peña 1987, 137). Littín's exilic films include *Letters from Marusia* (*Actas de Marusia*, 1975), about a mining company's exploitation of a small Chilean town, and *Alsino and the Condor* (*Alsino y el Condor*, 1982), about a boy's dream of flying in the context of Somoza's dictatorship in Nicaragua, both of which were nominated for the Best Foreign Film Oscar.

The strong presence and high productivity of Chilean filmmakers abroad created what was called a "Chilean cinema of resistance" in exile. However, as the cases of Iranians in the United States, Algerians in France, and Turks in

Germany demonstrate, the presence of a large displaced population from one country, including filmmakers, does not guarantee the emergence of a homogeneous or programmatic exilic cinema. The presence of a large number of Chilean filmmakers abroad also did not result in a cohesive film movement.[34]

Littín was not happy in exile, which he described in such painful terms as "tunnel of exile" (quoted in Marquez 1988, 23), "twilight of exile" (79), and "plague of exile" (86). In 1985, after twelve years of living in this dystopic realm, he took advantage of a hiatus in his work to put into action a long-held desire to return home. The problem was that his name had appeared on a list of 5,000 people permanently barred from returning. The solution he came up with was as dangerous as it was ingenious: return to a militarized Chile clandestinely and in disguise, accompanied by film crews hired to document the return. What followed was a bravura demonstration of politically motivated exilic doubling and parodic performance. He adopted the persona of a Uruguayan advertising executive and spent several weeks preparing himself: he shaved his trademark beard, dyed his hair and changed his hairstyle, shed some twenty pounds, practiced wearing contact lenses, worked on changing the way he walked and gestured, and practiced a Uruguayan accent. In addition, a false marriage was arranged with a female political activist who was instrumental in realizing the project, and he obtained the passport of a sympathetic Uruguayan national and adopted his name and identity.

With financing from an Italian producer, Littín hired three foreign film crews (French, Dutch, and Italian) and sent them to Chile to obtain official permission to film innocuous but plausible documentaries. He practiced the "drama of not being myself" by traveling with his new papers to several European cities and countries, where by answering custom agents' questions he gained confidence about his new identity. He arrived in Chile with his falsified papers and identity and with a pounding heart, but he gained a safe entry. He stayed there for six weeks, traveling from one part of the country to another, directing each foreign film crew as well as three locally hired crews. He made a point of appearing in his new persona in many of the shots filmed in public places to prove that he had been there. His transformation was so radical and his imitation of the businessman so real that close friends and relatives, including his mother, did not recognize him. Unable for security reasons to reveal his true identity to them (until at the very end, and only to his mother), he resigned himself "to not being me." Suppressing his innermost feelings, he "assumed the strange condition of an exile in my own country, the most bitter experience for me" (Marquez 1988, 34).

The six film crews audaciously recorded the daily lives of Chileans in cities and villages under the watchful eyes of the police (including Pablo Neruda's house and village in Isla Negra and the interior of the renovated presidential palace, which had been gutted during the coup). They also filmed interviews with members of the open and underground opposition. Understandably, the film's mode of production was clandestine, improvisational, and artisanal—even guerrilla-like. At times, the crews would carry two sets of equipment, the larger one for confiscation by the police and the smaller one for clandestine filming (Marquez 1988, 62). Littín himself carried a hidden tape recorder in his pocket to record the voices of ordinary people and passersby for later use as dialogue. During filming, he communicated with his crew by agreed-upon signals. Secrecy was built into all aspects of the project, which operated in a cellular fashion that resembled the structure of the guerrilla groups then fighting oppressive military regimes in the Third World. Only the chief of each crew knew Littín and was in on the project, and apparently no film crew was aware of the other crews. In addition, no rushes could be viewed during filming because the exposed footage was smuggled out for processing in Spain. As a result, there was no possibility of correcting mistakes. All in all, 105,616 feet of film was exposed, which Littín spent six month editing after leaving Chile. The result was *General Statement on Chile*, a four-hour television program, which was broadcast in many European countries. It won accolades at film festivals in Venice, Toronto, and Havana. Subsequently, he edited a two-hour version for theatrical distribution.

It is important in the context of the ethics of border crossing and traveling identities to note that Littín did not assume his persona of a "bourgeois mummy" willingly. It was forced upon him by his status as a "permanent exile." In addition, his masquerade was multifaceted and profound, involving the transformation of many dimensions of identity and personality, including personal name, legal status, behavior and habits, class affiliation, nationality, country of origin, past history, and marital status. Moreover, there was a very high price to be paid in case there was a slipup in the performative slippage of the camouflage. Not only his own life but also the lives of his film crews and members of the internal resistance, who were assisting him, were at stake. He could not afford to mimic the Uruguayan businessman; he had to be him. In other words, the copy and the original had to match perfectly. As a result, the kind of play and excess that characterize the more voluntary forms of doubling and masquerade, and which tend to reveal a criticism of that which is being imitated, could not develop in this case (at least not while he was in Chile). Consequently, he was enchained, not enchanted, by the doubling process. The tension that this produced became evident to Littín when he was passing by a childhood movie house: "I forgot my clandestine situation and returned for a moment to being myself. I had an irrational impulse to identify myself, to shout out my name, to tell the world that it was my right to be home" (Marquez 1988, 18). Despite the impulse, he did not risk breaking the disguise. Consequently, the tensions of the forced masquerade did not produce a subject at ease or a whole and jubilant subject. They also prevented his return from becoming the grand homecoming of which many exiles dream. Nevertheless, the disguise did accomplish its aim. Littín's plan, hatched during what he called "the chimerical sleeplessness of exile," had been to rediscover the country that he had "lost in a fog of nostalgia" and to thumb his nose at Pinochet (2–3). His success at entering and leaving the country unharmed, at filming a scathing record of life under the military regime, and at having it shown widely and internationally constituted a bold act of parody and sabotage against the invincible image of the great dictator. This turned the unbearable pain of doubling into welcome pleasure. As Littín states, making the film was tantamount to pinning a 105,616-foot-long tail on the donkey (114).[35]

The infected wound of exile continued to hurt even after Littín returned following the fall of the Pinochet's regime, as borne out by his first postexile film, *The Shipwrecked* (*Los Naufragos*, 1991), which deals with living with the memories of trauma and exile.

Film as Performance

A film may be regarded as the performance of the identity of its maker. By their choice of mise-en-scène, filming style, themes, characters, and editing, filmmakers inscribe themselves as author and enunciating subject of their films (Caughie 1981, 203–4). As such, filmmakers do not have to appear in their films, and their films need not be about them or be based on their lives for them to be considered as performances of identity. As interstitial authors, accented filmmakers use each of their films, intentionally or unintentionally, as an occasion for dramatizing themselves. They do this by "pacing, economics, juxtapositions, aggregations of tone, the whole conduct of the shaping presence" (Poirier 1992, 86–87). This shaping presence is made up of many private microdecisions made public, and it is both risky and highly empowering for the filmmakers—even though their films are often small, artisanal, and imperfect. Marker's narrator in *Sunless* muses: "I wonder how people remember who don't film, don't photograph, don't tape." To perform by making films is to remember, to memorialize yourself (and your community), and to remind others that you were there—even if you were in disguise.

A longitudinal study of the filmmakers' corpus can help chart not only the evolution of their style but also that of their personality and identity. Such a study of the careers of Egoyan and Zahedi, for example, shows their increasing ethnicization, while those of Sohrab Shahid Saless and Tefvik Baser show their gradual de-ethnicization. Taking note of these filmmakers evolution as social and historical agents can strengthen the textual study of their output. To discuss this point more fully, in the remainder of the chapter I will concentrate primarily on Egoyan's film corpus and on his own strategies of identity formation and social agency.

Close-Up: *Atom Egoyan's Films as Performance of Identity*

Ethnicization in Egoyan's films ranges from the veiling of his Armenian ethnicity to its full unveiling in his 1993 film *Calendar*, and finally to its near eradication in his latest works. However, even in films that engage in veiling, Armenian ethnicity and nationality are often present, but in latent or submerged forms. In *Next of Kin* (1984), ethnicity is not repressed; in fact, it is valorized in the way the ethnic Armenian family is privileged over a WASP family. In *Speaking Parts* (1989), Armenian ethnicity is submerged and its tell-tale sign is exposed only in Lisa's accented English. In *Family Viewing* (1987), the silent grandmother is Armenian, and the videotape of her grandson's home movies represents childhood in Armenia. In *The Adjuster* (1991), ethnicity is submerged, but there are delicate suggestions of Armenianness throughout the film: in the opening theme music, in the silent sister, in her photographs of Lebanon, which she burns, and in Hera's accented English. Latent Armenian ethnicity in *Exotica* (1994) and *The Sweet Hereafter* (1997) are primarily inscribed in the accented speech of key characters and in the films' extradiegetic music.

In the most directly ethnic of Egoyan's films, *Calendar*, we encounter the homeland in all its materiality and indexicality—its history, culture, people, language, monuments, and landscape. Centered on Armenia, this is a breakthrough film for Egoyan. Each of the three key characters represents one of the major states of Armenian national consciousness: those who are born in Armenia (represented by the guide), those Armenians born in diaspora who have grown up with a strong sense of affiliation and commitment to Armenia (represented by the translator), and those born in the diaspora who are assimilated in the host society (represented by the photographer) (Kricorian 1993–94, 27). The casting is very unusual for Egoyan, for each actor's part reflects his or her own ethnic and national biography. Ashot Adamian, the guide, is a native of Armenia who does not speak much English. Arsinée Khanjian, the translator and Egoyan's real-life spouse, was born and bred in an Armenian community in Beirut. Atom Egoyan, the photographer, was born in Egypt to an Armenian family but emigrated at age three to Canada, where he assimilated. The dynamics of the characters' relations also inscribe the pull-push of ethnic and national identity politics. As the film progresses, the wife and the guide, who are the most ethnic of the triangle, are attracted to each other, repelling the most assimilated of the three, who returns to Canada alone. *Calendar*, like *Next of Kin*, valorizes ethnic formation over the nuclear family. Indeed, the nuclear family is under threat in all of Egoyan's films.

The trajectory of ethnicization in Egoyan's films can be read as a reflection and a refraction of the dynamism of ethnicity and nationalism and of Egoyan's own increasing awareness of his tripartite identity as Egyptian, Canadian, and

Armenian. However, not all terms of this multiple identity are operational, publicized, or valorized equally. As a schoolboy in Victoria, Canada, Egoyan was teased and put down by his teachers as the "little Arab." To assuage the pain of difference, he tried to become assimilated by repressing all marks of his cultural baggage, including the Armenian language. As he told me: "Armenian was my mother tongue, but at a certain point it seemed absurd to me to continue speaking it. I didn't even want to speak it. I remember distinctly my parents speaking it to me, my grandmother in particular, and [my] closing my ears and not wanting to speak it because for me it was part of being called an Arab boy, it was part of what excluded me" (Naficy 1997a, 188). However, his attempt at passing was suddenly and irrevocably torn asunder by one statement from his mother. When he was about to board a plane to leave his family to go to Toronto for his university education, his mother told him, "You know, you can do anything you want with your life, but the one thing that you could do that would hurt me is if you marry a Turkish woman" (186). This statement, which to the young man's surprise seemed to have come out of nowhere, suddenly confronted him with the painful history of the Turkish genocide of Armenians in 1915. Awakened by his mother's remark, Egoyan became involved in Armenian nationalist politics in Toronto, which in the late 1970s was taking a radical, even extremist, turn that included acts of violent terrorism.

It was during this activist phase of his politics of identity, which depends on fixity and essentialism of a sort, that Egoyan became aware of the idea of national identity not as a fixed edifice but as a shifting, performing strategy. He not only adopted the derogatory stereotype in Canada of Armenians as "rug merchants" but also flaunted it (in *Next of Kin*, George Deryan is a rug merchant). Thomas Elsaesser's account of German émigrés and exiles in Hollywood shows that the adoption of cultural camouflages and national stereotypes is not restricted to today's postcolonial and postmodernist exiles. Lubitsch, the Korda brothers, Kurtiz, Lang, Wilder, Sternberg, and Stroheim, among others, attempted to fulfill the national imaginaries of Europeans and Americans of each other by reproducing those imaginaries in their own lives and films. Often this took the form of impersonating national stereotypes. Joseph von Sternberg and Erich von Stroheim, for example, fashioned themselves as European aristocrats, the former as an old-world dandy, the latter as an aristocratic military man. Such imitative self-fashioning, when deployed without irony, can become integrated into one's personality and biography, reversing the usual flow of influence in which the filmmaker's biography impacts his film. This was the case with Stroheim, as Elsaesser vividly describes:

> Son of a poor immigrant hatmaker, he lived not only the fiction of an aristocrat but also that of an Austro-Hungarian aristocrat, doubling the connotations of pretense, style and playacting, taking it from screen roles into his biography, and choosing for

his life and work a mode, in which the Prussian and the Austrian impersonations are not felt to be at all contradictory (as they were in history). Indeed, they almost cancel out the falsehood in both, to make one totally convincing persona. (1999, 112–13)

It is likely, however, that for Stroheim and the other émigré directors of the classical cinema era, as for many of the contemporary accented filmmakers such as Egoyan, ethnic and national masquerade did not produce a carefree subjectivity or an internally coherent identity, for masquerade always entails moments of surprised discovery, when the self is suddenly exposed to have become partially its other. In the case of Egoyan, his surprised discovery of his masquerade occurred when the father of a girl he loved wrote him a rejection letter because of his untrustworthy "Armenian merchant background." Egoyan wondered:

> What was he deriving that image from? My name? My looks? My behavior, or my mannerisms? What was it about those mannerisms that would have defined Armenian rug merchantness? I didn't know. So I think I went into this whole mode where I tried, on the one hand, to play that out and make fun of it, but on the other hand I was getting quite involved in more political, almost militant, Armenian nationalist activities through the student association. (Naficy 1997a, 191)

The adoption of the Armenian rug merchant identity must be seen as a strategy of mimicry, not imitation, for imitation involves identification with the other to the point of producing whole, identical subjects, where the original and the copy match (as was the case with Littín in Chile). Mimicry, on the other hand, involves the kind of overimitation or underimitation of the other that, in its surplus or deficit and in its irony, produces partiality of identity, where there is a slippage between the original and its copy. It is in this slipzone of unfitting that the critical tensions of exilic mimicry and irony can be deciphered. By mimicking and flaunting the Armenian rug merchant stereotype, Egoyan had unknowingly produced both excess and partiality, not wholeness and identity. These were misread by the girlfriend's father.

In exilic situations, especially for first-generation exiles, born in one country and reared in another, there is a prior identity, an original sense of the self at home, that they compare themselves with and to which many of them long to return. The juxtaposition of the originary self and the new evolving self creates hybridized performances, such as the tango-dy and the split characters in *Tangos: Exile of Gardel*. In such performances, the homeland is often the source of the true original identity to which exilic identity is a poor imitation.

If one were to generalize Butler's definition of gender identity as performance (1990b, 2), one could say that ethnic, diasporic, or exilic identities are performances that rely on certain practices of repetition that over time produce the effect of ethnic, diasporic, or exilic identity. But this repetition is inexhaustible, since it will never completely capture "identity" or "home." There will always exist a surplus drag in drag, an excess of mimicry in imitation, of posturing in posing, of inappropriateness in passing, of parody in camp, of obsequiousness in civility, of overmasking or underveiling in masquerade, and of homeward tensions in exile to point to the failure to either totally mask the original or to map a matched copy onto it. It is in the surplus and the deficit that escape the hermeticity of repetition that the fabricating mechanism of identity construction can be discerned.

Peter in *Next of Kin* pretends to be Pedros, who as a child was put up for adoption by his parents, the Deryans. For the Deryan family, who had not seen him for many years, the copy (Peter) and the original (Pedros) completely matched. There was no discomfiting surplus or partiality to tip them off. This made them vulnerable to Peter's manipulative game of pretense and identity (which represents his critique of his own blood family), while it forced him to be on constant guard against slipups. However, his impersonation of Pedros leads to spectator ambivalence for, on the one hand, we agree with his critique of his WASP family and, on the other hand, his duplicitous impersonation of a lost Armenian son prevents us from fully identifying with him.

Since discursive repetition in various spheres creates different identity effects, one can have a number of intersecting or evolving identities. However, because they have an impact on others, these identities are not without coercion, sanction, or reward. Consequently, discursive identities create sedimentation at individual, group, or national levels that cannot with impunity be erased, ignored, discarded, or replaced with new improved ones—as some proponents of postmodern fluidity seem to suggest. Performance of identity is not a free state because there is still a set of primary categories of belonging (sediments) to which one attaches in order not to become totally weightless, atomized, or alienated. In addition, one cannot join or leave an identity or a group formation without social sanction. As a result, cultural identity is neither a fixed essence nor all, or always already, a fabrication (Hall 1989: 71). Even in the most radical of exilically accented films, there are moments of sedimentation, moments of so-called authenticity, when the copy corresponds more or less fully to the original, bringing to a temporary end the chain of repetition, signification, and mediation. In Egoyan's *Speaking Parts* and in particular in Steven Frears's *My Beautiful Laundrette* (1986), that moment of total correspondence or bliss (or *petit mort*) is reached through a sincere and passionate love. What is more, at certain points in an exile's life—for political or personal reasons (such as the birth of a child)—it becomes important to reach for a firmer ground, to establish the facticity, not the fluidity, of identity. Because of the birth of his first child, for example, Egoyan began to reevaluate his "indulgence" in transgressive and doubling strategies (Naficy 1997a, 196).[36] This newfound understanding may be the reason for the dearth of doubling strategies in *The Sweet Hereafter*, which has been praised for its authenticity of feelings about a community's reaction to the loss of its children.

To establish facticity, many accented filmmakers avoid using performative strategies in their films, sometimes achieving a kind of emphatic realism. For example, in *Homage by Assassination*, Suleiman emphasizes the facticity and indexicality of identity by focusing on the minutest routines and rituals of his daily life in exile. As Iraq volleys Scud missiles onto Israel, threatening his hometown of Nazareth, and as the United States–led United Nations forces pulverize Iraq, Suleiman is helplessly ensconced in his claustrophobic New York City apartment, where he watches the milk boil over on the stove, laces up his boots, waits, types, and weighs himself on a scale several times, as if to ascertain that he weighs the same every time, that he is still alive. Likewise, the repetitious documentary images of New York City streets in Akerman's *News from Home*, punctuated by emphatic traffic noise, establish the indexical present of Akerman in her new world. At certain junctures in an exile's life, it becomes important, even mandatory, to stress the fixity, not fluidity, the weightiness, not weightlessness, of identity. The insistence in certain accented films, especially epistolary and calligraphic films, on using the verbal and written forms of native language, such as in Trinh's *Surname Viet Given Name Nam* and Hatoum's *Measures of Distance*, are examples of creating moments and signs of cultural fixity and sedimentation. Fixity, sedimentation, and weight may also be obtained by one's production mode—sometimes by adopting the accented modes (interstitial and collective), sometimes by moving into other alternative modes, and sometimes by opting for the center and the mainstream modes. Depending on the filmmakers' previous location, each of these modes is capable of setting them free or settling them down. In the case of Egoyan, since his increasing success with *Exotica*, his mode of production has evolved from interstitial to independent—a move that is similar to those made by Gregory Nava and Mira Nair.

This table may give the impression that the accented style is unitary or homogeneous and that all films made in this style contain all its components. This is not entirely true, for each film partakes of some or all of them in different measures.

TABLE A.1
Components of the Accented Style

Components	*Constituting Elements*
VISUAL STYLE	General characteristics:
	Simultaneously exhibits spontaneity and anxious formality
	Less driven by action than by words and emotions
	Uneven pacing, incompleteness, sometimes rough, amateur aesthetics, lacking definitive closure
Mise-en-scène	What is seen in frame:
Setting	Usually real locations
	Claustrophobic interiors, often ethnically coded
	Immense exteriors, homeland's landscapes, nature, monuments
	Transitional border spaces: airports and seaports, train and bus stations
Motivated props	Fetishized objects and icons of homeland and of past
Lighting scheme	Commensurate with the open and closed film forms
Filming Style	Characteristic of the image:
Framing	Closed form emphasizing claustrophobia, control, dystopia
	Open form stressing openness, possibility, euphoria
NARRATIVE STRUCTURE	Editing, relation of sound and image:
Orality	Emphasis on oral, aural, and vocal
Calligraphy/titling	Text on screen in native script or in translation
Multilinguality	More than one language spoken/titled in film
Multivocality	Several voices presented: direct, indirect, and free indirect
Asynchronicity	Intentional asynchronicity of sound and image
	Discontinuity of diegetic time and space made synchronous by epistolary media, memory flashbacks, longing narratives
Voice-over narration	Often provided by the filmmakers or their stand-ins
Native music	Used both diegetically and extradiegetically
Epistolarity	Inscribing means and acts of communication using letters, telephones, cassettes, computers

TABLE A.1 (cont.)
Components of the Accented Style

Components	Constituting Elements
Juxtaposition	Placing actualities/possibilities in analytic and critical juxtaposition
	Descent and consent relations are critically juxtaposed to compare place, time, cultures, societies
	Juxtaposition of public history with private memory
Narrative space and time	Inscribed in three modalities: timelessness/boundlessness, claustrophobia/contemporaneity, and transitional time/spaces
Self-reflexivity	Self-reflexivity about exile and filmmaking process
Memory/nostalgia	Memory of and nostalgia for childhood and homeland often drive the plot, flashbacks, and character actions
Incompleteness	Difficulty of achieving closure, completion
Incoherence	Relative tolerance for narrative incoherence and chaos
Structured absenses	Certain characters, people, and places are lost, absent
Border aesthetics	Multifocality, asynchronicity, fragmented narratives, multiple subjectivity, shifters, critical distance
Third Cinema aesthetics	Historically conscious, politically engaged, critically aware, generically hybridized, artisanal mode of production
Time lag	Between filming and editing, between filming and voice-over, between film projects
CHARACTERS/ACTORS	Character types and attributes:
Accented speech	Multilingual characters speak the dominant language with an accent
Identity and performance	Slippage between identity and performance of identity
Outsiders	Characters are often outsiders, alienated, illegal, alone, lonely
Shifters	Amphibolic characters who live contextually
Twoness	Sometimes characters are hybrid, double, split
Actors	Frequent use of nonactors, people playing themselves
	Filmmakers representing themselves on image and sound track
SUBJECT MATTER/THEME/PLOT	Recurring topics, themes, and plots:
Home-seeking journey	Events that caused departure and exile, search for home
Homelessness journey	Wandering, continual displacement, homelessness
Homecoming journey	Return, desire to return, impossibility of return, staging of return
Identity	Quest for wholeness, for healing of split identity
	Performativity of identity
Family	A unit that is under tremendous pressure
Historicization	Attempt to recount and account for personal/national past

TABLE A.1 (cont.)
Components of the Accented Style

Components	*Constituting Elements*
Reality	Ambiguity of and uncertainty about what is real and visible
Exile, displacement	Preoccupation with deterritorialization and unbelonging
STRUCTURES OF FEELING	Set of undeniable personal and social experiences of exile encoded in films:
Sensibilities	Oscillating between polar pairs: dysphoria/euphoria, dystopia/utopia, celibacy/celebration
	Recognition of and taking masochistic pleasure in ambivalence and asynchronicity
	Heightened sensuality, emotionality, nostalgic longing
Synaesthesia	Attention to all senses of the sensorium as markers of difference, loss, longing, and exile
Retrospectiveness	Characters and film look backward as plot moves forward
Prevailing mood	Melancholia, anomie, fear, panic
Liminality	Living between psychological states and social formations
Interstitiality	Located at the intersection of aesthetic systems, languages, nations, practices, cultures
Hybridity	Selectively appropriating other cultures and practices and keeping them in tension
Multifocality	Simultaneous awareness of and access to multiple cognitive systems and cultural orientations
Politicization	Interpreting all things politically, interjection of politics from inception to reception
Simultaneity	Recognition of simultaneity of space and time
Tactility	Perception based on distraction instead of contemplation
	Emphasis on textures of sound, screen, cultures, gestures, looks, nature
Nomadic sensibilities	Time is subjective, cyclical, simultaneous
	Strong sense of placelessness/displacement
	Belief in unseen forces, magic
Loneliness	Lonely characters and filmmakers, lonely mode of production
FILMMAKER'S LOCATION	Biographical/social/cinematic locations:
Cultural/social location	Filmmaker is liminal, interstitial figure
Autobiography	Filmmaker's biography, history, and subjectivity are inscribed
Self-inscription	Author, narrator, subject in film often coincide
Authorship	Filmmakers overdetermine authorship by performing multiple functions in films
MODE OF PRODUCTION	Production, distribution, exhibition, and reception of films and videos:

TABLE A.1 (cont.)
Components of the Accented Style

Components	Constituting Elements
Alternative/independent Minor practice of cinema	Artisanal, collective, and transnational modes Using deterritorialized language, political discourse, collective production and consumption
Integrated practice	Filmmaker involved in all phases, from preproduction to exhibition
Multiple function	Filmmaker serving multiple roles from beginning to end
Alternative distribution	By boutique, alternative, activist, ethnic, microdistributors
	Chiefly distributed on video, Internet webcasting on the rise
Exhibition venues	Repertory cinemas, art cinemas, museums, universities, ethnic/diasporic/exilic cultural organizations
Financing	Diverse sources: national and international TV channels, public and private funding agencies, ethnic and personal sources
Spectator positioning	Film addresses a variety of sometimes conflicting audiences: ethnic subjects, ethnic communities, national communities, international audiences
Spectatorial activity	Watching and reading the screen simultaneously

Appendix B

TABLE B.1
Sources of Funding for Atom Egoyan's Feature Films

FILM TITLE/(YEAR)	FUNDING SOURCES LISTED IN THE FILMS' ENDING CREDITS
The Sweet Hereafter (1997)	Ego Film Arts; Telefilm Canada, Alliance Communications Corp.; The Movie Network; Harold Greenberg Fund, Government of Canada; Canadian Film and Video Production Tax Credit
Exotica (1993)	Ego Film Arts; Alliance Communications Corp.; Telefilm Canada; Ontario Film Development Corp.
Calendar (1993)	Ego Film Arts; Armenian National Cinematheque; ZDF German TV
The Adjuster (1991)	Ego Film Arts; Telefilm Canada; Ontario Film Development Corp.; Alliance Communications Corp.
Speaking Parts (1989)	Ego Film Arts; Academy Pictures, Rome; Film Four International, London; Telfilm Canada; Ontario Film Development Corp.
Family Viewing (1987)	Ego Film Arts; Ontario Film Development Corp.; Canada Council; Ontario Arts Council; Union of Independent Filmmakers, Toronto
Next of Kin (1984)	Ego Film Arts; Canada Council; Ontario Arts Council; National Film Board of Canada, Ontario

Source: Compiled by the author from ending credits of the films.

TABLE B.2

Financial Profile of *Wedding in Galilée*, A Belgian-French Coproduction*

PRODUCTION BUDGET

Belgium:

The Belgian share constituted 60 percent of the film's budget,
obtained from the following multinational sources:

    La Société MARISA Film, Brussels

    Q.A Production, London

    ZDF television, Germany (TV transmission rights)

    Ministry of French Community in Belgium

Belgian contribution from above sources   4,260,000

France:

The French share of the budget was 40 percent, involving
funds from the following commercial and public sources in
France:

La société les productions audiovisuelles	620,000
Avidia Films (coproducor)	300,000
Canal Plus (TV transmission rights)	400,000
Lasa Films (distributor)	50,000
French Culture Ministry (advance from Centre nationale de la cinématographie)	1,600,000
French contribution	2,970,000
Total budget	7,230,000

PRODUCTION COST

Total cost of the film   7,420,000

The cost overrun of 190,000 francs was shared by the two contributing sides according
to the same 60/40 formula.

PUBLICITY/DISTRIBUTION

Publicity budget (in France)	600,000
Distribution budget (in both countries)	175,000

A total of ten film prints were made for distribution by Lasa Films, three of which were
paid for by the CNC fund of the Ministry of Culture.

PRODUCTION HISTORY

Filming took place in several villages in Galilée, the West Bank, and Jerusalem over
a nine-week period, from May 8 to July 19, 1986 (four were spent in the West Bank).
The film opened in France in November 1987 in five cinemas.

---

* All amounts are in French francs.
Source: Leclère 1988: 19.

Notes

Chapter One

1. I thank Bill Nichols for suggesting the parallel between exile and taboo. Also, see exile as "aesthetic gain" in Kaplan 1996, 33–41.

2. I have incorporated these and other attributes of exile and alterity to formulate a "paradigm of exile" (Naficy 1993a).

3. If Rushdie is an example of exilic hybridity, F. M. Esfandiary is an example of exilic virtuality. In the 1960s, Esfandiary wrote novels from exile about the horror of life in his homeland Iran (*The Identity Card* [1966]), but in the late 1980s he changed his name to FM-2030 and developed the concept of transhumanism, which dismissed all usual markers of continuity and identity. To be a transhuman is to be a universal "evolutionary being" (FM-2030 1989, 205).

4. This is particularly true for the Japanese-Americans whose loyalty to the United States was questioned during World War II and to the Muslim Americans whose loyalty is often questioned in contemporary times.

5. Peter Feng suggests removing the hyphen from "Asian-American," while Gustavo P. Firmat recommends replacing it with a plus sign for "Cuban + American" (1994, 16). Some insert a forward slash between the two terms. On the politics of the hyphen, especially for Asian-Americans, see Feng 1995, 1996; Lowe 1991.

6. These statistics should be understood in the following context. Many Middle Eastern filmmakers moved through several countries and across a number of identities. Some claimed multiple identities—both simultaneous and sequential—while others denied any form of particularistic identity. Some never returned, while others periodically visit their homelands, where they make films. Some moved among too many worlds, often leaving behind inadequately documented histories. A few deliberately obfuscated their history to conceal their tracks. Such fluidity and camouflaging, characteristic of exilic positionality, make it difficult to pin down some filmmakers' country of origin or residence, let alone their other markers of identity (such as their ethnic, religious, and political affiliations).

7. For sources on Middle Eastern and North African filmmakers in diaspora and exile, see the following: Arasoughly 1996; Armes 1996; Bodman and Bartholomew 1992; Bloom 1995; Brossard n.d.; *CinémAction*, no. 7; *CinémAction*, no. 8; *CinémAction*, no. 24; *CinémAction*, no. 56; *Iransk Film i Exil* 1993; Kaufman et al. 1991; Omid 1367/ 1988; *Palestinian Film Week* 1992; Pflaum and Prinzler 1993; Radvanyi 1993; Salloum 1996; *The Second Festival for Iranian Films in Exile* 1995; Tavenas and Volard 1989; and Thomas 1990.

8. Although "international," even "transnational," these directors—whom Douglas Gomery (1991) labels "the individual as international film artist"—are not considered "exilic" or "diasporic" by the definition used here.

9. In an earlier publication, I explored the promise of theorizing these films as a transnational "genre" (Naficy 1996g).

10. On regional exilic filmmaking, the following are notable studies: on Latin-American exile filmmakers, see Pick (1993, 157–85) and Burton (1986); on Chilean exile films, see King (1990); on Cuban exile films, see Lopez (1996); on cinemas of the black diaspora, see Martin (1995) and Ukadike (1994); on black British independent films, see Mercer (1994a), Diawara (1993b), and Fusco (1988); on black American diaspora films, see Diawara (1993a) and Reid (1991); on postcolonial and multicultural diasporic films, see Shohat and Stam (1994) and Sherzer (1996); on women and African and Asian diaspora films, see Foster (1997); on Caribbean exilic films, see Cham (1992); on Asian-American films, see Leong (1991); on Chicano/a cinemas, see Fregoso (1993) and Noriega (1992a); on Middle Eastern exile films, see Friedlander (1995) and Naficy (1995e); on Yiddish films, see Hoberman (1991a); on Iranian exile films, see Naficy (1993a); on Turkish exile films, see Naficy (1996g); on Soviet and Eastern European filmmakers in the West, see Petrie and Dwyer (1990); on exile and émigré cinema, particularly in France and Europe, including extensive filmographies, see the following special issues of *CinémAction* magazine: no. 7, "Cinéma contre racisme" (n.d.); no. 8, "Cinémas de l'émigration" (summer 1979); no. 24, "Cinémas de l'émigration" (n.d.); no. 56, "Cinémas métis: De Hollywood aux films beurs" (July 1990). On individual exilic filmmakers, consult the index or the close-up sections throughout the book.

11. On experimental diaspora cinema, see Marks 1994.

12. Even these two types of accented films are not fixed, for the works of some filmmakers may fall only partially into one or share attributes of both. This is another way in which these films are hybrid. For example, Solanas's *Tangos: Exile of Gardel* and Krishna's *Masala* may be categorized as hybrid films in their crossing of the boundaries and the mixing of elements of musical and melodrama, tragedy and comedy, narrative and nonnarrative, fictional and nonfictional, realism and surrealism, personal and national. However, both Solanas and Krishna make feature-length films, have high ambitions, and have large markets in mind. A key difference between them is that while *Masala* is a diaspora film, *Tangos* remains exilic, for it is focused solely on exile and on a binary relationship with the homeland. Likewise, Mekas's films share some of the characteristics of both feature films (their length) and experimental films (their aesthetics).

13. In the classical Hollywood cinema, the stars who retained their "foreign" accents fared differently. Some could not get parts because of their heavy accents. Scandinavian stars, particularly Greta Garbo, Sonja Henie, and Ingrid Bergman, were usually cast as European and Soviet foreign characters. Some British-born stars, such as Cary Grant, acquired a "transatlantic accent," so named perhaps because it was both readily comprehensible and hard to place (Jarvie 1991, 93).

14. For more on the phenomenon of exilic nostalgia and fetishization, see Naficy 1993a, chap. 4.

15. A point should be made here about the "exilic" status of the filmmakers who worked in the former Soviet Union, such as Paradjanov, Tarkovsky, Ilienko, and Pelechian. Of these, only Tarkovsky lived in external exile, where he made his last two films. Paradjanov lived in internal exile, some of it spent in prison. Whatever their differences, these filmmakers made their films under the state-run mode of production, not a subversive interstitial mode. The presence of Armenian ethnicity and regional identity in the films of Paradjanov and Pelechian had a lot to do with Soviet cinematic politics of fostering the so-called friendship of the peoples. The filmmakers' choice of theme was

often strategic. It might be more appropriate, therefore, to speak of filmmakers from the Soviet Union's "minority" republics as subaltern filmmakers instead of exilic filmmakers. I thank Susan Larsen for bringing these points to my attention.

16. These Latin-American and Third Cinema polemics and manifestos are collected in Martin 1997a.

17. For some of these, see Willemen 1989, 5–6; for others, see Martin 1995.

18. There is disagreement over what constituted the first and second cinemas. Gabriel, for example, assigned First Cinema to the products of the mainstream film industry in capitalist market economies, while consigning Second Cinema to the products of the communist/socialist command economies (1982, chap. 1).

19. Other middlemen figures in the border drama include sanctuary movement advocates who assist potential refugees to gain asylum in the United States.

20. I have borrowed this phrase from Pfeil 1988, 387.

21. For "influences" on Egoyan, see Brady 1993.

22. For books on and by Egoyan, see Desbarats et al. 1993; Egoyan 1993, 1995. On recurrent themes in Egoyan's films, see Harcourt 1995; Porton 1997; and Naficy 1997a.

Chapter Two

1. On the classical industrial mode of production, see Bordwell, Staiger, and Thompson 1985; Gomery 1986; and Schatz 1988.

2. The "merger mania" in 1995 occurred in anticipation of the 1996 United States telecommunication law that fundamentally restructured the communications industries.

3. In 1985, Third World Newsreel (TWN) created the "Journey across Three Continents Tour," a program of films from Africa and the black diaspora that toured to over a dozen sites in the United States (Bowser and Tajima 1985). TWN presented "Internal Exile," a program that showcased films and videos from Chile (Fusco 1990). In 1978, Göethe Institut of San Francisco organized a series of films made by German and Austrian émigré directors in Hollywood (Schürmann 1978), and in 1993 it organized "Homeless in the Homeland," a program of films made in Germany by émigré filmmakers and by German directors about immigrants living in Germany. In 1993, UCLA Film and Television Archive presented "Intercultural Europe," a series of films by émigré filmmakers in Europe. In 1995, the Archive presented "Constructing a Culture: Exile and Immigration in Southern California." In that same year, the Los Angeles Festival presented a program of films and videos by exile filmmakers working in Europe and the United States. Rice University's Media Center in Houston has presented several exile film programs, including "Cinema of Displacement" in 1995. In the 1990s, the Museum of Fine Arts, Houston, programmed "Jewish Worlds," a series of films made in Israel and in the Jewish diaspora.

4. Examples are the series "Voices from the Asian Diaspora" and "Voices from the African Diaspora," distributed by Third World Newsreel; "Video Titles from the Asian Diaspora," distributed by National Asian American Telecommunication Association; "Crossing Borders," distributed by New Day Films; and "Films and Videos on Race and Immigrant Experience," distributed by DEC Films in Toronto, Canada.

5. Women Make Movies groups a large number of films under the category "Cultural Identity," which includes such subcategories as Racism/Diversity, Latina, Native American, Asian American, and African American (Women Make Movies 1996).

6. In 1993, the University of Iowa's Center for International and Comparative Studies organized "Representing Nomadic Cultures," a symposium that included art exhibits, film screenings, and lectures on nomadism, exile, and allied topics. In 1994, the UCLA Center for Near Eastern Studies organized "Labyrinth of Exile," a series of lectures, musical performances, and films by and about Iranian exiles. In 1995, it put together another conference, "Cinema of Displacement: Middle Eastern Identities in Transition," that included lectures and screenings. In 1995, I organized at Rice University "House, Home, Homeland," a symposium on exile, consisting of a scholar's forum, art and photography exhibits, a film series, and a seminar course on exile cinema.

7. In recent years, the Society for Cinema Studies has designated a "special focus" for its annual conference. The topics, listed here, point to the organization's concern with alternative discourses. Special focus of 1991: MultiCulturalism; 1992: Oppression, Silencing, and the Production of Diverse Voices; 1993: Open Channels: Film, Television, and Multimedia; 1994: Emergences: New Identities/New Technologies; 1995: 100 Years of Cinema: Writing the Histories; 1996: Visual Cultures in the 1990s; 1997: Cinema(s) in Canada; 1998: Media on the Border; and 1999: Media Industries: Past, Present, Future. I thank Janet Staiger for supplying me with most of this list.

8. Until *Exotica*, Canadian filmmaker Atom Egoyan invested in his own films. Iranians Marva Nabili and Amir Naderi worked as film editors to raise money for their films. Chilean Raúl Ruiz and Iranian Parviz Kimiavi worked for French television, Palestinian Michel Khleifi made films for Belgian TV, Armenians Nigol Bezgian and Ara Madzounian produced ethnic TV shows in Los Angeles, and Wayne Wang worked on a Chinese-American children's TV program in California.

9. Iranian director Said Assadi, who made his first exile film, *Fata Morgana* (*Sarab*, 1991), in Sweden, had to act in the film because he could not find a Persian-Swedish bilingual actor (*Majalleh Sinemai-ye Film*, November 1992, no. 132, p. 84).

10. For example, the camera crew for Chantal Akerman's *A Couch in New York* (1996), a romantic comedy filmed in Paris and New York City, was multilingual and multicultural, consisting of a German cinematographer, a French camera operator, and an American focus puller (Bear 1995, H16). Multilinguality may also, and ironically, be a result of the dominance of one language, such as English in this case, that facilitated cross-cultural communication among a sizable, diverse crew of sixty people.

11. Despite working with low budgets, Egoyan has shown largesse with his award money toward other accented filmmakers. When his *Exotica* won the $25,000 first prize for best Canadian film at the 1995 Toronto Film Festival, he gave $5,000 of it in appreciation to the Chinese-Canadian filmmaker Mina Shum, whose first feature, *Double Happiness* (1995), had been praised by the festival (Benson 1995, H18).

12. One such ad announced that *The Sweet Hereafter* was "on over 250 critics' 10 best lists" and was "one of the best films of the decade" (*New York Times*, February 27, 1998, B17).

13. The features are *The Fertile Memory* (1980), *Wedding in Galilée* (1987), *Canticle of the Stones* (1990), *The Tale of Three Lost Jewels* (1994), and *Forbidden Marriages in the Holy Land* (1995).

14. For more on CNC, see Williams 1992; Tavenas and Volard 1989. For more on the funding mechanism and film and video distribution in France, see Bouquet 1994.

15. Ironically, this same support system may be partially responsible for the generally small and low-budget French films—factors that may have been responsible for driving scores of French film professionals to the United States (Hanania 1995).

16. Academic public screening includes film programs organized for the public by university film departments and by student-run film societies. Although these societies have decreased drastically because of competition from video, cable TV, and satellite TV, between 600 and 700 colleges still program films in this manner (Rubin 1993, 10). In addition, according to Pintoff, some 644 colleges and universities offer film classes nationwide (1994). These figures give an idea of the potentially large academic market for nontheatrical distribution.

17. Naficy 1996f and e-mail correspondence with WMM, February 11, 2000. Typically, WMM returns 40 percent of a film's revenues to its maker. It has returned more than $1 million to women producers in royalty payments.

18. The direct mailing of catalogs and publicity materials to 3,600 colleges and universities is manageable, but direct mail to over 100,000 high schools is not cost-effective for independent film distributors such as WMM.

19. WMM's price structure in fall 1996 was as follows: the average rental price for a thirty-minute 16mm film was $60 to $75; a sixty-minute film cost $125 to $150. The average rental fee for a thirty-minute video was $50 to 60; a sixty-minute video cost $75 to $125.

20. The rental and sale fees for a VHS copy of Trinh's *A Tale of Love* are $300 and $395, respectively. WMM's fees for foreign films are also higher than normal because of higher lab costs in Europe and Australia.

21. Copyright laws, designed rightly to protect the intellectual property of artists, also create anger and frustration within the academic community, which is faced with both decreasing film budgets and the increasingly aggressive tactics of some commercial distributors.

22. E-mail to the author from Debra Zimmerman, executive director, Women Make Movies, May 2, 1996.

23. Although nontheatrical distribution forms its most visible and financially successful activity, WWM also trains and fiscally sponsors women filmmakers, distributes and exhibits their films, and provides speakers for films.

Chapter Three

1. The communes, for example.

2. For example, civil rights, anti–Vietnam War, feminist, Third World liberation, and environmentalist movements.

3. Among these are rock music, the alternative press, Andy Warhol's Factory, Jonas Mekas's Anthology Film Archives, Jean-Luc Godard and Jean Pierre Gorin's Dziga Vertov Group, Chris Marker's SLON collective, activist video groups such as Videofreex and Top Value TV, and activist film groups such as the Newsreel. For more on Anthology Film Archives, see James 1992; on SLON (Société pour le Lancement des Oeuvres Nouvelles), see Van Wert (1979); and on SLON and Dziga Vertov groups, see Harvey 1978.

4. On Newsreel's history and evolution, see Nichols 1972; Renov 1987a, 1987b, 1984.

5. UCLA film graduates were instrumental in the emergence of another important minority film movement, the new independent black cinema; see Masilela 1993; James 1996b.

6. On representation of Asians and Asian-Americans on television, see Hamamoto 1994; on their representation in Hollywood films, see Marchetti 1993.

7. See the brochure *7th Annual Los Angeles Asian Pacific Film and Video*, May 7 to 17, 1992, 1.

8. According to Tong, who was born in Hong Kong but is a Canadian citizen, National Film Board of Canada supplied $80,000 of the budget, with the remainder provided by Asian communities in the United States and Canada.

9. Nair's documentaries are *Jama Masjid Street Journal* (1979), *So Far from India* (1982), *India Cabaret* (1985), and *Children of Desired Sex* (1986).

10. For extensive reviews of *Salaam Bombay!* see Nair and Taraporevala 1989.

11. The South Asians' protest was strong enough for the PBS outlet in New York City (WNET-TV) to cancel the airing of *India Cabaret* (Foster 1997, 113).

12. Nabili began her lengthy research for *Nightsongs* in 1979, wrote the screenplay in 1982 at the Sundance Film Institute, and completed the film in 1984.

13. For reviews of *Nightsongs*, see Thomas 1991; London 1984.

14. On the struggle for and against such overdetermination, involving cinema, see Naficy 1997f.

15. Denial is also a feature of Iranian exile literature, see Khorrami 1993, 186.

16. This includes the screening of Bahman Farmanara's *Smell of Camphor, Fragrance of Jasmine* (*Buy-e Kafur, Atr-e Yas*, 1999), Ramin Bahrami's *Strangers* (1999), and Babak Payami's *One More Day* (1999).

17. Amy Taubin (1989, 64) and Andy Klein (1989, B2) both called *The Suitors* a "rarity"; Mike McGrady noted that it "extracts high comedy from cultural shock" (1989, 7); Kathleen Carroll called it "a haunting tragicomedy" (1989, 38); and Jami Bernard praised its "disarming self-confidence" (1989).

18. One reviewer called *The Suitors* "anti-Iranian," and a "calamity," since its representation of Iranian exiles as "cruel, stupid, and pitiable" fit the pattern of colonialist conquest, which is based on negative portrayals of natives that justify intervention in their affairs and on their behalf (Pousti 1988). Another reviewer criticized it for "self-humiliation" aimed to appease the Americans (Shafa 1989, 86). In a letter published in an exile newspaper in London, a reader claimed that the film reinforced the negative image that the Islamic Republic's politics had created of Iranians as "barbarian," "uneducated," and "uncivilized savages." Dramatizing his disappointment with the film, the reader stated that he went to see it full of enthusiasm but returned to his car with "stooped shoulders and hesitant steps" (*Kayhan*, December 12, 1989, 9).

19. For a full list of these films, see Naficy 1993a, 231–32.

20. Southern California colleges and churches were active sites for screening anti-Shah documentaries and agitprop films. For these, see Naficy 1984, 46–53.

21. Similar reasons are cited for the gradual demise of ethnic movie houses among the more established ethnic populations such as Chinese-Americans (Chen 1998).

22. From 1979 to 1994, Iranian films were screened some 1,800 times in international festivals, garnering three awards in 1979 and thirty-three in 1993 (Farabi Cinema Foundation 1994, 68). For detailed analyses of the Iranian postrevolution cinema, see Naficy 1992b, 1994, 1995c; Issa and Whitaker 1999.

23. For the festival catalog, see UCLA Film and Television Archive 1990.

24. The following exile TV producers and filmmakers opposed the festival and called for its boycott: Mary Apik, Shohreh Aghdashlou, Hushang Baharlu, Shahrokh Golestan, Parviz Kardan, Marva Nabili, Parviz Sayyad, Barbod Taheri, and Houshang Towzi.

25. The festival cast a wide net in terms of the directors represented. Both the "old-timers" (those who had begun work during the preceding Pahlavi regime and continued on successfully) and the "newcomers" (those who had gained ascendancy under the Islamist regime) were represented. For the first time, women directors were represented. In terms of the whitewashing charge, none of the films was supportive of the Islamic government or of its politics; in fact, almost all of them were implicitly critical of either the pre- or the postrevolutionary societies. Most remarkably, there was a total erasure of the ruling clerics or clerical institutions in the films. Bill Nichols, who reviewed a dozen of them, came to a similar conclusion: "Absent are explicit references to religion and the state. Common Western stereotypes of fanaticism and zealotry are neither confirmed nor subverted. They are simply absent, of no local concern" (1994b, 21). This absence can be read as the filmmakers' resistance against the cleric-dominated government, in effect against the hands that fed them.

26. Filmmaker and entertainer Parviz Sayyad continued his one-man vitriolic crusade for over two decades by lecturing and publishing articles and a book (1996) containing many inaccuracies, misrepresentations, and malicious innuendos against the UCLA film festival and its organizers (including myself), the 1992 Los Angeles Festival and its organizers (including myself), the 1993 Chicago Film Festival, and other major festivals of quality films from the Islamic Republic.

27. These producers include Masud Assadollahi, Iraj Gorgin, Ali Limonadi, and Parviz Qaribafshar.

28. International Home Cinema, October Films, New Yorker Films, Miramax, and Gramercy Films handle theatrical distribution of Iranian films. Facets Multimedia in Chicago, Arab Film Distribution in Seattle, International Product Distribution in Orange County, California, and http://www.iranianmovies.com distribute them on video.

29. There have been other venues for showcasing Iranian exile films. In the United States, throughout the 1980s and the early 1990s, I organized the screening of a several exile-made films at UCLA, often with the filmmakers in attendance. Since 1995, Cinema-ye Azad organization has put on exile film festivals in Saarbrücken and other German cities. In 1995, the first U.S.-based International Tournée of Iranian Short Films in diaspora traveled to museum and university cinemas.

30. See *Iransk Film i Exil* (1993) and *The Second Festival for Iranian Films in Exile* (1995).

31. This cinematic development is paralleled by publication of periodicals about Iranian diasporic cinema. From the early 1980s, the active exile press in Europe and North America gave extensive coverage to Iranian films made at home and abroad. In the 1990s, two specialized film magazines—*Sinema* in Los Angeles and *Sinema-ye Azad* in Saarbrücken, Germany—dealt exclusively with these films. It is part of the political economy of exilic culture that the same companies that distributed Iranian films abroad and organized exile film festivals published these periodicals.

32. On these types of exile criticism of international festivals, see Nassibi 1995; Mahini 1995; Allamehzadeh 1991; and Sayyad 1995, 1996.

33. For example, in 1996 the Iranian film *The White Baloon* (*Badkonak-e Sepid*, 1995) directed by Jafar Panahi, which was being considered for a foreign-language Oscar, became embroiled in a political skirmish over a recently approved congressional plan (budgeted at $20 million) that directed the U.S. intelligence agencies to destabilize the Islamic Republic of Iran. The Ministry of Culture and Islamic Guidance announced that in the light of this plan, Iran would withdraw the film from consideration. The

Academy of Motion Picture Arts and Sciences, which issues the Oscar, responded that it would not permit a film to be "squeezed out because of politics" (Corliss 1996, 76), and, at any rate, the foreign-language film committee had already begun screening the film (Young 1996, 18). *The White Balloon* remained eligible and was favorably and widely discussed in the American press; later it was distributed commercially by October Films and aired repeatedly by Bravo cable channel, but it did not win the nomination.

34. On the collective production of *The Passion of Remembrance*, see Attille 1988; Attille et al. 1988; for the making of *Handsworth Songs*, see Akomfrah et al. 1988.

35. The controversy about the collectives' works included attempts at censoring them. On Independent Broadcasting Authority's attempt to "censor" Ceddo's films, see "Ceddo: *The Peoples' Account*," *ICA Documents*, no. 7 (1988): 58–59.

36. On Julien's works, see Arroyo 1991, Grundmann 1995.

37. On the black British cinema in this period, see Pines 1988; Mercer 1988.

38. For a brief survey of these directors' works, see Blackwood and Givanni 1988.

39. See Diawara 1993b; Mercer 1994b (introduction and chap. 2); Fusco 1988, 1995.

40. On the dynamics of South Asian/Punjabi *bhangra* music and ethnic TV in England, see Gopinath 1995; Gillespie 1995.

41. Indeed, *sankofa* resonates in the works of other African filmmakers, among them in Haile Gerima's *Sankofa* (1993), which is built on the *sankofa*'s connotation of returning to the past in order to go forward.

42. On using independent ethnic films to teach history, see Abrash and Egan 1992.

43. For Channel 4's policy on supporting film, see Aukin 1995; Fountain 1988. For more on the channel's relations to the film industry, see Hill 1996a; Grade 1996.

44. Among the accented films it supported are the following: *El Norte* (Gregory Nava, 1983); *Paris-Texas* (Wim Wenders, 1984); *Bangkok Bahrain* (Amos Gitai, 1984); *Born of Fire* (Jamil Dehlavi, 1984); *My Beautiful Laundrette* (Stephen Frears, 1985); *Vagabonde* (Agnès Varda, 1986); *The Passion of Remembrance* (Sankofa Film and Video Collective, 1986); *Playing Away* (Horace Ové, 1986); *Esther* (Amos Gitai, 1986); *The Sacrifice* (Andrei Tarkovsky, 1986); *Sammy and Rosie Get Laid* (Stephen Frears, 1987); *Salaam Bombay!* (Mira Nair, 1988); *Speaking Parts* (Atom Egoyan, 1989); *Berlin-Jerusalem* (Amos Gitai, 1989); *Canticle of the Stones* (Michel Khleifi, 1989); *Homage by Assassination* (Elia Suleiman, 1991); *Bhaji on the Beach* (Gurinder Chadha, 1993); *In the Valley of Wupper* (Amos Gitai, 1993); and *Three Colors: Red, White, Blue* (Krzysztof Kieslowski, 1993–94).

45. For example, Frears received 100 percent of the budget for *My Beautiful Laundrette* and 29 percent for *Sammy and Rosie Get Laid*; Nava received 7 percent of the budget for *El Norte*; and Egoyan received 13 percent of the budget for his *Speaking Parts* (1989) (compiled by author from Pym 1992).

46. In writing this section on *beur* cinema, I benefited from Peter Bloom's unpublished essay (1995). I thank him for putting it at my disposal. See also Bloom 1999.

47. These films are distributed by the Audiopradif collective. For more on the Mohammed Collective, see Mohamed 1981; Bosséno 1982.

48. To support French films and to ward against foreign products, especially those of American pop culture, current French law requires that 50 percent of all films and TV fictions aired by the five networks be French, and that 40 percent of popular music broadcast by French radio stations between 6:30 A.M. and 10:30 P.M. be French (Ross 1996, H23).

49. According to Bosséno, more than 100,000 people saw *Tea in the Harem* in theaters in the greater Paris area alone (1992, 56).

50. Gatlif's films are *Gypsies: The Princes* (*Les Princes*, 1982), an angry film about a desperate Gypsy family in a Parisian suburb; *Latcho Drom* (*Safe Journey*, 1993), a lyrical musical history of Gypsy life in Europe; *Mondo* (1997) a modern fairy tale about an eleven-year-old Gypsy boy living in the streets of Nice, France, who touches everyone with whom he comes into contact; and *Mad Foreigner* (*Gadjo Dilo*, 1997), about a young Parisian who returns to rural Romania to trace the origin of a Gypsy song.

51. For more on *raï*, rap, and world music, see Chambers 1994; Gross, McMurray, and Swedenburg 1994; Roberts 1992.

52. Other notable examples of *banlieue* feature films are François Richet's *L'état des lieux* (1995); Karim Dridi's *Pigalle* (1994) and *Bye, Bye* (1995); Thomas Gilou's *Raï*; and Malik Chibane's *Hexagone* (1994) and *Douce France* (1995). For more on *banlieue* films, see Reynaud 1996; Boubeker and Abdallah 1993.

Chapter Four

1. Among them are Frank Borzage's *A Farewell to Arms* (1933), William Wyler's *The Letter* (1940), Ernst Lubitsch's *The Shop around the Corner* (1940), Henri-Georges Clouzot's *The Raven* (*Le Corbeau*, 1943), William Dieterle's *Love Letters* (1945), Max Ophuls's *Letter from an Unknown Woman* (1948), Jacques Tati's *Jour de Fete* (1948), and Joseph L. Mankiewicz's *A Letter to Three Wives* (1948).

2. There is debate about what the direct, indirect, and free-indirect discourses should be called. For convenience and variety, I have randomly switched between the designation discourse, style, speech, and voice. For a full discussion, see Pascal 1977; McHale 1978; Ducrot and Todorov 1983; and Gates 1988.

3. Epistolaries may be classified into subcategories based on how they affect the plot and narration. There are, for example, films that feature undelivered letters (William Cameron's *Address Unknown*, 1944), misdelivered letters (Joseph Losey's *The Go-Between*, 1971), incriminating letters (Alfred Hitchcock's *Suspicion*, 1941), lost letters (Tay Garnett's *Cause for Alarm*, 1951), indiscreet letters (Joseph L. Mankiewicz's *A Letter to Three Wives*, 1948), letters that bridge the years (Elia Kazan's *Sea of Grass*, 1947), or posthumous letters (Max Ophuls's *Letter from an Unknown Woman*, 1948). I have borrowed some of the types of epistolary films from Halliwell (1977, 434) and Valot (1989).

4. On voice-over in fiction films, see Kozloff 1988; Silverman 1988; on voice-over in nonfiction films, see Nichols 1991, 1994a. In "image-over" films, voice-over sound is primary, but it is not necessarily a priori to the visual—although in some cases, as in Godard/Gorin's *Letter to Jane* and in Marker's *Letter to Siberia*, it may be. On "image-over," see Green 1994.

5. For the text of the manifesto, see Martin 1997a. For Solanas's other publications, see Mraz 1990.

6. Quoted in the publicity package accompanying *Tangos: Exile of Gardel*.

7. From *The Journey*'s press package, entitled: *El Viaje: La Aventura de Ser Joven*, 19.

8. Solanas wrote the music and the lyrics of two tangos performed in the film: "Tango, Tango" and "Solo." He wrote the lyrics for three other tango numbers: "Hijos del Exilio," "Los Tangos del Exilio de Gardel," and "Vals del Regreso." In addition, he acted in the film as the character named Angel.

9. The result of Varda's trip to Iran was an additional short film (six minutes long), *Palisir d'amour en Iran* (1976), which features Pauline and her Iranian lover in an affectionate tribute to Iranian mosque and house architecture.

10. For more on Varda, see Wakeman 1988; Gussow 1997.

11. For examples, see the following films (distributed by Women Make Movies): Neesha Dosanjh's *Beyond/Body/Memory* (1993), Frances Negrón-Muntaner's *Bricando El Charco: Portrait of a Puerto Rican* (1994), Michelle Mohabeer's *Coconut/Cane & Cutlass* (1994), Pratibha Parmar's *Flesh and Paper* (1990) and *Khush* (1991), Prem Kalliat's *Jareena, Portrait of a Hijda* (1990), Noski Deville's *Loss of Heat*, Susana Muñoz's *Susana* (1980), and Meena Nanji's *Voices of the Morning* (1992).

12. For more on Akerman's films, see Mayne 1990; McRobbie 1993; Rosenbaum 1983a; Walker Art Center 1995. In addition to *News from Home* and *Je Tu Il Elle*, Akerman's other epistolary films include *Lettre d'un Cinéaste* (*Letter from a Filmmaker*, 1984), and *Letters Home* (1986).

13. The structure of some epistolary films, such as Marker's *Sunless*, is not only palimpsestical and serial but also rhizomatic—a topic that is worth further exploration.

14. See also Masri and Chamoun's *Under the Rubble* (1983), about the siege of Lebanon, including the massacre of Palestinians at the Sabra and Chatilla refugee camps.

15. Erik Barnouw called the makers of these films "prosecutors" (1983), while Jay Leyda characterized the purpose of the films as "trial by document" (1964).

16. The film won the Best First Feature award at the Venice Film Festival.

17. For more on Suleiman and Salloum's films, see the following: Marks 1991; Salloum and Hankwitz 1996; Hankwitz 1995; Sandiford 1994/95; and Shohat and Stam 1994.

18. On the influence of oral narratives in African cinema, see Ukadike 1994; Diawara 1989; Malkmus and Armes 1991, 177–84; and Gabriel 1989a. For the influence of African oral tradition on African-American cinema, see Taylor 1988. On *Ceddo*'s collectivity, see Rosen 1993. On the griot in African cinema and on Sembene himself as a cinematic griot, see Pfaff 1984; Ukadike 1994. On Jean Rouch as a cinematic griot, see Stoller 1992.

19. Sometimes this interplay involves a postcolonial struggle over national identity by means of language that spans a filmmaker's career. That of Ousmane Sembene demonstrates the dynamics of such interplay. His first feature, *Black Girl*, was entirely in French. The next film, *The Money Order* (*Mandabi*, 1968), financed partly by Centre national de la cinématographie, was made in two, versions, French and Wolof. Since 1968, however, all his features—*Émitaï* (1972), *Xala* (1974), *Ceddo, Camp de Thiaroye* (1988), and *Guelwaar* (1993)—have employed Senegalese dialects and languages, such as Wolof and Diola.

20. In the United States, dubbing and subtitling of foreign films has created a paradoxical situation: distributors do not want to dub films into English because American audiences apparently do not appreciate the "lip-flapping" that results, and they do not want to subtitle foreign films because that automatically reduces the film's market. Hence, the preference for remaking popular foreign films as English-language films (Pristin 1986).

21. The hermeneutic density becomes apparent in Trinh's screenplay of *Surname Viet Given Name Nam*, which forced her to create an elaborate typeface and layout to

differentiate the sources of the spoken texts, the voices that speak the words, and the on-camera speakers (Trinh 1992).

22. Godard's deconstructive uses of graphic and calligraphic textuality since his landmark film *La Chinoise* (*The Chinese Girl*, 1967) are strategies that subvert the cinematic state of dominant cinema.

23. The official voice calls the internment camps "relocation centers," while the personal voice calls them "concentration camps."

24. Such a consoling bond is obtained in other daughter-films by the physical proximity of mothers and daughters. In one scene in Akerman's *Les Rendez-vous d'Anna* (1978), she and her mother lie together in a hotel bed. Akerman uses the occasion to confess to her lesbian affairs, and her mother advises her not to reveal the secret to her father. Onwurah's *The Body Beautiful*, too, is bracketed by scenes that show mother and daughter basking in such symbiosis.

25. This is based on the assumption that both sets of letters are "documentary," that is, they are real letters sent to the filmmakers by their mothers.

26. Freud also wrote about the telephone, but as a metaphor for transference (1953–74, 12:115–16).

27. In its treatment of simultaneity and multifocality, *Homage by Assassination* is exilic, while Jim Jarmusch's *Night on Earth* (1991) is transnational. The former is paralyzed by temporal disjuncture and split subjectivity, while the latter celebrates and appropriates time differences and multiple subjectivity.

28. Naderi named Tom Ryan after Tom Joad of John Steinbeck's *Grapes of Wrath*, who in the end walks off to an unknown destination (Anderson 1993). Modeling Steinbeck's novel, Naderi critiques the socioeconomic dislocation of urban America in the 1990s.

29. The genre of "black telephone" films, which emerged in Italy in the wake of neorealism, centered on the life of the lower classes and the problems of crime, honor, and emigration. It countered the "white telephone" films, an earlier genre of escapist melodramas and comedies about the upper classes (Dalle Vacche 1992).

30. ZDF, the German television network, which had given Egoyan $100,000 to make *Calendar*, required him to deliver the completed film in twelve months (MacInnis 1993).

31. Against this tight claustrophobic narrative grid, this hermetic and ambiguous system within which all the film's characters are trapped, the footage of churches and Armenian landscape provides an antidote of immensity, openness, and clarity (Brown 1994).

32. In many of Egoyan's films, video represents an absent, often an exilic, figure.

33. Two other letter-films are worth mentioning. *Kuch Nai* (1993) is about a journey by a member of the San Francisco Silt collective to India, from where he dispatched letters and super-8 footage to his colleagues in California. They in turn processed, rephotographed, slowed down, superimposed, and hand-colored the footage to create from India a highly visual but unrecognizably abstract India. Ilan Ziv's *Tango of Slaves* (1994) poses itself as a letter from the filmmaker to his two young daughters about their grandfather's experience of the Nazi era holocaust in Poland. Narrated by Ziv himself, the film begins with the Christie's auction of the 1941 Warsaw Ghetto photographs. Ziv tells his daughters that, sadly, he has only one photo of his prewar family. The film's basic problematic centers on this photograph and on its discourse on photography. On

the one hand, the filmmaker expresses deep regret for not having more records and photos of his family. On the other hand, he levels a strong criticism against both the Nazis for manipulating photographs of the Jews and the contemporary culture for reducing history to visual representation. The problem with this overly long film is its apparent unawareness of how it, too, is participating in this visual overinvestment and reductionism.

34. For a comprehensive source on Mekas's films, see James 1992. For Mekas's own "story," see Mekas 1991. For a collection of his early writings on film and film culture, see Mekas 1972. For an affectionate filmic "take" on Mekas, his modus operandi, and his films (including many clips from them), see Peter Sempel's *Jonas in the Desert* (1994), which Sempel characterized as "a documentary psychomusic film."

35. In Peter Sempel's *Jonas in the Desert*, Mekas passionately describes his efforts at turning the Anthology Film Archives into a "museum," of independent avant-garde cinema: "All museums are established and run by businessmen and millionaires or governments. But this museum is run by a poor poet. And it's built brick by brick, penny by penny, and it's taking us as long a time as it took for some of the Renaissance cathedrals to be built. But it will be built, I promise you that. It will be built like a poem."

36. Unlike the work of many exilic filmmakers, Mekas's films are generally monolingual: both their voice-overs and their titles are in English.

37. This storytelling approach is constitutive of Mekas's accented style, as he told me in an interview: "I don't want suspense, I want the audience to know what's coming" (Naficy 1995b).

38. One of Mekas's achievements is that his dogged resistance often counterbalances deep nostalgia. The resulting films, in Jonathan Rosenbaum's characterization, are not "texts of stalemate but of dialectical vision and live wire tension" (1983b, 115).

39. Mekas has said that *Lost, Lost, Lost* "describes the mood of a Displaced Person who hasn't yet forgotten the native country but hasn't gained a new one" (Film-Maker's Cooperative 1989, 364). In *I Had Nowhere to Go*, he asks: "Am I a Gypsy, a citizen of the world, an eternal D.P.?" (Mekas 1991, 328).

40. This is reflected in the critics' difficulty in naming Marker's filmmaking style. They have called his films "philosophical report," "essay film," "cultural documentary," and "deconstructed travelogue" (Quandt 1993). "Factography" might be another suitable label, a term that the Russian exile novelist Viktor Shklovsky applied to his own writing style (see Kauffman 1992, 14).

41. Marker has used this approach of posing as a traveler sending back letter-films in a number of films before and after *Letter from Siberia*, among them *Sunday in Bejing* (*Dimanche à Pékin*, 1955), *Description of a Struggle* (*Description d'un Combat*, 1960), *Cuba Si!* (1961), and *Sunless* (*Sans Soleil*, 1982).

42. For *Letter from Siberia*'s commentary, accompanied by many photographs and cartoons from the film, see Marker 1961.

43. The film is mute about this point, but Marker is a pseudonym for Christian François Bouche-Villeneuve, who has always been fond of complication, subterfuge, and disguise to the point of variously giving his place of birth as Ulan Bator (Mongolia), Bellville (an Arab quarter in Paris), and Neilly-sur-Seine, Paris (most probably the real place of his birth) (Wakeman 1988, 649; Quandt 1993b, 2).

44. In analyzing *Sunless*, Allan Casebier tells of a traditional Japanese diary form called *utanikki* in which a woman narrates the diary. Whether Marker adopted this form is open to speculation, but some of the characteristics of the Japanese diary form are uncannily similar to those in *Sunless* (Casebier 1988, 36).

45. For extended extracts of *Sunless*'s narration, see Marker 1984.

46. *Sunless* calls Hitchcock's *Vertigo* "raging impossible memory, insane memory."

47. For further analysis of Marker's editing style, in addition to Branigan 1992, see Rafferty 1993; Walsh 1989.

48. Edward Branigan calls *Sunless* a "hyperindex" (1992, 216).

Chapter Five

1. In time, these dyadic constructions of home and exile evolve and become more nuanced, and they may even be reversed. People who were previously unselfconscious about their place in the world often become ardent nationalists upon their exile, while others disavow all bonds or choose to form new webs of group affiliation. One of the privileges of exile is the freedom and opportunity to self-consciously construct one's place in the world.

2. Some exiles carry with them a sample of their homeland's earth as a reminder of their rootedness in the land. It is reputed that when Reza Shah Pahlavi of Iran and his son Mohammad Reza Shah were forced into exile (in 1940 and 1979, respectively), each carried with him a potful of the Iranian soil. Both died in exile. If one reads F. W. Murnau's *Nosferatu* (1922) as a tale of exile, with Dracula as an exilic figure (who carries the earth of his homeland, Transylvania, in his coffin on his mission to England), it becomes more poignant than horrific. As an exilic figure he can rest and find peace only on his home country's soil.

3. Reference to such icons of harmonious timelessness and boundlessness may produce in the wavering exiles a feeling of permanence and expansion—what Gaston Bachelard called "intimate immensity" (1969, 184). The production of such expansiveness may also be read as their attempt to counter the time-space compression resulting from globalization and deterritorialization.

4. Ana Thomas calls "dream realism" a style of telling stories that has roots in the Mayan culture (Insdorf 1984, 17).

5. Although Pelechian made *Seasons* in his homeland, Armenia, and under the Soviet Union's centralized system of funding and filmmaking, it is discussed here as an accented film insofar as it expresses the intense longing for Armenian nature, bucolic life, and tradition that characterize accented films. In addition, under the Soviets, Armenia was an occupied land, and its people lived in a sort of exile in situ.

6. A serious weakness of the film is that the mountain fulfills her prayer in too predictable a fashion.

7. Mountain films deeply affected the German exiles, particularly Siegfried Kracauer, who waxed eloquent about the films' depiction of the mountains in his famous "psychological history" of the German cinema (1947). He saw in the submission to the elemental forces of nature, which these films inscribed, an anticipation of mass submission of the Germans to the potent force of Nazism.

8. According to newspaper accounts, Turkey's government revoked his citizenship, although Ariç has not been told this officially. However, as he told me, the films in

which he had acted have been heavily edited to decrease his presence in them and to reduce the films' political import. All biographical and production information about Ariç and his exilic film is from an interview I conducted with him and his partner-wife, Christine Kernich (Naficy 1997b). I thank Christine for translating during the interview.

9. Ariç had this to say about the security of mountains and caves for the Kurds: "I did not do this cave scene because of intellectual consideration but on account of sentiments and intuition. Kurds are used to living in the mountains, mountains are part of our life, and we are comfortable there. For us mountains and caves are shelter" (Naficy 1997b).

10. The most notorious and ghastly of these operations was the gassing of the town of Halabjah on March 17–18, 1988. Hundreds of inhabitants, including many children, perished.

11. I thank Stella Grigorian for bringing this point to my attention.

12. Not only Ararat but the whole chain of the Caucasian mountains are beloved by Armenians and have inspired filmmakers, in particular Paradjanov. For a fascinating nonfiction film about Paradjanov and the importance of the Caucasus landscape in his art, see *Memories of the Caucausus (Kavkazskie Capriccio, 1991)*, directed by Georgii Vlasenko.

13. The distribution of Palestinians in the Middle East is as follows: Lebanon, 349,773; Syria, 342,507; Jordan, 1,328,768; West Bank, 524,207; and Gaza Strip, 700,789 (Jehl 1997: A11).

14. For an early important film on the refugee situation, see *Gaza Ghetto: Portrait of a Family, 1948–1984* (Pea Holmquist and Joan Mandel, 1984).

15. His feature documentary *Fertile Memory* (1981) is also about the land issue in Israel, focusing on a widow whose land has been expropriated by Jews who plan to build a kibbutz on it. The film "constitutes the best study of the situation of women in the occupied Palestine" (Elena 1993, 242).

16. The film is taking historical license here. Palestinian villages within Israel are not under military occupation, but those in the Occupied Territories have been.

17. However, in Farida Ben Layazid's fiction film *A Door to the Sky* (1989) and Jennifer Fox's feature documentary *Beirut: The Last Home Movie* (1988), the house serves primarily to reterritorialize female returnees from exile.

18. For more on the meanings of house, home, and homeland in contemporary times and the media's role in their construction, see Naficy 1999.

19. According to Al Haq, a Palestinian human rights group in the West Bank, the Israeli army has demolished 564 houses of suspects since 1980 and sealed 475 others, either completely or in part (Haberman 1995, 3).

20. For the latest example of this policy in the Har Homa/Jabal abu Ghneim section of East Jerusalem, see Miller 1997, A6.

21. A film that provides an important discourse on the meaning of homeplace for African-Americans is Charles Burnett's fascinating but undervalued *To Sleep with Anger* (1990), in which homeplace for urban blacks is considered to be not only the home in which they live here and now (in South Central Los Angeles) but also the living and disturbing memories of the South, which haunt the émigrés and their descendants from the South.

22. Tarkovsky's words about his mother when he was making *Mirror* demonstrate her powerful hold on him: "I cannot reconcile myself to the thought that my mother will ever die. I will protest and shout that she is immortal. I want to convince others of her individuality and uniqueness" (quoted in Turovskaya 1989, 61).

23. For example, he was able to reshoot most of *Stalker* (1979), either because the film's negative had accidentally been destroyed in a lab (Mitchell 1986–87, 103) or because he was dissatisfied with the cameraman (Christie 1989, x).

24. This latter charge refers to the alleged role that the conservative Soviet director Sergei Bondarchuck played as a jury member in preventing *Nostalgia* from receiving the Grand Prix at Cannes International Film Festival in 1983.

25. Tarkovsky dedicated *Nostalgia* to the memory of his mother, who "gave me everything that we probably won't manage to give our children, namely a severity and moral strictness towards ourselves and others" (quoted in Mitchell 1986–87, 105).

26. The musician returned to Russia, became an alcoholic, and eventually committed suicide. Return is thus ruled out, leaving quest and exile as the twin conditions of contemporary existence.

27. In a symbolic reading, the motel, with its four walls looking onto an enclosed yard, can be regarded as the Ark, while Noah can be taken as the prophet Noah. His sexual relations with the inhabitants, however, subvert the religious narrative. This reading brings up a national connection as well, for it is widely believed that Noah's Ark landed on Mount Ararat, the symbol of Armenian national identity.

28. Atilla Dorsay made this remark during the conference "Images of the East in Western Films," Hawaii International Film Festival, December 1992. A similar point is made by Basutcu 1992–93.

29. Likewise, in *A Season in Hakkâri* (1983), made by exile director Erden Kiral, the chronotope of Turkish nature and rural life during harsh winter is one not of an idyll but of a prison (Cullingworth 1984).

30. Kurds in Turkey form some 12 million of a total population of 65 million, roughly one-fifth of the country's population (Bohlen 1995, 9). Turkey's government has refused to accept Kurdish ethnic identity and has closed Kurdish newspapers, banned the use of Kurdish language in public places and media, jailed Kurdish politicians, and murdered hundreds of Kurdish civilians by death squads—leaving the radical Marxist Kurdish Workers Party (PKK) as the only alternative for representing Kurdish national aspiration (Kinzer 1997a).

31. These government tactics continued even under the elected, nonmilitary regimes in recent years. In 1994, some 13,000 Kurds fled from southeastern Turkey after the army either forced them out of their villages or burned them. The antigovernment Kurdish guerrilla war has killed 15,000 between 1985 and 1995 alone (Hedges 1995, A6).

32. Once Güney was stripped of his citizenship, his films (even those made in Turkey before his exile) were considered foreign imports and had to be officially approved as such for exhibition within Turkey. Attempts by leftist and pro-Kurdish organizations to gain permission to "import" them were denied by the Ministry of Culture for years until an appeal to the Supreme Administrative Court removed the prohibition on *Umut* in the early 1990s ("Hope Deferred," *Index on Censorship* 3 [1991]: 11). The ban on *Yol* was lifted in 1992, but the film was screened publicly in a dozen theaters in Istanbul only years later, in February 1999, to enthusiastic crowds.

33. From an interview with Yilmaz Güney, included in the press packet for *The Wall*, distributed by Kino International Corporation, 2.

34. An example that ties closed spatiality to exilic performing arts and to queer sensibilities and politics is the confrontational performance of Turkish-German-American choreographer Mehmet Memo Sander, who called himself "HIV⁺ and Queer choreographer from Istanbul" (Segal 1992, 52). He constructed relentlessly oppressive and claustrophobic physical processes and spaces, release from which tested his own and his dancers' endurance, even survival skills. His performances may symbolize the trauma of coming out of ethnic enclaves and homosexual closets. Being inside the closet or coming out of the closet entails and unleashes claustrophobic and agoraphobic spatialities and, as Eve Sedgwick has noted, certain "performative work" (1990, 3–4). Another example that shows that closed spatiality is limited neither to the exilic cinema nor to heterosexual women nor to Turkish artists is the powerful theatrical performance of the Iranian-American director Reza Abdoh, who died of AIDS in the mid-1990s. In one of his last confrontational productions, *Bogeyman* (1993), the audience witnessed through the windows of a three-story apartment house violent discussions and activities among various gay and other sexually "transgressive" people. Soon the entire front of the building was lifted away to reveal the disturbing interiors of these small confining worlds. What came across strongly was the explosive desire to break out of the socially defined spatial, gendered, and sexual categories and roles. The lifting of the building's facade could be read as a metaphor for coming out of the closet to face and to expose oneself to a hostile homophobic world. A film that astutely ties agoraphobia, claustrophobia, "closetedness," and commodification is *Agora* (1992), directed by two gay brothers, Robert and Donald Kinney, about a gay agoraphobe who is paralyzed by fear of being found out. His agoraphobia is engendered not only by fear of the public spaces, or fear of coming out, but also by the relentless advertising that surrounds him.

Chapter Six

1. Losey's prophetic remaking of *M* in the 1950s America turned out to be a protoexilic film for him, in the same way that the original 1931 version of *M* was a protoexilic film for Fritz Lang in Germany. Both films anticipated, even perhaps expedited, the exile of their respective directors (Dimemberg 1997, 22).

2. This siege configuration in the Israeli cinema, which is based on the Israelis' real fears and anxieties, has evolved over the years with the fluctuation of the Israeli-Arab and Israeli-Palestinian conflicts. Significantly, however, its inscription in the liberal-leftist films of the 1980s, for example, in Uri Barabash's *Beyond the Walls* (*MeAkhorei baSoragim*, 1984) and Shimon Dotan's *The Smile of the Lamb* (*Khiukh BaGdi*, 1986), often served not to repel but to promote Israeli-Palestinian reconciliation, turning the Massada syndrome on its head. On the politics of Israeli cinema, see Shohat 1989; Kronish 1996; and Ben-Shaul 1997.

3. In many of his early films, Greek-born French director Constantin Costa-Gavras has exposed and protested such bureaucratization and militarization.

4. Television played an instrumental role in this nation-building task. Since 1994, a Kurdish satellite channel in England, MED-TV, which was sympathetic to PKK and its nationalistic project, aired Kurdish-language programs, projecting across Europe and into Turkey not only a diasporic Kurdish identity but also a pan-Kurdish national iden-

tity. In the process, it caused diplomatic tensions between Britain and Turkey, which caused its closure in the late 1990s. For more on MED-TV and Kurdish media cultures, see Hassanpour 1995, 1996.

5. On nationalist Kurds' anti-Turkish violence in Germany, see Cowell 1995; A1 and Chapin 1996.

6. The Turkish dialogue is translated into English from the film's German subtitles. I thank Gudrun Klein for translating.

7. For a history of the representation of physical disability in cinema, see Norden 1994.

8. This is a reference to *Lotte H. Eisner's Long Vacation* (*Die Langen Ferien der Lotte H. Eisner*, 1979), Shahid Saless's affectionate film about the Jewish German film scholar who, upon leaving Nazi Germany by train for a permanent French exile, had declared that she was going on a long vacation.

9. Quoted in the film's publicity package, without date or page number.

10. The claustrophobic overcrowding of dwelling places is both a reality of émigré life and a theme in the accented cinema. A recent example is Udayan Prasad's *Brothers in Trouble* (1997), about a young Pakistani immigrant in London who is crammed into a dingy house with seventeen other Pakistani "illegals" who huddle together in fear of being discovered and deported. The film depicts powerfully the claustrophobic and panic-stricken atmosphere of the house.

11. As he said to me, "I saw my mother only once, in Austria, when I was eighteen years old, and we ended up having a fight" (Naficy 1997f).

12. According to Shahid Saless, the income from these films' residuals largely sustained him and his stepmother in the United States in the 1990s.

13. He told me that he removed his name from *Hans—A Boy from Germany* (*Hans—Ein Junge in Deutscheland*, 1983) because of the producers' demand that he shorten the three-and-a-half-hour film. He refused. The film was broadcast without his name, until four years later when he finally shortened the film to his liking and allowed his name to be used (Naficy 1997f).

14. Although his latest films, particularly *Roses for Africa*, show some stylistic changes in terms of faster pacing, they are still recognizable as his works because of what he calls his individual "handwriting" (*dastkhat*) (Naficy 1997f). It is this handwriting, or signature, that gives his films not only a Shahid Salessian but also an exilic accent.

15. There is only one book chapter about him in German, one monograph in French, and in the half dozen books in English on the new German cinema, he garners only brief mentions. For German sources, see Erenz 1988; Netenjakob 1994; for French sources, see McMullin 1983; Schneider 1990; for English sources, see Shahid Saless 1988, 1993; *German Film* (October 1979); and *Film International* (summer 1998); and for Persian sources, see *Kelk* 1992; Dehbashi 1992, 1999; Ruhani 1992; and *Mahnameh-ye Sinemai-ye Film* (August 1998/20 Tir 1377).

16. Another critical exilic filmmaker who made many of his films in Germany is Romanian-German Harun Farocki, whose works have been widely acclaimed. However, his critical films are stylistically very different from Shahid Saless's. Focusing on various topics, from photography and surveillance to social turmoil and revolutions in Europe, many of them are nonfictional, essayistic films that cross generic and typological boundaries. For more on Farocki's works, see Silverman 1993; Farocki 1993; Kratzer-Juilfs 1996.

17. Its URL is http://www.thesync.com/ram/walls28.ram.

18. For more on Snow's art and cinema, see Monk et al. 1994; Shedden 1995; Mac-Donald 1993.

19. For example, in *Magdalena Viraga: Story of a Red Sea Crossing* (1986), the prostitute protagonist has sex with nine different men in nine very long takes of her face only, and there is a seventeen-minute sequence of relentless card dealing in *Queen of Diamonds* (1990).

20. For Ivens's life and films, see Ivens 1974; Delmar 1979; Thomas 1990; Barnouw 1983; and Gelly 1989.

21. Ivens's passport was officially restored in 1985 when he was made an honorable citizen of his birth town and his career was celebrated with a huge retrospective (Silcock 1988, 41).

22. Another film by a First World filmmaker that documents and embodies the winds of a Third World country is Albert Lamoriss's celebrated *A Lovers' Wind* (*Bad-e Saba*, 1969). It dramatizes the Iranian landscape from the points of view of the various winds that according to folklore inhabit the land. Over 80 percent of this visually stunning feature-length film is shot from a roving helicopter, with a first-person voice-over narration that personifies the winds even further. Lamoriss was killed in a helicopter crash in Iran while completing an addendum to the film.

23. Hassan Hosseini-Kaladjahi, in his comparative study of the émigré populations in Sweden (Chileans, Finns, Iranians, and Poles), shows that the low international status of originating countries and their cultural distance from the receiving countries negatively impacts the acculturation of their émigrés (1997).

Chapter Seven

1. His brother Adolfas Mekas made his own return film, called *Going Home* (1971).

2. Among Brazilian films that narrativize the African slaves' escape to create maroon communities in Brazil or their desire to return to the African motherland are Carlos Diegues's *Ganga Zumba* (1963) and *Quilombo* (1984) and Raquel Gerber's *Orí* (1988).

3. Many scenes exemplify the meliorative properties of return. In one, Mekas tastes the water from his mother's well, which elicits this voice-over remark: "We went to the well to drink some water, the water that tastes like no other water. O cool water of Semeniskiai, no wine ever tasted better anywhere." In another, he visits his old schoolhouse and a friend's farm, eliciting the following comment: "Where are you now my old childhood friends? How many of you are around? Where are you scattered through the graveyards, through the torture rooms, through the prisons, through the labor camps of the Western civilization? But I see your faces just like they used to be. They never change in my memory. They remain young. It's me who is getting older."

4. *Chronicle of a Disappearance* won the Best First Feature Award at the Venice International Film Festival in 1997.

5. A letter also lures a Turkish worker in Shahid Saless's *Far from Home* (1975) into an unwanted return home.

6. In the aftermath of recent, creeping fragmentation and deterritorialization, the border places have become a sort of last-resort semipermanent home for the homeless. In urban centers, homeless people have traditionally found shelter in doorways, subways, train stations, and bus depots. Airports have been less used, perhaps because of

their distance from city centers. However, JFK International Airport in New York has had a history of homeless people living in its vast, cavernous spaces, some for as long as four years (Holloway 1995).

Occasionally, because of legal and other complications, airports have become the abode of international homeless, or stateless, persons. One of the most remarkable recent cases is that of Mehran Karimi Nasseri, a fifty-six-year-old man from Iran, who has lived in the Charles de Gaulle Airport in Paris since the late 1980s (Valente 1994). The reasons were many, but, in a nutshell, he had no real home because he disavowed his Iranian nationality, and no other nation recognized him as its subject. Caught in a twilight zone, he has lived for twelve years (so far) out of suitcases and has been fed and clothed by airport and airline personnel and passengers, who consider him a man of honesty and dignity. During this time he became the darling of some members of the American and European print and broadcasting media, who were sympathetic and intrigued by his liminal situation and sensationalized his story.

However, as Hamid Rahimian's documentary film *Sir Alfred* (2000) shows, Nassiri, who has changed his name to Sir Alfred Mehran, is far from a victim of international bureaucratic mistake or insensitivity. Among other things, he appears to be ashamed of his Iranian background, blaming Iran for all his troubles, and is determined to erase all traces of it by engaging in various games of ethnic camouflage, denial, and passing. When in 1999 Belgium confirmed that it had granted Alfred a refugee card and France gave him an international residency permit and a French residency, he refused both because they listed him as an Iranian ("Alfred Not Leaving the Airport," *Iran Times*, September 24, 1999, 1). Like many characters in the accented films, such as the prostitutes in Shahid Saless's *Utopia* who feel more safe in their claustrophobic spaces and are reluctant to leave them, Alfred has so far refused to leave the airport now that he can. According to the airport's medical director, "He is scared to leave this bubble world he has been living in. Finally getting the papers has been a huge shock to him, as if he was just thrown from his horse" (Daley 1999, A4).

7. Charles Chaplin's *The Immigrant* (1917) was an arrival film that took a critical jab at the treatment of immigrants. A deep fear most immigrants shared was arriving at a strange port without having someone to meeting them. *Adrift in a Great City* (1914) shows how the failure of an immigrant to meet up with his wife and daughter forces them to beg to survive.

8. One such film, *Emigranten* (1910), shows how the dream of plenitude in America causes a farmer and his wife to undertake a difficult journey, only to receive a barren piece of land instead of a lush farm. Deeply disappointed, they pack their belongings and return home (Brownlow 1990, 304–7).

9. Iglesias also reported that between 1936 and 1996 a total of 300 border films were made in Mexico (1998).

10. These are based on Iglesias's formulation, quoted in Fregoso (1999, 189–90), which I have modified considerably.

11. *Newsweek* quoted a border patrol agent who called the United States–Mexican border "a war zone, nothing less" (July 7, 1997, 8). On militarization of borders, also see Dillon 1996.

12. Among the celebrated non-Chicano border films are Orson Welles's *Touch of Evil* (1958), Sam Peckinpah's *The Wild Bunch* (1969), Tony Richardson's *The Border* (1982), and John Sayles's *Lone Star* (1996).

13. Tunnels and tunneling are regularly featured in prison escape films. Of the films that combine tunneling with the escape of refugees, *The Tunnel* is noteworthy. Produced by Reuven Frank for NBC News, and aired in 1962, the documentary focused on East German dissidents who dug a tunnel under the Berlin Wall to escape to West Berlin.

14. *The Runner* was made during the eight-year Iran-Iraq war, after the port city of Abadan fell to the Iraqi forces. Consequently, as he told me in an interview, Naderi had to shoot the film in eleven different locations near the war zone, where the crew could hear gunfire and bombing in the distance. He edited the footage seamlessly to give the impression of a single location (Naficy 1996d).

15. For a description of Naderi's films and career in English, see Golmakani 1993. For an extensive anthology of essays on his works, see Haidari 1991.

16. For more on the dynamics of the "veiled look" or "averted look" in cinema, see Naficy 1994.

17. After the success of *Lolita*, Nabakov lived with his wife in a penthouse suite of the luxurious Montreux Palace Hotel, overlooking Lake Geneva, where he died. FM-2030 (aka F. M. Esfandiari), who advocates transhumanism, prefers large hotels, since for him houses are too domestic and claustrophobic (Raffat 1994, 34).

18. Rafigh Pooya incorporated a great deal of this show trial's footage into his documentary *In Defense of People* (*Dar Defa' az Mardom*, 1981). Pooya also produced Allamehzadeh's *The Guests of Hotel Astoria*.

19. The biographical information about Allamehzadeh's postrevolutionary film activities is from my interview with him (Naficy 1988).

20. These include *Death to Imperialism* (*Marg bar Amperialism*, 1979–80) and *From Dust to Dust* (*Ba Khak Ta Khak*, 1980?).

21. Zahedi has said that his mother "would never consent" to being in the film (Skyler 1994, 9).

22. Zahedi has exaggerated these technical failures to enhance the film's drama (Mordler 1994, 41).

23. As Zahedi told me, two other factors in addition to this film contributed to his ethnic realignment toward Iranian culture: his exposure to recent Iranian cinema, particularly to Abbas Kiarostami's films, which deal with a similar blurring of documentary and fictional boundaries, and his reading of the mystic poetry of the Persian Sufi poet Mowlana Jalal Al-Din Rumi (Naficy 1997g).

24. Similar to Güney's *Yol*, Sayyad's protoexilic *Dead-End* was completed a year before his exile. The film posits the Iranian society under Shah Mohammad Reza Pahlavi as a prison, whose inhabitants are under constant police surveillance. It centers on the story of a young woman who is pursued by a man she thinks is a suitor but who turns out to be a security agent tailing her brother. Watching from her window overlooking the cul-de-sac, she misreads with disastrous consequences the surveying gaze of the state police as the desirous look of a potential suitor. The film's structure of confinement is both national and gendered. While her window promises freedom, the cul-de-sac suggests an obstacle to freedom (Akrami 1987, 147).

25. Spike Lee's *Get on the Bus* (1996) is a refreshing counternarrative to Sayyad's film. It uses the bus ride of some twenty African-Americans from South Central Los Angeles to Washington, D.C., to participate in the 1995 "Million Man March," organized by the Nation of Islam, as an occasion and a vehicle with which to turn weakness into empowerment and polarity into plurality. He explores many aspects of Jewish and

African-American, black and white, and black and black politics. He also creates a number of well-rounded figures who are moved by personal convictions and are transformed by their own experiences of riding on the bus. In this way, unlike Sayyad but like Zahedi, Lee succeeds in turning the forced association of disparate people in the vehicle's enclosed space into an expansive space of discourse and understanding.

26. In February 1997, French protesters against a proposal limiting immigration carried suitcases to symbolize the expulsion of the immigrants that the law would bring about.

27. Personal correspondence from Mitra Tabrizian, November 11, 1997.

28. Such performance strategies include veiling and unveiling (Naficy 1994), masking (Fanon 1967), masquerading (Doan 1982, 1988; Holmlund 1993), drag (Butler 1990a, 1990b), camp (Newton 1972; Sontag 1982) haggling (Naficy 1993a), cleverness and guile (Beeman 1986), sly civility, mimicry, and hybridity (Bhabha 1994), and performativity (Butler 1990a, 1990b; Dyer 1979).

29. These include Fyodor Dostoevsky in *The Double* (1866), Robert Lewis Stevenson in *The Strange Case of Dr. Jekyl and Mr. Hyde* (1886), Oscar Wilde in *The Picture of Dorian Gray* (1890), Mark Twain in *Pudd'nhead Wilson* (1894), Joseph Conrad in *Secret Sharer* (1912), Franz Kafka in *Metamorphosis* (1946), Vladimir Nabakov in *Despair* (1932) and *Lolita* (1954), and Sadegh Hedayat in *The Blind Owl* (1937).

30. Krzysztof Kieslowski's *The Double Life of Véronique* (*La Double vie de Véronique*, 1991), filmed in Poland and France, contains two characters (Weronika and Véronique, respectively) who are each other's doubles without knowing one another. However, they are in touch, as Kieslowski states, by means of "intuition," "presentiment," and "sensibility" (quoted in Stok 1993, 173). These methods of communication, of being in touch, are part of the tactile optic of exile.

31. Woody Allen's *Zelig* (1983), about a chameleon-like Jew named Zelig, provides an insightful, if flawed, treatment of ethnically driven doubling and duplicity.

32. This is also true of the various adjusters in *The Adjuster*.

33. For more elaboration on this type of self-othering by Iranian exile filmmakers, entertainers, and wrestlers, see Naficy 1997h, 1995d, 1993c.

34. For more on why the Chilean cinema in exile did not become a movement, see Pick 1987.

35. In the way it deflated the regime of the Chilean junta, Littín's *General Statement on Chile* is similar to Constantin Costa-Gavras's influential film *Z* (1969), which mocked and exposed the ruthless regime of the Greek generals in his home country.

36. Egoyan made an affectionate short film (4½ minutes) about his son, *A Portrait of Arshile* (1995), in which he and his wife provide the bilingual Armenian and English voice-over narration, which addresses Arshile. Named after the great Armenian painter Arshile Gorky, whose mother died in his lap when he was fifteen, the film repeatedly reminds the child of his namesake—his double!

Bibliography

Abrash, Barbara, and Catherine Egan. 1992. *Mediating History: The Map Guide to Independent Video by and about African American, Asian American, Latino, and Native American People.* New York: New York University Press.

Affron, Charles. 1982. *Cinema and Sentiment.* Chicago: University of Chicago Press.

Ahmad, Aijaz. 1994. *In Theory: Classes, Nations, Literatures.* New York: Verso.

Akomfrah, John, et al. 1988. "An Interview with Black Audio Film Collective." *ICA Documents,* no. 7: 60–62. [Special issue on black film, British cinema].

Akrami, Jamsheed. 1987. "The Blighted Spring: Iranian Cinema and Politics in the 1970s." In *Film and Politics in the Third World,* edited by John D. H. Downing. 131–44. New York: Praeger.

Al-Ariss, Ibrahim. 1996. "An Attempt at Reading the History of Cinema in Lebanon: From Cinema to Society and Vice Versa." In *Screens of Life: Critical Film Writing from the Arab World.* Vol. 1, edited and translated by Alia Arasoughly, 19–39. Quebec: World Heritage Press.

Alekseychuk, Leonid. 1990–91. "A Warrior in the Field." *Sight and Sound* 60, no. 1: 22–26.

Alexander, Livia. 1995. "Wedding in Galilee." Unpublished paper.

Allamehzadeh, Reza. 1991. *Sarab-e Sinema-ye Eslami-ye Iran.* Saarbrücken, Germany: Nawid Verlag und Offsetdruck.

Allen, Robert C., and Douglas Gomery. 1985. *Film History: Theory and Practice.* New York: Knopf.

Altman, Janet Gurkin. 1982. *Epistolarity: Approaches to a Form.* Columbus: Ohio State University Press.

Altman, Rick. 1989. *The American Film Musical.* Bloomington: Indiana University Press.

Anderson, Benedict. 1983. *Imagined Communities.* London: Verso.

Anderson, John. 1993. "He'll Take Manhattan," *New York Newsday,* March 19.

Andrew, Dudley. 1995. *Mists of Regret: Culture and Sensibility in Classic French Cinema.* Princeton, N.J.: University of Princeton Press.

Ansen, David. 1992. "A Holiday from Hype." *Newsweek,* June 29, 64.

———. 1984. "Homeless on the Range." *Newsweek,* November 19, 132.

Anyidoho, Kofi. 1997. "Prison as Exile/Exile as Prison." In *The Word Behind Bars and the Paradox of Exile,* edited by Kofi Anyiodo, 1–17. Evanston, Ill.: Northwestern University Press.

Anzaldúa, Gloria. 1987. *Borderlands/La Frontera: The New Mestiza.* San Francisco: Spinsters.

Appadurai, Arjun. 1996. *Modernity at Large: Cultural Dimensions of Globalization.* Minneapolis: University of Minnesota Press.

Arasoughly, Alia, ed. and trans. 1996. *Screens of Life: Critical Film Writing from the Arab World.* Vol. 1. Quebec: World Heritage Press.

Aresu, Bernard. 1992. *Substance,* no. 69. [Special issue entitled "Translations of the Orient: Writing the Maghreb."]

Armes, Roy. 1996. *Dictionary of North African Film Makers.* Paris: Editions ATM.

———. 1987. *Third World Film-Making and the West.* Berkeley: University of California Press.

Armstrong, Toni, Jr., and Dell Richards. 1992. "The Little Feminist Idea That Could: Women Make Movies." *Hot Wire,* May, 22–24.

Aronson, Sydney H. 1977. "Bell's Electrical Toy: What's the Use? The Sociology of Early Telephone Usage." In *The Social Impact of the Telephone,* edited by Ithiel de Sola Pool, 1–39. Cambridge, Mass.: MIT Press.

———. 1971. "The Sociology of the Telephone." *International Journal of Comparative Sociology* 12, no. 3: 153–67.

Arroyo, José. 1991. "The Films of Isaac Julien Look Back and Talk Back," *Jump Cut,* no. 36: 98–108.

Asher, R. E. ed. 1994. *The Encyclopedia of Language and Linguistics.* Vol. 1. New York: Pergamon Press.

Astruc, Alexander. 1968. "The Birth of a New Avant-Garde: La Caméra Stylo." in *The New Wave: Critical Landmarks,* edited by Peter Graham, 17–23. New York: Doubleday.

Atamian, Christopher. 1991. "Emotion in Fast Forward: For Filmmaker Atom Egoyan, It's Veni, Video, Vici." *AIM,* August–September, 70.

Attille, Martina. 1988. "*The Passion of Remembrance*: Background." *ICA Documents,* no. 7: 53–54. [Special issue on black film, British cinema.]

Attille, Martina, et al. 1988. "Interview with Sankofa Film Collective," *ICA Documents,* no. 7: 55–57. [Special issue on black film, British cinema.]

Aukin, David. 1996. "Channel Four's Policy toward Film." In *Big Picture, Small Screen: The Relations between Film and Television,* edited by John Hill and Martin McLoone, 183. Luton, Bedfordshire, UK: John Libbey Media/University of Luton.

Austin, David F. 1990. *What's the Meaning of "This"? A Puzzle about Demonstrative Belief.* Ithaca, N.Y.: Cornell University Press.

L'Avant Scène Cinéma 372 (June): 1988. [Special issue on Michel Khleifi's film *Wedding in Galilée.*]

Bachelard, Gaston. 1969. *The Poetics of Space.* Trans. Maria Jolas. Boston: Beacon Press.

Baert, Renee. 1993. "Desiring Daughters." *Screen* 34, no. 2:109–23.

Bahloul, Joëlle. 1996. *The Architecture of Memory: A Jewish-Muslim Household in Colonial Algeria, 1937–1962.* Trans. Catherine Du Perloux Ménagé. New York: Cambridge University Press.

Bakhtin, Mikhail. 1981. *The Dialogic Imagination: Four Essays.* Ed. Michael Holquist. Trans. Caryl Emerson and Michael Holquist. Austin: University of Texas Press.

Ball, Donald W. 1968. "Toward a Sociology of Telephones and Telephoners." In *Sociology and Everyday Life,* edited by Marcello Truzzi, 59–75. Englewood Cliffs, N.J.: Prentice-Hall.

Balley, Cameron. 1989. "Scanning Egoyan." *CineAction,* spring, 45–51.

Barnouw, Erik. 1983. *Documentary: A History of the Non-fiction Film.* New York: Oxford University Press.

Barsam, Richard M. 1992. *Nonfiction Film: A Critical History.* Revised and expanded. Bloomington: Indiana University Press.

Barthes, Roland. 1978. *A Lover's Discourse: Fragments.* Trans. Richard Howard. New York: Hill and Wang.

————. 1977. *Image, Music, Text.* Trans. Stephen Heath. New York: Hill and Wang.

————. 1975. *The Pleasure of the Text.* Trans. Richard Miller. New York: Hill and Wang.

————. 1974. *S/Z: An Essay.* Trans. Richard Miller. New York: Hill and Wang.

Basutcu, Mehmet. 1992–93. "The Power and Danger of the Image." *Cinemaya*, nos. 17–18: 16–19.

Battegay, Alain, and Ahmed Boubeker. 1993. *Les Images publiques de l'immigration: Média, actualité, immigration dans la France des années 80.* Paris: Éditions L'Harmattan.

Bauman, Zygmunt. 1991. "Modernity and Ambivalence." In *Global Culture: Nationalism, Globalization and Modernity,* edited by Mike Featherstone, 143–69. London: Sage.

Bazin, André. 1973. *Jean Renoir.* Ed. François Truffaut. Trans. W. W. Halsey II and William H. Simon. New York: Delta Books.

Bazter, John. 1976. *The Hollywood Exiles.* New York: Taplinger.

Bear, Liza. 1995. "Berlin to Paris, with an All-Important Stopover in Brooklyn." *New York Times,* July 9, H16.

Beeman, William O. 1986. *Language, Status, and Power in Iran.* Bloomington: Indiana University Press.

Benjamin, Walter. 1978. "The Author as Producer." *In Reflections: Essays, Aphorisms, Autobiographical Writings,* 220–38. Trans. Edmund Jephcott. New York: Schocken Books.

Ben-Shaul, Nitzan S. 1997. *Mythical Expressions of Siege in Israeli Films.* Lampeter, Wales: Edwin Mellen Press.

Benson, Sheila. 1995. "Chinese but Not Chinese, and Revealing the Difference." *New York Times,* July 23, H18.

Bernard, Jami. 1989. "Moslem Mayhem Manhattan-Style." *New York Post,* May 17.

Bernbaum, Edwin. 1990. *Sacred Mountains of the World.* San Francisco: Sierra Club Books.

Bernstein, Mathew. 1993. "Hollywood's Semi-independent Production." *Cinema Journal* 32, no. 3:41–54.

Bhabha, Homi K. 1994. *The Location of Culture.* London: Routledge.

————. 1989. "The Commitment to Theory." In *Questions of Third Cinema,* edited by Jim Pines and Paul Willemen, 111–32. British Film Institute.

Bhabha, Homi K., Paul Gilroy, and Stuart Hall. 1991. "Threatening Pleasures." *Sight and Sound,* n.s., 1, no. 4:17–19.

Bharucha, Rustom. 1989. "Haraam Bombay!" *Economic and Political Weekly,* June 10, 1275–79.

Blackwood, Maureen, and June Givanni. 1988. "Black Film-Making in Europe." *Screen* 29, no. 4: 114–18.

Bloom, Peter. 1999. "Beur Cinema and the Politics of Location: French Immigration Politics and the Naming of a Film Movement." *Social Identities* 5, no, 4:469–87.

————. 1995. "Locating Beur Cinema: Social Activism, Immigration Politics and the Naming of a Film Movement." Paper presented at the Tenth Triennial Symposium on African Art, New York University, New York, April.

Bloom, Peter. 1990. "Some Reflections on the Iranian Film Festival: 'A Decade of Iranian Cinema, 1980–1990.'" *Jusur* 6: 95–99.

Bodman, Ellen-Fairbanks, and Ronald L. Bartholomew. 1992. *Middle East and Islamic World Filmography*. Chapel Hill: University of North Carolina, Nonprint Materials Collection.

Boettinger, Henry M. 1977. "Our Sixth-and-a-Half Sense." In *The Social Impact of the Telephone*, edited by Ithiel de Sola Pool, 200–207. Cambridge, Mass.: MIT Press.

Bohlen, Celestine. 1995. "In Turkey, Open Discussion of Kurds is Casualty of Effort to Confront War." *New York Times*, October 29, 9.

Borau, José Luis. 1983. "Without Weapons." *Quarterly Review of Film Studies* 8, no. 2:85–90.

Bordo, Susan. 1993. *Unbearable Weight: Feminism, Western Culture, and the Body*. Berkeley: University of California Press.

Bordwell, David. 1989. *Making Meaning: Inference and Rhetoric in the Interpretation of Cinema*. Cambridge, Mass.: Harvard University Press.

———. 1997. *On the History of Film Style*. Cambridge, Mass.: Harvard University Press.

———. 1985. *Narration in the Fiction Film*. Madison: University of Wisconsin Press.

Bordwell, David, and Kristin Thompson. 1993. *Film Art: An Introduction*. 4th ed. New York: McGraw-Hill.

Bordwell, David, Janet Staiger, and Kristin Thompson. 1985. *The Classical Hollywood Cinema: Film Style and Mode of Production to 1960*. New York: Columbia University Press.

Bosséno, Christian. 1992. "Immigrant Cinema: National Cinema—the Case of Beur Film." In *Popular European Cinema*, edited by Richard Dyer and Ginnette Vicendeau, 47–57. London: Routledge.

———. 1982. " 'Le Garage,' 'Zone immigrée,' 'La mort de Kadar': Des film provocaterus." *CinémAction* 24: 128–31.

Boubeker, Ahmed, and Mongniss H. Abdallah. 1993. "*Douce France*: La Saga du Mouvement Beur, 1983–1993." *IM'média*, fall–winter. [Special issue is on *Douce France*.]

Bouquet, Stéphane. 1994. "Distribution: Le maillon faible." *Cahiers du Cinéma*, September. 45–53.

Bowser, Eileen. 1990. *The Transformation of Cinema, 1907–1915*. New York: Scribner's.

Bowser, Pearl, and Renee Tajima. 1985. *Journey across Three Continents*. New York: Third World Newsreel.

Bozorgmehr, Mehdi. 1997. "Iranians." In *Encyclopedia of American Immigration Cultures*, edited by David Levinson, 442–48. New York: Macmillan.

Bozorgmehr, Mehdi, Claudia Der-Martirosian, and Georges Sabagh. 1996. "Middle Easterners: A New Kind of Immigrant." In *Ethnic Los Angeles*, edited by Roger Waldinger and Mehdi Bozorgmehr, 345–78. New York: Russel Sage Foundation.

Bozorgmehr, Mehdi, and Georges Sabagh. 1991. "Iranian Exiles and Immigrants in Los Angeles." In *Iranian Refugees and Exiles since Khomeini*, edited by Asghar Fathi, 121–44. Costa Mesa, Calif: Mazda.

Brady, Shirley. 1993. "Atom Egoyan Out of the Margins." *Shift* 1, no. 4:10–13, 37.

Branigan, Edward. 1992. *Narrative Comprehension and Film*. London: Routledge.

———. 1984. *Point of View in the Cinema: A Theory of Narration and Subjectivity in Classical Film*. New York: Mouton.

Breslau, Karen. 1992. "Screening Out the Dark Past." *Newsweek*, February 3, 30.

Brooks, John. 1977. "The First and Only Century of Telephone Literature." In *The Social Impact of the Telephone*, edited by Ithiel de Sola Pool, 208–24. Cambridge, Mass.: MIT Press.

———. 1976. *Telephone: The First Hundred Years*. New York: Harper and Row.

Brooks, Linda. 1992. "Interview: Nina Menkes," *Art Papers* 16, no. 2:1–7.

Brossard, Jean-Pierre. N.d. "Dictionnaire des principaux cinéastes." In *L'Algérie vue par son cinéma*, 173–78. Locarno: Tisca Nova SA.

Brown, George. 1994. "Daily Bread." *Village Voice*, April 15.

Brownlow, Kevin. 1990. *Behind the Mask of Innocence*. New York: Knopf.

Buñuel, Luis. 1983. *My Last Sigh*. Trans. Abigail Israel. New York: Vintage.

Burgeson, Scott. 1994. "Zen and the Art of Movie Maintenance." *Art Brut* 2, no. 30.

Burgin, Victor. 1994. "Paranoiac Space." In *Visualizing Theory: Selected Essays from V.A.R., 1990–1994*, edited by Lucien Taylor, 230–41. New York: Routledge.

Burnett, Ron. 1995. *Cultures of Vision: Images, Media and the Imaginary*. Bloomington: Indiana University Press.

Burton, Julianne, ed. 1986. *Cinema and Social Change in Latin America: Conversations with Filmmakers*. Austin: University of Texas Press.

Butler, Judith. 1990a. *Gender Trouble: Feminism and the Subversion of Identity*. New York: Routledge.

———. 1990b. "Lana's 'Imitation': Melodramatic Repetition and the Gender Performative." *Gender*, no. 9: 1–18.

Cameron, Dan. 1997. "Boundary Issues." In *Mona Hatoum*, edited by Jessica Morgan, 25–46. Chicago: Museum of Contemporary Art.

Cameron, Ian. 1962. "I Am Writing to You from a Far Country. . . ." *Movie*, October, 14.

Canby, Vincent. 1993. "Staying Hot on the Trail of a Cooled Friend." *New York Times*, April 12.

Canoni, Rachel E., and Rebecca Hellerstein. 1994. "50 Years after Bretton Woods: What Is the Future for the International Monetary System? An Overview." *New England Economic Review*, July/August, 65–73.

CAPI Films Presents. N.d. *A Tale of the Wind by Joris Ivens and Marceline Loridan*. Paris, France: Capi Films. [Publicity package for the film.]

Carroll, Kathleen. 1989. "A Dark Comedy That Would Have Made Hitchcock Laugh." *Daily News*, May 17, 38.

Cartwright, Lisa. 1994. "Interview with Ngozi Onwurah." Unpublished manuscript.

Casebier, Allan. 1988. "A Deconstructive Documentary." *Journal of Film and Video* 40, no. 1:34–39.

Casson, Herbert N. 1910. *The History of the Telephone*. 3d ed. Chicago: A. C. McClurg.

Caughie, John, ed. 1981. *Theories of Authorship: A Reader*. London: Routledge and Kegan Paul.

Ceddo. 1986. "Ceddo Film-Video Workshop." In *Conference Speakers, Biographical Lists and Additional Biographical Material*. Edinburgh: Third Cinema: Theories and Practices Conference (August 11–13).

Cham, Mbye B. 1992. *Ex-Iles: Essays on Caribbean Cinema*. Trenton, N.J.: Africa World Press.

Chambers, Iain. 1994. *Migrancy, Culture, Identity*. London: Comedia.

Chambless, Diane L. 1982. "Characteristics of Agoraphobia." In *Agoraphobia: Multiple Perspectives on Theory and Treatment*, edited by Diane L. Chambless, and Alan J. Goldstein, 1–18. New York: Wiley.

Chanan, Michael. 1983. *Twenty-five Years of the New Latin American Cinema*. London: British Film Institute.

Chapin, Wesley D. 1996. "The Turkish Diaspora in Germany." *Diaspora* 5, no. 2:275–301.

Chen, David W. 1998. "Movie House, and an Era, Go Dark in Chinatown." *New York Times*, June 14, A1, A26.

Chen, Nancy N. 1992. " 'Speaking Nearby': A Conversation with Trinh T. Minh-ha." *Visual Anthropology Review* 8, no. 1: 82–91.

Christie, Ian. 1989. "Introduction: Tarkovsky and His Time." In *Tarkovsky: Cinema as Poetry*, edited by Ian Christi ix–xxvi. Trans. Maya Turovskaya and Natasha Ward. London: Faber and Faber.

Ciment, Michel. 1985. *Conversations with Losey*. London: Methuen.

CinémAction, no. 7. (n.d.). [Special issue: "Cinéma contre racisme."]

CinémAction, no. 8 (summer 1979). [Special issue: "Cinémas de l'émigration."]

CinémAction, no. 24 (n.d.). [Special issue: "Cinémas de l'émigration 3."]

CinémAction, no. 56 (n.d.). [Special issue: "Cinémas métis: De hollywood aux films beurs."]

CinémAction, no. 69 (1993). [Special issue: "Les Revues de cinéma dans le monde."]

Clifford, James. 1997. *Routes: Travel and Translation in the Late Twentieth Century*. Cambridge, Mass.: Harvard University Press.

Coan, Peter Morton, ed. 1997. *Ellis Island Interviews: In Their Own Words*. New York: Facts on File.

Cohen, Robin. 1997. *Global Diasporas: An Introduction*. London: UCL Press.

Cohen, Roger. 1999. "Germany Makes Citizenship Easier for Foreigners to Get." *New York Times*, May 22, A3.

Corliss, Richard. 1996. "Balloon Story." *Time*, February 12, 76.

Cotter, Holland. 1997. "Pangs of Exile and Lost Childhood." *New York Times*, December 5, B27.

Cowell, Alan. 1995. "Germans Fear Slipover of Conflict in Turkey." *New York Times*, March 27, A1, A4.

Cripps, Thomas. 1993a. *Making Movies Black: The Hollywood Message Movie from World War II to the Civil Rights Era*. New York: Oxford University Press.

———. 1993b. "Oscar Micheaux: The Story Continues." In *Black American Cinema*, edited by Manthia Diawara, 71–79. New York: Routledge.

———. 1988. " 'Race Movies' as Voices of the Black Bourgeoisie: *The Scar of Shame* (1927)." In *American History/American Film: Interpreting the Hollywood Image*, edited by John E. O'Connor and Martin A. Jackson, 39–56. Expanded edition. New York: Ungar.

———. 1978. *Black Film as Genre*. Bloomington: Indiana University Press.

———. 1977. *Slow Fade to Black*. New York: Oxford University Press.

Crump, Ted. 1991. "Westphal's Agoraphobia." *Journal of Anxiety Disorders*. 5:77–86.

Crusz, Robert. 1985. "Black Cinemas, Film Theory and Dependent Knowledge." *Screen*, 26 nos. 3–4:152–56.

Crystal, David. 1991. *A Dictionary of Linguistics and Phonetics*. 3d ed. New York: Blackwell.

Cullingworth, Michael. 1984. "Behind the Mountains." *Sight and Sound* 53, no. 3:208–10.

Dabashi, Hamid. 1993. "Introduction: Parviz Sayyad and His Theater for the Diaspora." In *Theater of Diaspora*, edited by Parviz Sayyad, xi–xxiv. Costa Mesa, Calif.: Mazda Publishers.

Daley, Suzanne. 1999. "11 Years Caged in an Airport; Now He Fears to Fly." *New York Times*, September 27, A4.

Dalle Vacche, Angela. 1992. *The Body in the Mirror: Shapes of History in Italian Cinema*. Princeton, N.J.: Princeton University Press.

Daws. 1991. "A Little Stiff." *Daily Variety*, June 24. 3.

Dayal, Samir. 1992. "The Subaltern Does Not Speak: Mira Nair's *Salaam Bombay!* as a Postcolonial Text." *Gender* 14 (fall): 16–32.

Dean, Peter. 1992. "Colonists and Pirates." *Sight and Sound*, n.s., 2, no. 3.

Dehbashi, Ali. 1999. *Yadnameh-ye Sohrab Shahid Saless*. Tehran: Nashr-e Shahab va Entesharat-e Sokhan.

———. 1992. "Goftogu ba Sohrab Shahid Saless." *Kelk* 40: 175–217.

Delaney, Marshall. 1985. "Ethnic Humor." *Saturday Night*, June, 53–54.

De las Carreras, Maria Elena. 1995. "'Contemporary Politics in Argentine Cinema, 1981–1991." Ph.D. diss., UCLA.

Deleuze, Gilles. 1992. "Postscript on the Societies of Control." *October*, no. 59 (winter): 3–7.

Deleuze, Gilles, and Félix Guattari. 1986. *Kafka: Toward a Minor Literature*. Trans. Dana Polan. Minneapolis: University of Minnesota Press.

Delmar, Rosalind, ed. 1979. *Joris Ivens: Fifty Yeas of Film-Making*. London: British Film Institute.

Dempsey, Michael. 1981. "Lost Harmony: Tarkovsky's *The Mirror* and *The Stalker*." *Film Quarterly* 35, no. 1:12–17.

Derrida, Jacques. 1981. *Writing and Difference*. London: Routledge.

———. 1980. *The Post Card: From Socrates to Freud and Beyond*. Trans. Alan Bass. Chicago: University of Chicago Press.

Desbarats, Carole, Daniele Riviere, Jacinto Lageria, and Paul Virilio, eds. 1993. *Atom Egoyan*. Paris and Toronto: Editions Dis Voir and Ontario Ministry of Culture, Tourism and Recreation.

Dhillon-Kashyap, Perminder. 1988. "Locating the Asian Experience." *Screen* 29, no. 4:120–26.

Dhoukar, Hedi. 1990. "Les Thémes du cinéma beur." *CinémAction* 56 (July): 152–60.

Diawara, Manthia. 1993a. *Black American Cinema*. New York: Routledge.

———. 1993b. "Power and Territory: The Emergence of Black British Film Collectives." In *Fires Were Started: British Cinema and Thatcherism*, edited by Lester Friedman, 147–60. Minneapolis: University of Minnesota Press.

———. 1992. *African Cinema: Politics and Culture*. Bloomington: Indiana University Press.

———. 1989. "Oral Literature and African Film: Narratology in *Wend Kuuni*." In *Questions of Third Cinema*, edited by Jim Pines and Paul Willemen, 199–211. London: British Film Institute.

Dick, Bernard F. 1990. *Anatomy of Film*. 2d ed. New York: St. Martin's Press.

Dickstein, Morris. 1995. "Imitations of Mortality." *New York Times Book Review*, July 23, 6.

Dieckmann, Katherine. 1984–85. "Wim Wenders: An Interview." *Film Quarterly* 38, no. 2:2–7.

Dija, Eddie. 1995. *BFI Film and Television Handbook 1996*. London: British Film Institute.

Dillon, Sam. 1996. "Illegal Migrants Warned: Stay South of the Border." *New York Times*, January 7, A3.

Dimemberg, Edward. 1997. "Film Noir and the Space of Modernity." Unpublished manuscript.

Doan, Mary Anne. 1988. "Masquerade Reconsidered: Further Thoughts on the Female Spectator." *Discourse* 11, no. 1:42–53.

———. 1982. "Film and Masquerade: Theorizing the Female Spectator." *Screen* 23, nos. 3–4: 74–87.

Doraiswamy, Rashmi. 1992–93. "Joris Ivens' *A Tale of the Wind*." *Cinemaya*, nos. 17–18: 92–93.

Dowlatabadi, Zahra. 1989. "Goft va Shonudi ba Qasem Ebrahimian." *Par*, no. 45: 28–32.

Drummond, Philip, Richard Patterson, and Janet Willis. 1993. *National Identity and Europe: The Television Revolution*. London: British Film Institute.

Ducrot, Oswald, and Tzvetan Todorov. 1983. *Encyclopedic Dictionary of the Sciences of Language*. Trans. Catherine Porter. Baltimore: Johns Hopkins University Press.

Dunn, Ashley. 1995. "Skilled Asians Leaving U.S. for High-Tech Jobs at Home." *New York Times*, February 21, A1, A11.

Durgnat, Raymond. 1985. "Letter from Siberia." In *Magill's Survey of Cinema: Foreign Language Films*. Vol. 4, edited by Frank N. Magill, 1774–79. Englewood Cliffs, N.J.: Salem Press.

Dyer, Richard. 1979. *Stars*. London: British Film Institute.

Eagleton, Terry. 1982. *The Rape of Clarissa: Writing, Sexuality and Class Struggle in Samuel Richardson*. Minneapolis: University of Minnesota Press.

———. 1970. *Exiles and Émigrés: Studies in Modern Literature*. London: Chatto and Windus.

Easton, Nina J. 1989. "Threats Spur Police Aid for Film Maker," *Los Angeles Times*, April 4, pt. 6, p. 1.

Egoyan, Atom, ed. 1995. *Exotica*. Toronto: Coach House Press.

———. 1993. *Speaking Parts*. Toronto: Coach House Press.

Elena, Alberto. 1993. *El cine del Tercere Mundo: Dictionario de realizadores*. Madrid: Ediciones Turfan.

Ellis, Jack C. 1990. "Marker, Chris." In *International Dictionary of Films and Filmmakers*. Vol. 2, *Directors*, edited by Nicholas Thomas, 552–54. 2d ed. Chicago: St. James Press.

Elsaesser, Thomas. 1999. "Ethnicity, Authenticity, and Exile: A Counterfeit Trade? German Filmmakers and Hollywood." In *Home, Exile, Homeland: Film, Media and the Politics of Place*, edited by Hamid Naficy, 97–123. New York: Routledge.

Elsaesser, Thomas. 1992. "Tales of Sound and Fury: Observations on Family Melodrama." In *Film Theory and Criticism: Introductory Readings*, edited by Gerald Mast, Marshall Cohen, and Leo Braudy, 512–35. 4th ed. New York: Oxford University Press.

Erenz, Benedikt. 1988. "Uhr ohne Zeiger." In *Harte Ziele, Weiche Ziele*, 127–33. Berlin: Karl H. Henssel Verlag.

Ewen, Stuart, and Elizabeth Ewen. 1982. *Channels of Desire: Mass Images and the Shaping of American Consciousness*. New York: McGraw-Hill.

Fabrikant, Geraldine. 1996. "T.T.C. and Time Warner Reach Accord on Acquisition of Turner." *New York Times*, July 18, A1, C20.

Fanon, Frantz. 1968. *The Wretched of the Earth*. Trans. Constance Farrington. New York: Grove Press.

———. 1967. *Black Skin, White Masks*. Trans. Charles Markmann. New York: Grove Press.

Farabi Cinema Foundation. 1994. *A Selection of Iranian Films 1994*. Tehran: Farabi Cinema Foundation.

Farassino, Alberto. 1993. "Gitai the Nomadic Image." In *The Films of Amos Gitai: A Montage*, edited by Paul Willemen, 16–18. London: British Film Institute.

Farocki, Harun. 1993. "Commentary from the Film *Bilder der Welt und Inschrift des Kreiges* (*Images of the World and Inscription of the War*)," *Discourse* 15, no. 3:78–92.

Feeney, F. X. 1983. "The Iranian Master." *L.A. Weekly*, July 5–21, 27–28.

Fehrenbach, Heide. 1995. *Cinema in Democratizing Germany: Reconstructing National Identity after Hitler*. Chapel Hill: University of North Carolina Press.

Feng, Peter. 1996. "Being Chinese American, Becoming Asian American: Chan Is Missing." *Cinema Journal* 35, no. 4:88–118.

———. 1995. "In Search of Asian American Cinema." *Cinéaste* 21, nos. 1–2:32–36.

Fernandez, Sergio. 1984. "Nina Menkes' *Great Sadness of Zohara*." *Daily Bruin*, January 27, 12.

Film-Maker's Cooperative Catalogue No. 7. 1989. New York: Film-Maker's Cooperative.

Firmat, Gustavo Pérez. 1994. *Life on the Hyphen: The Cuban-American Way*. Austin: University of Texas Press.

Fish, Sandra L. 1990. "Therapeutic Uses of the Telephone: Crisis Intervention vs. Traditional Therapy." In *Talking to Strangers: Mediated Therapeutic Communication*, edited by Gary Gumpert and Sandra Fish, 154–70. Norwood, N.J.: Ablex.

Flitterman-Lewis, Sandy. 1996. *To Desire Differently: Feminism and the French Cinema*. Expanded edition. New York: Columbia University Press.

FM-2030. 1989. *Are You a Transhuman?* New York: Warner Books.

Forman, Milos, and Jan Novak. 1994. *Turnaround: A Memoir*. New York: Villard Books.

Foster, Gwendolyn Audrey. 1997. *Women Filmmakers of the African and Asian Diaspora: Decolonizing the Gaze, Locating Subjectivity*. Carbondale: Southern Illinois University Press.

Foucault, Michel. 1979. *Discipline and Punish: The Birth of the Prison*. Trans. Vlan Sheridan. New York: Vantage.

———. 1978. *The History of Sexuality: Vol. 1: An Introduction*. Trans. Robert Hurley. New York: Vintage.

———. 1977. *Language, Memory, Practice*. Ed. D. F. Bouchard. Oxford: Basil Blackwell.

Fountain, Alan. 1988. "Channel 4 and Black Independents." *ICA Documents*, no. 7:42–44. [Special issue on black film, British cinema.]

Fregoso, Rosa Linda. 1999. "Recycling Colonial Fantasies on the Texas Borderlands." In *Home, Exile, Homeland: Film, Media, and the Politics of Place*, edited by Hamid Naficy, 167–92. New York: Routledge.

———. 1993. *The Bronze Screen: Chicana and Chicano Film Culture*. Minneapolis: University of Minnesota Press.

Freud, Sigmund. 1953–74. "Recommendations to Physicians Practising Psycho-Analysis." (1912). In *The Standard Edition of the Complete Psychological Works of Sigmund Freud*, edited by James Strachey. London: Hogarth Press.

Friedlander, Jonathan, ed. 1995. *The Cinema of Displacement: Middle Eastern Identities in Transition*. Los Angeles: UCLA Center for Near Eastern Studies.

Fusco, Coco. 1995. "Black Filmmaking in Britain's Workshop Section." In *Cinemas of the Black Diaspora: Diversity, Dependency, and Oppositionality*. Edited by Michael T. Martin, 304–17. Detroit: Wayne State University Press.

———. 1990. *Internal Exiles: Nexw Films and Videos from Chile*. New York: Third World Newsreel.

———. 1988. *Young British and Black: A Monograph on the Work of Sankofa Film/Video Collective and Black Audio Film Collective*. Buffalo, N.Y.: Hallwalls.

———. 1987–88. "The Tango of Esthetics and Politics." *Cinéaste* 16, nos. 1–2:5, 58–59.

Gabler, Neal. 1988. *An Empire of Their Own: How the Jews Invented Hollywood*. New York: Crown.

Gabriel, Teshome, H. 1993. "Ruin and the Other: Toward a Language of Memory." In *Otherness and the Media: The Ethnography of the Imagined and the Imaged*, edited by Hamid Naficy and Teshome Gabriel, 211–20. New York: Harwood.

———. 1989a. "Third Cinema as Guardian of Popular Memory: Towards a Third Aesthetics." In *Questions of Third Cinema*, edited by Jim Pines and Paul Willemen, 53–64. London: British Film Institute.

———. 1989b. "Towards a Critical Theory of Third World Films." In *Questions of Third Cinema*, edited by Jim Pines and Paul Willemen, 30–52. London: British Film Institute.

———. 1988. "Thoughts on Nomadic Aesthetics and the Black Independent Cinema." In *Blackframes: Critical Perspectives on Black Independent Cinema*, edited by Mbye B. Cham and Clair Andrade-Watkins, 62–79. Cambridge, Mass.: MIT Press.

———. 1987. "Black British Cinema: An Introduction." In *Black Independent Cinema: Britain and America*. Los Angeles: UCLA Film and Television Archive. [Brochure for a film series.]

———. 1982. *Third Cinema in the Third World: The Aesthetics of Liberation*. Ann Arbor, Mich.: UMI Research Press.

Gains, Jane. 1993. "Fire and Desire: Race, Melodrama, and Oscar Micheaux." In *Black American Cinema*, edited by Manthia Diawara, 49–70. New York: Routledge.

Garbowsky, Maryanne M. 1989. *The House without the Door: A Study of Emily Dickinson and the Illness of Agoraphobia*. Rutherford, N.J.: Fairleigh Dickinson University Press.

Gates, Anita. 1995. "There Are Movies, and Then There Are *Movies*." *New York Times*, January 15, H1, H22.

Gates, Henry Louis, Jr. 1988. *The Signifying Monkey: A Theory of African-American Literary Criticism.* New York: Oxford University Press.

Gelly, Violaine. 1989. "Le Rapport du plus vaste et du plus intime." *La Croix*, March 16, 20.

Giannetti, Louis. 1990. *Understanding Movies.* 5th ed. Englewood Cliffs, N.J.: Prentice Hall.

Gibson, Michael. 1989. "Ivens, Filming the Impossible." *International Herald Tribune*, March 3, 7, 9.

Gidden, Anthony. 1990. *The Consequences of Modernity.* Cambridge: Polity Press.

Giles, Paul. 1993. "History with Holes: Channel Four Television Films of the 1980s." In *Fires Were Started: British Cinema and Thatcherism*, edited by Lester Friedman, 70–91. Minneapolis: University of Minnesota Press.

Gillespie, Maire. 1995. *Television, Ethnicity and Cultural Change.* London: Routledge.

Gilroy, Paul. 1993. *The Black Atlantic: Modernity and Double Consciousness.* Cambridge, Mass.: Harvard University Press.

———. 1991. *"There Ain't No Black in the Union Jack": The Cultural Politics of Race and Nation.* Chicago: University of Chicago Press.

———. 1988. "Nothing But Sweat inside My Hand: Diaspora Aesthetics and Black Arts in Britain." *ICA Documents*, no. 7: 44–46. [Special issue on black film, British cinema.]

Gilroy, Paul, and Jim Pines. 1988. "*Handsworth Songs*: Audiences/Aesthetics/Independence." *Framework*, no. 35:9–18.

Givani, June. 1988. "In Circulation: Black Films in Britain." *ICA Documents*, no. 7:39–41. [Special issue on black film, British cinema.]

Glucksman, Mary. 1995a. "The More Things Change." *Filmmaker* 3, no. 2:23–28.

———. 1995b. "Pushing Films." *Filmmaker* 3, no. 3:21–24.

———. 1994. "State of Things." *Filmmaker* 3, no. 1:23–26.

Golmakani, Houshang. 1993. "Amir Naderi: The Loneliness of a Long Distance Runner." *Film International* 1, no. 4:16–25.

Gomery, Douglas. 1992. *Shared Pleasures: A History of Movie Presentation in the United States.* London: British Film Institute.

———. 1991. *Movie History: A Survey.* Belmont, Calif.; Wadsworth.

———. 1986. *The Hollywood Studio System.* New York: St. Martin's Press.

Gómez-Peña, Guillermo. 1988. "Documented/Undocumented." In *Multi-cultural Literacy: Opening the American Mind*, edited by Rick Simonson and Scott Walker, 127–34. Saint Paul, Minn.: Graywolf Press.

Gong, Stephen. 1991. "A History in Progress: Asian American Media Arts Centers, 1970–1900." In *Moving Image: Independent Asian Pacific American Media Arts*, edited by Russell Leong, 1–9. Los Angeles: UCLA Asian American Studies Center.

Gopinath, Gayatri. 1995. " 'Bombay, U.K., Yuba City': Bhangra Music and the Engendering of Diaspora." *Diaspora* 4, no. 3:303–22.

Grade, Michael. 1996. "Getting the Right Approach: Channel Four and the British Film Industry." In *Big Picture, Small Screen: The Relations between Film and Television*, edited by John Hill and Martin McLoone, 177–82. Luton, Bedfordshire, UK: John Libbey Media/University of Luton.

Graffy, Julian. 1997. "Tarkovsky: The Weight of the World." *Sight and Sound* 7, no. 1:18–22.

Green, Peter. 1984–85. "The Nostalgia of *Stalker*." *Sight and Sound* 54, no. 1:50–54.

Green, Ronald J. 1994. "The Illustrated Lecture." *Quarterly Review of Film and Video* 15, no. 2:1–23.

———. 1993. " 'Twoness' in the Style of Oscar Micheaux." In *Black American Cinema*, edited by Manthia Diawara, 26–48. New York: Routledge.

Greenberg, Joel. 1995. "Palestinian 'Martyrs': Defiant and So Willing." *New York Times*, January 25, A6.

Greenhouse, Linda. 1998. "High Court Awards New Jersey Sovereignty over Most of Ellis I." *New York Times*, May 27, 1, A21.

Grillo, Virgil, and Bruce Kawin. 1981. "Reading the Movies: Subtitles, Silence, and the Structure of the Brain," *Post Script: Essays in Film and the Humanities* 1, no. 1:25–32.

Gross, Joan, David McMurray, and Ted Swedenburg. 1994. "Arab Noise and Ramadan Nights: Raï, Rap, and Franco-Maghrebi Identity." *Diaspora* 3, no. 1:3–40.

Grundmann, Roy. 1995. "Black Nationhood and the Rest of the West: An Interview with Isaac Julien." *Cinéaste* 21, nos. 1–2:28–31.

Gunning, Tom. 1991. "Heard over the Phone: The Lonely Villa and the de Lorde Tradition of the Terror of Technology." *Screen* 32, no. 2:184–96.

Gusso, Mel. 1997. "A Filmmaker at High Tide since France's New Wave." *New York Times*, October 2.

Haberman, Clyde. 1995. "Israel Resumes Sealing of Houses as Punishment." *New York Times*, December 4, 3.

Haidari, Gholam, ed. 1991. *Mo'arrefi va Naqd-e Filmha-ye Amir Naderi*. Tehran: Sohail Publisher.

Hall, Stuart. 1996. "The Question of Cultural Identity." In *Modernity: An Introduction to Modern Societies*, edited by Stuart Hall et al., 594–634. London: Blackwell.

———. 1994. "Cultural Identity and Diaspora." In *Colonial Discourse and Post-colonial Theory: A Reader*, edited by Patrick Williams and Laura Chrisman, 392–403. New York: Columbia University Press.

———. 1992. "European Cinema on the Verge of a Nervous Breakdown." In *Screening Europe: Image and Identity in Contemporary European Cinema*, edited by Duncan Petrie, 45–53. London: British Film Institute.

———. 1989. "Cultural Identity and Cinematic Representation." *Framework*, no. 36:68–81.

———. 1988. "New Ethnicities." *ICA Documents*, no. 7: 27–31. [Special issue on Black film, British cinema.]

Halliwell, Leslie. 1977. *The Filmgoer's Companion*. 6th ed. New York: Avon.

Hamamoto, Darrell Y. 1994. *Monitored Peril: Asian Americans and the Politics of TV Representation*. Minneapolis: University of Minnesota Press.

Hanania, Joseph. 1995. "Fleeing a Fallow France for Greener U.S. Pastures." *New York Times*, October 22, H14.

Handling, Piers. 1993. "Allegories of Alienation: The Films of Atom Egoyan." *Cinematheque Ontario*, March 18–May 27, 8.

Hankwitz, Molly. 1995. "Jay Salloum." *Art Papers*, May and June, 38–39.

Hansen, Miriam. 1991. *Babel and Babylon: Spectatorship in American Silent Film*. Cambridge, Mass.: Harvard University Press.

Hanson, Ellis. 1995. "The Telephone and Its Queerness." In *Unnatural Acts*, edited by Sue-Ellen Case, Philip Brett, and Susan Foster, 35–58. Bloomington: Indiana University Press.

Haraway, Donna J. 1991. *Simians, Cyborgs, and Women: The Reinvention of Nature.* London: Routledge.

Harcourt, Peter. 1995. "Imaginary Images: An Examination of Atom Egoyan's Films." *Film Quarterly* 48, no. 3:2–14.

Hargreaves, Alec G. 1990. *Voices from the North African Immigrant Community in France: Immigration and Identity in Beur Fiction.* New York: Berg.

———. 1989. "*Beur* Fiction: Voices from the Immigrant Community in France." *French Review* 62, no. 4:661–67.

Harlow, Barbara. 1991. "Sites of Struggle: Immigration, Deportation, Prison, and Exile." In *Criticism in the Borderlands*, edited by Héctor Caldrón and José David Saldívar, 149–63. Durham, N.C.: Duke University Press.

———. 1987. *Resistance Literature.* New York: Methuen.

Harvey, David. 1992. *The Condition of Postmodernity: An Enquiry into the Origins of Cultural Change.* Cambridge: Blackwell.

———. 1989. *The Condition of Postmodernity.* Oxford: Blackwell.

Harvey, Sylvia. 1978. *May '68 and Film Culture.* London. British Film Institute.

Hassanpour, Amir. 1996. "The Creation of Kurdish Media Culture." In *Kurdish Culture and Identity*, edited by Philip G. Kreyenbroek and Christine Allison, 48–84. London: Zed Books.

———. 1995. "MED-TV, Britain, and the Turkish State: A Stateless Nation's Quest for Sovereignty in the Sky." Unpublished manuscript presented at the Frei Universitat, Berlin, November 7.

Hebdige, Dick. 1979. *Subculture: The Meaning of Style.* London: Methuen.

Hedges, Chris. 1995. "Turks Plan to Keep 35,000 Troops in Iraq." *New York Times*, March 24, A6.

Heilbut, Anthony. 1983. *Exiled in Paradise: German Refugee Artists and Intellectuals in America, from the 1930s to the Present.* Boston: Beacon Press.

Heim, Michael. 1993. *The Metaphysics of Virtual Reality.* New York: Oxford University Press.

Henderson, Brian. 1991. "The Civil War: Did It Not Seem Real?" *Film Quarterly* 44, no. 3:2–14.

Heung, Marina. 1993. "Daughter-Text/Mother-Text: Matrilineage in Amy Tan's *Joy Luck Club*." *Feminist Studies* 19, no. 3:597–616.

Hicks, D. Emily. 1991. *Border Writing: The Multidimensional Text.* Minneapolis: University of Minnesota Press.

Hill, John. 1996. "British Television and Film: The Making of a Relationship." In *Big Picture, Small Screen: The Relations between Film and Television*, edited by John Hill and Martin McLoone, 151–76. Luton, Bedfordshire, UK: John Libbey Media/University of Luton.

———. 1994. "The Future of European Cinema: The Economics and Culture of Pan-European Strategies." In *Border Crossing: Film in Ireland, Britain and Europe*, edited by John Hill, Martin McLoone, and Paul Hainsworth, 53–80. Belfast: Queens University.

Hill, John, and Martin McLoone, eds. 1996. *Big Picture, Small Screen: The Relations between Film and Television*. Luton, Bedfordshire, UK: University of Luton Press.

Ho, Christine G. T. 1993. "The Internationalization of Kinship and the Feminization of Caribbean Migration: The Case of Afro-Trinidadian Immigrants in Los Angeles." *Human Organization* 52, no. 1:32–40.

Hoberman, J. 1997. "Endangered Species." *Village Voice*, June 3, 65.

———. 1991a. *Bridge of Light: Yiddish Film between Two Worlds*. New York: Museum of Modern Art.

———. 1991b. "Paradjanov and Protégé." *Premiere*, September, 36–37.

———. 1988. "Man from Galilee." *Village Voice*, June 28, 84.

Hobsbawm, E., and T. Ranger, eds. 1983. *The Invention of Tradition*. Cambridge: Cambridge University Press.

Hohenadel, Kristin. 2000. "Where Television Sponsors the Film Industry." *New York Times*, June 11, AR31.

Holden, Stephen. 1993a. "A Joint Struggle, Adolescence and Disability," *New York Times*, March 23, B2.

———. 1993b. "Technology, a Tripod, a Romantic Triangle." *New York Times*, October 16, 18.

Holloway, Lynette. 1995. "Airport Homeless: A Long, Pleasant Layover." *New York Times*, February 3, A1, A13.

Holmlund, Chris. 1993. "Masculinity as Multiple Masquerade: The 'Mature' Stallone and the Stallone Clone." In *Screening the Male: Exploring Masculinities in Hollywood Cinema*, edited by Steven Cohan and Ina Rae Hark, 213–29. New York: Routledge.

Hondo, Abid Med. 1987. "The Cinema of Exile." In *Film and Politics in the Third World*, edited by John D. H. Downing, 69–76. New York: Praeger.

hooks, bell. 1990. *Yearning: Race, Gender, and Cultural Politics*. Boston: South End Press.

Hosseini-Kaladjahi, Hassan. 1997. *Iranians in Sweden: Economic, Cultural and Social Integration*. Stockholm: Almqvist & Wiksell International.

Hui, Ann. 1991. "*Song of the Exile*." *Cinemaya* 12: 56–57.

Hurston, Zora Neale. 1937/1978. *Their Eyes Were Watching God*. Urbana: University of Illinois Press.

Ibrahim, Youssef, M. 1995a. "Chirac Orders French Border Tightened over Bombs," *New York Times*, September 6, A6.

———. 1995b. "A Wary France Cracks Down on Its Muslims." *New York Times*, September 7, A3.

Iglesias, Norma. 1998. "Representations of the Frontier." Paper presented at Society for Cinema Studies Conference, San Diego, April 4–7.

———. 1991. *Entre yerba, polvo y plomo: Lo fronterizo visto por el cinemexicao*. Tijuana, Mexico: El Colegio de la fronternorte.

Ilal, Ersan. 1987. "On Turkish Cinema." In *Film and Politics in the Third World*, edited by John D. H. Downing, 119–29. New York: Praeger.

Insdorf, Annette. 1990a. "Gypsy Life Beguiles a Film Maker." *New York Times*, February 4, H18, H25.

———. 1990b. "Image Problems: A Director's Specialty." *New York Times*. February 11, 25H.

Insdorf, Annette. 1984. " 'El Norte': On Screen and in Reality, a Story of Struggle." *New York Times*, June 8, 17, 26.

Iransk Film i Exil. 1993. Festival catalog, Göteborg, Sweden, October 7–14.

Iris, no. 9 (spring 1989). [Special issue on "Cinema and Cognitive Psychology."]

Issa, Rose, and Sheila Whitaker, eds. 1999. *Life and Art: The New Iranian Cinema.* London: National Film Theatre.

Ivens, Joris. 1974. *The Camera and I.* New York: International Publishers.

Jackman, Jarrell C. 1983. "German émigrés in Southern California." In *The Muses Flee Hitler: Cultural Transfer and Adaptation, 1930–1945*, edited by Jarrel C. Jackman and Carla M. Border, 95–110. Washington, D.C.: Smithsonian Institution Press.

Jamal, Mahmood. 1988. "Dirty Linen." *ICA Documents*, no. 7:21–22. [Special issue on black film, British cinema.]

James, Caryn. 1989. "A Film Maker's Witty and Poetic Last Word." *New York Times*, September 25.

———. 1988. "Mira Nair Combines Cultures to Create a Film." *New York Times*, October 17, 3.

James, David E. 1996a. "Introduction: Socialist Questions in a Rented World." In *Power Misses: Essays across (Un)Popular Culture*, David James, 1–23. London: Verso.

———. 1996b. "The Most Typical Avant-Garde: Film in Los Angeles/Los Angeles in Film." Unpublished manuscript.

———. 1992. *To Free Cinema: Jonas Mekas and the New York Underground.* Princeton, N.J.: Princeton University Press.

———. 1989. *Allegories of Cinema: American Film in the Sixties.* Princeton, N.J.: Princeton University Press.

Jameson, Fredric. 1992. *The Geopolitical Aesthetic: Cinema and Space in the World System.* Bloomington: Indiana University Press.

———. 1989. "Nostalgia for the Present." *South Atlantic Quarterly* 88, no. 2:517–37.

———. 1988. "Cognitive Mapping." In *Marxism and the Interpretation of Culture*, edited by Cary Nelson and Lawrence Grossberg, 347–57. Urbana: University of Illinois Press.

———. 1986. "Third-World Literature in the Era of Multinational Capitalism." *Social Text* 15 (fall): 65–88.

———. 1984. "Periodizing the 60s." In *The 60s without Apology*, edited by Sohnya Sayers et al., 178–209. Minneapolis: University of Minnesota Press.

Jarvie, Ian C. 1991. "Stars and Ethnicity: Hollywood and the United States, 1932–51." In *Unspeakable Images: Ethnicity and the American Cinema*, edited by Lester Friedman, 82–111. Urbana: University of Illinois Press.

Jay, Martin. 1993. *Downcast Eyes: The Denigration of Vision in Twentieth-Century French Thought.* Berkeley: University of California Press.

Jehl, Douglas. 1997. "Hard Life Gets Harder for Palestinians in Lebanon." *New York Times*, March 9, A11.

Johnson, Brian D. 1991. "Bleak Beauty." *Maclean's*, September 30, 68.

Johnson, Vida T., and Graham Petrie. 1994a. *The Films of Andrei Tarkovsky: A Visual Fugue.* Bloomington: Indiana University Press.

———. 1994b. "Tarkovsky." In *Five Filmmakers: Tarkovsky, Forman, Polanski, Szabó, Makavejev*, edited by Daniel J. Goulding, 1–49. Bloomington: Indiana University Press.

Jones, Steven G., ed. 1995. *Cybersociety: Computer-Mediated Communication and Community.* Thousand Oaks, Calif.: London: Sage.

Julien, Isaac, and Colin MacCabe. 1991. *Diary of a Young Soul Rebel.* London: British Film Institute.

Kael, Pauline. 1985. *State of the Art.* New York: Dutton.

Kaes, Anton. 1989. *From Hitler to Heimat: The Return of History as Film.* Cambridge, Mass.: Harvard University Press.

Kaleta, Kenneth C. 1998. *Hanif Kureishi: Postcolonial Storyteller.* Austin: University of Texas Press.

Kapchan, Deborah A. 1995. "Hybrid Genres, Performed Subjectivities: The Revoicing of Public Oratory in the Moroccan Marketplace." *Women and Performance* 7, no. 2–8, no. 1:53–85.

Kaplan, Caren. 1996. *Questions of Travel: Postmodern Discourses of Displacement.* Durham, N.C.: Duke University Press.

Kaufman, Deborah, Rena Orenstein, and Janis Plotkin, eds. 1991. *Independent Filmmakers: Looking at Ourselves. A Guide to Films Featured in the Jewish Film Festival.* Berkeley: Jewish Film Festival.

Kauffman, Linda S. 1992. *Special Delivery: Epistolary Modes in Modern Fiction.* Chicago: University of Chicago Press.

———. 1986. *Discourse of Desire: Gender, Genre, and Epistolary Fiction.* Ithaca, N.Y. Cornell University Press.

Kazan, Elia. 1979. "The View from a Turkish Prison." *New York Times Magazine,* February 4, 33–35, 48–50.

Kazin, Alfred. 1983. "The European Writers in Exile." In *The Muses Flee Hitler: Cultural Transfer and Adaptation, 1930–1945,* edited by Jarrel C. Jackman and Carla M. Border, 123–34. Washington, D.C.: Smithsonian Institution Press.

Kelk, no. 40 (1992). [Persian journal of art and literature, contains a long interview with and several articles about Sohrab Shahid Saless.]

Kempley, Rita. 1990. " 'Parts,' Video as Big Brother." *Washington Post,* February 3.

Khorrami, Mohammad Mehdi. 1993. "Qesseh va Qessehnevisi dar Tab'id: Tarikhcheh-ye Esteqlal-e Adabi." *Iranshenasi* 5, no. 1:183–94.

Kibbey, Ann. 1993. "The Moving Image of a Woman." Unpublished manuscript.

Kinder, Marsha. 1993. *Blood Cinema: The Reconstruction of National Identity in Spain.* Berkeley: University of California Press.

King, John. 1990. "Chilean Cinema in Revolution and Exile." In *Magic Reels: A History of Cinema in Latin America,* 169–87. New York: Verso.

Kinzer, Stephen. 1998. "Turk-Kurd War Begins to Spill Refugees into Europe" *New York Times,* January 6, A9.

———. 1997a. "Kurdish Rebels in Turkey Are Down but Not Out." *New York Times,* March 8, 1, 3.

———. 1997b. "Kurds No Longer X-Rated Topic in Turkish Film." *New York Times,* May 15, A4.

———. 1997c. "Turks Say Bonn Is Encouraging Racist Attacks." *New York Times,* April 5, 3.

Klein, Andy. 1989. "Iranian Immigrant's N.Y. Nightmare." *Los Angeles Herald Examiner,* May 17, B2.

Klein, Irma. 1993. "An Architectonics of Responsibility." In *The Films of Amos Gitai: A Montage*, edited by Paul Willemen, 24–36. London: British Film Institute.

Kolker, Robert Phillip. 1988. *A Cinema of Loneliness: Penn, Kubrick, Spielberg, Altman.* 2d ed. New York: Oxford University Press.

———. 1973. "Angle and Reality: Godard and Groin in America," *Sight and Sound* 42, no. 3:130–33.

Kolson, Ann. 1992. "They're in the Movies to Relay Life's Untold Stories." *Philadelphia Inquirer*, April 3, D1, D3.

Kozloff, Sarah. 1988. *Invisible Storytellers: Voice-Over Narration in American Fiction Film.* Berkeley: University of California Press.

Kracauer, Siegfried. 1947. *From Caligari to Hitler: A Psychological History of the German Film.* Princeton, N.J.: Princeton University Press.

Kratzer-Juilfs, Silvia. 1996. "Exile Cinema as National Cinema: Re-defining German National Cinema (1962–1995)." Ph.D. diss., UCLA.

———. 1994. "Exiled Inside Out: Memory and Remembrance in (East) German Documentary Film." *Spectator* 14, no. 2:53–67.

Kricorian, Nancy. 1993–94. "Too Far for Home." *Filmmaker*, winter, 27.

Kristof, Nicholas D. 1996. "Today's History Lesson: What Rape of Nanjing?" *New York Times*, July 4, A6.

Kronish, Amy. 1996. *World Cinema: Israel.* Trowbridge, Wiltshire, UK: Flicks Books.

Kuhn, Annette, and Susannah Radstone, eds. 1990. *Women in Film: An International Guide.* New York: Fawcett Columbine.

Kureishi, Hanif. 1988. "England, Bloody England." *ICA Documents*, no. 7, 24. [Special issue on black film, British cinema.]

Lacan, Jacques. 1977. *Écrits.* London: Tavistock.

Laclau, Ernesto. 1990. *New Reflections on the Revolution of Our Time.* London: Verso.

Larsen, Neil. 1991. "Foreword." In *Border Writing: The Multidimensional Text*, D. Emily Hicks, xi–xxi. Minneapolis: University of Minnesota Press.

Lawrence, Amy. 1994. "Women's Voices in Third World Cinema." In *Multiple Voices in Feminist Film Criticism*, edited by Diane Carson, Linda Dittmar, and Janice Welsch, 406–20. Minneapolis: University of Minnesota Press.

Leclère, Jacques. 1988. "Droit et économie du cinéma la production." *l'Avant Scène Cinéma* 372 (June): 19.

Lee, Benjamin. 1995. "Metalinguistics, Subjectivities, and the Public Sphere." Unpublished manuscript.

Le Fanu, Mark. 1990. *The Cinema of Andrei Tarkovsky.* London: British Film Institute.

Lefevre, Henri. 1991. *The Production of Space.* Trans. Donald Nicholson-Smith. Oxford: Blackwell.

Leggewie, Claus. 1996. "How Turks Became Kurds, Not Germans," *Dissent*, summer, 79–83.

Lejeune, Phillipe. 1989. *On Autobiography.* Ed. Paul Eakin. Minneapolis: University of Minnesota Press.

Leong, Russell, ed. 1991. *Moving the Image: Independent Asian Pacific American Media Arts.* Los Angeles: UCLA Asian American Studies Center.

Lev, Peter. 1993. *The Euro-American Cinema.* Austin: University of Texas Press.

Lewis, Neil A. 1997. "Arab-Americans Protest 'Profiling' at Airports." *New York Times*, August 11, A10.

Leyda, Jay. 1964. *Films Beget Films: A Study of the Compilation Film.* New York: Hill and Wang.

Liehm, Mira. 1984. *Passion and Defiance: Film in Italy from 1942 to the Present.* Los Angeles: University of California Press.

List, Chris. 1989. "*El Norte*, Ideology and Immigration." *Jump Cut* 34 (March): 27–31.

Lombardi, Fred. 1993. "Manhattan by Numbers." *Variety*, April 5, n.p.

London, Michael. 1984. "Miracles at Filmex: Women Independents," *Los Angeles Times*, July 6, pt. 6, pp. 1, 14.

Longfellow, Brenda. 1993. "Lesbian Fantasy and the Other Woman in Ottinger's *Johanna d'Arc of Mongolia*." *Screen* 34, no. 2:124–36.

Lopez, Ana M. 1996. "Greater Cuba." In *The Ethnic Eye: Latino Media Arts*, edited by Chon A. Noriega and Ana M. Lopez, 38–58. Minneapolis: University of Minnesota Press.

Lourdeaux. Lee. 1990. *Italian and Irish Filmmakers in America: Ford, Capra, Coppola, and Scorsese.* Philadelphia: Temple University Press.

Lowe, Lisa. 1991. "Heterogeneity, Hybridity, Multiplicity: Making Asian American Difference." *Diaspora* 1, no. 1:24–44.

MacDonald, Scott. 1998. *A Critical Cinema 3: Interview with Independent Filmmakers.* Berkeley: University of California Press.

———. 1993. *Avant-Garde Film Motion Studies.* New York: Cambridge University Press.

———. 1992. *A Critical Cinema. Vol. 2, Interviews with Independent Filmmakers.* Berkeley: University of California Press.

———. 1988. *A Critical Cinema. Vol. 1, Interviews with Independent Filmmakers.* Berkeley: University of California Press.

MacFarquhar, Neil. 1996. "Portrait of a Suicide Bomber: Devout, Apolitical and Angry." *New York Times*, March 18, A1, A5.

Machida, Margo. 1994. "Out of Asia: Negotiating Asian Identities in America." In *Asia/America: Identities in Contemporary Asian American Art*, edited by the Asia Society Galleries, 65–111. New York: New Press.

MacInnis, Craig. 1993. "Egoyan's *Calendar* Is Simply Wonderful." *Toronto Star*, April 8.

MacPherson, Robin. 1986. "Introducing Scottish Workshops." In *Fortieth Edinburgh International Film Festival Catalogue*, 32–33. Edinburgh, Scotland.

Mahini, Hossein. 1995. "Introduction." *The Second Festival for Iranian Films in Exile, 6–13 October*, vi–v. Götenborg, Sweden, Exile-Film Festival.

Malekpour, Jamshid. 1363/1984. *Adabiat-e Namayeshi dar Iran: Dowran-e Enqelab-e Mashruteh* [Iranian Literature of Performance: Constitutional Revolution Period]. Tehran: Entesharat-e Tus.

Malik, Sarita. 1996. "Beyond 'the Cinema of Duty'? The Pleasures of Hybridity: Black British Film of the 1980s and 1990s." In *Dissolving Views: Key Writings on British Cinema*, edited by Andrew Higson, 202–15. London: Cassell.

Malkmus, Lizbeth, and Roy Armes. 1991. *Arab and African Film Making.* London: Zed Books.

Marchetti, Gina. 1993. *Romance and the "Yellow Peril": Race, Sex, and Discursive Strategies in Hollywood Fiction.* Berkeley: University of California Press.

Marcus, George E. 1994. "The Modernist Sensibility in Recent Ethnographic Writing and the Cinematic Metaphor of Montage." In *Visualizing Theory: Selected Essays from V.A.R, 1990–1994*, edited by Lucien Taylor, 37–53. New York: Routledge.

Marker, Chris. 1984. "Sunless." *Semiotext(e)* 4, no. 3:33–40.

———. 1961. "Lettre de Sibérie." In *Commentaires 1*, 41–79. Paris: Éditions du Seuil.

Marks, Isaac M. 1987. *Fear, Phobias, and Rituals: Panic, Anxiety, and Their Disorders.* New York: Oxford University Press.

Marks, Laura U. 1997. "Video Haptics and Erotics." Unpublished manuscript.

———. 1996. "The Skin of the Film: Intercultural Cinema, Embodiment, and the Senses." Ph.D. diss., University of Rochester.

———. 1994. "A Deleuzian Politics of Hybrid Cinema." *Screen* 35, no. 3:244–64.

———. 1991. "The Language of Terrorism," *Framework*, no. 38/39:64–73.

Márquez, Gabriel García. 1988. *Clandestine in Chile: The Adventures of Miguel Littín.* Trans. Asa Zatz. New York: An Owl Book.

Martin, Michael, ed. 1997a. *New Latin American Cinema.* Vol. 1, *Theory, Practices and Transcontinental Articulations.* Detroit: Wayne State University Press.

———. 1997b. *New Latin American Cinema.* Vol. 2, *Studies of National Cinemas.* Detroit: Wayne State University Press.

———. 1995. *Cinemas of the Black Diaspora: Diversity, Dependence, and Oppositionality.* Detroit: Wayne State University Press.

Masilela, Ntongela. 1993. "The Los Angeles School of Black Filmmakers." In *Black American Cinema*, edited by Manthia Diawara, 107–17. New York: Routledge.

Maslin, Janet. 1995. "Bucking the System, but Still Part of the Buzz: Atom Egoyan May Have His Breakthrough in *Exotica*." *New York Times*, March 5, H13, H17.

———. 1990. "Coming of Age as a Gypsy with a Turkey for a Friend." *New York Times*, February 9.

———. 1989. "On Forging Relationships by Electronic Intermediary." *New York Times*, September 29, C16.

Mayne, Judith. 1990. *The Woman at the Keyhole: Feminism and Women's Cinema.* Bloomington: Indiana University Press.

McBride, Joseph. 1991. "Foreign Oscar Hopeful Tongue-Tied." *Variety*, October 28, 3.

McGrady, Mike. 1989. "Iranians in Culture Shock." *New York Newsday*, May 17, 7.

McHale, Brian. 1978. "Free Indirect Discourse: A Survey of Recent Accounts." *Poetics and Theory of Literature* 3: 249–87.

McMullin, Corine. 1983. *Sohrab Shahid Saless.* Paris: Göethe Institut and Cinématheque Française.

McRobbie, Angela. 1993. "Chantal Akerman and Feminist Film-Making." In *Women and Film: A Sight and Sound Reader*, edited by Pam Cook and Philip Dodd, 198–203. Philadelphia: Temple University Press.

Mehrabi, Massoud. 1994. "47th Cannes Film Festival." *Film International* 2, no. 3:28–36.

Mekas, Jonas. 1996. *There Is No Ithaca: Idylls of Semeniskiai and Reminiscences.* Trans. Vyt Bakaitis. New York: Black Thistle Press.

———. 1991. *I Had Nowhere to Go: Diary of a Displaced Person.* New York: Black Thistle Press.

———. 1987. "The Diary Film." In *The Avant-Garde Film: A Reader of Theory and Criticism*, edited by P. Adam Sitney, 190–98. New York: Anthology Film Archive.

Mekas, Jonas. 1972. *Movie Journal: The Rise of the New American Cinema, 1959–1971*. New York: Collier Books.

———. 1970. "The Other Direction." In *The Movies as Medium*, edited by Lewis Jacobs, 313–19. New York: Farrar, Straus, and Giroux.

Mercer, Kobena. 1994a. "Diaspora Culture and the Dialogic Imagination: The Aesthetics of Black Independent Film in Britain." In *Welcome to the Jungle: New Positions in Black Cultural Studies*, 53–68. London: Routledge.

———. 1994b. *Welcome to the Jungle: New Positions in Black Cultural Studies*. London: Routledge.

———. 1988. "Recoding Narratives of Race and Nation." *ICA Documents*, no. 7: 4–14. [Special issue on black film, British cinema.]

Messick, Brinkley. 1993. *The Calligraphic State: Textual Domination and History in a Muslim Society*. Los Angeles: University of California Press.

Michelson, Annette. 1987. "Toward Snow." In *The Avant-Garde Film: A Reader of Theory and Criticism*, edited by P. Adam Sitney, 173–83. New York: Anthology Film Archives.

Miller, Judith. 1996. "Artists and Arts Groups Angered by New Rules for Federal Grants." *New York Times*, February 20, A1, A10.

Miller, Marjorie. 1997. "Israel Closes Four Palestinian Offices in E. Jerusalem." *Los Angeles Times*, March 6, A6.

Mitchell, Tony. 1986–87. "Andrei Tarkovsky and *Nostalghia*." *Film Criticism* 11, nos. 1–2:101–10.

Mizrahi, Simon. 1988. "Interview with Fernando Solanas." In *Sur: A Fernando E. Solanas Film*, 9–16. Cannes, France: Cannes International Film Festival.

Modarressi, Taghi. 1992. "Writing with an Accent." *Chanteh* 1, no. 1:7–9.

Mohamed. 1981. "Un outil d'enquête." *CinémAction* 7:86–88.

Monk, Philip, Dennis Reid, and Louise Dompierre. 1994. *Visual Art: The Michael Snow Project*. Toronto: Alfred A. Knopf Canada.

Moore, Margaret. 1994. "International Film Co-production Tax and Subsidy Mechanism." *COMM/ENT* (Hastings Communications and Entertainment Law Journal) 16, no. 3:287–310.

Mordler, Michael. 1994. "Privacy Last." *Filmmaker* 2, no. 3:41–42, 58.

Morgan, Jessica. 1997. "The Poetics of Uncovering: Mona Hatoum in and out of Perspective." In *Mona Hatoum*, edited by Jessica Morgan, 1–24. Chicago: Museum of Contemporary Art.

Morley, David, and Kevin Robins. 1995. *Spaces of Identity: Global Media, Electronic Landscapes and Cultural Boundaries*. London: Routledge.

Mraz, John. 1990. "Solanas, Fernando E., and Octavio Getino." In *International Dictionary of Films and Filmmakers-2 Directors*. edited by Nicholas Thomas, 793–94. 2d ed. Chicago: St. James Press.

Mulvey, Laura. 1992. "Pandora: Topographies of the Mask and Curiosity." In *Sexuality and Space*, edited by Beatriz Colomina, 53–71. Princeton, N.J.: Princeton University Press.

Muscarella, Daphne. 1989. "*Suitors*: Strangers in a Strange Land." *American Cinematographer* 70 (January): 42–43.

NAATA CrossCurrent Media. 1995. *Asian Pacific American Film, Video and Audio Collection, 1995–1996*. San Francisco: NAATA.

Nabokov, Vladimir. 1977. *Lolita*. New York: Berkeley Books.

Naficy, Hamid. 2000. "Parallel Worlds." In *Shirin Neshat*, 42–53. Vienna/London: Kunsthalle Wien/Serpentine Gallery.

———. 1998a. Interview with Mitra Tabrizian, August 12, London.

———. 1998b. "Narrowcasting in Diaspora: Middle Eastern Television in Los Angeles." In *Living Color: Race and Television in the United States*, edited by Sasha Torres, 82–96. Durham, N.C.: Duke University Press.

———. 1997a. "The Accented Style of the Independent Transnational Cinema: A Conversation with Atom Egoyan." In *Cultural Producers in Perilous States: Editing Events, Documenting Change*, edited by George E. Marcus, 179–231. Chicago: University of Chicago Press.

———. 1997b. Interview with Nizamettin Ariç, March 17, translated by his partner and wife, Christine Kernich, Los Angeles.

———. 1997c. Interview with Shirin Etessam, February 28, San Francisco.

———. 1997d. Interview (telephone) with Ara Madzounian, March 2, Los Angeles.

———. 1997e. Interview (telephone) with Nina Menkes, February 2, Los Angeles.

———. 1997f. Interview with Sohrab Shahid Saless, April 10, 11, 12, Los Angeles.

———. 1997g. Interview (telephone) with Caveh Zahedi, July 31, Houston.

———. 1997h. "Self-Othering: A Postcolonial Discourse on Cinematic Film Contact." In *New Directions in So-Called Postcolonial Studies*, edited by Fawzia Afzal-Khan and Kalpana Seshadri-Crooks. 292–309. Durham, N.C.: Duke University Press.

———. 1996a. "Identity Politics and Iranian Exile Music Videos." In *Middle Eastern Diaspora Communities in America*, edited by Mehdi Bozorgmehr and Alison Feldman, 104–23. New York: New York University, Hagop Kevorkian Center for Near Eastern Studies.

———. 1996b. Interview with Jean Pierre Jeancolas, March 12, Houston.

———. 1996c. Interview (telephone) with Erica Jordan, October 25, Houston.

———. 1996d. Interview with Amir Naderi, October 25, Houston.

———. 1996e. Interview with Nancy Tong, February 20, Houston.

———. 1996f. Interview (telephone) with Debra Zimmerman, executive director, Women Make Movies, April 22, Houston.

———. 1996g. "Phobic Spaces and Liminal Panics: Independent Transnational Film Genre." In *Global/Local: Cultural Productions and the Transnational Imaginary*, edited by Rob Wilson and Wimal Dissanayake, 119–44. Durham, N.C.: Duke University Press.

———. 1996h. "Theorizing 'Third World' Film Spectatorship." *Wide Angle* 18, no. 4:3–26. [Special issue on "The Media and *Moi*."]

———. 1995a. Interview with Bahram Baizai, April 2, Houston.

———. 1995b. Interview with Jonas Mekas, March 6, New York City.

———. 1995c. "Iranian Cinema under the Islamic Republic." *American Anthropologist* 97, no. 3:531–41.

———. 1995d. "Mediating the Other: American Pop Culture Representation of Postrevolutionary Iran." In *The U.S. Media and the Middle East: Image and Perception*, edited by Yahya R. Kamalipour, 73–90. Westport, Conn.: Greenwood Press.

———. 1995e. "Recurrent Themes in the Middle Eastern Cinema of Diaspora." In *The Cinema of Displacement: Middle Eastern Identities in Transition*, edited by Jonathan Friedlander, 3–63. Los Angeles: UCLA Center for Near Eastern Studies.

Naficy, Hamid. 1994. "Veiled Vision/Powerful Presences: Women in the Postrevolutionary Iranian Cinema." In *In the Eye of the Storm: Women in Post-revolutionary Iran*, edited by Mahnaz Afkhami and Erika Friedl, 131–50. London and Syracuse: I. B. Taurus and Syracuse University Press.

———. 1993a. *The Making of Exile Cultures: Iranian Television in Los Angeles*. Minneapolis: University of Minnesota Press.

———. 1993b. "Narrowcasting and Nationality: Middle Eastern Television in Los Angeles." *Afterimage* 20, no. 7: 9–11.

———. 1993c. "Sinema va Hovviat-e Melli," [Cinema and National Identity] *Kankash* [USA] 10 (fall): 137–69.

———. 1992a. Interview with Caveh Zahedi, May 26, Los Angeles.

———. 1992b. "Islamizing Film Culture in Iran." In *Iran: Political Culture in the Islamic Republic*, edited by Samih K. Farsoun and Mehrdad Mashayekhi, 173–208. London: Routledge.

———. 1988. Interview with Reza Allamehzadeh, October 7, Los Angeles.

———. 1987. "History, Memory, and Film: Voices from Inside Lebanon." *Jusur* 3: 95–102. [Interview with Mai Masri and Jean Chamoun.]

———. 1985. "The Sealed Soil." In *Magill's Survey of Cinema: Foreign Language Films*, edited by Frank Magill, 2677–81. Los Angeles: Salem Press.

———. 1984. *Iran Media Index*. Westport, Conn.: Greenwood Press.

———, ed. 1999. *Home, Exile, Homeland: Film, Media, and the Politics of Place*. New York: Routledge.

Naficy, Hamid, and Teshome Gabriel, eds. 1993. *Otherness and the Media: The Ethnography of the Imagined and the Imaged*. New York: Harwood Academic Publishing.

Nair, Mira, and Sooni Taraporevala. 1989. *Salaam Bombay!* New Delhi: Penguin Books.

Nassibi, Bassir. 1995. "Sinema-ye Moqavemat dar Barabar-e Takhrib-e Farhangi." *Suresrafil*, June, 13.

Neale, Stephen. 1983. *Genre*. London: British Film Institute.

Nelson, Joyce. 1988. *The Colonized Eye: Rethinking the Grierson Legend*. Toronto: Between the Lines.

Netenjakob, Egon. 1994. *TV-Filmlexikon: Regisseure, Autoren, Dramaturgen, 1952–1992*. Frankfurt: Fischer Taschenbuch Verlag.

Newman, Kathleen. 1993. "National Cinema after Globalization: Fernando Solanas's *Sur* and the Exiled Nation." In *Mediating Two Worlds: Cinematic Encounters in the Americas*, edited by John King, Ana Lopez, and Manuel Alvarado, 242–57. London: British Film Institute.

Newton, Esther. 1972. *Mother Camp: Female Impersonators in America*. Chicago: University of Chicago Press.

Ngugi, Wa Thiongo. 1989. *Decolonising the Mind: The Politics of Language in African Literature*. London: James Currey.

Nichols, Bill. 1994a. *Blurred Boundaries: Questions of Meaning in Contemporary Culture*. Bloomington: Indiana University Press.

———. 1994b. "Discovering Form, Inferring Meaning: New Cinemas and the Film Festival Circuit." *Film Quarterly* 47, no. 3:16–30.

———. 1991. *Representing Reality: Issues and Concepts in Documentary*. Bloomington: Indiana University Press.

Nichols, William James. 1972. "Newsreel: Film and Revolution." Master's thesis, University of California, Los Angles.

Niney, Françoise. 1993. "Artavazd Pelechian ou la réalité déterminée." In *Le Cinéma Armenien*, edited by Jean Radvanyi, 87–88. Paris: Centre Georges Pompidou.

Norden, Martin F. 1994. *The Cinema of Isolation: A History of Physical Disability in the Movies*. New Brunswick, N.J.: Rutgers University Press.

Noriega, Chon. 1996. "Imagined Borders: Locating Chicano Cinema in America/America." In *The Ethnic Eye: Latino Media Arts*, edited by Chon A. Noriega and Ana M. Lopez, 3–21. Minneapolis: University of Minnesota Press.

———. 1992a. *Chicanos and Film: Essays on Chicano Representation and Resistance*. New York: Garland.

———. 1992b. "This Is Not a Border." *Spectator* 13, no.1:4–11.

Noriega, Chon A., and Ana M. Lopez, eds. 1996. *The Ethnic Eye: Latino Media Arts*. Minneapolis: University of Minnesota Press.

O'Grady, Gerald. 1973. "Our Space in Our Time: The New American Cinema." In *The American Cinema*, edited by Donald E. Staples, 228–44. Washington, D.C.: U.S. Information Agency.

Omid, Jamal. 1367/1988. *Farhang-e Sinema-ye Iran. Zendeginameh-ye Kargardanan, Tahiyehkonandegan, Filmnamehnevisan, Bazigaran, Filmbardaran, Tadvinkonandegan, Ahangsazan, Tarrahan-e Sahneh, va . . .* Tehran: Negah.

Ong, Walter J. 1982. *Orality and Literacy: The Technologizing of the Word*. London: Routledge.

Onishi, Norimitsu. 1996. "New Sense of Race Arises among Asian-Americans." *New York Times*, May 30, A1, A16.

Oswald, Helga. 1991. "The Dark Realities of Nina Menkes." *Montage Magazine*, summer, 26–29, 34.

Palestinian Film Week. 1992. Jerusalem: Jerusalem Film Institute. [Film catalog.]

Parks, Louis B. 1995. "Viewers Play Sleuths in Unusual 'Exotica.' " *Houston Chronicle*, March 25, 3c.

Parmenter, Barbara McKean. 1994. *Giving Voice to Stones: Place and Identity in Palestinian Literature*. Austin: University of Texas Press.

Pascal, Roy. 1977. *The Dual Voice: Free Indirect Discourse and Its Functioning in the Nineteenth-Century European Novel*. Manchester, UK: Manchester University Press.

Passek, Jean-Loup, ed. 1993. *Le Cinéma Armenien*. Paris: Centre de Georges Pompidou.

Peña, Richard. 1987. "Images of Exile: Two Films by Raoul Ruiz." In *Reviewing Histories: Selections from New Latin American Cinema*, edited by Coco Fusco, 136–45. Buffalo, N.Y.: Hallwalls Contemporary Art Center.

Pendakur, Manjunath. 1990. *Canadian Dreams and American Control: The Political Economy of the Canadian Film Industry*. Detroit: Wayne State University Press.

Peteet, Julie. 1996. "Identity and Community in Exile." *Critique: Journal for Critical Studies of the Middle East* 8 (spring): 1–15.

Peters, John. 1999. "Exile, Nomadism, and Diaspora: The Stakes of Mobility in the Western Canon." In *Home, Exile, Homeland: Film, Media, and the Politics of Place*, edited by Hamid Naficy, 17–41. New York: Routledge.

Petric, Vlada. 1989–90. "Tarkovsky's Dream Imagery." *Film Quarterly* 43, no. 2:28–34.

Petrie, Duncan. 1992. *Screening Europe: Image and Identity in Contemporary European Cinema*. London: British Film Institute.

Petrie, Graham, and Ruth Dwyer, eds. 1990. *Before the Wall: Society and East European Filmmakers Working in the West.* Lanhan, Md.: University Press of America.

Pfaff, Françoise. 1984. *The Cinema of Ousmane Sembene, a Pioneer of African Film.* Westport, Conn.: Greenwood Press.

Pfanner, Helmut F. 1983. *Exile in New York: German and Austrian Writers after 1933.* Detroit: Wayne State University Press.

Pfeil, Fred. 1988. "Postmodernism as a 'Structure of Feeling.'" In *Marxism and the Interpretation of Culture,* edited by Cary Nelson and Lawrence Grossberg, 381–403. Urbana: University of Illinois Press.

Pflaum, Hans Günther, and Hans Helmut Prinzler. 1993. *Cinema in the Federal Republic of Germany.* Bonn: Inter Nationes.

Philip, Craig. 1994. *Last Stands: Famous Battles against the Odds.* Greenwich, Conn.: Dorset Press.

Phillips, Julie. 1990. "Romany Holiday." *Village Voice,* February 13, 77.

Pick, Zuzana M. 1993. "Exile and Displacement." In *The New Latin American Cinema: A Continental Project,* 157–85. Austin: University of Texas Press.

———. 1989. "The Dialectical Wandering of Exile." *Screen* 30, no. 4:48–64.

———. 1987. "Chilean Cinema in Exile (1973–1986)." *Framework* 34 (1987): 39–57.

Pines, Jim. 1988. "The Cultural Context of Black British Cinema." In *Blackframes: Critical Perspectives on Black Independent Cinema,* edited by Mbye B. Cham and Claire Andrade-Watkins, 26–36. Cambridge, Mass.: MIT Press.

Pintoff, Ernest. 1994. *The Complete Guide to American Film Schools and Cinema and Television Courses.* New York: Penguin Books.

Poirier, Richard. 1992. *The Performing Self: Compositions and Decompositions in the Language of Contemporary Life.* New Brunswick, N.J.: Rutgers University Press.

Pool, Ithiel de Sola. 1977. *The Social Impact of the Telephone.* Cambridge, Mass.: MIT Press.

Poonam, Arora. 1994. "The Production of Third World Subjects for First World Consumption: *Salaam Bombay* and *Parama.*" In *Multiple Voices in Feminist Film Criticism,* edited by Diane Carson, Linda Dittmar, and Janice Welsch, 293–304. Minneapolis: University of Minnesota Press.

Porton, Richard. 1997. "Family Romances: An Interview with Atom Egoyan." *Cinéaste* 23, no. 2:8–15.

Portuges, Catherine. 1992. "Border Crossings: Recent Trends in East and Central European Cinema." *Slavic Review* 51, no. 3:531–35.

Pousti, Said. 1988. "Hich Zedd-e Irani Nemitavanest in Chenin Iran va Irani ra Zir-e So'al Bebarad." *Fogholadeh* [Los Angeles], n.d., n.p.

Pribram, Deidre E. 1993. "Straight Outta Money: Institutional Power and Independent Film Funding." *Afterimage* 21, no. 1:3–5.

Pristin, Terry. 1986. "Will Dubbing Fly in the U.S.? Read My Lips." *New York Times,* February 19, C1, C4.

Pym, John. 1992. *Film on Four, 1982/1991: A Survey.* London: British Film Institute.

Quandt, James. 1993a. "Calendar." *Cinématheque Ontario Programme Guide* 3, no. 3:9.

———. 1993b. "Grin without a Cat: Films and Videos by Chris Marker." *Cinématheque Ontario Programme Guide* 4, no. 1:2.

Qukasian, Zaven. 1992a. *Goftogu ba Bahram Baiza'i* [Interview with Bahram Baiza'i]. Tehran: Agah Publishers.

Qukasian, Zaven. 1992b. *Majmu'eh-ye Maqalat dar Naqd va Mo'arreffi-ye Asar-e Bahram Baiza'i* [An Anthology of Articles Critiquing and Introducing the Works of Bahram Baiza'i]. Tehran: Agah Publishers.

Radvanyi, Jean, ed. 1993. *Le Cinéma Arménien*. Paris: éditions du Centre Pompidou.

Raffat, Donné. 1994. "Jet-Lagged in an Imagined Land or Is There Exile in the Age of E-Mail?" *Critique* 5 (fall): 31–40.

Rafferty, Terrence. 1993. "Chris Marker." In *The Thing Happens: Ten Years of Writing about the Movies*, 63–74. New York: Grove Press.

Rakow, Lana R. 1992. *Gender on the Line: Women, the Telephone, and Community Life*. Urbana: University of Illinois Press.

Ranvaud, Don. 1979. "Argentina." *Framework* 10 (spring): 34–38.

Ray, Robert. 1985. *A Certain Tendency of the Hollywood Cinema, 1930–1980*, Princeton, N.J.: Princeton University Press.

Reid, Mark A. 1993. *Redefining Black Films*. Berkeley: University of California Press.

———. 1991. "African and Black Diaspora Film/Video." *Jump Cut*, no. 36: 43–46.

Reingold, Howard. 1993. *The Virtual Community: Homesteading on the Electronic Frontier*. Reading, Mass.: Addison-Wesley.

Renov, Michael. 1996. "Video Confessions." In *Resolutions: Contemporary Video Practices*, edited by Michael Renov and Erika Suderburg, 78–101. Minneapolis: University of Minnesota Press.

———. 1989. "The Subject in History: The New Autobiography in Film and Video." *Afterimage* 17, no. 1:4–7.

———. 1987a. "The Construction of a Political Imaginary for the New Left." *Afterimage* 14, no. 7:12–15.

———. 1987b. "Newsreel: Old and New—Towards an Historical Profile." *Film Quarterly* 41, no. 1:20–33.

———. 1984. "Newsreel's Re-search for a Radical Film Practice." *Wide Angle* 6, no. 3:82.

Rentschler, Eric. 1990. "Mountains and Modernity: Relocating the *Bergfilm*." *New German Critique* 51 (fall): 137–61.

———. 1984. *West German Film in the Course of Time: Reflections on the Twenty Years since Oberhausen*. New York: Redgrave.

Revkin, Andrew C. 1997. "Motherly? Not Her! Nature Is Trying to Kill You." *New York Times*, April 20, H13, H19.

Reynaud, Bérénice. 1996. "Le 'Hood: Hate and Its Neighbors." *Film Comment*, March–April, 54–57.

Rich, B. Ruby. 1991. "Tangles Argentina." *Village Voice*, July 30, 64.

Riding, Alan. 1997. "A Fable Rooted in Gypsy Lore." *New York Times*, May 25, H16.

———. 1996. "Berlin Fires Up Its Film Festival with Star Power." *New York Times*, February 22, B1, B6.

———. 1995a. "Czech Wields Hatchet on the Arts." *New York Times*, November 14, B1, B4.

———. 1995b. "The Last Film for Director from Bosnia." *New York Times*, December 5, B3.

Roberts, Martin. 1992. " 'World Music' and the Global Cultural Economy." *Diaspora* 2, no. 2:229–42.

Robertson, Roland. 1995. "Globalization: Time-Space and Homogeneity-Heterogeneity." In *Global Modernities*, edited by Mike Featherstone, Scott Lasch, and Roland Robertson, London: Sage.

Robinson, Amy. 1994. "It Takes One to Know One: Passing and Communities of Common Interest." *Critical Inquiry* 20 (summer): 715–36.

Robinson, Marc, ed. 1994. *Altogether Elsewhere: Writers on Exile*. San Diego: A Harvest Book.

Rohter, Larry. 1997. "Central Americans Feel Sting of New U.S. Immigration Law." *New York Times*, April 9.

Rooney, David. 1994. "*I Don't Hate Las Vegas Anymore.*" *Variety*, February 14–20.

Rose, Gillian. 1993. *Feminism and Geography*. Cambridge, Mass.: Polity Press.

Rosello, Mireille. 1996. "Third Cinema or Third Degree: The 'Rachid System' in Serge Meynard's *L'oil au beurre noir*." In *Cinema, Colonialism, Postcolonialism: Perspectives from the French and Francophone Worlds*, edited by Dina Sherzer. 147–72. Austin: University of Texas Press.

Rosen, Miriam. 1989. "The Uprooted Cinema: Arab Filmmakers Abroad." *Middle East Report*, July–August, 34–37.

Rosen, Philip. 1993. "Making a Nation in Sembene's Ceddo." In *Otherness and the Media: The Ethnography of the Imagined and the Imaged*, edited by Hamid Naficy and Teshome Gabriel, 147–72. New York: Harwood Academic Publishing.

Rosenbaum, Jonathan. 1983a. "Chantal Anne Akerman." In *Film: The Front Line 1983*, 30–36. Denver, Colo.: Arden Press.

———. 1983b. "Jonas Mekas." In *Film: The Front Line 1983*, 112–23. Denver, Colo: Arden Press.

———. 1983c. "Michael Snow." In *Film: The Front Line 1983*, 176–87. Denver, Colo.: Arden Press.

Ross, Alex. 1996. "A Musical Flood, but Not Unwelcome." *New York Times*, January 14.

Rubin, Mike. 1993. "Film Threat: The Demise of Campus Film Societies." *Village Voice Film Special*, May 25, 10–14.

Ruby, Jay. 1988. "The Image Mirrored: Reflexivity and the Documentary Film." In *New Challenges for Documentary*, edited by Alan Rosenthal, 64–77. Berkeley: University of California Press.

Ruhani, Omid. 1992. "Khab dar Chem-e Taram Mishekanad." *Kelk* [Tehran] 40:225–35.

Rushdie, Salman. 1991. *Imaginary Homelands: Essays and Criticism, 1981–1991*. London: Granta.

———. 1988. "Songs Doesn't Know the Score." *ICA Documents*, no. 7:16–17. [Special issue on black film, British cinema.]

———. 1982. *Midnight's Children*. New York: Avon Books.

Rushkoff, Douglas. 1994. *Cyberia: Life in the Trenches of Hyperspace*. San Francisco: Harper.

Sackville-West, Vita. 1990. *Passenger to Teheran*. New York: Moyer Bell.

Sadoul, Georges. 1972. *Dictionary of Film Makers*. Trans. Peter Morris. Berkeley: University of California Press.

Safran, William. 1991. "Diasporas in Modern Societies: Myths of Homeland and Return." *Diaspora* 1 no. 1:83–99.

Said, Edward W. 1994. "Intellectual Exile: Expatriates and Marginals." In *Representations of the Intellectual: The 1993 Reith Lectures*, 35–48. New York: Vintage.

Said, Edward W. 1990a. "Narrative, Geography and Interpretation." *New Left Review*, no. 180: 81–97.

———. 1990b. "Reflections on Exile." In *Out There: Marginalization and Contemporary Cultures*, edited by Russell Ferguson, Martha Gever, Trinh T. Minh-ha, and Cornel West, 357–66. Cambridge, Mass.: MIT Press.

———. 1979. *The Question of Palestine*. New York: Vintage Books.

Salloum, Jayce, ed. 1996. *East of Here: (Re)Imagining the "Orient."* Catalogue of an exhibition held at YYZ Artists' Outlet, Toronto, November 20–December 14.

Salloum, Jayce, and Molly Hankwitz. 1996. "Occupied Territories: Mapping the Transgressions of Cultural Territory." *Felic: A Journal of Media Arts and Communication* 2, no. 1:113–22.

Sandiford, Judith. 1994/95. Interview with Jayce Salloum: Making Pictures in Lebanon." *Artworld*, winter, 33–38.

Santner, Eric L. 1990. *Stranded Objects: Mourning, Memory, and Film in Postwar Germany*. Ithaca, N.Y.: Cornell University Press.

Sarris, Andrew. 1976. "Toward a Theory of Film History." In *Movies and Methods*, edited by Bill Nichols, 237–51. Los Angeles: University of California Press.

———. 1962–63. "Notes on the Auteur Theory in 1962." *Film Culture* 27 (winter): 1–8.

Sayyad, Parviz. 1996. *Rah-e Doshvar-e Sinema-ye dar Tab'id*. Los Angeles: Parsian.

———. 1995. "Cham va Khamha-ye Jomhuri-ye Eslami ba Sinema-ye dar Tab'id." *Rouzegar-e Now* [France] February–March, 58–64.

Schama, Simon. 1995. *Landscape and Memory*. New York: Knopf.

Schatz, Thomas. 1993. "The New Hollywood." In *Film Theory Goes to the Movies*, edited by Jim Collins, Hilary Radner, and Ava Preacher Collins, 9–36. New York: Routledge.

———. 1988. *The Genius of the System: Hollywood Filmmaking in the Studio Era*. New York: Pantheon.

———. 1981. *Hollywood Genres: Formulas, Filmmaking, and the Studio System*. Austin: University of Texas Press.

Schneider, Roland. 1990. "D'*Utopia* a *La Femme Flambée*: Un regard iranien et un regard allemand sur l'aliénation." *CinéAction* 56 (July): 89–91.

Schürmann, Ernst. 1978. *German Film Directors in Hollywood: Film-Emigration from Germany and Austria*. San Francisco: Göethe Institut.

Schwartzman, Karen. 1995. "National Cinema in Translation: The Politics of Film Exhibition Culture." *Wide Angle* 16, no. 3:66–99.

The Second Festival for Iranian Films in Exile, 6–13 October. 1995. Göteborg: Sweden: Exile-Film Festival.

Sedgwick, Eve Kosofsky. 1990. *Epistemology of the Closet*. Berkeley: University of California Press.

Seed, Patricia. 1999. "The Key to the House." In *Home, Exile, Homeland: Film, Media, and the Politics of Place*, edited by Hamid Naficy, 85–94. New York: Routledge.

Segal, Aaron. 1993. *An Atlas of International Migration*. London: Hans Sell Publishers.

Segal, Lewis. 1992. "Young Turk." *Los Angeles Times Calendar*, July 12, 52.

7th Annual Los Angeles Asian Pacific Film & Video. May 7 through 17, 1992. Film catalog.

Shafa, Sa'id. 1989. "Sinemagaran-e Borunmarzi-ye Iran." *Simorgh* 6:82–88.

Shahid Saless, Sohrab. 1993. "Sohrab Shahid Saless and a Private Agony." *Film International* [Tehran] 1, no. 4:60–65.

———. 1988. "Culture as Hard Currency or: Hollywood in Germany (1983)." In *West German Filmmakers on Film: Visions and Voices*, edited by Eric Rentschler, 56–58. New York: Holmes and Meir.

Shedden, Jim. 1995. *The Films of Michael Snow, 1956–1991: Presence and Absence*. Ontario: Art Gallery of Ontario and Alfred A. Knopf.

Sherzer, Dina, ed. 1996. *Cinema, Colonialism, Postcolonialism: Perspectives from the French and Francophone World*. Austin: University of Texas Press.

Shiri, Keith. 1992. *Directory of African Film-Makers and Films*. Westport, Conn.: Greenwood Press.

Shohat, Ella. 1991. "Ethnicities-in-Relation: Toward a Multicultural Reading of American Cinema." In *Unspeakable Images: Ethnicity and the American Cinema*, edited by Lester D. Friedman, 215–250. Urbana: University of Illinois Press.

———. 1989. *Israeli Cinema: East/West and the Politics of Representation*. Austin: University of Texas Press.

———. 1988. "Wedding in Galilee." *Middle East Report* 154 (September–October): 44–46.

Shohat, Ella, and Robert Stam. 1994. *Unthinking Eurocentrism: Multiculturalism and the Media*. London: Routledge.

Shorts, John Rennie. 1991. *Imagined Country: Society, Culture and Environment*. New York: Routledge.

Siberok, Martin. 1997. "Gatlif Focuses on the Plight of the Gypsies." *Globe and Mail* [Montreal], September 4, C2.

Signaté, Ibrahim. 1994. *Un Cinéaste rebelle: Med hondo*. Paris: Présence Africaine.

Silcock, Lisa. 1988. "The Old Man and the Wind." *Observer*, November 6, 41.

Silverman, Kaja. 1993. "What Is a Camera? or: History in the Field of Vision." *Discourse* 15, no. 3:3–56.

———. 1988. *The Acoustic Mirror: The Female Voice in Psychoanalysis and Cinema*. Bloomington: Indiana University Press.

Simpson, Janice C. 1992. "Focusing on the Margins." *Time*, March 2, 67.

Sims, Calvin. 1997. "Argentina's Bereft Mothers: And Now, a New Wave." *New York Times*, November 18, A4.

———. 1995. " 'Dirty War' Admission Ungags Argentines." *New York Times*, April 27, A5.

Sinclair, John, Elizabeth Jacka, and Stuart Cunningham, eds. 1996. *New Patterns in Global Television: Peripheral Vision*. New York: London: Oxford University Press.

Singer, Benjamin D. 1980. *Social Function of the Telephone*. Palo Alto, Calif.: R & E Research Associates.

Sitney, P. Adam. 1990. "Mekas, Jonas." In *International Dictionary of Films and Filmmakers*. Vol. 2, *Directors*, edited by Nicholas Thomas, 565–66. 2d ed. Chicago: St. James Press.

Sklar, Robert. 1994. *Movie-Made America: A Cultural History of American Movies*. Revised and updated. New York: Vintage Books.

Skyler, Lisanne. 1994. "Gambling with Movie-Making." *Release Print*, June, 8–9, 17–18, 20–22.

Smith, Roch C. 1995. "Open Narrative in Robbe-Grillet's *Glissments progressifs du plaisir* and Wim Wenders's *Paris, Texas.*" *Film Literature Quarterly* 23, no. 1:32–38.

Sobchack, Vivian. 1999. " 'Is Any Body Home?': Embodied Imagination and Visible Evictions." In *Home, Exile, Homeland: Film, Media and the Politics of Place*, edited by Hamid Naficy, 45–61. New York: Routledge.

Soja, Edward. 1996. *Thirdspace: Journeys to Los Angeles and Other Real-and-Imagined Places*. Cambridge: Blackwell.

———. 1989. *Postmodern Geographies: The Reassertion of Space in Critical Social Theory*. London: Verso.

Sollors, Werner. 1986. *Beyond Ethnicity: Consent and Descent in American Culture*. New York: Oxford University Press.

Sontag, Susan. 1982. "Notes on Camp." In *A Susan Sontag Reader*, 105–20. New York: Vintage.

Sorlin, Pierre. 1991. *European Cinemas, European Societies: 1939–1990*. London: Routledge.

Spivak, Gayatri Chakravotry. 1993. *Outside in the Teaching Machine*. New York: Routledge.

———. 1990. *The Post-colonial Critic*. Ed. S. Harasym. London: Routledge.

———. 1988. "Can the Subaltern Speak?" In *Marxism and the Interpretation of Culture*, edited by Cary Nelson and Lawrence Grossberg, 271–313. Urbana: University of Illinois Press.

———. 1985. "The Rani of Simur." In *Europe and Its Others*. Vol. 1, edited by Francis Barker, Peter Hulme, Margaret Iversen, and Diana Loxley, 128–51. Colchester, UK: University of Essex.

Stam, Robert. 1991. "Bakhtin, Polyphony and Racial/Ethnic Representation." In *Unspeakable Images: Ethnicity and the American Cinema*, edited by Lester Friedman, 251–76. Urbana: University of Illinois Press.

———. 1989. *Subversive Pleasures: Bakhtin, Cultural Criticism, and Film*. Baltimore: Johns Hopkins University Press.

Stevenson, Richard W., and Jeff Gerth. 1997. "I.M.F.'s New Look: A Far Deeper Role in Lands in Crisis." *New York Times*, December 8, A1, A10.

Stok, Danusia, ed. 1993. *Kieslowski on Kieslowski*. Boston: Faber and Faber.

Stoller, Paul. 1992. *The Cinematic Griot: The Ethnography of Jean Rouch*. Chicago: University of Chicago Press.

Stone, Judy. 1983. "An Iranian's Mission to Expose Hypocrisy." *San Francisco Sunday Examiner and Chronicle Datebook*, November 20.

Stoneman, Rod. 1996. "Nine Notes on Cinema and Television." In *Big Picture, Small Screen: The Relations between Film and Television*, edited by John Hill and Martin McLoone, 118–32. Luton, Bedfordshire, UK: John Libbey Media/University of Luton.

Stout, Janis P. 1983. *The Journey Narrative in American Literature: Patterns and Departures*. Westport, Conn.: Greenwood Press.

Street, G. S. 1913. "While I Wait." *Living Age*, March 15, 696–97.

Stukator, Angela. 1993 "Critical Categories and the (Il)logic of Identity." *Canadian Journal of Film Studies/Revue Canadienne d'étude Cinématographiques* 2, nos. 2–3: 117–28.

Suner, Asuman. 1998. "Speaking the Experience of Political Oppression with a Masculine Voice: Making Feminist Sense of Yilmaz Güney's *Yol.*" Unpublished manuscript.

Tajima, Renee. 1991. "Moving the Image: Asian American Independent Filmmaking 1970–1990." In *Moving Image: Independent Asian Pacific American Media Arts,* edited by Russell Leong, 10–33. Los Angeles: UCLA Asian American Studies Center.

Tarkovsky, Andrey. 1987. *Sculpting in Time: Reflections on the Cinema.* Trans. Kitty Hunter-Blair. Austin: University of Texas Press.

Tarr, Carrie. 1993. "Questions of Identity in Beur Cinema: From Tea in the Harem to Cheb." *Screen* 34, no. 4:321–42.

Taubin, Amy. 1993. "New Directors' Risky Business." *Village Voice,* March 23, 63.

———. 1992. "Burning Down the House." *Sight and Sound,* n.s., Z, n. 2:18–19.

———. 1989. "Foreign Affairs." *Village Voice,* May 29, 64.

Taussig, Michael. 1992. "Tactility and Distraction." In *Reading Cultural Anthropology,* edited by George E. Marcus, 8–14. Durham, N.C.: Duke University Press.

Tavenas, Stéphane, and François Volard. 1989. *Guide of European Cinema.* Trans. David Clougher. Paris: éditions Ramsey/Eurocinéma.

Taylor, Clarke. 1983. "Film Maker Runs into Controversy." *Los Angeles Times,* July 1.

Taylor, Clyde. 1988. "Les Grands axes et les sources africanes du Nouveau cinéma noir." *CinémAction,* no. 46: 84–92. [Special issue on "le cinéma noir américain."]

Taylor, Julie. 1998. *Paper Tangos.* Durham, N.C.: Duke University Press.

———. 1992. "Tango." In *Reading Cultural Anthropology,* edited by George E. Marcus, 377–89. N.C.: Durham: Duke University Press.

Third World Newsreel. 1995. *Third World Newsreel Film/Video Catalogue.* New York: Third World Newsreel.

Thomas, Kevin. 1991. "Bleak View of Immigrant Experience." *Los Angeles Times,* June 7.

———. 1987a. "Busload of Iranians Stuck in 'Checkpoint.'" *Los Angeles Times,* November 20, pt. 4, p. 32.

———. 1987b. "An Exhilarating *Runner* from Iran." *Los Angeles Times,* March 7.

Thomas, Nicholas, ed. 1990. *International Dictionary of Films and Filmmakers.* 2d ed. Chicago: St. James Press.

Tölölyan, Khachig. 1996. "Rethinking Diaspora(s): Stateless Power in the Transnational Moment." *Diaspora* 5, no. 1:3–36.

Toubiana, Serge. 1989a. "Entretein avec Joris Ivens et Marceline Loridan." *Cahiers du Cinéma,* March, 36–39.

———. 1989b. "L'Image c'est du vent." *Cahiers du Cinéma,* March, 34–35.

Trinh, T. Minh-ha. 1992. *Framer Framed.* London: Routledge.

———. 1989. "Outside In Inside Out." In *Questions of Third Cinema,* edited by Jim Pines and Paul Willemen, 133–49. London: British Film Institute.

Truffaut, François. 1976 [1954]. "A Certain Tendency of the French Cinema." In *Movies and Methods,* edited by Bill Nichols, 224–37. Los Angeles: University of California Press.

Turner, Craig. 1997. "Canadian Official Ready for War on Hollywood." *Los Angeles Times,* February 11, A3, A8.

Turovskaya, Maya. 1989. *Tarkovsky: Cinema as Poetry.* Ed. Ian Christie. Trans. Natasha Ward, London: Faber and Faber.

UCLA Film and Television Archive. 1990. *A Decade of Iranian Cinema, 1980–1990.* Los Angeles: UCLA.

Ukadike, Nwachukwu Frank. 1994. *Black African Cinema*. Berkeley: University of California Press.

United Nations. 1996. *World Population Monitoring 1993 with a Special Report on Refugees*. New York: United Nations.

United Nations High Commissioner for Refugees. 1995. *The State of the World's Refugees 1995*. New York: Oxford University Press.

Valente, Judith. 1994. "The Man without a Country Resides at Charles de Gaulle." *Wall Street Journal*, October 7, A1, A6.

Valot, Jacques. 1989. "Écrans épistolaires." *La Revue du Cinema*, January, 87–88.

Van Wert, William F. 1979. "Chris Marker: The SLON Films." *Film Quarterly* 32, no. 3:38–46.

Verhovek, Sam Howe. 1997. " 'Silent Deaths' Climbing Steadily as Migrants Cross Mexico Border." *New York Times*, August 24, 1, 18.

Vidler, Anthony. 1991. "Agoraphobia: Spatial Estrangement in Georg Simmel and Siegfried Kracauer." *New German Critique* 54 (fall): 31–45.

Vincendeau, Ginnette. 1996. *The Companion to French Cinema*. London: British Film Institute.

Voskeritchian, Taline. 1993. "A View from Within." In *The Films of Amos Gitai: A Montage*, edited by Paul Willemen, 37–41. London: British Film Institute.

Wakeman, John, ed. 1988. *World Film Directors*. Vol. 2, *1945–85*. New York: H. W. Wilson.

Walker Art Center. 1995. *Bordering on Fiction: Chantal Akerman's* D'Est. Minneapolis, Minn.: Walker Art Center.

Wall, Karen. 1993. " 'Déjà vu/jamais vu': *The Adjuster* and the Hunt for the Image." *Canadian Journal of Film Studies* 2, nos. 2–3:129–44.

Walsh, Michael. 1993. "Allegories of Thatcherism: The Films of Peter Greenaway." In *Fires Were Started: British Cinema and Thatcherism*, edited by Lester Friedman, 255–77. Minneapolis: University of Minnesota Press.

————. 1989. "Around the World, Across All Frontiers: *Sans Soleil* as Dépays." *CinéAction*, fall, 29–36.

Weinraub, Bernard. 1996. "Mavericks Adapting to Power of Studios." *New York Times*, June 24, B1, B4.

Werckmeister, O. K. 1991. *Citadel Culture*. Chicago: University of Chicago Press.

Wexelblat, Alan, ed. 1993. *Virtual Reality: Applications and Explorations*. Boston: Academic Publishers Professional.

Willemen, Paul, ed. 1993. *The Films of Amos Gitai: A Montage*. London: British Film Institute.

————. 1989. "The Third Cinema Question: Notes and Reflections." In *Questions of Third Cinema*, edited by Jim Pines and Paul Willemen, 1–29. London: British Film Institute.

Williams, Allan. 1992. *Republic of Images: A History of French Filmmaking*. Cambridge, Mass.: Harvard University Press.

Williams, Carol J. 1991. "New Picture for Hungary's Filmmakers." *Los Angeles Times*, March 3.

Williams, Lena. 1996. "Aimed at Terrorists, Law Hits Legal Immigrants." *New York Times*, July 17, A1, B12.

Williams, Raymond. 1977. "Structure of Feeling." In *Marxism and Literature*, 128–35. London: Oxford University Press.

Williamson, Judith. 1988. "Two Kinds of Otherness: Black Film and the Avant-Garde." *Screen* 29, no. 4:106–12.

Willis, Holly. 1992. "An Interview with Nina Menkes." *Film Quarterly* 45, no. 3:7–12.

Women Make Movies. 1996. *Film and Video Catalogue*. New York: Women Make Movies.

Wood, Michael. 1993. "Buñuel in Mexico." In *Mediating Two Worlds: Cinematic Encounters in the Americas*, edited by John King, Ana M. Lopez, and Manuel Alvarado, 40–51. London: British Film Institute.

Woolley, Benjamin. 1992. *Virtual Worlds: A Journey in Hype and Hyperreality*. Oxford: Blackwell.

Yari, Abbas. 1994. "A Second Generation of Iranian [*sic*] in America Turns to Independent Filmmaking." *Film International* 2, no. 3:54–56.

Yarovskaya, Marianna. 1997–98. "Underground." *Film Quarterly* 51, no. 2:50–54.

Young, Josh. 1996. "The Usual Spats over Nominees for Foreign Films." *New York Times*, February 11, 18.

Yung. 1988. "Une histoire de vent." *Variety*, September 28.

Index